Contextual Development Economics

The European Heritage in Economics and the Social Sciences

Edited by: Jürgen G. Backhaus
University of Erfurt
Frank H. Stephen
University of Manchester

http://www.springer/series/5902

Matthias P. Altmann

Contextual Development Economics

A Holistic Approach to the Understanding of Economic Activity in Low-Income Countries

Springer

Dr. Matthias P. Altmann
Cologne
Germany
altmann.matthias@t-online.de

ISBN 978-1-4419-7230-9   e-ISBN 978-1-4419-7231-6
DOI 10.1007/978-1-4419-7231-6
Springer New York Dordrecht Heidelberg London

© Springer Science+Business Media, LLC 2011
All rights reserved. This work may not be translated or copied in whole or in part without the written permission of the publisher (Springer Science+Business Media, LLC, 233 Spring Street, New York, NY 10013, USA), except for brief excerpts in connection with reviews or scholarly analysis. Use in connection with any form of information storage and retrieval, electronic adaptation, computer software, or by similar or dissimilar methodology now known or hereafter developed is forbidden.
The use in this publication of trade names, trademarks, service marks, and similar terms, even if they are not identified as such, is not to be taken as an expression of opinion as to whether or not they are subject to proprietary rights.

Printed on acid-free paper

Springer is part of Springer Science+Business Media (www.springer.com)

"We can't solve problems by using the same kind of thinking we used when we created them."

Albert Einstein (1879–1955)

Acknowledgements

This book arrives at new insights by connecting old ideas from early European schools of economics with contemporary thinking in development research and policymaking. I am clearly indebted to both, the authors that more than a century ago developed the concepts and methods of research that today can help modern development economists regain a more holistic understanding of economic life in poor countries, as well as the authors whose recent analyses of the effectiveness of past development policies have led them to recognise the need for a new development economics that yields more policy-relevant conclusions and context-specific solutions to the problems of low-income countries.

This monograph is a revised version of my doctoral dissertation written under the supervision of Jürgen Backhaus and Erik Reinert, and completed *summa cum laude* at the University of Erfurt's Faculty of State Sciences in January 2010. In preparing the thesis, I benefited greatly from my studies in economics, first at the University of Hohenheim and then, with a truly international scope, at Maastricht University, the Netherlands. At Maastricht, I met Jürgen Backhaus who taught me to study economics as a science of reality, and exposed me to the writings of the Historical School of Economics. He supervised my Master's thesis, and his steady confidence in my work has been a great source of encouragement also for embarking on my doctoral dissertation, for which he, by then at the University of Erfurt, became first promoter. His virtually inexhaustible knowledge and thought-provoking questions have always had a stimulating effect on my work. I owe much to his advice and support. I was fortunate that Jürgen Backhaus introduced me to Erik Reinert, who kindly accepted to be the second promoter of my dissertation. As a leading development economist, he masters the art of generating policy-relevant and context-sensitive conclusions from a deep qualitative understanding of processes of economic change. I am most grateful for the time he spent discussing my work with me at Hvasser, Norway. Although I have approached my position independently of his, I realised in our discussions a deep intellectual bond we share with regard to both the motivation and assumptions behind our respective views and ideas.

Studying for my Ph.D. at the University of Erfurt's Faculty of State Sciences was an exceptional experience in yet another respect. Problems of development are usually researched in parallel discourses in separate disciplines. At Erfurt, the disciplines of economics, law and sociology are integrated under the umbrella of a single Faculty of State Sciences, allowing for interdisciplinary research of the economic, legal and social dimensions of a problem – all of which are clearly relevant also for the study of economic life in low-income countries. This approach could clearly be felt at the doctoral colloquia meetings, and I am grateful to all colloquia participants and faculty colleagues for their valuable comments and advice, in particular Helge Peukert, Ringa Raudla, Arne Weiss and Heike Grimm.

Outside Erfurt, I equally enjoyed the exchange of experiences and mutual encouragement from friends who did their doctorates at about the same time as I, namely, Johanna Witte, Stefan Kolev, Matthias Hauser, Tilman Läppchen and Niels Beisinghoff. I also wish to thank Inge Kaul for examining my research findings with the critical eye of a development expert who combines the professional realism of a former United Nations director with the analytical rigour of a researcher and policy adviser on issues of global governance. A big thank you finally goes to Elspeth MacGregor, who has been an interested and careful reader of many parts of this book, and greatly helped to improve its readability.

Besides my academic studies and research, this book has to a substantial part been inspired by my professional experience from working with KPMG and, more recently, with Fairtrade Labelling Organizations International. At KPMG, my position in a business unit specialised on the acquisition and management of EU and World Bank funded development assistance projects gained me a profound understanding of the workings of the international aid bureaucracy, and it triggered many questions that I set out to explore in this book. At Fairtrade, I enjoyed the possibility to practically apply my research findings to the benefit of small producers and traders in the global South. A general expression of thanks must be offered to all the colleagues and business partners who shared their knowledge with me and from whose experience I have learnt so much.

I also wish to thank Friedrich Naumann Foundation for Liberty for funding parts of my research through a dissertation fellowship. As a Naumann Fellow, I benefited greatly also from the foundation's non-material support that opened-up the possibility for me to initiate and coordinate a development project in Malawi with a group of fellow students of European and African origin. The project aims at improving maternal health care in the district of Nkhotakota through the training of traditional birth attendants. These remarkable women tirelessly complement main functions of the formal health care system, and even substitute for public health services as these are frequently unavailable at all in rural areas. Financial support for field research in Malawi and South Africa from the Friedrich Naumann Foundation for Liberty is gratefully acknowledged as well. It allowed me to conduct an enterprise survey among domestic owners of local businesses on the occasion of the 19th Malawi International Trade Fair in Blantyre in 2007, which was extremely useful for gaining a qualitative understanding of the organisation and governance of economic activities in the context of a low-income country. I thank all the interviewees who enthusiastically shared with me their strategies, business models and experiences from successfully operating on the Malawian and neighbouring markets, while coping creatively with the region's difficult framework conditions.

Furthermore, I would like to thank my editor Jon Gurstelle at Springer Science+Business Media, New York, for his friendly guidance and patience in bringing the manuscript to publication.

Finally, I wish to express my deep gratitude to my mother for always accepting and supporting whatever I set out to do. My greatest personal debt, however, is to my wife Franziska. I could always trust on her love, advice and understanding. This book is dedicated to her and our two wonderful sons Raphael and David.

Contents

1 **Introduction**.. 1
  1.1 The Need for a Contextual Approach to Development
      Economics.. 2
  1.2 Premises of Research 5
  1.3 Structure and Method of the Study 6

Part I   Economic Characteristics of Low-Income Countries

2 **Poverty** 13
  2.1 The Multiple Dimensions of Poverty 16
      2.1.1 Income and Consumption Pattern 16
      2.1.2 Health and Education 20
      2.1.3 Social Exclusion.. 21
      2.1.4 Insecurity... 22
  2.2 The Problem of Measuring Poverty 23

3 **Transaction Costs**... 29
  3.1 Transaction Costs and the Organisation of Economic Activity 30
  3.2 Transaction Costs and the Institutional Environment 31
  3.3 Definition and Measurement of Transaction Costs........................ 34
      3.3.1 The Cost of Regulation 36
      3.3.2 Infrastructure Costs... 38
      3.3.3 Informal Institutional Determinants
            of Transaction Costs.. 40
      3.3.4 Historical Determinants of Transaction Costs 40

4 **Private Governance**... 43
  4.1 Foundations of Private Economic Governance.............................. 46
      4.1.1 Morality... 47
      4.1.2 Personal Trust 49
      4.1.3 Reputation 50

4.2	Alternative Institutions for Contract Enforcement		52
	4.2.1	Group Structure	52
	4.2.2	Contractual Structure	56
	4.2.3	Coordinated Arrangements and Private Third Parties	58
4.3	Alternative Institutions for Property Rights Protection		62
	4.3.1	The Definition of Property Rights	62
	4.3.2	Sources of Property Rights Violations	63
	4.3.3	Private Protection of Property Rights	65
4.4	The Scope and Limits of Informal Enforcement Institutions		66
	4.4.1	The Relationship Between Informal Enforcement and the Scope of Exchange	66
	4.4.2	Natural Limits of Private Governance Mechanisms	68
	4.4.3	Natural Advantages of Private Governance Mechanisms	69

5 Informal Economic Activity ... 73
   5.1 Defining and Measuring the Informal Economy ... 74
      5.1.1 The Size and Growth of the Informal Economy and How It Can Be Estimated ... 77
   5.2 Private Support Institutions for Informal Firms ... 83
   5.3 The Role and Implications of Informality for Economic Development ... 86
      5.3.1 Different Interpretations of Informal Economic Activity and the Merits of Formalisation ... 87

Part II Development Economics: The Past 70 Years

6 The First Generation of Development Economists ... 93
   6.1 Modernisation Theories ... 95
      6.1.1 Paul Rosenstein–Rodan: Industrialisation and the "Big Push" ... 95
      6.1.2 Arthur Lewis: The Dual Sector Model ... 96
      6.1.3 Ragnar Nurkse: Balanced Growth, Capital Formation and the Primacy of Domestic Action ... 97
      6.1.4 The Analysis of Typical Growth Paths by Clark, Kuznets, Rostow and Gerschenkron ... 100
   6.2 Structuralist Approaches to Development Economics ... 101
      6.2.1 Albert O. Hirschman: The Strategy of Unbalanced Growth ... 102
      6.2.2 Gunnar Myrdal: Development as a Cumulative Process of Circular Causation ... 104
      6.2.3 Hans W. Singer: The International Distribution of Gains from Trade and Investment ... 105
      6.2.4 Raú Prebisch: Import Substitution as Strategy for Development ... 108

	6.2.5	Excursus: Friedrich List and the German Zollverein	112
	6.2.6	Peter T. Bauer: A Class of His Own	114

7 The Second Generation: Return to the Mainstream 117
  7.1 Neoclassical Development Economics 117
  7.2 Methodological Considerations 121
  7.3 Neoclassical Welfare Economics and Methods
      of Project Appraisal 125
      7.3.1 Social Cost: Benefit Analysis 125
      7.3.2 Shadow Pricing 126
      7.3.3 Time Discounting 127
      7.3.4 Choice of the Time Horizon 128
      7.3.5 Implications of Neoclassical Welfare Economics 129
  7.4 Development Policies and the "Washington Consensus" 132

**8 The Third Generation: Institutional Turn
and the "New Development Economics"** 135
  8.1 Imperfect Information and the "New Development
      Economics" 136
  8.2 The New Institutional Economics and Development 138
      8.2.1 The Concept of Transaction Costs
            in Institutional Theory 139
      8.2.2 The Process of Institutional Change 140
      8.2.3 Institution-Building and Policy Reform 141
  8.3 Empirical Literature on Institutions and Growth 143
  8.4 The Good Governance Agenda 146

**9 Conclusions from the Past and the Agenda
for a New Generation of Development Economics** 149
  9.1 The Challenge of Igniting Growth in Low-Income Countries 149
  9.2 Why Context Matters 151
      9.2.1 Operational Guidance to Policymakers:
            An Often Neglected Objective
            of Development Research 154
      9.2.2 The Balance and Sequence of Empirical
            and Theoretical Analysis in Development
            Economics 158
  9.3 The Danger of Bureaucratic Failure in the Administration
      of Development Assistance 163
      9.3.1 Problems of Accountability and Feedback 165
      9.3.2 Adverse Behaviour of Aid Bureaucrats 166
      9.3.3 Informational and Motivational Problems
            Associated with the Provision of Aid 168
  9.4 Summary of Conclusions from the Review
      of Development Economics 171

**Part III In Search of an Analytical Framework for the Study
of Low-Income Countries: The Style-Economic Approach**

10 Emerging New Directions in Development Economics........................ 177
    10.1 Confessions of Humility and Ignorance 178
    10.2 Planners vs. Searchers... 180
    10.3 Behavioural Development Economics.. 184
    10.4 Trends at the Level of Research Methods
         and Analytical Techniques... 187
         10.4.1 Analytic Narratives 188
         10.4.2 Growth Diagnostics.. 190
         10.4.3 Experimental Methods... 192

11 German Historical Economics as Development Economics................ 195
    11.1 Scope and Scientific Method of the German
         Historical School... 196

12 From Stage Theories to the Concept of Economic Styles..................... 203
    12.1 Stage Theories and the Idea of Economic Systems 203
         12.1.1 Historical Stage Theories... 203
         12.1.2 Werner Sombart and the Concept
                 of Economic Systems... 205
    12.2 Spiethoff's Concept of the Economic Style.................................... 206
         12.2.1 Methodological and Theoretical
                 Foundations of Spiethoff's Economic Styles.................... 210
    12.3 The Concept of Economic Styles in the Literature
         Since Spiethoff.. 216
         12.3.1 Evaluation and Critique by Eucken 216
         12.3.2 The Concept of Economic Styles
                 in the Contemporary Literature... 220
    12.4 Parallel Contributions of the "Old" Institutional
         School of Economics 222

**13 The Relevance of the Historical School for the Study
of Low-Income Countries**.. 225
    13.1 Methodological Contributions 227
         13.1.1 Inductive and Deductive Reasoning.................................. 228
         13.1.2 Positive and Normative Research 228
         13.1.3 Nature and Scope of Research 229
         13.1.4 Models of Man and Behavioural Assumptions................. 230
    13.2 The Style-Based Approach to the Understanding
         of Economic Activity in Low-Income Countries........................... 233
         13.2.1 Culture and Style in Economic Analysis 235
         13.2.2 Economic Style and Institutional Diversity 242
         13.2.3 Some Applications and Fields for Further Research 245

14 Conclusions 249

Bibliography 255

Author Index 275

Subject Index 281

List of Figures

Fig. 9.1   Actors and linkages in the International Aid System 168

Fig. 10.1 The growth diagnostics methodology 191

Fig. 12.1 Different approaches to economic analysis 211

List of Tables

Table 2.1	Indicators of income- and non-income dimensions of poverty	26
Table 3.1	A taxonomy of transaction costs	35
Table 3.2	Selected indicators of the cost of doing business	37
Table 5.1	The size of the informal economy	81
Table 12.1	Elements and characteristics of economic systems according to Sombart	207
Table 12.2	Basic elements and characteristics of economic styles according to Spiethoff	208
Table 14.1	Methodological differences between mainstream and contextual approaches to development economics	250

Chapter 1
Introduction

Low-income countries are the focus of this book. They comprise the world's poorest nations, more than two thirds of which are concentrated in Africa south of the Sahara. Most people in these countries are as poor today as their grandparents were at the time when development economics emerged as a new sub-discipline within the economic sciences, and when Western governments started to provide billions of dollars worth in development assistance to the developing world.[1]

The persistence of poverty in low-income countries represents one of the greatest conundrums of our time. Low-income countries not only differ markedly in their economic characteristics from advanced economies but also in the developing world, they represent a discrete group of countries. What distinguishes them is in particular the fact that they have hardly seen any sustained rises in income levels over the last half century. While the developing world as a whole is shrinking as large parts of it, especially in South and East Asia, converge with advanced economies, the countries with the lowest income levels are actually diverging from the rest. The problems of these countries are very different from those that development economists and aid agencies have primarily addressed over the past six decades. Efforts at promoting economic growth and poverty reduction in developing countries have, in fact, been most successful in countries that had already experienced growth accelerations in the past. The much more difficult task, however, is to assist low-income countries in creating the conditions for getting growth started. The challenge of igniting growth in low-income countries defines the current frontier of development economics. This book is meant as a contribution to meeting this challenge.

How can poor people in low-income countries be assisted in finding their way out of poverty? Change will have to come from within the societies of these countries, but the international community can ensure that these efforts are more likely to be

---

[1] Since the 1960s, the proportion of people in sub-Saharan Africa who live in extreme poverty (defined by a consumption level of less than 1.25 US dollars per day at 2005 PPP) remained unchanged at a rate of more than 50% of the total population, while the absolute number of the extreme poor has even risen due to high population growth in the region (Chen and Ravallion 2008). For further poverty statistics and their underlying definitions, see Chap. 2.

undertaken and to succeed. However, as this book will show, past development theories have provided little guidance on the kind of policies that can encourage change in today's low-income countries. More current proposals intended to confront this challenge also tend to pass by the root of the problem. In view of the ineffectiveness of their aid to low-income countries, donor agencies now prefer to allocate their aid budgets more selectively to only those countries with a good existent institutional and policy environment. However, the danger is that those countries are being left behind, which have a high rate of poverty precisely because they are lacking the institutional preconditions for sustained growth and poverty reduction.

1.1 The Need for a Contextual Approach to Development Economics

The main thesis that will be examined in this book is that low-income countries differ markedly from advanced economies in their economic characteristics and development paths. It will be shown that for this reason, a contextual approach to the theoretical explanation of their economic realities is required that yields context specific and hence more policy-relevant solutions to the development problems of low-income countries. To understand how poor countries differ from more advanced economies, the study investigates the ways in which people in low-income countries become economically active and the conditions under which they organise their economic relations.[2]

Private enterprise is the engine for sustainable growth and a dominant source of new employment opportunities worldwide. But in low-income countries, private sector activity is often constrained by poorly performing government institutions and the resulting insecurity of property rights, lawlessness, corruption, policy unpredictability and limited access to reliable public services. Under such conditions, it is generally assumed that markets either do not exist or perform very poorly. Yet, this book finds that private economic activity can develop in spite of the adverse institutional framework conditions that characterise poor countries. In particular, it shows that privately governed institutional arrangements have evolved in these countries as functional equivalents for the necessary economic governance unavailable from markets and government institutions. For instance, where dysfunctional markets prevent impersonal forms of exchange, informal networks linked through

---

[2]Throughout the analysis, economic activity refers to private efforts by individuals or groups which make productive use of their abilities and resources, and thereby exploit gains from specialisation and trade. This includes economic activities of households, micro-entrepreneurs, owners of small and medium-sized businesses or members of other corporate or cooperative bodies. Private economic activity can, for instance, include engagement in subsistence farming, manufacturing or long-distance trade. In the context of low-income countries, economic activity as defined here encompasses the largest part of their domestic private sector activity and represents areas with the greatest potential for employment creation and poverty alleviation.

shared norms and values, reputation or trust based on repeated transactions provide an alternative way of doing business. Likewise, in the absence of an effective court system, contract enforcement and commercial dispute settlement can be made possible through various forms of private ordering arrangements.

Yet, it is important to note that the conceptualisation of privately governed institutional arrangements as functional equivalents to the institutions of the market and the state does not imply that they represent better or relatively more efficient forms of economic governance. By whatever alternative institutional arrangement economic activity in low-income countries may be governed, it will always tend to involve higher transaction costs than would otherwise be the case if markets operated efficiently and property rights and contracts were enforced by a well-functioning state. Yet, in the absence of such formal institutions, informal alternatives are often the most efficient of all available strategies for enabling private economic activity. An understanding of the rationalities behind poor people's efforts in coping with the circumstances they live in, and of the context in which they evolve, may indeed serve development economists and policymakers as a promising new point of departure for finding more effective ways of encouraging policy reforms in low-income countries that help to create the conditions for enhanced productivity and sustained growth.

Previously, development economists have largely been ignorant both of the diversity of the institutional forms that support economic activity in low-income countries, and of their underlying context-specific constraints and structures. While some early development economists had still been conscious of the distinct characteristics of economic life in developing countries, mainstream thinking in development economists had soon turned towards general theories of development based on universal assumptions and models of the economy. Following this approach, realities in developing countries were explained by inference from theories and models that had originally been derived from observations of economic life in advanced economies, just as most policy advice was, and often still is, inspired by lessons from the historical experience of developed Western nations. The expectation that meeting the challenge of getting growth started in low-income countries could be achieved with recourse to general economic theories and universal policy prescriptions actually rests upon the implicit belief that economic development could be achieved by assisting poor countries in doing what rich countries did on their way to prosperity. It is true that development economists have attempted to adapt their models and assumptions to the circumstances of developing countries. But their crucial assumptions, especially the postulate of rational, self-interested behaviour, have been retained throughout as premises in development research, as has the deductive method of logically deriving from these general assumptions and laws of theoretical conclusions about the behaviour of economic phenomena in low-income countries.

By contrast, this study argues that the factors in which low-income countries differ most significantly from advanced Western economies are historically and culturally derived. Different societies have internalised different social norms, cultural beliefs and values that reflect the cumulative learning experiences of past and present generations. They make their actions path dependent and determine how their institutions evolve and change. The cultural underpinnings of societies thereby also influence the structure and performance of their economies. It is in fact the ignorance of cultural and historical influences on economic life that has led to the illusive belief that economic realities in low-income countries could be explained by general theories derived from a chain of deductive reasoning.

The limits of general theory in development economics have recently become obvious in view of the distinct development paths on which once poor countries like China, India, Vietnam or Chile have achieved a significant reduction in poverty over the last decades. These countries' development experiences have provided two kinds of important lessons: first, international development assistance has played almost no role in the early stages of reforms that have helped these countries in getting growth started. Instead, economic change has been incepted by internal political groups devoted to modernising their countries and to improving the performance of their economies. The other lesson is that economic reforms in these countries have deviated substantially from the policy prescriptions advocated by mainstream development economists and international aid agencies.

The study does not deny the validity in particular cases of the premises and axioms of general economic theory in the neoclassical, rational choice tradition. Many economic phenomena in the context of a developed market economy actually possess essential characteristics consistent with the general models of neoclassical theory. But the study sets out to challenge the claim for universal validity of the assumptions and general laws on which neoclassical economics is founded. To make development economics a more realistic, context-minded science, a new analytical framework will have to be conceived, one that has the prospect of increasing the explanatory power of development theory and to yield more relevant, context-specific solutions to the economic problems of low-income countries. This framework that will be proposed takes inspiration from the theoretical concept of the "economic style", which can be traced back to the method and research by members of the Historical School of Economics, who significantly shaped the economic discourse in Continental Europe until the early twentieth century. The fundamental idea behind the style-economic approach is to conceptualise discrete patterns of interdependent economic, cultural and political factors as elements of a particular economic style, and to define the context to which the elements of that style apply as the domain within which generalisations about the behaviour of economic phenomena are possible. The value of this approach unfolds specifically in areas where economic outcomes are significantly determined not only by economic variables, but also by their interaction with cultural, psychological and political factors, and where, for this very reason, conventional economic theories have only limited explanatory power.

Underlying the objective to rethink the methods and approaches to development research is the recognition that in order to increase the explanatory power and policy relevance of their theoretical conclusions, development economists will have to shift their focus more on questions of *how* they do development research and policy advice, rather than on *what* to research and advise on. This study argues that success in devising effective strategies for igniting growth in low-income countries is above all a matter of applying appropriate methods of empirical and theoretical research. At this level, the aim must be to enable development economists identifying the context-specific factors that determine the organisation and governance of economic activity, and that are central for understanding how the specific cultural and institutional environment in low-income countries influences economic behaviours and outcomes. Adopting a contextual perspective will change the way in which development policies are designed and implemented – beginning with the realisation that the development objectives which enjoy a broad consensus today are actually confronted by a multitude of ways of implementation.

It follows from the search for new methods and approaches for the economic analysis of economic life in low-income countries that a considerable part of the discussion will centre on problems of economic methodology. But the study does not deal with them in an abstract way. Rather, the consideration of methodological questions is dictated by the character of the economic problems of low-income countries and the urgent need to gain a better understanding of the nature and causes of persistent poverty and economic stagnation in the world's poorest regions.

It is important to note that the use of the concept of economic styles as a vehicle for the advancement of a contextual approach to the understanding and explanation of economic realities in low-income countries does not imply that this approach is constructed and suitable for this specific group of countries alone. Instead, the application of a contextual approach to economics through the conceptualisation of certain regular and uniform characteristics of economic life in a specific time or region as elements of an economic style is principally possible for every society, country or group of countries. For instance, one may think as well of an Islamic economic style that synthesises specific but significant institutional patterns of Muslim societies. Furthermore, the concept of economic styles can be instrumental for capturing the discrete institutional characteristics that explain China's economic development. Also the Western capitalist system has many features that are bound to European history and culture and are thus specific to the contexts of Western industrial countries. Some authors even believe to having identified a discrete French, Italian, Spanish or Russian economic style.[3] In the present analysis, the concept is applied as an element in a contextual approach to the study of economic realities in low-income countries, or subgroups thereof, as they are the focus of this book.

1.2 Premises of Research

The argument so far has conjectured a positive relationship between growth and poverty reduction. This assumption will be retained, albeit with some necessary qualifications. First, growth is not understood as an ultimate goal, but as a means

---

[3] See Sect. 12.3.2 for references to these applications.

to several ends, above all poverty reduction and human development. Second, the study focuses on the conditions that help advance the economic participation and opportunities of the poor. It is therefore the quality of growth that matters above a country's rate of growth. Growth becomes a goal worth pursuing especially when it results from the productive activities of the poor themselves or when it directly improves their own income-earning opportunities and capabilities. Third, in the case of today's low-income countries, the primacy of international economic integration as an engine of growth has to be met with some reservations. Ironically, it turns out that the success of especially South and East Asia's emerging economies in fostering growth through global economic integration has made it much more difficult for today's low-income countries to enter the global market and to gain a competitive edge by taking advantage from their backwardness.

The discussion, furthermore, rests upon the conviction that in spite of the limited effectiveness of foreign aid to low-income countries, abandoning international efforts aimed at assisting the development of poor countries is not an option. Getting growth started in low-income countries does not just matter for the majority of their populations that lives in extreme poverty. It also matters to rich countries. As Kaul and Conceição (2006) point out, freedom from extreme poverty is a global public good as it often cannot or will not be adequately addressed by individual countries alone. It belongs as a policy goal into the global public domain. Conversely, if the growing divergence between advanced and low-income countries is allowed to persist, the situation of poor countries is likely to turn in a global public "bad", the consequences of which will increasingly been felt in the rich world too.

1.3 Structure and Method of the Study

The book approaches its subject matter in three main steps. In Part I of the analysis, careful observation of economic realities in low-income countries is allied with descriptive analysis of a range of phenomena that represent regular and essential characteristics of economic life in today's low-income countries. In particular, the following topics will be explored: how a high incidence of poverty determines the conditions, choices and preferences of large parts of society (Chap. 2); how high transaction costs influence the modes of organisation and governance of economic activity (Chap. 3) and how individuals and firms respond to the absence of necessary formal institutions by resorting to alternative, privately governed arrangements and the informal economy (Chaps. 4 and 5). In all these areas, the inquiry focuses primarily on "micro" issues, namely those involving the circumstances of specific households, enterprises, communities or markets. The empirical results of Part I have been obtained through the review and assessment of the more recent empirical literature on low-income countries and through the use of data from household surveys, case studies and analytic narratives. Moreover, the discussions draw on an original field research carried out by the author in May and June 2007 in Malawi,

1.3 Structure and Method of the Study

consisting of a survey among owners of domestic, mostly small-scale enterprises, as well as participatory observations of economic and societal life in several villages in remote rural areas of the Nkhotakota district.

In Part II, the analysis turns from empirical observation to theoretical explanation. By adopting a retrospective view on post-war development thinking, the relevance of past development theories for explaining the specific characteristics and determinants of economic life in low-income countries is evaluated. Gains of insight can be expected from this review in at least two important respects: First, it will be asked why past theories mostly failed to deliver the policy conclusions and reform strategies to effectively assist low-income countries in entering into a process of sustainable growth and social progress. Second, the analysis of what worked and what didn't in development theory and policy is intended to uncover omissions and missing elements in the existing theoretical framework and guide development research into new directions in order to accommodate the many unsettled questions that still need to be fully understood and resolved.

Three generations of development economists are identified and discussed, ranging from the early pioneers, whose work helped development economics to emerge as an independent area of inquiry some 70 years ago (Chap. 6), over contributions to development economics in the neoclassical tradition (Chap. 7) and to the results from more recent work on the role of institutions on development outcomes (Chap. 8). Part II closes with an analysis of the lessons learned from past experiences and a discussion of their implications for the future of development theory and policy (Chap. 9).

Part III is dedicated to the development of an analytical framework that addresses the theoretical implication of the need to explain cultural influences on economic outcomes and the observed institutional diversity among countries. Moreover, this framework is designed to accommodate the methodological demands on development research that have been extracted as lessons from the retrospective appraisal of development theories and policies. The analysis emanates from the recognition that context matters in the explanation of economic phenomena, and that theoretical research of these phenomena has to be based on a methodology that is capable of identifying, in the diverse realities of countries, regular and essential, but nonetheless context-specific influences and behaviour.

Similarly motivated attempts at making theoretical conclusions in development economics more policy relevant and adaptive to the specific circumstances of low-income countries are gradually emerging in both the development literature and in the strategies of development institutions. They will be discussed at the beginning of Part III with a view to assess their potential for transcending well-established paradigms in development thinking (Chap. 10). Surprisingly, unnoticed in these recent contributions remains the fact that the problem of context specificity had already been fully recognised in the eighteenth and early nineteenth centuries by the Historical School of Economics that had placed it at the centre of the theoretical discourse in Continental Europe for more than 100 years. Based on a review of the primary literature, a discussion of the Historical School's empirical and inductive method will be taken as an important source of insight for the formulation of a new contextual approach to development economics (Chap. 11). Particular inspiration is obtained from contributions by members of the "youngest" Historical School, and especially from their concept of the "economic style" (Chap. 12). Based thereon, a style-theoretical approach to the economic analysis of the interdependent economic, cultural and political determinants of economic life in low-income countries is proposed in Chap. 13 as the methodological core of a new, contextual development economics.

Part I
Economic Characteristics of Low-Income Countries

The chapters in this part present observations of phenomena that characterise economic life in today's low-income countries, with a specific focus on countries in Africa south of the Sahara.[1] The objective is to identify and understand these characteristics, and to discuss how they are conceptualised and measured in economics and neighbouring social sciences. By being descriptive in its method, the analysis in this part does not purport to deliver causal explanations of the observed characteristics, or to predict their consequences for the development of low-income countries. The task of theoretical analysis, and the prior search for an analytical framework capable of explaining economic realities in low-income countries, will be approached in the subsequent parts of the analysis. The purpose of this part is to receive a picture of economic life in low-income countries that delineates the space to which theoretical explanations and meaningful predictions about the behaviour of the observed economic phenomena are to be confined. In this respect, the discussion is also intended to serve as a basis for the later analysis of why some theories worked better in explaining characteristic problems of low-income countries while others did not. As will be seen from the retrospective assessment of development theories in the second part of the book, development economists have long but misleadingly taken the behaviour of economic phenomena in rich economies as models for explaining economic realities in low-income countries – as the former were thought to provide a clear example of development paths that could, at least theoretically, be open to the developing world as well. Theoretic models relevant for advanced economies were thus generalised and extended to developing countries without specifying in their assumptions the often significant differences between the economic characteristics of advanced and less developed countries.

---

[1]Thirty-three out of the 49 countries currently classified as low-income countries are located in Sub-Saharan Africa (for a country listing see footnote 3). African countries deserve particular attention also because the identified characteristics that go along with their low income levels per head are more enduring than in most other regions of the world.

Against this experience, a clear analytic distinction between the characteristics of developing and developed economies seems vitally important.² This shall neither disguise the fact that less developed economies in themselves represent a very diverse group of countries, nor does the observation of commonalities in the economic characteristics of low-income countries imply that these characteristics have unique underlying causes. The factors that contribute to the emergence of certain common characteristics can, in fact, vary widely with each country's specific cultural roots, colonial history, territorial and demographic size, natural endowments, degree of ethnic heterogeneity, form of government, or with regard to many other context-specific factors. In other words, contextual diversity among countries relates primarily to the endogenous processes that bring about certain common characteristics or outcomes. As will be discussed at the end of Part II, this limits not only the scope for deriving broad policy conclusions from the commonly observed characteristics of low-income countries. Conversely, it also implies that broadly framed development policies can lead to very divergent results in different developing countries, unless they are accompanied by individual implementation arrangements that accommodate a country's context-specific conditions.

Before individual economic characteristics of low-income countries will be discussed in the chapters that follow, it seems sensible to look at how this group of countries is conventionally defined. Developing countries are usually classified by their low level of income per capita relative to that of advanced industrialised economies. Most international organisations use gross national income (GNI) per capita as classification criterion in their formal definitions of developing countries. However, as GNI by itself does not constitute a measure of welfare or success in development, these official definitions are often supplemented by indicators for the quality of social and human life. The group of developing countries is generally subdivided in low- and middle-income economies. The World Bank currently classifies economies with a GNI per capita at or below 935 US$ per year as low-income countries.³ Those countries with a GNI per capita between US $936 and 3,705 are

---

²The economic characteristics of developing and advanced economies often differ markedly both in their degree and in their kind. For example, informal economic activity (the subject of Chap. 5 below) is a phenomenon that can be observed in low-income and high-income countries alike. But while the informal sector sometimes accounts for the largest part of output and employment in low-income economies, it has often only negligible effects on economic outcomes in industrialised countries. Moreover, informality in low-income countries and high-income countries differs substantially in its forms and underlying causes: Whereas informal economic activity in advanced economies occurs mostly as a form of tax evasion, it is in low-income countries primarily a strategy to cope with the absence or poor performance of formal legal and juridical institutions.

³As per 2009, 49 countries are belonging to the group of low-income countries. These are: Afghanistan; Bangladesh; Benin; Burkina Faso; Burundi; Cambodia; Central African Republic; Chad; Comoros; Congo, Dem. Rep.; Côte d'Ivoire; Eritrea; Ethiopia; Gambia, The; Ghana; Guinea; Guinea-Bissau; Haiti; Kenya; Korea, Dem. Rep.; Kyrgyz Republic; Lao PDR; Liberia; Madagascar; Malawi; Mali; Mauritania; Mozambique; Myanmar; Nepal; Niger; Nigeria; Pakistan; Papua New Guinea; Rwanda; São Tomé and Principe; Senegal; Sierra Leone; Solomon Islands;

classified as lower middle-income countries, and the group of countries with a GNI per capita between US $3,706 and 11,455 as upper middle-income countries.[4]

A more elaborate definition of the poorest countries is given by the UN's classification for Least Developed Countries (LDCs). According to UNCTAD (2008), a country is classified as LDC if it meets inclusion thresholds on three criteria: (1) a low-income criterion (a GNI per capita below US $750); (2) a weak human assets criterion (measured by a composite index based on indicators of nutrition, health, school enrolment and literacy); and (3) an economic vulnerability criterion (measured by a composite index based on indicators of instability in agricultural production, instability in exports of goods and services, the share of manufacturing and modern services in GDP, economic concentration, economic smallness and economic remoteness).[5]

Based on the World Bank's classification, latest statistics of 2007 suggest that nearly 84% of the world's population lived in low- and middle income countries which together produced 26% of the world's output. The group of low-income countries alone accounted for 20% of the world's population in 2007, but produced just 1.5% of the world's statistically recorded output of that year (World Bank, 2009). At a first glance, this output share of low-income countries is so low that one might be tempted to conclude that virtually no economic activity is performed in the world's poorest countries. That is not the case at all. Poor people engage in exchange and production activities in many different ways and forms, albeit often at only subsistence or small-scale levels. But just as the outcomes of these activities are hardly accounted for in international statistical compilations, so have the motivations and forms that characterise economic activity in low-income countries only incompletely been understood and addressed in mainstream development thinking.

Somalia; Tajikistan; Tanzania; Togo; Uganda; Uzbekistan; Vietnam; Yemen, Rep.; Zambia; and Zimbabwe. Although the term "low-income countries" has been chosen in this book to refer to the world's poorest countries, the analysis is not restricted to the countries included into the group of countries classified as low-income by the World Bank. An additional criterion for consideration of a country or region in this study is in particular the absence of major historical growth accelerations across a variety of interlinked sectors that also increased economic opportunities for the poorest parts of society.

[4]Figures correspond with data on 2007 GNI per capita using the "atlas conversion factor" to reduce the impact of exchange rate fluctuations (World Bank, 2009). Note that higher income values are usually obtained by calculating GNI per capita in purchasing power parity units, as prices tend to be lower in poor countries (thus a dollar of spending there is worth more).

[5]The differences in classification criteria have the effect that 14 countries (Angola; Benin; Bhutan; Djibouti, Equatorial Guinea; Kiribati; Lesotho; Maldives; Samoa; Sudan; Timor–Leste; Tuvalu; and Vanuatu) are considered LDCs by the UN but not as low-income countries by the World Bank. Conversely, another thirteen low-income countries according to the World Bank's definition (Benin; Côte d'Ivoire; Ghana; Kenya; Korea, Dem. Rep.; Kyrgyz Republic; Nigeria; Pakistan; Papua New Guinea; Tajikistan; Uzbekistan; Vietnam; Zimbabwe) are not considered LDCs according to UN criteria.

Against this background, the following chapters are intended to illuminate some of the conditions that have influenced the emergence of seemingly idiosyncratic but functioning forms and processes of economic activity in low-income countries. The common characteristics that are identified in this part, and discussed with regard to their economic implications, include persistent poverty (Chap. 2), high transaction costs (Chap. 3), private economic governance in responses to poorly performing governments (Chap. 4), and the widespread informalisation of economic relations (Chap. 5). The focus is mainly on the micro-level because it is at this level where the specific conditions of low-income countries affect economic choices and hence the specific forms in which economic activity is organised and governed. Macroeconomic factors are taken into account to the extent in which they affect the conditions that define the incentive structure of individuals and their responses to changes in the broader policy and institutional environment. Apart from that, the topics of the following chapters have been chosen as low-income countries are believed to differ especially in the occurrences of these phenomena from more advanced countries – with far-reaching implications for development theory, policy and operations as later parts of this book will show.

Chapter 2
Poverty

> Poverty is hunger. Poverty is lack of shelter. Poverty is being sick and not being able to see a doctor. Poverty is not being able to go to school and not knowing how to read. Poverty is not having a job, is fear for the future, living one day at a time. Poverty is losing a child to illness brought about by unclean water. Poverty is powerlessness, lack of representation and freedom.[1]

Poverty is the most distressful characteristic of economic underdevelopment. Poverty and underdevelopment are closely associated, and poverty reduction is by now an integral part of poor countries' development strategies as well as the overriding goal of international development assistance.[2] As reflected in the quote from the World Bank's *PovertyNet* that opens this chapter, poverty can be associated with a multitude of different factors. In all its dimensions, poverty has manifold implications for the behaviour of people and for the way in which an economy functions. Both the multi-dimensional nature of poverty and the heterogeneity of those defined as poor have made the operationalisation of poverty in development economics and policy an inherently difficult task. Related problems of measuring poverty in its various dimensions pose additional challenges.

Beyond the analytical challenges involved in defining and measuring poverty, a yet more fundamental problem concerns the often striking discrepancy between the concept of poverty of those engaged in the international fight against poverty and the self-perception of those who are, by the former's definition, considered as poor. The developed world tends to look at poverty in the South primarily in terms of

---

[1] Source: World Bank, *PovertyNet* website: http://go.worldbank.org/RQBDCTUXW0 (permanent URL).

[2] Overcoming poverty was first named as the key goal of the World Bank by Robert McNamara, then president of the bank, in his annual meeting speech in Nairobi in 1974. James Wolfensohn, who took office as the bank's president in 1995, renewed the institution's focus on poverty reduction, which has since then been embraced by most international and bilateral development institutions. More recently, international commitment to global poverty alleviation was reinforced by the international agreement of the Millennium Development Goals (MDGs) as part of the road map for implementing the UN Millennium Declaration adopted at the UN Millennium Summit in New York in September 2000. The goals include halving the proportion of population in extreme poverty between 1990 and 2015. See Table 2.1 for further details on the MDGs.

people's deficient living conditions and deprivation of basic needs, from which a moral imperative for action to fight poverty is inferred. A more dynamic concept of poverty can be encountered in poor (especially rural) communities in low-income countries, where poverty is not regarded as a fault, but rather as a state of minimum satisfaction of people's endogenous needs – a perspective that entails the potential for increases in human well-being.[3] In many poor countries, a distinction is, in fact, being made between leading a poor but dignified life, and living in destitution and misery. The former concept refers to situations where people have little but still have hope, while the latter means poverty without hope. Given the vulnerability of the poor to external shocks and insecurity, the line between poverty and destitution is sometimes very thin. Yet, it is important to note that differences in the perception of the poor, and in the assumptions about the nature of their poverty, can result in very different poverty reduction strategies and policies. These differences in the perception of poverty, and their implications on assumptions about the needs of the poor, have to be kept in mind if in the remainder of the analysis reference is made to "poverty" or "the poor".

The conventional approach for distinguishing the poor from the non-poor is to specify a poverty line in terms of a certain benchmark level of income or consumption below which people are defined as poor. National poverty lines reflect what is considered minimally sufficient to sustain a family in terms of food, housing, clothing or medical needs, and may vary against the background of a country's specific economic and social circumstances. Using the latest available data from national household surveys, almost half the population of low-income countries was living in households with per capita consumption or income levels below their respective country's national poverty line (World Bank 2009).[4]

To measure poverty across countries, international poverty lines set at 1.25 and 2 US dollars per day of standard purchasing power in 2005 prices are used.[5] According to

---

[3] A radical plea for the rehabilitation of poverty as a positive value can be found in the book *Poverty, Wealth of Mankind* by Beninese economist, politician and UN official Albert Tévoédjrè (1978).

[4] Among those low-income countries for which data are available, this headcount index ranges from around 30% of population below the national poverty line in Benin (1999), Ghana (2006) and Uganda (2004) to around 70% in Madagascar (1999), Sierra Leone (2004) and Zambia (2004).

[5] The 1.25 U.S. dollars per day line measures absolute (or extreme) poverty. The figure of 1.25 U.S. dollars a day was chosen because it is very close to the mean of the national poverty lines for the poorest 15 countries in terms of consumption per capita (i.e., 1.27 U.S. dollars per day at 2005 PPP prices). According to this standard, people are counted as poor if their daily consumption expenditure has less purchasing power than 1.25 U.S. dollars had in the United States in 2005. It has previously been set at 1 U.S. dollar per day at 1993 PPP, and the MDG 1, which tracks progress in absolute poverty reduction through 2015, is still based on this older international reference line. The revision of the absolute poverty line to 1.25 U.S. dollars followed the availability of updated PPP estimates after a new round of international price surveys in 2005. While also after the revision national poverty lines remain the same in local currency units, the incidence of poverty in the world is found to be higher than past estimates have suggested, as the 2005 price survey data suggest that past PPPs had implicitly underestimated the cost of living in most developing countries. The 2 U.S. dollars a day reference line counts poverty as defined by standards more typical of middle-income countries. It represents the median poverty line found amongst developing countries at 2005 prices. For more technical details on the methodology behind these poverty calculations, see Chen et al. (2008) as well as Chen and Ravallion (2008). For a critical assessment of the World Bank's approach to poverty measurement see Pogge and Reddy (2005).

newest estimates by the World Bank (Chen and Ravallion 2008), about 1.4 billion people – more than a quarter of the population of the developing world – were living with less than the equivalent of 1.25 US dollars a day in 2005, and more than 2.6 billion people had consumption levels below 2 US dollars per day. Compared with the numbers of the poor in 1981, there are today about 500 million fewer people who live with less than 1.25 US dollars a day – even as the developing countries' population grew by 1.78 billion people between 1981 and 2005. During the same period, the number of those that are defined as poor by the 2 US dollars a day standard has been constant at about 2.5 billion, implying that number of people living between 1.25 and 2 US dollars a day has actually risen sharply over 1981–2005, from about 600 million to 1.2 billion.

But this aggregate picture hides important regional trends in the poverty rate over the last 25 years. Almost the entire decline in extreme poverty actually happened in China, and to a lesser extent in India. Accordingly, the incidence of poverty (measured by the percentage of population below 1.25 US dollars per day) declined in East Asia from 77.7% in 1981 (by then the highest in the world) to 16.8% in 2005, and in the South Asia region from 59.4 to 40.3%. At the same time, in sub-Saharan Africa, where most of today's low-income countries are located, the percentage of population living below 1.25 US dollars a day fell only slightly from 53.7% in 1981 to 51.2% in 2005, with a peak of 58.7% in 1996 (ibid.).

The identification of poor populations through such income- or consumption-based reference lines represents a definition of poverty in the monetary space alone. Even though this is the most operational way for economists to conceptualise poverty, it has often made them blind for the many non-income related aspects that influence the living conditions of the poor as well. Analysing poverty also in its non-income related dimensions is important to understand the wide range of factors which contribute to poverty, and which can provide critical areas of intervention for antipoverty policies. But it is also necessary to account for the multiple dimensions of poverty because an income-based definition alone disguises the complex influences of poverty on the motivations and constraints which govern economic decisions of the poor, and which may ultimately help to explain why poverty persists and what can be done about it.

Initial efforts have been made to develop approaches by which poverty can be defined and measured in its multiple dimensions. As these approaches often identify different groups as poor, poverty rates may differ significantly depending on the approach adopted.[6] In the remainder of this chapter, poverty will be discussed in its multiple income and non-income related dimensions. Moreover, it will be shown that the non-income related indicators that have been developed to account for the multiple dimensions of poverty are still insufficient in terms of both their measurability and their value to convey an understanding of poverty as actually lived in everyday experience in low-income countries. Even the one-dimensional income-based poverty measures presented above are associated with considerable technical and methodological difficulties, which warrant cautious treatment of any measure of the rate of poverty on both national and global levels.

---

[6] See Laderchi et al. (2003) for a comparison of results from different approaches to poverty measurement.

2.1 The Multiple Dimensions of Poverty

Any attempt to understand the realities of low-income countries must remain incomplete if it concentrates on only visible and objectively measurable outcomes. It is the quantifiability that has made income or consumption levels the most frequently invoked criteria for defining poverty. However, people suffer from poverty in many more respects than just through the immediate consequences of their low levels of income or consumption. Good health, a long life expectancy, education, social status, having a voice in matters that affect ones living conditions, security, freedom from harm, violence and disaster are all valued elements of individual welfare too, and deprivation from these constitutes important non-income dimension of poverty.

In the following subsections, poverty will be discussed by looking at the implications of low income and consumption levels on the economic activities of the poor, as well as by examining the effects of three additional non-income dimensions of poverty: (1) poor health and education; (2) social exclusion and (3) insecurity. All these dimensions are essential complements to the concept of income poverty in so far as they directly or indirectly affect the income-earning capability of the poor, and thus also the extent of their material well-being.

2.1.1 Income and Consumption Pattern

As said before, a low level of income or consumption represents the most visible and objectively quantifiable dimension of poverty. It captures poor people's deprivation from material goods such as food, clothing and housing, as well as their deficient command over productive resources, including natural endowments such as land, crops, animals, clean water and air, as well as other productive assets like equipment, machinery or information.

But poor people's low levels of income and consumption expenditure also have important implications on their economic decisions and demand pattern, which in turn influence the structure of the economic system in which they interact. The economic structure of low-income countries is in large parts that of a subsistence economy. Subsistence or near-subsistence activities are common where the only productive resource that people possess is their human capital and – in the case of subsistence farming – often also a small plot of land. Subsistence activities mostly take place entirely outside the monetary economy, i.e., poor people consume what they produce with no or only little surplus production left for exchange.

An immediate consequence of the subsistence economy is the low purchasing power of the poor, which means they can only afford to buy small amounts of goods at a time. For example, the author observed people in Malawi buying single cigarettes, single sheets of paper, single razor blades or soap in chunks. Peter Bauer (2000) reports from Nigeria that the sale of one box of matches is at times a wholesale transaction, as the buyer resells the box in little bundles of only a few matches together with parts of the striking surface of the box. The large success of mobile telephone operators in Africa can also be attributed to the fact that it is commensurate with the demand pattern of the poor. Whereas the donor-assisted installation of landline telephone networks failed in many parts of Africa south of the Sahara because of the high and regular cost of individual subscriptions, mobile phone operators sell airtime for their prepaid services in small units worth only a few dollar cents.[7] Prepaid airtime is even being used by the poor as a way of transferring money. In its most simple form, this works in that the sender buys prepaid airtime of the desired amount, sends the scratch card code via SMS to the recipient who then exchanges the value of the airtime for money at a specialised agent who usually uses the airtime to run a "telephone bureau" where people can make calls for money. Some mobile phone operators are now also offering more sophisticated mobile payment services. In any way, these new technologies make financial service accessible to poor people who would otherwise not have had any chance to open a bank account.[8]

The demand patterns of the poor also determine the structures by which products are supplied to them. The demand for basic products that poor people cannot produce themselves is satisfied in low-income countries by a large number of mostly informal vendors and traders, who operate on a small scale and far away from major commercial centres. They themselves often receive their supplies from regional traders who again procure their goods from even other middlemen or international traders. Most development economists would agree that this fragmented supply structure hurts the poor as it leads to inefficient marketing and means that the poor pay higher prices per unit than they would pay for bulk purchases on markets. But one has to consider that these vendors' and traders' modes of organisation and marketing are a reflection of the structure of the demand they satisfy. No formal retail business, let alone foreign traders, would service the poor in a way these small-scale internal traders do. Bauer (1991, 2000) was among the first to emphasise the important role that these traders play in helping to transform low-income countries' subsistence economies into exchange economies. He even conjectured that "had [internal] trading activity and its effects been properly appreciated, mainstream development economics would have been radically different" (Bauer 2000, 5).

Small-scale internal traders and vendors do not only add to the economic opportunities of the poor by offering a supply structure through which they can satisfy their demand for basic manufactured goods, but they also open up for them the possibility to exchange their own surplus production. It is mostly the poor themselves

---

[7] Africa's leading mobile operator is Zain Group (formerly Celtel), which has about 20 million subscribers in 15 countries in Africa south of the Sahara. It employs around 8,000 people directly, but indirectly provides jobs to around 170,000 people in Africa who resell prepaid airtime or operate telephone bureaus (The Economist 2007a).

[8] In Africa, mobile telephony and the various support services that have become available with it has unleashed a wave of wealth-creating entrepreneurship, even among some of the poorest people. In Malawi, for instance, the Malawi Agriculture Commodity Exchange (MACE), an independent government-sponsored organisation, makes prices on a wide range of agricultural commodities from main national markets available to small-scale farmers on a daily basis through a short messaging service.

who engage in small-scale trade to market the surplus from their subsistence or near-subsistence activities in farming or home-based production. But because of a lack of cash reserves and storage facilities, marketable outputs are provided in only small quantities and at irregular intervals. Just as with the distribution of goods to the poor, these conditions make the physical collection, storage, bulking and transport of poor people's surplus production inherently labour intensive. But as the supply price of labour and the barriers to enter into informal trading activities are low, engagement in internal trade does in fact make economic sense.[9]

Besides their engagement in exchange, poor people also make investments of various kinds. These investments include the clearing, improvement and cultivation of fallow land, the self-construction of dwellings or the breeding of livestock. Yet, these forms of capital formation are effectuated by the poor largely through the investment of their human capital. They involve no or only very little monetary expenditure and are therefore ignored in official statistics as well as by both mainstream development economists and policymakers. In fact, as Bauer (2000) notes, these overlooked categories of investment are highly significant in the economic context of low-income countries because they make up the predominant form of domestic investment in a subsistence-style economy, and particularly in subsistence farming. Moreover, these non-monetary investments represent an archetypical form of capital formation that can be a crucial basis for the advancement to more modern forms of investment and exchange.

In spite of poor people's low income and consumption levels, these basic forms of carrying out economic activities represent endogenous strategies for poverty reduction that rely on the poor's own potential. The challenge lies in increasing the scale of individual operations through greater specialisation and a deepening in the division of labour to raise productivity. Yet, investment into a specialised occupation requires capital – in fact not only long-term investment capital, but especially short-term financing. As the results from a survey carried out by the author in 2007 among indigenous small-scale enterprises in Malawi confirm, the foremost obstacle to the growth of production activity in low-income countries appears to be a lack of working capital, that is the short-term finance needed by small-scale farmers to bridge the time between the planting and harvesting season, or between the purchase of primary products and the sale of assembled goods made from them, for instance, in the case of processing activities. If such needs were more properly appreciated, there could be a meaningful role for development assistance here. But donors and international

---

[9] It has yet to be noted that the important function that internal traders perform by connecting small-scale producers to markets can have a downside if producer–trader relations are characterized by an asymmetric distribution of power. This can happen, for instance, when only one buyer faces many sellers and thus uses his monopsony power to drive prices down. This is a frequent characteristic of the coffee sector where small-scale farmers in remote locations depend on local middlemen who purchase their raw coffee at a fraction of its value (these middlemen are hence known as "coyotes" in Latin America). In situations like these, fair trade schemes can provide a way to correct such market failures. By cutting the middlemen out of the supply chain, alternative trade organisations provide small-scale produces with direct access to domestic and international markets at predetermined prices that are set to guarantee farmers a living wage.

development banks have largely been reluctant to establish appropriate channels through which the needed working capital could be allocated to the poor. Development banks are scarcely prepared for the provision of especially short-term finance. Where they have managed to implement financing schemes for small and medium-sized firms in low-income countries, they came mostly in the form of global credits provided to domestic banks which then offer them to local firms as long-term capital backed by the assets into which they are being invested. Short-term financing is rarely provided. This is in part due to obvious misconceptions of the structures and needs of poor people's small-scale economic operations, and also because short-term micro-finance is considered as too risky a business since stocks of products and production work in progress are not recognised as collateral by most commercial banks.

The private sector has actually been more effective in anticipating and servicing the needs of the poor. An example is the growing micro-credit market especially in South Asia. Grameen Bank in Bangladesh was the first to demonstrate that lending to the poor can be economically viable if oriented at poor people's needs and the indigenous structures of their economic activities. By providing small loans to self-help groups of mostly woman micro-entrepreneurs, it relies on these group's internal monitoring mechanisms to ensure that its members honour their joint liability for repayment of the loan.[10]

The benefits that micro-lending provides to the businesses of the poor and micro-credit institutions alike have paved the way for the discovery of the poorest parts of the population as a particular customer group also for other products and services. The case for profitably serving the untapped market of almost three billion people living on less than 2 US dollars per day in the developing world has first been articulated by C. K. Prahalad and Stuart Hart in 2002.[11] In their article, they advise multinational corporations to rethink their emerging market strategies: instead of servicing the few wealthy and emerging middle-class consumers, they should focus on the developing world's poorest, but largest socio-economic group. In low-income countries, this "base of the pyramid" (BoP) market segment indeed accounts for the vast majority of total household expenditure on food, energy, health, housing, transportation and communication services. But the BoP market cannot just be entered with conventional product portfolios or by replicating Western marketing strategies. It needs, instead, to be built by thoroughly re-engineering existing business processes, products and distribution channels to reflect the specific needs, circumstances and consumption patterns of the poor. As discussed above, large mobile phone operators were among the first to successfully tap into the BoP market by offering prepaid services at very low unit costs. Many more examples of products serving the needs of the poor exist which range from dairy products that don't require refrigeration like margarine and powdered milk to affordable commercial solutions that bring modern lighting

---

[10] See Sect. 4.2.2 for a more detailed analysis of the approach to micro-lending adopted by Grameen Bank.

[11] See their article "The Fortune at the Bottom of the Pyramid" (published in Strategy+Business, Issue 26, 2002). Both further developed the idea separately in Prahalad (2010) and Hart (2007).

technologies to the estimated 1.6 billion people in developing countries that lack access to electricity. While claims that servicing the BoP market represents a new blueprint for poverty reduction are disputed, more inclusive business models of multinational corporations that respond to the needs of those at the base of the pyramid have indeed great potential for empowering the poor. Benefits come from a greater choice of goods and services available to the poor without a "poverty penalty" as the result of local monopolies, inadequate market access or poor distribution. Moreover, the BoP market offers opportunities for establishing linkages between developing world producers and major retailers in the developed world, for instance, where BoP business models include buying from or distributing through local producers, microentrepreneurs and internal traders. The most promising property of BoP business models, however, is that they are build on the principle of mutual value creation and empowerment of the poor as opposed to the model of dependence that still characterise many aid-financed poverty reduction programmes.

The described patterns of economic activity by the poor have the potential of being a nucleus of endogenously induced growth in low-income countries. Yet, these efforts by the poor are fragile as they still remain vulnerable to other aspects of poverty like diseases, natural disasters, uncertainty and insecurity.

2.1.2 Health and Education

Education and health are necessary human resources that determine poor people's opportunities and capabilities to earn an income, in particular as their human capital is often the only productive asset they possess. The positive effect of education on labour earnings at the individual level is a well-researched finding of the empirical literature on economic growth.[12] Empirical studies also show that health and nutritional status have a positive effect on wages and labour productivity, and that this linkage is stronger for poor workers than for wealthier ones.[13] But health also determines poor people's productivity through its effect on education. School attendance and performance is lower for children who suffer from disease or malnutrition, hence leading to a lower income-earning capacity later on. Not only does health determine educational attainment, the reverse is also true. For instance, the education of mothers has been found to have a strong positive impact on their children's health. The interpretation is that mothers with at least some years of schooling are better able to process health-related

---

[12] As Murphy et al. (1990) show, this effect is less significant at the aggregate level, however. They argue that the effect of education on individual productivity will only translate into economic growth if educated workers engage in productive activities. It does not if they use their skills, for instance, for rent-seeking activities or for getting employed in the informal sector.

[13] This has important effects also at the aggregate level: malaria alone is estimated to reduce GDP growth rates by 0.5 per year on an average in sub-Saharan Africa, and in the countries hardest hit by the HIV/AIDS epidemic (such as Botswana, Zimbabwe, South Africa and Lesotho), the average lifespan was cut short by more than ten years (World Bank 2002).

information that helps them to protect their children from diseases.[14] Similarly, education plays an important role in the prevention of HIV/AIDS. These interrelations show that malnourishment, poor health and low educational attainment are not only consequences of poverty but they are also important causes of it. This has also important policy implications: If economic growth increases the income-earning opportunities of the poor, they will only be able to fully benefit from these opportunities if they enjoy good health and educational status. Thus, for economic growth to be pro-poor, it has to be accompanied by improvements in health and education.

2.1.3 Social Exclusion

Social exclusion refers to poor people's limited access to institutions and public services. Exclusion from the access to formal institutions can be the result of corrupt or unaccountable state officials who are not responsive to poor people's needs, public service providers that discriminate against the poor or legal and juridical systems that fail to protect the weakest in the society. The presence of other aspects of poverty may also constrain poor people's participation in economic and political life. For instance, illiteracy and weak health are barriers to the access to labour and product markets. Furthermore, with little formal education, poor people lack the information that is required for their participation in economic and political processes, for the use of the media or for gaining knowledge about their rights or economic opportunities potentially open to them.

Exclusion from the benefits of formal institutions constrains people in fully realising the potential they actually have to escape from poverty. For instance, the holder of a productive asset may not be able to realise an income from it if he is denied the legal title which establishes his property right to that asset. And a farmer, whose crops exceed his own household needs may not be able to sell his surplus production if he lacks access to physical infrastructure and transport services that connect him with product markets. Exclusion from the merits of formal institution is a dimension of poverty that poor people express as a sense of helplessness and dependency, and as the lack of power and voice in the institutions of state and society (World Bank 2001a).

Where access to formal institutions is denied, informal arrangement at the community or family level can serve as an important substitute for the functions that formal institutions fail to perform for the poor. These informal institutions include networks, associations and social connections governed by customary or cultural rules.[15] But community relationships and their informal arrangements are seldom open-access endowments. Instead, they are built from common traits, trust and recip-

---

[14] See Kanbur and Squire (2001) for a discussion of the empirical literature on both the effects of health and education on income and on the interrelations between health and education.

[15] See Chaps. 4 and 5 for a more detailed discussion of types and functions of informal institutions and arrangements in the context of low-income countries.

rocal relations among people who often share same cultural, ethical or religious backgrounds. Inclusiveness of membership in informal arrangements based on social divisions excludes all those who are distinct from the main group in terms of their gender, ethnicity, religion, race, caste or social status. Members of minority groups are thus often deprived from the opportunity to take part in community life, to participate in social activities and to have a sense of belonging to a larger group.

In the more recent literature on social development, social exclusion is often related to the concept of social capital.[16] Elinor Ostrom (1997) defines social capital broadly as "the shared knowledge, understandings, institutions, and patterns of interaction that a group of individuals bring to any activity" (ibid., 158). Other contributions to this field have used different terms and definitions for social capital. Ritzen et al. (2000) focus on social cohesion which they define as "a state of affairs in which a group of people [...] demonstrate an aptitude for collaboration that produces a climate for change" (ibid., 6). Amartya Sen (1999) discusses "social opportunity" as one of five distinct instrumental freedoms which help to enhance the general capability of a person, and which contribute to the overall freedom he has to live the way he would like to live. Sen relates social opportunities to the arrangements that society makes to enable everyone's effective participation in economic and political activities – a description which closely approximates to what other researchers mean by social capital, and which makes evident that the concept of social capital embraces relationships with both formal and informal institutions.[17] There is considerable overlap among the concept of social capital and social exclusion. Indeed, social exclusion can be understood as deprivation from the returns on social capital.[18]

2.1.4 Insecurity

Insecurity is not an aspect of poverty alone. It is a widely observable characteristic of developing countries and associated, among others, with conditions of political and macroeconomic instability that may result from limitations in the rule of law, corruption, natural disasters, domestic violence from war or civil conflict or macroeconomic phenomena such as inflation or market collapses. However, poor people are particularly vulnerable to adverse changes in their environment. If people lack assets which could be used to make provisions against emergencies, the probability of being exposed to the risk of adverse shocks results in a strong sense of insecurity.

---

[16] The concept of social capital originally emerged within political science and sociology. Notable contributors have been James Coleman (1990) and Robert Putnam et al. (1993).

[17] While the essence of the concept of social capital is widely accepted, several authors question its denotation as capital, because many of the characteristics of physical capital do not apply to social assets (e.g., divisibility, non-negative value, the possibility for establishing ownership, depreciation from use, etc.). However, similar qualifications could easily be made also with regard to the widely accepted notion of "human capital".

[18] For a comparative discussion of both concepts, see Narayan (1999).

Insecurity resulting from an inability to cope with risks also means uncertainty about the future, and explains why short-term decision-making often dominates among poor people over long-term planning for escaping poverty. Moreover, insecurity reinforces dependency arising from unequal relationships with landlords, creditors, vendors, employers, government institutions or bread-winning family members.

In the absence of effective protection through formal state institutions, public safety nets and effective insurance markets, the acquisition of social capital in informal networks or traditional communities represents an important alternative means of insurance for poor people. As will be discussed in more detail in Chap. 4, the participation in relation-based informal arrangements, like local community associations, can enhance the ability of households to better cope with uncertainty and to adapt to changing circumstances.

2.2 The Problem of Measuring Poverty

Poverty measures add to the understanding of the nature of poverty important quantitative information about the incidence and depth of the problem. Measuring poverty permits to evaluate the relevance of poverty as a characteristic element of developing countries, is indispensable for the formulation and testing of hypotheses on the causes of poverty, and makes it possible to monitor the development of poverty rates over time and across countries. But poverty measures are instrumental for these purposes only to the extent in which it is possible to measure the multiple dimensions of poverty in an accurate, robust and consistent way. Unfortunately, a combination of data gathering problems and methodological questions makes this a particularly difficult task.

As discussed above, the traditional way economists think of and operationalise the standard of living is in terms of income or consumption levels. Correspondingly, the most common measures of poverty are based on real income or some monetary value of consumption.[19] This has been justified in two different ways. First, income-based poverty measures are compatible with (cardinal) utility theory, which assumes the maximisation of utility as an objective of consumers, and their expenditures on commodities as a reflection of the marginal utility they derive from their consumption. Utility thus defines well-being and is measured by either expenditure or income data. Second, those who reject the notion of income as a monetary measure of utility, instead justify the use of income-based indicators through the assumption that income most appropriately approximates other

---

[19] Consumption expenditure is generally viewed as a more adequate welfare indicator than income. However, income data are more widely available than data on consumption levels. In such cases, the preferred approach for estimating consumption levels used by the World Bank and other international organisations is to multiply income data by the share of aggregate private consumption in national income obtained from national accounts data (World Bank 2001a).

(non-income) aspects of poverty.[20] Finally, the measurement of poverty in terms of income levels is so common because data on income are just most widely available, allowing for relatively robust and consistent poverty measures across countries and over time.

These comfortable features of income-based poverty measures are yet obscured by several technical and methodological difficulties. They are in particular evident where monetary measures are used for welfare comparisons across countries, as is being done in the case of the "1 US dollar a day" international poverty line.[21] Problems start with the choice of the data source to which poverty measures are anchored. Income and consumption data can either be drawn from national accounts or from household surveys. Theoretically, both sources of data should yield similar results, but practically, the do not. On the one hand, the level of absolute poverty (as measured by the global 1 or 1.25 US dollars a day poverty lines) is much lower when income per head is measured by data from national accounts, while survey data yield higher poverty counts. Ravallion (2004a) argues that studies which use GNI from national accounts to measure average income per person of households actually capture not only household consumption (with data obtained through household surveys) but also investment and government spending. Relative to the 1 or 1.25 US dollars a day poverty lines, this method must give lower poverty counts as it overstates the average incomes of the poor. On the other hand, national account data indicate a significant decline in global poverty over the last two decades, while this trend is much more moderate when poverty measures are obtained from survey data. Two explanations for these contradicting results are suggested by Deaton (2004). First, much of the discrepancy is probably due to the fact that, as people get better off, they are likely to understate their income in household surveys. As a result, income growth is to a lesser extent reflected in survey data than in data from national accounts. Second, unlike national account data, household survey data also capture informal economic activities or non-market transactions such as the value of poor peoples' own subsistence production, intra-family services or in-kind contributions from local community groups. These components of households' consumption pattern usually account for a larger share of total consumption the poorer a household is. As economies grow, the share of income from informal activity decreases, which narrows the discrepancies between survey and national accounts estimates. In other words, income data from national accounts rise faster than income data gathered through household surveys, thus implying a faster decline in poverty rates. Note also that meaningful comparisons of average income or consumption growth rates from national account statistics with survey data on income or consumption are only possible if the distribution of income or consumption has remained unchanged over the observation period. If economic growth is associated

---

[20] This view has been challenged by studies which show that income usually explains very little of the variations in non-money metric welfare indicators. See, for instance, Appleton and Song (1999).

[21] It has recently been raised to 1.25 U.S. dollars at 2005 PPP following the availability of improved price survey data on the basis of which international price comparisons used in poverty accounting are being made. For further details, see footnote 5 above.

2.2 The Problem of Measuring Poverty

with growing inequality, consumption of the poor does not rise as fast as average consumption, and hence national accounts data overestimate the poverty reducing effect of economic growth.[22]

Another set of methodological difficulties with income-based welfare comparisons across countries relates to the fact that international poverty lines are expressed in Purchasing Power Parity (PPP) terms to account for differences in prices of commodities traded on local markets. This is done to hold the real value of the poverty line constant across countries. This method does not, however, allow accounting for intra-country differences in the cost of living, which may be significant in particular between rural and urban areas. Furthermore, the use of PPP conversion factors is questioned because PPP refers to a fixed reference basket of commodities and thus accounts neither for differences in national consumption pattern nor for the fact that a poor household's typical consumption needs may differ from the goods and services contained in the relevant international reference basket.[23] The use of a universal international poverty line may be instrumental for monitoring progress in reducing global poverty. But for the design and effective implementation of policy interventions towards poverty alleviation, more context-specific assessments of the situation of the poor are needed that not only account for the different dimensions and causes of poverty, but also for regional conditions and the individual needs and preferences of different social groups.

An even greater challenge poses the task of measuring poverty in its multiple non-income dimensions. Unlike income or consumption expenditure, non-income aspects of deprivation are, by definition, very difficult to measure in monetary terms, as no market prices are available for them. Approximating them instead by conventional income or consumption-based metrics is as well difficult, as no general correlation can be established between all income and non-income elements of deprivation. The prevalence of each individual dimension of poverty is therefore more appropriately measured by separate independent indicators. An overview of the indicators that are presently used to monitor various health, education and environment-related aspects of poverty is presented in Table 2.1. Many of the indicators are also used for measuring progress against the seven poverty-related Millennium Development Goals (MDGs), which commit the international community to promote human development.

---

[22] The neglect of income distribution actually represents another serious shortcoming of GNI per head as poverty indicator. Advances in the generation of data on income inequality in recent years have made it possible to construct well-being measures that combine average income with some measure of inequality [see, for instance, Grün and Klasen (2003) and Deininger and Squire (1996)]. Above that, as has been suggested most prominently by Amartya Sen, the uneven distribution of incomes may have an independent negative effect on the aggregate well-being of the poor if economic inequality is in itself considered as a dimension of poverty.

[23] In order to better anticipate the characteristics of poor households in future poverty estimations, efforts are being made in the framework of the International Comparison Program (ICP) to prepare data that reflects expenditure patterns of poor people that can be used to compute specific "poverty PPPs". The ICP, which was initiated in 1968 by Irving Kravis, Alan Heston and Robert Summer on behalf of the World Bank, regularly produces internationally comparable price levels, expenditure values and PPP estimates based on national surveys that price nearly 1,000 products and services.

Table 2.1 Indicators of income- and non-income dimensions of poverty

Poverty dimension	Indicators
Income-poverty (MDG 1)	Percentage of population below 1 US dollar (PPP) a day
	Poverty gap ratio (mean percentage distance below poverty line)
	Share of poorest quintile in national consumption
Malnutrition and hunger (MDG 1)	Prevalence of underweight children under 5 years of age
	Proportion of population below minimum level of dietary energy consumption
(Primary) education (MDG 2)	Net enrolment ratio in primary education
	Proportion of pupils starting grade 1 who reach grade 5
	Literacy rate of 15–24-year-olds
Gender equality (MDG 3)	Ratio of girls to boys in primary, secondary and tertiary education
	Ratio of literate women to men, 15–24-year–olds
	Share of women in wage employment in the non-agricultural sector
	Proportion of seats held by women in national parliament
Health (children and mothers) (MDGs 4 and 5)	Under five mortality rate
	Infant mortality rate
	Proportion of 1-year-old children immunised against measles
	Maternal mortality ratio
	Proportion of births attended by skilled health personnel
Health (prevalence of HIV/Aids, malaria and other diseases) (MDG 6)	HIV prevalence among pregnant women aged 15–24 years
	Condom use rate of the contraceptive prevalence rate
	Ratio of school attendance of orphans to school attendance of non-orphans aged 10–14 years
	Prevalence and death rates associated with malaria
	Proportion of population in malaria-risk areas using effective malaria prevention and treatment measures
	Prevalence and death rates associated with tuberculosis
	Proportion of tuberculosis cases detected and cured under directly observed treatment short course (DOTS)
Access to, and preservation of environmental resources (MDG 7)	Proportion of land area covered by forest
	Ratio of area protected to maintain biological diversity to surface area
	Energy use (kg oil equivalent) per 1 US dollar of GDP (in PPP)
	Carbon dioxide emissions per capita and consumption of ozone-depleting chlorofluorocarbons (ODP tons)
	Proportion of population using solid fuels
	Proportion of population with sustainable access to an improved water source, urban and rural
	Proportion of population with access to improved sanitation, urban and rural
	Proportion of households with access to secure tenure

Poverty dimensions that are addressed by one of the Millennium Development Goals (MDG) are identified by the abbreviation *MDG* and the number of the respective goal in *parentheses*.
Source: UNDP (2007)

The greatest disadvantage of using separate indicators for each aspect of being poor is that this method does not allow for the simultaneous evaluation of poverty in all its dimensions. An attempt to overcome this drawback has been made in 1990 by Mahbub ul Haq of the United Nations Development Programme (UNDP), who introduced the now widely recognised Human Development Index (HDI). This index combines three dimensions of human well-being (or poverty defined as lack of human development) in terms of a single composite measure: (1) a long and healthy life as measured by life expectancy at birth; (2) access to knowledge as measured by a combination of the adult literacy rate and gross enrolment in primary, secondary and tertiary level education and (3) the standard of living as measured by GDP per capita in PPP US dollars (UNDP 2007). It has to be noted, however, that the HDI does not produce absolute measures of poverty. It is instrumental only for ranking different countries with regard to their relative level of human development. Moreover, the aggregation of several dimensions of poverty into a single index makes weakens the power of the HDI as a poverty measure. Apart from the loss of information associated with aggregation, the selection of weights associated to each component of the summary index involves value judgements about the relative utility that individuals derive from the attainment of each measured aspect of human development. A rise in the index suggests that each of its components (life expectancy, literacy and income) improve. If there are movements in opposite directions, however, the index yields ambiguous results.[24] The main achievement of the HDI yet is that it raised awareness and global recognition of the equal importance of both the income and non-income dimension of poverty or human development, respectively.

Measuring poverty in the dimensions of social exclusion and insecurity is not without difficulty either. The World Bank (2001a) suggests evaluating voicelessness and powerlessness as associated with social exclusion by a combination of the results from participatory group discussions, polls and national surveys on qualitative variables, such as the extent of civil liberties, political rights, the transparency of the legal system and the existence of an independent media.

Moreover, the effects from insecurity and vulnerability to shocks can be identified, for instance, through fluctuations in people's income and consumption levels or through variations in their health or housing situation. These dynamics cannot be measured by one-time observations, however. Instead, household panel data are required that survey the same sample of households several times over a prolonged period. Yet, for the proposal of strategies to protect the poor against external shocks, it is even more important to find indicators that help to identify a household's exposure to risk beforehand. Possible indicators are those which capture factors that help households to cope with risks, like the presence of physical assets (as a means of self-insurance that can be sold to compensate for temporary loss of income), the level of education (where better education implies a higher ability to manage risk), the degree of income diversification or links to formal and informal support networks.[25]

---

[24] As Kanbur (2003) notes, a way to overcome this conceptual weakness could be to find a meta-concept of well-being that is determined by the components of the HDI. Amartya Sen's "capability approach" provides a leading attempt in this direction.

[25] See World Bank (2001a) for a discussion of the complexities involved in measuring vulnerability.

Chapter 3
Transaction Costs

In neither in advanced economies, nor in developing countries are economic transactions without cost. But the lower these costs are, the more exchange is possible, and the greater are a society's gains from trade and specialisation. It is well known since the early days of classical economics that a major cause for the wealth of nations is the ability of both countries and firms to exploit comparative advantages through specialisation and the division of labour. However, the division of labour requires that everyone can exchange his specialised output for other products. Although the importance of the exchange economy is well recognised, it has long been assumed to operate at no cost. Accordingly, economic development was conventionally attributed to changes in production factors and technology alone.

More recent research on transaction costs demonstrates, instead, that the level and composition of the cost of doing business conveys important information about how economic activity is organised in a society, and how the productivity and performance of an economic system is determined by the transaction cost properties of alternative modes of organising economic interactions. The transaction cost approach is part of an emerging new body of research on the role and importance of institutions for the performance of an economic system. Within this New Institutional Economics,[1] it contributes in particular to the understanding of institutional arrangements that govern cooperation and exchange in a given institutional environment. Another theme within the New Institutional Economics centres on the institutional environment upon which institutional arrangements are based. It specifically asks how changes in a society's formal rules and informal norms of behaviour affect cost and incentive structures and hence the performance of the economic system.[2] Understanding transaction costs in developing countries requires the study

---

[1] See Sect. 8.2 for a more detailed discussion of the theoretical foundations of the New Institutional Economics and its application to development problems.

[2] Within this branch of institutional theory, the economics of property rights deal with the part of the institutional environment that is concerned with the rules that govern economic activity in the private sector. Correspondingly, the public choice literature has developed from research on the rules and mechanisms that determine the performance of public institutions.

of both the organisation and governance structures of contractual relations within a given institutional environment and the performance characteristics of that institutional environment itself.

3.1 Transaction Costs and the Organisation of Economic Activity

The role of transaction costs in explaining the structure of market and non-market forms of economic organisation was first acknowledged by Coase (1937) in his *The Nature of the Firm*. Accordingly, economic exchanges are organised in ways to reduce the cost of contracting among the parties to an exchange. The organisational form of exchange is therefore determined by the nature of the transaction. Williamson (1979) associates various attributes of transactions with their most economical mode of exchange.[3] Accordingly, transactions are performed through markets if they concern recurrent or occasional exchanges of standardised goods for which generic demand and supply sources are large. Such non-specific transactions are associated with relatively low transaction costs and are hence best executed through impersonal exchange on markets.[4] In contrast, high transaction costs are likely to come along with highly specific transactions in which the identity of the parties to the exchange matters, which require individually negotiated agreement of the terms of exchange and joint contract execution or which involve other kinds of transaction-specific investments. If any of these conditions predominate, exchanges might be executed at lower costs if it is organised outside the market under either bilateral or unified governance structures. In bilateral structures, which represent a hybrid form between impersonal exchange on markets and hierarchically structured transactions, the autonomy of the parties to an exchange is maintained. Examples include joint ventures, franchise operations, value chains or other forms of long-term contracting relationships. Unified or hierarchical governance structures provide an alternative mode of organising economic activity in the presence of highly specific transactions. In this case, transactions are placed under unified ownership, i.e. both sides to an exchange are within the same enterprise. A typical form of such hierarchical or unified structures is the vertical integration of successive stages in production and distribution into a single legal entity. Unlike impersonal exchanges on markets, such highly specific governance structures involve fixed costs as a result of the

---

[3] Williamson (1979) refers to mode of exchange as the governance structure under which a transaction is executed, i.e., the institutional arrangement within which the integrity of a transaction is decided. The idea that transactions and governance modes are aligned in a way to economise transaction costs was later formulated in Williamson (1996) as the discriminating alignment hypothesis.

[4] In these cases, transaction costs are low because, for instance, the verification of a product's price and quality parameters is easy, or because exchanges are executed with reference to standard terms and conditions which help to keep contracting costs low.

specific investments needed to set up the institutional arrangement for exchange. For that reason, bilateral or unified governance structures are more likely to evolve where transactions are recurrent in order to allow the set-up cost of the specialised structure to be recovered. Similarly, highly specific structures are superior to markets if transactions are executed under high uncertainty, because they allow better for adaptations in contractual relations once they become necessary in reaction to unforeseen events.

In low-income countries, in which unreliable formal legal and juridical systems are prevalent, economic interactions are inherently transaction specific. Without the possibility of recourse to formalised statutory proceedings, mutual trust and commitment to the terms of an exchange have to be acquired in the process of repeated transactions, on the basis of shared values, through participation in the institutions of a homogeneous group or through other shared features that create strong bonds between exchange partners.[5] In either case, the investment into an economic relation constitutes an asset the value of which is lost if the relationship breaks down. Long-standing relationships are in fact conceptually comparable with investments in specific assets. Highly specific assets represent sunk costs that have relatively little value beyond their use in the context of a specific contractual relation (Williamson 1979). If exchanges display features of asset specificity, transaction costs can be lowered if the exchange partners integrate. Relation-based transactions and other forms of privately governed modes of exchange that are common in low-income countries can thus be understood as transaction cost minimising arrangements. However, relation specificity in economic transactions can also have negative economic implications. For instance, if the institutional environment that gave rise to investments in relation-specific modes of exchange changes, the asset specificity characteristics can make informal relations path dependent in that agents prefer to continue exchange with partners they trust even if more profitable exchange opportunities outside the established relationship arise. Such cases, in which the transaction cost properties of an existing mode of economic organisation change in response to changes in the institutional environment, are addressed in the following section.

3.2 Transaction Costs and the Institutional Environment

The central concern of transaction costs economics is to explain the organisation and governance structure of contractual relations within a given institutional environment. From this perspective, the only influence economic agents have on the transaction costs they face is through their choice of the institutional arrangement that governs their transactions. However, a transaction cost-based perspective on

---

[5]See Chap. 4 for a discussion of the forms and functions of privately governed exchange arrangements that have evolved in contexts of low-income countries.

economic performance is incomplete if it is not complemented by an analysis of how changes in the institutional environment influence the transaction cost structures of different modes of organising economic activity. Whereas the study of alternative modes of exchange helps to explain how productivity can be increased by organising transactions in their most economical way in a given institutional setting, the analysis of the institutional environment delivers important insights on how the level and composition of transaction costs depend on the performance of a country's legal, political and social institutions.

Both perspectives are thus closely related. The institutional environment determines the structure and intensity of transaction costs in an economy. It constitutes an external constraint which influences the kind of institutional arrangements individuals enter to conduct economic transactions in the most economical way. Each institutional environment thus supports distinctive modes of organising economic activities. Changes in the institutional environment shift the comparative costs of governing institutional arrangements and thus generally imply a reorganisation of economic activities. For instance, a government that reforms its regulatory policies to simplify administrative procedures for businesses shifts the transaction cost constraints of the entire economic system. It means lower costs of transacting for all businesses that operate in the formal economy, and is supposed to translate into a higher productivity and performance of the economy.[6] However, differences in the economic performance of countries are not only a matter of different formal regulatory and enforcement systems. Informal institutions like the customs, conventions and attitudes of economic actors define a country's institutional background conditions as well. They can have very similar effects on the level and composition of transaction costs as formal institutions, but are much more difficult to influence through deliberate policy reforms.[7]

How does the institutional environment matter to the individual entrepreneur? To him, transaction costs are an artificial concept. He is concerned with the total costs of production, and his objective in choosing the location, organisational mode and technology for an investment is to economise on the sum of transformation and transaction costs incurred. If this sum exceeds expected benefits, the investment

---

[6] Expressed in technical terms, transaction cost economies that result from aligning specific types of transactions with their most economical governance structure could be interpreted as movements towards a given production possibility frontier (PPF), whereas institutional change that results in a lower overall level of transaction costs in an economy has the effect of shifting the PPF outwards, implying a more productive use of available resources. Expressed in the terms of constitutional economics, the distinction between attaining transaction cost economies through optimising the institutional form of exchange, or through a deliberate change of the institutional environment would correspond to making choices within constraints, as opposed to the choice of constraints.

[7] It is important to understand that in the context of low-income countries, reforms that only affect the formal institutional environment are likely to remain ineffective as large parts of population of these countries operate outside the official economy. This point is further developed in Sect. 5.3.1 on policy options for formalising informal economic activity as well as in Sects. 8.2.2 and 13.2.1 on the role of informal norms and values in the process of (formal) institutional change.

3.2 Transaction Costs and the Institutional Environment

will not take place. The total costs of production depend on the quality and price of productive inputs that are needed for both transaction and transformation activities. How much of these input factors are used in the transformation process is determined by the production technology. The share of total costs of production that is consumed for transaction-related activities depends on the governance structure of production and exchange activities and on the institutional environment. The total costs of production are thus jointly determined by the cost of productive inputs, the production technology and the institutional environment.

Productive inputs are expensive if they are low in supply. In developing countries, labour is abundant and its relatively low price is often the single most important competitive advantage of low-income economies.[8] The availability of investment capital depends on a country's propensity to save, but also upon the attractiveness of local investment opportunities. Low savings rates are indeed a common characteristic of developing countries, but could be remedied if profitable domestic investment opportunities attracted sufficient foreign capital.[9] Technological advances are embodied in new capital, but realising the productive potential unleashed by the adoption of new technologies requires congruent institutional background conditions.[10] The institutional environment therefore matters to the individual entrepreneur through its effect on both transformation and transaction costs. In fact, when assessing a country's business environment, investors primarily value issues that relate to a country's institutional environment, namely a sound legal and regulatory framework that promotes competition, good public governance and an efficient bureaucracy, as well as access to key financial and infrastructure services.[11] This again confirms the link between a country's institutional environment, the level and structure of transaction costs incurred by domestic enterprises and the effect of both on the country's economic performance.

---

[8] This applies to unskilled labour whereas the availability of skilled labour (human capital) and entrepreneurial talent often represents an investment constraint. This explains why investments in human capital through education can enhance productivity as much as physical capital investments do. Both categories thus warrant analogous treatment.

[9] In lack of the latter, a major rational for international development aid has long been to supply the capital necessary for filling a country's domestic savings gap. For development theories that support this proposition see Chap. 6.

[10] Features of the institutional environment that are of particular relevance for the diffusion and acquisition of new technologies include the available stock of knowledge and the physical infrastructure, but also behavioural attributes, formal regulations and production standards. On the interactions between technological and institutional change, see North and Wallis (1994) and North (1997).

[11] See, for instance, the findings from the World Bank Group's World Business Environment Surveys (WBES), which are presented, among others, in Batra et al. (2003), as well as the International Finance Corporation's Investment Climate Assessments which represent comprehensive country reports that draw upon the results of World Bank's business environment surveys and other available diagnostic tools.

3.3 Definition and Measurement of Transaction Costs

The literature on transaction costs interprets its subject of analysis in diverse ways. A broadly accepted, unified terminology has not yet emerged. At a high level of generality, transaction costs are defined as the cost of exchanging ownership titles (Demsetz 1968), the cost of running the economic system (Arrow 1969), the cost of making and enforcing contracts or the cost of capturing the gains from specialisation and the division of labour (Wallis and North 1986). In order to reduce these definitions' broad inclusiveness, associational assumptions are often made. For instance, Demsetz (1968) assumes that titles to assets exist and that all parties to an exchange are informed about their respective intensions and decisions and about the general nature of their market.

Definitions of greater empirical value are those applied in studies that aim at quantifying the level of transaction costs in an economy. An early attempt to develop an empirical definition of transaction costs is that by Wallis and North (1986). Their approach is to isolate from all economic activities those that are primarily associated with mediating, facilitating or managing economic transactions. In so doing, they invoke the rule that, to the consumer, transaction costs are all costs related to the purchase of goods or services that are not transferred to the seller. For the producer, they define transaction costs as the costs which he would not incur were he selling the good to himself. Actually observable, however, are only the costs related to marketed transaction activities, i.e. the transaction services provided by independent lawyers, accountants or by insurance, real estate and other agents. Conceptual difficulties arise with regard to transaction activities that are carried out within firms. Wallis and North approximate these internalised transaction services by the value of compensations of private sector employees in transaction-related occupations, including managers, accountants, in-house counsels, salesmen, inspectors and clerical staff. By combining the value of market-based and in-house transaction services with estimates for the value of compensations of government employees in transaction-related occupations, they found that 45% of national income of the United States was devoted to transacting in 1970, and that the size of the transaction sector has steadily grown since 1870.

But for the study of low-income countries, comparative estimates of the relative costs of doing business in different countries matter more than absolute measures of the size of transaction-related activities in an economy. Specifically, the interest is in identifying the costs that determine domestic economic opportunities and hence the relative competitiveness and performance of countries. These transaction costs can either be defined from the perspective of individuals and firms that operate under a given institutional structure or they can be approached by comparing the transaction cost implications of alternative institutional environments.

In analyses that are concerned with the comparative cost of alternative forms of organising contractual relations, transaction costs are most commonly defined with reference to the cost of successive transaction-related activities throughout the process of production and exchange. According to this definition, transaction costs associated with individual exchanges of goods and services include ex ante search and information costs, the cost of drafting, negotiating and enforcing the terms of exchange, as well as the ex post costs of contract alignment or dispute settlement that arise when omissions or unanticipated disturbances require adjustments of the terms of exchange.[12] Moreover, the costs associated with setting up and running the structure that governs production and exchange processes represent a further category of transaction costs. They include the cost of managing customised long-term contractual relations within or between firms, which are more significant the more specific these transactions are. Managerial transaction costs substitute for exchange-related ones if transactions along the supply chain are removed from the market and instead are performed in-house under unified ownership and control. Note that this substitution effect may partially offset the intended transaction cost economies of organising specific exchanges under hybrid or hierarchical governance structures. The different types of transaction costs are summarised in Table 3.1.

Table 3.1 A taxonomy of transaction costs

Cost component	Definition
Institutional perspective	
Information costs	The cost of measuring the price, quality and logistical attributes of the goods or services exchanged, as well as the credibility of agents
Search costs	The cost of finding fitting and credible exchange partners; the cost of marketing of goods or services
Contract drafting and negotiation costs	The cost of specifying the terms of exchange; the cost of ex ante planning of provisions for future contingencies
Enforcement costs	The cost of monitoring performance and ensuring compliance with the terms of a transaction; the cost of ex post contract alignments; legal costs of dispute settlement or arbitration
Managerial costs	The cost of coordination within firms or of overseeing and safeguarding contractual relations between firms
Institutional environment	
Market entry and exit costs	The cost of formally registering and/or closing a business
Transaction costs related to obtaining productive factors	The cost of getting credit; hiring and dismissing employees; the cost of registering property and obtaining titles to land
Costs of security	The cost of safeguarding against crime
Infrastructure costs	Transportation and communication costs; natural resources provision and distribution costs

---

[12] In economic analysis, the possibility that contracts are incomplete and may thus require ex post realignments is a consequence of assuming that individuals experience limits in foreseeing and processing all relevant information and future contingencies when formulating and solving complex problems. These limits unavoidably place bounds on the rationality of individual actions. For a more detailed discussion of bounded rationality and related behavioural implications, see Sects. 10.3 and 13.1.4.

If the interest is in the transaction cost implications of changes in the institutional environment over time or across countries, then a definition of transaction costs is most operational that reflects the performance characteristics of a country's economic, legal, political and social institutions. Of relevance for the study of low-income countries are in particular the transaction costs which relate to the way in which government institutions perform the basic functions that are considered as preconditions for the efficient functioning of markets or, in their absence, the effectiveness of alternative modes of governing contractual relations.[13]

3.3.1 The Cost of Regulation

The transaction costs associated with a country's formal institutional environment are largely those that result from government regulation of private businesses. In the context of low-income countries, important related categories include the cost associated with both the incomplete definition and enforcement of property rights, and ineffective formal contract enforcement institutions. These regulatory costs of private business activity find empirical representation in the indicators of the Doing Business project that provides objective measures of the cost associated with business regulations and their enforcement in 181 economies around the world (as of 2009). These data are compiled by the World Bank and the IFC through annual surveys among local government officials, lawyers, business consultants and other professionals who are engaged in administering or advising on legal and regulatory requirements in their respective countries. The data thus measure actual regulatory practices and outcomes rather than describing abstract stipulations of written laws and regulations. Table 3.2 compares average values for selected business regulation and enforcement measures for 2008 between low-income economies and OECD countries.[14]

---

[13] Note that the interpretation of transaction costs from the point of view of a country's institutional environment just describes another approach of defining the cost of transacting in an economy. Whereas the perception of transaction costs from the point of view of different modes of organising economic activity breaks down transactions costs according to different types of transaction activities, the institutional environment view defines transaction costs in terms of their distinct origins. For instance, the cost of obtaining a credit is a component of transaction costs that are determined by the institutional environment (in this case by the performance characteristics of financial institutions), but at the same time these costs can also be interpreted as the sum of information and negotiation costs involved in signing a credit agreement.

[14] As a source of cross-country comparative data on the outcomes of different forms and approaches to business regulations, the Doing Business Project is of great value for private investors, policymakers and academic researchers. But the data are also increasingly used to benchmark regulatory practices and outcomes across countries and as such function as a motivating device for national policymakers who are competing for foreign capital and investors. But giving priority to a particular reform on the basis a country occupying a low rank in terms of regulatory outcomes may be an unsound method of making choices about policy reforms in developing countries. The reason is that choosing reforms based on international benchmarking hides from the view the possibility for context-specific arrangements that are hardly susceptible to international best practice. For further elaborations on the context-specific nature of development problems and outcomes see Sect. 9.2.

3.3 Definition and Measurement of Transaction Costs

Table 3.2 Selected indicators of the cost of doing business

	Country group averages[a]	
	Low income	OECD
Starting a business		
Number of procedures	10	6
Time (days)	49	13
Cost (% of income per capita)	107.9	4.9
Registering property[b]		
Number of procedures	6.9	4.7
Time (days)	107	30.3
Cost (% of property value per capita)	8.95	4.7
Trading across borders[c]		
Number of documents for export (import)	8 (9.2)	4.5 (5.1)
Time for export (import) (days)	38.5 (43.7)	10.7 (11.4)
Enforcing contracts[d]		
Number of procedures	39.8	30.8
Time (days)	617.5	462.6
Cost (% of debt)	52.5	18.8
Closing a business[e]		
Time (years)	2.7	1.6
Cost (% of estate)	15	8.6
Recovery rate (cents on the dollar)	15.3	68.6
Country group characteristics		
GNI per capita (atlas method, current USD)	578	39,177
Total population of group (millions)	1,295.7	965.3

Data of all sets of indicators are for 2008. All data on costs and procedures refer to a hypothetical domestically owned limited liability company with 50 employees that operates in the respective country's most populous city. It is assumed that information on legal requirements is readily available to the entrepreneur and that all entities in the process function efficiently and without corruption

[a] Non-weighted arithmetic means
[b] The indicators refer to the purchase of land and a building in a peri-urban area by a business. Every procedure, whether it is the responsibility of the seller or the buyer, is included
[c] The indicators assume a standardised cargo of traded products by ocean transport in a dry-cargo, 20-foot, full container load
[d] The indicators assume a commercial sale dispute before local courts in which the buyer opposes the seller's claim, saying that the quality of the goods is not adequate
[e] The insolvent business is assumed to be 100% domestically owned and has a downtown real estate as its main asset on which it runs a hotel that is used as a security for the bank loan from which it was bought. Twelve out of forty-seven low-income countries covered have no practice for closing a business in place
Source: World Bank, IFC (2008)

These indicators of regulations and their associated costs represent only the measurable fraction of transaction costs that are determined by the quality of a country's formal institutional environment, however. Immediately associated with regulation are also the information costs that the individual entrepreneur incurs to learn about the particulars of all applicable laws and regulations, such as their individual requirements, the number and sequence of procedures or the different public agencies to consult. Furthermore, policy uncertainty that stems from unpredictable interpretation and application of regulations by officials is frequently reported by investors as a costly obstacle to doing business in developing countries.[15] Also corruption adds to the cost of regulation. Every additional procedure that involves interaction with government officials increases the potential for corruption. This applies ever more the less transparent, predictable and consistent regulatory processes are administered.[16] It has finally to be noted that the regulatory cost discussed above represents only the cost of firms that operate in the formal economy. Informal firms face very different kinds of cost that will be discussed in more detail in Chap. 5. However, there is a clear relationship between the cost of doing business in the official economy and the size of the informal sector, as a high regulatory burden represents a high barrier of entry into the formal sector which forces especially small enterprises to operate in the informal economy.

3.3.2 Infrastructure Costs

Infrastructure services represent another element of the institutional environment. They involve basic services that are necessary for everyday life, such as water, sanitation, energy, roads and other aspects of transport, as well as access to modern telecommunication and information networks. They may influence the level of transaction costs, for instance, if getting connected to telecommunication services, water or electricity involves costly bureaucratic procedures and delays associated with them, or when income is lost due to frequent power outages. Poor transport services translate into higher transaction costs as firms have to hold large inventories because delivery of inputs is unreliable or where poorly maintained roads increase vehicle operating costs.[17] Furthermore, trade-related transaction costs contain a substantial infrastructure-related component in many low-income countries.

---

[15] According to the World Bank's Investment Climate Surveys carried out since 2001 among senior managers in 53 developing countries, more than 70% of respondents in Latvia, Georgia, Russia, Belarus and Moldova disagreed with the statement that the interpretation of regulations by officials was predictable in their country. The lowest percentage of managers who disagreed with the statement was surveyed in Bangladesh (21.4%) and China (33.7%) (World Bank 2004).

[16] For instance, the public posting of price schedules for legal fees required to register a company has helped to fight administrative corruption in India (World Bank and IFC 2004).

[17] The inclusion of the infrastructure services in a definition of transaction costs is conceptually disputed. Some (e.g. North and Wallis 1986) argue that their cost should actually be regarded as part of the electricity, telecommunications or transportation industries' respective costs of sales (thus belonging to the class of "transformation costs"). This view is justified to the extent in which transportation, communication and distribution services represent individual input factors for other commodities. Similar arguments apply to the value of national taxes and custom duties. They determine a country's relative cost structure, but do so primarily through their effect on the price of productive inputs. Nevertheless, transaction costs are also affected as dealing with tax authorities or clearing customs for imports and exports represent resource-consuming transaction-related activities.

3.3 Definition and Measurement of Transaction Costs

Freight charges and other logistical expenses often represent a greater obstacle to trade than tariffs. The transaction costs associated with national borders may actually crowd out the intended effects of efforts at trade liberalisation as these costs cannot be eliminated even if tariffs and capital controls are.

Transportation and communication costs can become prohibitively high where whole regions are disconnected from infrastructure networks. Limited access to infrastructure services is a particular characteristic of many African economies in which relative land abundance and a low population density are associated with small and highly scattered settlements. With no all-weather roads to remote rural areas, agricultural expansion is prevented because producers cannot connect with markets.[18] The insulation of large parts of Africa's productive forces from domestic and international markets does not only cause gains from trade and specialisation to remain unexploited. It also explains why, for instance, agricultural market reforms implemented in Africa upon the advice of international development institutions have had no or only very limited impact on output because farmers in rural areas did not respond to incentives from price changes and marketing reforms on distant markets. But low population densities in land abundant countries not only increase transport and infrastructure costs. Some authors even consider these patterns, that are typical especially for African countries, as the single most important barrier to technological progress and argue that low population densities reduce incentives to invest in more productive methods of (agricultural) production (Boserup 1981; Platteau 2000). This view actually also challenges the widely held belief that population growth negatively affects economic development.[19]

---

[18] The unavailability or poor quality of Africa's transport infrastructure may actually surprise given the considerable efforts undertaken by most colonial powers to improve the situation through the construction of railways and roads. They had indeed been quite aware of the effects of infrastructure investments on lowering transaction costs and fostering trade and development. However, as Boserup (1981) notes, these infrastructure investments were heavily biased towards external commerce. Most of the African railways network built in the colonial period actually connected interiorly located mines and extraction fields to a coastal harbour. The transportation infrastructure inherited from the colonial powers thus contributed little to improve intra-African trade as it failed to interlink the various regions of the African continent.

[19] The consequences of a poor transport infrastructure in countries with a low population density are well illustrated, for instance, by the difficulties that the United Nations experienced in assisting the preparations for the Democratic Republic of Congo's referendum about its new constitution, which laid the groundwork for the country's first democratic elections since independence in 1960. The country, which makes up two-thirds the size of Western Europe, has scarcely any decent roads. Consequently, material for the referendum had to be air-lifted by helicopters, ferried by dug-out canoes and carried through the jungle on people's heads (The Economist 2006). The referendum was made even more difficult by the lack of a communication infrastructure necessary to inform people about the purpose and consequences of their vote.

3.3.3 Informal Institutional Determinants of Transaction Costs

Even more difficult than the cost associated with a country's formal institutions are informal constraints to define. They relate to peoples' behavioural attributes and preferences which are in turn shaped by a society's values and cultural beliefs. The influence of informal institutions on a country's transaction cost structure and economic performance is among the less well researched and understood issues in institutional economics. It is postulated that informal factors led societies to develop distinct formal institutional structures. For that reason, informal norms and cultural values affect a country's transaction cost structure indirectly through their influence on the evolution of a country's formal institutions.[20]

3.3.4 Historical Determinants of Transaction Costs

Since cultural and historical influences are able to explain why different countries prefer different ways of dealing with problems of regulating business activity, they are clearly relevant also for understanding why countries differ in their transaction cost structures. For instance, a country's legal tradition can explain the efficiency of contract enforcement through its court system. Common-law countries in the English legal tradition are characterised by lower procedural complexity than civil-law countries. Among the countries where contract enforcement is primarily governed by civil law, Nordic countries have the fewest procedures, the shortest time and the second-lowest cost of contract enforcement (after Germanic countries). Countries in the French legal tradition have the most procedures and the second most time intensive and costly court procedures. Conversely, the legal and juridical systems in Germanic countries operate at relatively low costs but demand long periods of time (World Bank and IFC 2004).

An interesting account of the historical origins of distinct legal traditions is provided by Backhaus (2000). He discusses how Europe's rise to technological and economic leadership in the nineteenth century was brought about by the unique circumstances created by the Peace Treaties of Westphalia of 1648, which in turn supported the development of the economic–political doctrine of Cameralism and its application to public policy and administration in Continental Europe. The Treaties of Westphalia, which ended the Thirty Years'*** War, provided the constitutional framework in which a large number of competing jurisdictions had to cooperate.

---

[20] See Chap. 4 for an illustration of how informal norms can support business transactions, Sect. 8.2.2 for a discussion on the role of informal norms and values in the process of institutional change, and Sect. 13.2.1 for the effects of cultural influences on economic processes and outcomes.

Unlike mercantilist countries, which sought to maximise their wealth through colonial expansion, the states on the European continent had to seek revenues through the development of their own territories. The Cameralists provided the methods of public administration to achieve this by making best possible use of their state's domestic resources, for instance, through the foundation of universities and the promotion of internal trade and commerce. Thereby, the Cameralist doctrine established the ground for many constitutional rules that are characteristically in particular for the German and Nordic legal traditions. Examples include the concept of the welfare state or the subsidiarity principle that today guides the division of responsibilities within the European Union.

Chapter 4
Private Governance

Economic development is impossible to achieve without exchange and investment. To enable both, a market-based economy needs two distinct sets of institutions: those that encourage trust and commitment in economic relations, and those that define and secure property rights.[1] In the previous chapter, the implications of high transaction costs for the level and organisation of economic activity in low-income countries have been discussed. A specific source of transaction costs, which arises if the institutional environment is characterised by weekly performing formal institutions, is the cost of protection against opportunistic behaviour in exchange relations,[2] and the cost to protect ones property against theft and expropriation.

Exchange will be carried out only if it is perceived as mutually beneficial. In determining whether the exchange of a good is beneficial, individuals consider not only its price, its physical attributes and logistical factors, but also the identity of the other party to the transaction. If they have reasons to expect that their exchange partner will not fulfil his or her part of the agreement, the transaction will not take place. To avoid opportunistic breach of contract *ex-post*, the parties to an

---

[1] Contract enforcement and property rights are the most fundamental, but not the only institutional prerequisites for the functioning of markets. Rodrik (2005) developed a taxonomy of market-sustaining institutions in which he classifies property rights and contract enforcement institutions as market-creating institutions. Besides them, the formal institutional framework that sustains markets includes market-regulating institutions (e.g. regulatory bodies and other mechanisms for correcting market failures), market-stabilising institutions (e.g. monetary and fiscal institutions, as well as institutions of prudential regulation and supervision) and market-legitimising institutions (e.g. democracy as well as social protection and social insurance systems). The discussion here will primarily be concerned with the category of market-creating institutions.

[2] Dixit (2004) defines opportunistic behaviour as actions by one party that increase his or her own gain while lowering the other party's gain by a greater amount. Such behaviour may include the supply of defective goods, shirk on the job, or renege on payment, and arises whenever exchange is carried out in a sequence of actions (as opposed to the case of simultaneous and instantaneous exchange in goods with immediately verifiable attributes and qualities). Opportunism can be interpreted as a kind of negative externality in that it involves privately profitable but socially dysfunctional behaviour. The term was originally introduced by Williamson (1979), who defines opportunism as "self-interest seeking with guile".

exchange have to demonstrate credibly their commitment to their mutual agreement *ex ante*. In advanced economies, impartial contract enforcement and dispute resolution through effective formal legal and juridical institutions provides the incentives for compliances that lend credibility to contractual commitments. Without contract enforcement institutions that perform these functions effectively, uncertainty and unpredictability arising from a lack of credible commitment and incentives for compliance make voluntary exchange extremely costly if not impossible.[3]

Secure property rights are equally fundamental for the operation of a market-based economy. Without effective protection of property rights, it may take less effort to steal a property than to create it. Theft and other privately profitable but socially dysfunctional behaviour thus constitutes a strong disincentive to invest in the creation and maintenance of private property.

To enable economic exchange and investment, any economic system needs an order that governs exchange relations, provides for contract enforcement, and protects private property rights. Economists and legal scholars have traditionally associated such an order exclusively with the formal laws and juridical institutions that govern private commercial activities in modern market economies. This has led to the assumption that private economic activity cannot develop in the absence of such formal, state-governed institutions. Yet, contemporary evidence from low-income countries, as well as historical records of commercial trade in late-medieval Europe, suggest the possibility for private economic activity to take place without a centrally provided system of formal laws and courts. These cases document how entrepreneurs find ways to exploit potential gains from trade and specialisation by making use of privately governed (i.e. informal) enforcement arrangements that provide proper incentives for gathering information, honouring agreements and settling disputes. The emergence of alternative institutional forms that perform these functions provides the conditions for lower transaction costs and helps to make the pursuit of available business opportunities potentially more profitable.

The study of such privately governed enforcement institutions makes clear that there is no unique correspondence between the functions that economic institutions perform and the form that such institutions take.[4] Appropriate contract enforcement and protection of property rights can in fact be provided through diverse institutional arrangements. The implications of an absent or ineffective state-governed legal framework for private economic activity in low-income countries are then not necessarily that economic interactions have to break down in chaos and dispute. The absence of effective formal enforcement institutions rather implies that economic actors are denied one of many alternative forms to structure their interactions and to resolve their disputes.[5]

---

[3] Whereas some authors define the term contract only with regard to explicit bilateral agreements that are supported by formal state law, the term is used more broadly here to include all voluntary agreements between two or more parties that impose rights and obligations on each party. They can be formal or informal, explicit or implicit, rigid or flexible.

[4] This assertion builds on, and reinforces, the conclusions reached in Rodrik (2007). See also Sect. 9.4 for an elaboration of the implications of this finding.

[5] As further discussed in Sect. 4.4, private enforcement institutions may, however, not be sufficient to accommodate all jointly profitable business opportunities.

A recent attempt at integrating the contributions to the understanding of institutional substitutes for state law from various social sciences into a multidisciplinary research area is provided by Avinash Dixit in a research area that he tentatively entitles "Lawlessness and Economics" (Dixit 2004). His approach is relevant to the present analysis as it delivers a theory of economic activity under the assumption of absent economic governance by the state. By this assumption, the approach takes up a rather extreme situation. Cases in which a government is completely absent and has hence no impact at all on economic transactions are actually very rare. More widespread are situations in which a government is unable or unwilling to protect property rights and enforce contracts through appropriate state-governed legal and juridical institutions. In some cases, the government is even likely to exert a deliberately negative influence on private sector activity, for example, if it creates widespread corruption, socially costly regulations, or commits acts of extortion.

The purpose of this chapter is to identify and analyse the economic implications of weak or absent state-sponsored governance of private sector activity, which characterise the economic realities of many low-income countries. Thereby, limited statehood is understood primarily as the ineffective operation or absence of the whole body of formal private and commercial law, including contract law, property law and laws of liability and tort, which are usually either produced by lawyers and judges in a common law system, or interpreted by them in a system of codified civil law. The implications of weak governance by the state extend, of course, beyond, private law. They also include a broad range of economic policies and business regulation with which the discussions in Chaps. 3 and 5 are mainly concerned.[6]

In the contemporary world, economic activity that is governed by private arrangements outside the formal law can be found in two occurrences. The first is the extreme and rather rare case of complete absence of state-governed law and order that describes the reality of a number of so-called failed states. In these countries, a government is either absent or lacks the capacity or inclination to carry out its legislative, executive and juridical functions. Somalia, which has no central government since 1991, is probably the most prominent contemporary example of a failed state.[7] But also the Democratic Republic of Congo, Burundi, the Central

---

[6]Note that in the context of the analysis, conditions of limited statehood, or lawlessness, are not necessarily meant to include other implications that are often also associated with weak states such as anarchy, violent conflict or unbridled crime.

[7]In a study on private sector responses to the absence of government institutions, Nenova and Harford (2004) report that even in places like Somalia, private firms have been surprisingly innovative in finding ways to engage in economic transactions, to strengthen property rights and even to operate basic systems of finance and sporadic infrastructure services. Specifically, the authors found that Somali entrepreneurs have used three methods to compensate for the lack of effective government regulation: First, they are "importing" governance by relying on foreign institutions in areas like airline safety, currency stability and company law. Second, they are using clans and other local networks of trust for contract and property rights enforcement. Finally, they simplify transactions to minimise the need for effective mechanisms of contract enforcement.

African Republic, Zimbabwe, Liberia and parts of Afghanistan, Iraq and Sudan, to name only a few, qualify in various respects as failing or failed states.[8]

More widespread are cases of developing countries in which, despite that they formally have a state-backed legal and juridical system, most economic activity takes place outside the law in the informal sector. The problem of these countries is that their formal institutions are ineffective in governing economic relations in an efficient, accountable and reliable manner. As a result, formal legal institutions and courts are inaccessible or lack legitimacy for the majority of enterprises and workers. The conditions that determine the size and growth of the informal sector and the economic consequences of informal business activity will be the subject of Chap. 5. In the context of the present discussion, the interest is in the emergence and form of alternative, private modes of economic governance, and their capacity to support economic activity in low-income countries.[9]

4.1 Foundations of Private Economic Governance

The neoclassical notion of anonymous, impersonal exchange presupposes the existence of an economic order that solves all inherent information and commitment problems in an almost invisible and costless manner. This ideal model may represent a sufficiently good approximation for the conditions found on a range of markets in advanced countries. But in the absence of condition that allow for impersonal, anonymous exchange, the identity of exchange partners matters. People will engage in exchange only if they expect each other to behave in a trustworthy and honest manner. The formation of expectations about the future actions of others requires information about their identity, their past conduct, as well as their interests and motivations. To obtain such information, exchange partners must be somehow related to each other, for instance, through a history of repeated interactions, membership in the same community, adherence to the same norms and conventions, or through otherwise shared ethical, religious or cultural beliefs. If social relations can create incentives for cooperation and compliance, the enforcement of obligations in exchange relations becomes possible even without the governance from formal legal institutions.

Incentives for compliance in relation-based contracting are founded upon three main aspects of human behaviour that play a role in every system of informal contract

---

[8] According to the Brookings Institution's Index of State Weakness in the Developing World (Rice and Patrick 2008).

[9] A third area in which the absence of state-governed legal and juridical institutions creates scope for alternative private governance mechanisms is the field of international trade and commerce. Although international law has some bearing on economic transactions, it is incomplete in so far as it lacks an inherent power to impose sanctions. Private modes of arbitration and mediation therefore often dominate in the resolution of conflicts in international trade relations.

enforcement. These aspects are morality, personal trust and reputation. Their underlying concepts will be analysed here before the discussion turns to concrete examples of informal contract enforcement arrangements that govern economic exchanges in many low-income countries.

4.1.1 Morality

Moral behaviour can be defined as actions that are oriented not only towards ones own benefit, but also towards the well-being of others or towards the common good. People who internalise moral behaviour inflict costs on themselves (or forego personal profit) for the sake of conforming to some principles or norms. In other words, moral norms shape an individual's preferences in that they constrain purely self-interested behaviour.

Moral norms are culturally derived and can vary widely across different social groups and societies. Moral norms that are universally applicable to a vast range of social relations beyond the narrow circle of personal acquaintances (i.e. to all members of a society, cultural area, or even to all of humanity) are often referred to as norms of generalised morality. They are developed mainly through the internalisation of values especially in the process of primary socialisation. They include, for instance, implicit agreements to certain kinds of regard for others that are essential to the working of a society. Conversely, limited morality exists where moral norms are applied discriminately only to the members of a specific social group or network of relations.[10]

An alternative, though related, typology of morality in economic relations is offered by Jens Beckert (2005). He distinguishes between four forms of morality-based behaviour: cooperation, group solidarity, blocked exchange and altruism. Beckert defines cooperation as moral behaviour that takes one's own well-being and the well-being of others into consideration – a definition that roughly corresponds with the notion of generalised morality in the above discussion. Group solidarity differs from cooperation in that it involves the application of moral norms only towards members of a culturally specified group. Group solidarity in Beckert's typology thus describes a type of limited morality. The third kind of moral behaviour in Beckert's typology is blocked exchange. It refers to the morally defended prohibition or restriction of exchange of certain goods or services, like limitations on the charging of interest for money-lending in the Muslim world, or other religious taboos. Finally, the fourth type of moral behaviour in economic relations,

---

[10] Note that moral norms are not equivalent to social norms. They rather are a subset of the latter. Platteau (2000) distinguishes between social and moral norms as follows: Social norms are "endogenous outcomes of interactions among individuals acting strategically within a given framework". Moral norms, instead, are viewed as "cultural beliefs that are able to modify preferences and payoffs by restricting people's set of available strategies to those that conform to their moral beliefs" (ibid., p. 291).

altruism, is characterised as a person's voluntary commitment to behaviour that inflicts costs on him for the benefit of others. The voluntary internalisation of otherwise externalised costs falls into this category which is observable, for instance, where firms commit themselves to international labour standards, protect the natural environment, or engage in community development programmes. Yet, such behaviour could equally be motivated by genuine self-interested considerations, for instance, where firms commit to voluntary standards in order to forestall compulsory government regulation, or if they act socially responsible to build customer confidence or to avoid conflicts with important stakeholders. In such cases, apparently moral conduct reveals as a form of Trojan altruism, a fifth type of behaviour that extends Beckert's typology. Trojan altruism is defined as the "parasitic" use of altruism that does not find moral legitimisation as it aims at gaining advantage from actions that are justified on moral grounds, but are actually motivated by narrow self-interest.

As Platteau (2000) notes, morality will be capable of establishing order in exchange relations only if concerns for others are based on identity or loyalty feelings towards a clearly specified reference group. Because generalised morality refers to a broad group of abstract people, it is questionable whether it is sufficient to sustain cooperative behaviour in exchange relations without the help of other enforcement institutions.[11] Morality can instead be an effective basis for cooperation in exchange relations if it guides behaviour towards concrete people within restricted groups. This has several reasons: First, homogeneous social groups, whose members share common values, find it easier to reach a consensus about what is considered as morally justified behaviour. Second, this consensus evolves best within groups of people that interact and communicate frequently. Communication, in particular, reinforces cooperative behaviour because it stimulates empathy and hence increases someone's ability to adopt the other's viewpoint. Moreover, feelings of guilt are stronger if one cheats a concrete person instead of an abstract stranger.

What motivates people to voluntarily accept and apply moral norms? One explanation is the tendency of humans to derive utility from acting according to the values they have acquired in the course of their socialisation and education. But people do not just want to follow practices that they approve; they also do so in particular if they can expect similarly situated others to follow the same moral norms too. The exercise of morality thus depends on the moral behaviour by others as well. The fact that one behaves the way in which one would like others to behave exhibits a strong element of reciprocity in interpersonal relations. This property of moral norms can guide economic exchange relationship in a mutually beneficial way. It underpins the self-enforcing character of the moral code in the sense that people not only voluntarily accept it as a standard for their own behaviour, but also feel inclined to monitor and sanction immoral behaviour by others. If someone's

---

[11] From this perspective, the correspondence of generalised morality with cooperation in Beckert's typology is somewhat misleading in the present context.

own willingness to cooperate influences the predisposition of others to cooperative behaviour, and vice versa, then a cooperative relationship can be possible even without the support from a long history of repeated interactions or other arrangements designed to generate trust.

4.1.2 Personal Trust

Trust is central to solving the commitment problem inherent to the enforcement of obligations in economic exchange relations. This problem arises whenever there is a time lag between the performances of actions agreed by each party to a transaction.[12] Economic exchanges involve a set of reciprocal promises and expectations that lead to mutually beneficial trade only if they are accompanied by trust in the honest and cooperative behaviour on each side of the agreement. In the absence of trust-based mechanisms that deter cheating and dishonest behaviour, the only feasible strategy for doing business is to avoid all transactions that involve delayed obligations which make opportunistic behaviour possible. Practically, such a mode of transacting means to inspect the good on the spot, pay cash and walk away with it. Fafchamps and Minten (2001) associate such instantaneous modes of exchange with a "flea market economy" in which placement of orders, invoicing, or granting of trade credit and product warranty do not exist.

The political scientist Francis Fukuyama defines trust as "the expectation that arises within a community of regular, honest, and cooperative behaviour, based on commonly shared norms on the part of other members of that community" (Fukuyama 1995, p. 26). This definition embodies three main elements that are essential for establishing trust: First, trust is associated with regular behaviour that creates stability in economic and social relations. The expectation of regular behaviour, in turn, is the result of a process of learning and knowledge creation in the course of repeated interactions within a given institutional environment. Second, such regular behaviour must be honest and conductive to cooperation. The expectation that people will regularly cheat their fellows would actually lead to a deficit of trust in their relations. Third, honest and cooperative behaviour becomes effective through a set of shared values and norms. These norms can be derived from deep-seated cultural beliefs, traditional customs or moral habits, as well as from professional standards or codes of conduct. Repeated interaction and reference to a set of commonly shared values and norms are two forces in the creation of trust that actually reinforce each other. Repeated transactions are important to form personal trust

---

[12] Imperfect information is a further condition that contributes to commitment and contract enforcement problems. Without perfect information about an agent's past conduct, expectations about his future compliance are difficult to build. Moreover, information asymmetries that generate moral hazard and adverse selection problems make compliance with contractual obligations hard to verify by third-party enforcement agents.

on the individual level. The general propensity to establish trust in relationships, instead, is determined by a society's shared social norms and cultural beliefs.

Even formal laws and contracts can become a common basis for trust in economic exchanges. However, the more formalised these norms are, the less are they capable of generating personal trust. Instead, they enable exchanges through a kind of institutionalised trust, that is, through peoples' general confidence in the rule of law and the regulations and procedures of the formal legal and juridical system. But if institutionalised trust prevails, a minimum level of personal trust is indispensable for making the economic system run smoothly and at low transaction costs. Nevertheless, it is fair to say that what personal trust alone can achieve in pre-modern societies on the basis of shared, social norms, is gradually being replaced in modern societies by institutionalised trust in formal law and its enforcement systems. The distinction between personal and institutionalised trust is important as both forms of trust apply to very different institutional contexts. While trust is essential with regard to both formal and informal contract enforcement, only personal trust based on social relations is capable of sustaining economic exchange if formal contract enforcement institutions are absent or ineffective in governing economic transactions.

4.1.3 Reputation

In frequent and enduring bilateral exchanges, economic actors accumulate knowledge and information about each other from which they gradually build their reputation. The information embodied in an agent's reputation has a value as long as the relationship is continued. Therefore, the repeated engagement in exchanges with the same partner facilitates exchange not only because it promotes trust through the creation of stable expectations about an agent's future behaviour. Repeated transactions also create strong incentives for cooperative behaviour, because dishonest agents would risk losing the value represented by the accumulated information embodied in their bilateral reputation.

An agent's reputation also has a value beyond a specific bilateral exchange relationships if suitable mechanisms exist through which information about his past behaviour can be made available to a larger community of potential exchange partners. Milgrom, North, and Weingast (1990) assert that for such a multilateral reputation mechanisms to serve as an adequate bond for honest behaviour, it is not necessary that each pair of traders comes together frequently (as it is required for the operation of bilateral reputation mechanisms). Rather, it is sufficient that each individual agent trades frequently enough with the community of traders, and that all members of the community can be kept informed about each other's past behaviour. This latter condition, however, is hard to achieve without some kind of collective information sharing mechanism. As it can be extremely costly to keep every agent of a community informed about everybody's past behaviour, such a mechanism is unlikely to emerge spontaneously. Instead, a third party will have to be entrusted with the collection and dissemination of information about each community member's reputation. Several historical and contemporary cases of multilateral reputation mechanisms are known in which the information sharing function has indeed been assumed by private but collectively maintained institutions.[13]

However, an institutional solution to the information sharing problem may not be sufficient to ensure honest behaviour in contractual relations. Multilateral reputation mechanisms that rely solely on information pooling are only incomplete substitutes for formal contract enforcement if, for example, the cost of information queries about a potential exchange partner's reputation is higher than the gains of having an honest deal, or if, for other reasons, the advantages from behaving opportunistically are larger than the expected gains from future trade with members of the community. Under such conditions, dishonest behaviour can only be effectively deterred if information about an agent's reputation is supplemented by the credible threat of sanctions against the dishonest agent. This requires that every participating agent commits himself to refrain from dealing with dishonest agents, even if he himself has not been cheated, or if not dealing with a dishonest agent would mean to him the loss of income from a potentially profitable transaction. As has been noted above, this commitment problem can be solved by homogenous social groups in a decentralised manner through their members' common reference to a system of shared norms, values and conventions.[14]

But even if a reputation system involves mechanisms for collective punishment, the price of losing ones reputation is not limited to the income lost from future transactions or other material sanctions alone. Incentives for cooperation may actually also be reinforced by the prospect of facing non-material consequences of one's dishonest behaviour. For instance, punishment through exclusion from the group is associated with the loss of social status and recognition by others. If being part of a larger community is assumed a fundamental desire of human beings, then the threat of social exclusion can provide a strong additional incentive for cooperative behaviour. As Platteau (2000) notes, a similar reinforcement effect may work through shame feelings that are triggered by the emotion of contempt in other group members. This holds in particular for closed, homogenous groups in which the operation of reputation effects and strong common identity feelings create incentives for its members to refrain from opportunistic behaviour.

---

[13] See Sect. 4.2.3 for the discussion of such cases.

[14] Milgrom, North and Weingast (1990) assert that "theoretically, the main condition that enables anonymous exchange is not the coercive power of a formal third party, but the availability of information at the society level". Mechanisms of information pooling can indeed function without the central authority of a formal third party. But given the gain from concealment and the noise in the system, information pooling alone may not suffice to sustain a cooperative equilibrium. Practically, the possibility for dishonest behaviour cannot fully be ruled out. A residual commitment problem thus remains that requires mechanisms for the multilateral implementation of sanctions against dishonest agents – a function that a collective information sharing system alone cannot fulfil.

4.2 Alternative Institutions for Contract Enforcement

The following discussion describes a variety of informal institutional arrangements that are capable of creating commitment in economic relations under conditions of limited economic governance by the state. The reviewed cases draw on historical accounts as well as on contemporary observations in low-income countries. They all represent strategies for coping with situations where effective state-backed legal institutions are lacking. These strategies may differ with respect to the institutional arrangements by which the relevant economic relations are governed, the degree of internal coordination that is required to generate a cooperative outcome, or the nature of the parties that are involved in an economic exchange. Not all discussed enforcement strategies and institutions are mutually exclusive, however. In reality, most enforcement systems rather contain different elements of the presented forms.

4.2.1 Group Structure

In the above sections, morality, personal trust and reputation were discussed in the context of social groups, communities and networks the members of which share common values, conventions or cultural beliefs. These values and beliefs, and the social norms based on them, create a strong bond between exchange partners and can therefore generate incentives for cooperative behaviour. Therefore, homogeneity concerning the exchange partners' preferences, expectations and attachment to norms is thus an important property of groups and networks through which the spontaneous emergence of informal contract enforcement mechanisms can be facilitated.[15]

Backhaus (1980) defines homogeneity as the result of restrictions on the action sets of individuals by an obligatory social order. He asserts that these restrictions on individual behaviour can reduce the cost of transactions among homogenous group members, including the social cost of collective decision-making within the group. A condition through which homogeneity lowers transaction costs is that the reduction of individual action sets implicates a reduction in uncertainty, which in turn increases the predictability of individual behaviour. According to Backhaus, exchange is enabled in homogenous social groups through the operation of a common reference system (based on shared social norms, values or beliefs), the consequent standardisation of behaviour and modes of conduct, and the compatibility of the ends of individuals that interact within the group.

---

[15] A very basic function through which homogeneity facilitates exchange is that it provides homogenous partners with an information advantage: Even if they have not previously known each other, they do not enter exchange as complete strangers, since the attributes they commonly share provide them with initial information about each other. This information advantage facilitates exchange by making the behaviour of contracting partner more predictable.

4.2 Alternative Institutions for Contract Enforcement

Social groups, communities or networks can be homogeneous with regard to many different characteristics that their members share. The extent to which the homogeneity of exchange partners can support economic activity and lower transaction costs depends on the nature of their commonly shared norms, and on the social structure under which their interactions take place.[16] It is therefore important to analyse the emergence of informal contract enforcement institutions in the context of the distinctive forms of relationships that prevail in intra-group interactions. Two basic types of homogenous social groups can be distinguished. First, the extended family, in which economic relations are defined and structured on the basis of kinship ties; and second, groups formed through voluntary association on the basis of common ethic values, religious beliefs or otherwise shared norms, interests and motivations.

Following Putnam et al. (1993), the two types of homogenous groups differ in the structure of their intra-group relations. Accordingly, vertical (i.e. hierarchical) social ties are an attribute of relationships in extended family groups, whereas groups based on voluntary association are usually characterised by horizontal relationships among individuals with equal social status. An even more important distinguishing feature, however, is the fact that membership in the kin group is based on common ancestry (i.e. blood relations). In effect, a member's social and economic roles are predetermined in the context of the family's internal hierarchy. This prescription of roles and actions, and the predictability of individual behaviour that follows from it, are the primary causes for cooperation in extended family groups.[17] But these foundations of cooperation in groups based on family ties do not extend to people outside the kin system. Therefore, extended family groups have a weak ability to engage in exchange with unrelated people because they lack a basis for trusting them. In contrary, groups which generate mutual trust from commonly shared values and norms alone are principally open to everyone who voluntarily commits itself to act in accordance with the group's internal values and norms.

Whereas social cohesion among members of kinship groups is continually reinforced through daily interactions within the family household and with other relatives, it requires the acquisition of a particular capability to establish cohesion among voluntarily associated group members. This capability of people to cooperate for common ends on the basis of shared norms and values has often been referred to as the social capital of a group or community. Broadly defined, social capital is present in all kinds of associations among people whose interactions are

---

[16] By social structure, sociologists describe some kind of instilled and recurrent patterns of interaction between individuals, which are maintained through common norms and values and the sanctioning mechanisms that originate from them. The concept of social structure is thus useful to describe the culturally induced pattern of behaviour by which different types of groups, communities or networks can be distinguished.

[17] Note, however, that the threat of exclusion is a less effective means to discourage opportunistic behaviour within family groups, because kinship creates a natural bond that cannot easily be broken deliberately in response to dishonest behaviour by the individual family member.

governed by mutual trust. Yet, with regard to the extended family group, social capital is static in that it is naturally given and restricted to interactions among family members. Non-kin groups, instead, have to acquire social capital as a precondition for their voluntary association.

Such differences in group structures have important implication for the ability of economically active communities to adjust to changing external circumstances, and to broaden the scope of their economic relations in response to new opportunities that arise outside the group. The latter point is of particular importance for assessing the role and extent to which a private governance structure is capable of promoting society-wide economic activity beyond the boundaries of a specific group, community or network. In fact, Putnam et al. (1993) conclude from a study in which they compare different patterns of regional development across Italy, that an economy performs less well if it relies heavily on intra-family and intra-hierarchical exchange, while they found that especially strong horizontal ties are essential for the emergence of a modern market economy. In a related analysis, Fukuyama (1995) contrasts the societies of China, France, Italy and South Korea with those of Japan, Germany and, as a specific case, the United States. He maintains that the first group of countries are familistic in the sense that the family constitutes the basic unit of economic organisation, whereas the second group are high-trust societies. According to Fukuyama's historical analysis, familistic societies had a much harder time to create large-scale private organisations that go beyond the family, and often gave the state a role in promoting enduring, globally competitive firms.[18] Conversely, high-trust societies, in which voluntary association outside the kinship group is the norm, were earlier able to create large, professionally managed and internationally competitive firms. These observations point at important areas of research that is necessary to better understand how differences in the social structure of societies lead to different paths of their development. The attempt at developing an appropriate framework for the analysis of this and related questions will be made in the third part of this study.

The purpose of the present section finally demands for a closer look at the evidence on the structures of economically active groups, communities and business networks in low-income countries. The available empirical data on groups, whose governance structures have evolved as functional equivalents for the absent functions of a formal legal and juridical system, mostly result from case studies undertaken in a number of low-income countries in Sub-Saharan Africa. This evidence is complemented by more general observations of social scientists about the contemporary structures of informal exchange relationships in selected developing economies.

---

[18] As the economic success of China shows, familism is not necessarily a barrier to growth. It is rather a factor that influences the character of economic growth in terms of the role that the state plays in it and the types of organisations and sectors of the economy the development of which is commensurate with the structures of family-based societies. China is also a good example to demonstrate how a lack of social capital in kin-based societies can constrain the development of democratic structures.

4.2 Alternative Institutions for Contract Enforcement

A team of 12 economists (Bigsten et al. 2000) examined contractual practices of African manufacturing firms by using survey data collected in six African countries (Burundi, Cameroon, Côte d'Ivoire, Kenya, Zambia and Zimbabwe). They show that relational contracting is the norm between manufacturers, their suppliers, and their clients. Firms mitigate the risk of opportunistic breach of contract by largely limiting exchange on transactions with business partners with whom they share a common ethnic or religious background, or which they know from long-term repeated transactions. Bigsten et al. (2000) found that more than 70% of all surveyed firms procured their inputs from a single supplier, with whom they did business for already 9½ years on average.

Fafchamps (2003) observed that members of non-indigenous ethnic communities dominate manufacturing and agricultural trade in several African countries, in spite of the fact that they represent only tiny minorities of their host countries' populations. For instance, in many West African countries like Cote d'Ivoire or Sierra Leone, ethical Lebanese and Syrian entrepreneurs are particularly successful in import–export trade. Immigrants from South Asia own the majority of light industries in East Africa (especially in Kenya and Zambia). Similarly, firm owners of European origin dominate manufacturing and agricultural sectors in many southern African countries (especially in Zimbabwe, Namibia and South Africa). Finally, collective systems of contract enforcement based on religious affiliation are found, for instance, among Muslim brotherhoods in northern Sudan. In all these cases, ethnically or religiously homogenous groups not only have the most efficient informal forms of collective contract enforcement; their members are also reportedly among the most successful entrepreneurs in their country and business sector.[19]

Concentrations of business activity on non-indigenous ethnic groups are also common in Asia. For instance, many entrepreneurs in Indonesia, Malaysia and Singapore originate from China (Fafchamps 2004). Andersson (2004) reports that most informal moneylenders in the Philippines and in other East Asian countries are ethnic Indians. In the Philippines, they are referred to as "Bumbays" after the Indian city of Bombay (now Mumbai). They operate mostly in the squatter settlements of large cities where they provide small loans to home-based workers and micro-entrepreneurs. Although they lend money without contract or security and at high interest rates (their terms are usually "five for six", i.e. an interest rate of 20%), they experience few defaults, as they are able to effectively monitor their borrowers and exclude those with a poor credit history from future lending. The necessary exchange of information about their borrowers is facilitated through the moneylenders' close ties that result from their common ethnic origin.

---

[19] It must be noted, however, that in the case of southern African countries, the white minority's commercial success is largely built on privileges retained from the period of their colonial rule.

4.2.2 Contractual Structure

A common strategy to cope with situations of absent or ineffective formal contract enforcement institutions is to structure business agreements *ex ante* in ways that help to forestall disputes *ex-post*. The intention behind such arrangements is to create incentive structures that make contractual obligations self-enforcing. Straightforward examples include barter trades and the agreement of advance payments or other safeguards that provide sufficient incentives for compliance with obligations in sequential transactions.

A simple and widely practiced way of coping with various non-performance risks in economic exchanges is the flexible and often implicit arrangement of contractual obligations. Bigsten et al. (2000) found that contractual flexibility is the preferred form of sharing the risk of late delivery or non-payment in several African countries south of the Sahara.[20] In the case of unforeseen events, this approach leaves both sides to an agreement enough flexibility to adjust their obligations in accordance with their ability to conform to the agreement. Although this may actually have the effect of a partial default, it represents a superior strategy to the alternative possibility of a complete breach of contract. A logical consequence of the flexible arrangement of exchange agreements is that negotiation is a preferred method of conflict resolution. Almost 80% of all firms surveyed by Bigsten et al. resolve their disputes through bilateral negotiation, while only large firms use confrontational dispute settlement through lawyers and counts if negotiation fails (ibid.).[21]

In addition, specific contractual structures can be used to prevent *ex-post* conflicts in bilateral exchange. One possibility to control opportunistic behaviour in exchange relationships is to integrate both parties to an exchange into a unified ownership structure. Thereby, the potential "external effect" that the cheated party experience from the other party's opportunistic behaviour is internalised in a single ownership entity that spans both sides of the transaction. A joint profit-maximisation problem then evolves subject to an agreement on how the profit from the internalised transaction is distributed. An example of how a joint ownership structure

---

[20] However, African's elastic definition of flexibility also explains why many foreign firms find it hard to do business with African partners.

[21] A notable exception from this observation is Zimbabwe. Before the Zimbabwean government started its controversial fast-track land reform in 2000 that drove the country into its current economic and humanitarian crisis, the country had relatively well developed legal institutions. As a result, an unusually high number of firms in Zimbabwe used lawyers or the courts for purposes of contract enforcement and dispute settlement. But in the same time, Zimbabwean firms reported almost twice as many cases of non-compliance with contractual obligations than firms in the other surveyed African countries. The favoured interpretation by Bigsten et al. (2000) is that good legal institutions and formal dispute settlement mechanisms encourage firms to engage in riskier and less flexible contractual relations, which consequently leads to more cases of non-compliance and hence more frequent recourses to lawyers and counts.

can facilitate production and exchange is the pooling of resources and bargaining power in member-owned cooperatives, which will be discussed in more detail in Chap. 5.

Another form of economic organisation that can help to facilitate economic activity in contexts of low-income countries is sharecropping. It describes a contractual arrangement for the distribution of returns through which non-performance risks can be controlled in situations of imperfect information and limited formal risk-sharing possibilities. Sharecropping has originally been used as a system of agricultural contracting in which employee farmers work a parcel of land in return for a fraction of the parcel's crops. Sharecropping arrangements represent a synthesis between a rental system, in which the agent (i.e. the worker or tenant) bears all the performance risk of his work and investment, and the wage system, in which the principal (i.e. the landlord or employer) bears all risk associated with the worker's performance. The relative advantage of a sharecropping arrangement becomes evident if one assumes the case of a crop season that has yielded poor returns. Under a rental contract, this situation may force the agent to default on his rent liability. Conversely, under an employment arrangement, the principal may breach the contract by not paying the agreed wage. These non-performance risks are mitigated in a sharecropping system, since the agent's liability towards the principal, just as his own returns, depend directly on his output.[22]

An example for a contractual arrangement by which relations between lenders and borrowers are structured is group lending. It provides a functional substitute for a banking system in an environment in which formal financial institutions are unwilling or unable to operate because of high costs of borrower monitoring, as well as informational problems such as adverse selection or moral hazards. Group lending takes advantage of the local knowledge and monitoring capacity of groups or communities those members know each other well from a history of repeated interactions, or which are bound by the informal order of a system of commonly shared norms and values that allows them to exert social control to deter opportunistic behaviour by individual group members. The arguably most successful model of group lending that also attracted considerable academic interest in recent years is the Grameen Bank in Bangladesh (Yunus and Jolis 1999; Stiglitz 1990; Besley 1995). The Grameen Bank gives small loans to self-formed groups of about five borrowers who are usually either from the same neighbourhood, or otherwise related, and thus able to monitor the actions of each other.[23] The incentives for such peer monitoring are provided by the fact that all group members are jointly liable for repaying their loans, and by the requirement that new loans can only be obtained when all existing loans are repaid. The inherent incentive structure of the loan

---

[22] The incentive properties of sharecropping arrangements have been a longstanding interest to development economists. Stiglitz (1986) demonstrates that in situations of imperfect information (in which agents are risk-averse, and supervision of agent performance as well as contract enforcement is costly), sharecropping represents a rational and efficient form of economic organisation.

[23] Note that another condition for the effectiveness of group lending is that the group members who co-sign a loan agreement share similar risk characteristics.

agreement thus assures compliance in borrower–lender relations, a fact that is confirmed by the very low default rates of group lending schemes in general, and that of Grameen Bank in particular.[24]

4.2.3 Coordinated Arrangements and Private Third Parties

In the absence of effective enforcement systems through a formal third party, self-enforcing exchange arrangements are among the most efficient informal alternatives for governing contractual relations. Self-enforcing agreements either require strong first-party enforcement through the contract partners' *ex-ante* self-commitment to honest cooperation, or must rely on mechanisms that allow the cheated party to sanction his dishonest contract partner effectively in the course of contract implementation (second-party enforcement). As stated, strong norms of morality that restrict the exchange partners' action-set to cooperative behaviour are necessary to enable first-party enforcement. Similarly, second-party enforcement involves the exchange partners' common reference and commitment to a system of shared norms, values or conventions. The self-enforcing character of first and second-party enforcement is even stronger if their underlying social norms induce others to sanction dishonest behaviour by members of the same group, even if they have not themselves been part to the agreement, or have otherwise been harmed by the cheater. Of all discussed enforcement mechanisms, such collective punishment systems represent the closest functional equivalent to third-party enforcement.

However, in situations in which the economic space broadens beyond the reach of the individual sanctioning power of people that are part of self-enforcing arrangements, morality, shared norms or enduring relations cannot be relied upon as the only basis for contract enforcement.[25] In some instances, the self-enforcing property of first and second-party enforcement systems can be restored through an institution that coordinates the implementation of multilateral punishment strategies. Such a coordinating institution can be regarded as a third-party enforcer. Unlike formal third-party enforcement backed by the state's coercive power as its means of punishment, private coordinating third parties rely on the norms that govern long-term relations among the members of their jurisdictions. The ability of a private third party to punish opportunistic behaviour is thus limited to the indirect

---

[24]Grameen Bank, which formally began its lending operations in 1983, now provides about 380 million US-Dollars annually in low-interest loans with an average loan size of around 100 US-Dollars to poor, mostly female landless farmers and micro-entrepreneurs in rural areas of Bangladesh without requiring collateral. More than 98% of its loans are repaid in time and only 0.5% are outright defaults.

[25]Such situations arise, for instance, in exchange transactions within large groups, over long distances, or in exchanges by members of a homogenous group with outside parties.

4.2 Alternative Institutions for Contract Enforcement

imposition of costs, for instance, by tarnishing the reputation of a dishonest agent, or by otherwise depriving him of the benefits from future transactions.[26]

Numerous studies confirm the empirical relevance of informal contract enforcement through coordinated mechanisms and the use of private third parties. These case studies and analytic narratives draw either on historical accounts or use contemporary observations from today's developing countries. For instance, Greif, Milgrom and Weingast (1994) relate the development of the late medieval merchant guild in Europe to the ineffectiveness of second-party enforcement mechanisms in governing relations between merchants and the rulers of medieval trade centres. They recognise that under bilateral reputation (i.e. second-party enforcement) mechanisms, the ruler lacked the incentives to protect the rights of a visiting merchant in the long-run, and was rather interested in reaping short-run gains from expropriating his property. This meant that the immediate gain from expropriation, or the opportunity cost of protection that could be withheld, were valued higher by the ruler than the future benefits that he forwent as the merchant withdrew his trade from the ruler's territory. Greif, Milgrom and Weingast thus conclude that as long as ruler–merchant relations were based on bilateral enforcement, trading activity could not expand to its efficient level because withdrawal of trade was the only possible way for individual merchants to sanction the ruler.

In light of this, the expansion of medieval long-distance trade thus required an institution that was able to effectively coordinate and enforce the merchants' responses to a ruler's opportunistic behaviour. Between the tenth and fourteenth centuries, Europe indeed experienced a period of commercial expansion that was supported by the institution of merchant guilds, most prominently among them the Hanseatic League, which developed as an association of traders active in international commerce. Often described as a mercantile league of medieval towns in northern Germany and the Baltics, the *Hanse* was never a closely managed formal organisation. Its main purpose was rather to protect and enforce the rights of its member merchants abroad. Merchants that participated in the Hanseatic privileges abroad could thus rely on the rulers of their Hanseatic home towns, and their dispatched negotiators, to protect and defend their rights and interests towards the rulers of foreign towns, in which they maintained trading posts or *Kontore* (Dollinger 1998). Through these arrangements, the Hanseatic League was able to enforce agreements with foreign rulers, and thereby overcame the commitment problem present in alternative bilateral or second-party enforcement systems.

While the need for governance in ruler–merchant relations was primarily responsible for the development of merchant guilds like the Hanseatic League, its administrative and legal bodies also performed important coordination and enforcement functions as a private third party in contractual relations among merchants. Besides the legal protection abroad, the Hanseatic privileges actually also included the commitment to a common body of law (Henn 1999). In the same time, local

---

[26]Note that punishment through exclusion from future trade is effective only if the trade relation is considered to be continued, and if it is sufficiently valued by the punished agent (i.e. if the present value of the returns from future exchanges is higher than the immediate gain from cheating).

guilds often had exclusive trade privileges in their hometown, like monopoly rights over retail trade within the territory of the town. Such benefits from guild membership leant not only credibility to the threat of exclusion of opportunistic members, but also assured that all members committed to collective action, which in turn facilitated the operation of the League's multilateral reputation mechanism.[27]

The operation of a multilateral reputation mechanism has also been observed by Avner Greif in his historical analysis of long-distance trade by a group of Jewish merchants in the Mediterranean region in the eleventh century (Greif 1993). These Jewish merchants, known as Maghribi traders due to their origin from the western part of the Muslim world, managed their long-distance trade through the employment of overseas agents. To ensure that agents were committed to act on behalf of the merchants, rather than to misappropriate their goods, the Maghribi traders formed a coalition that organised sanctions against agents that had cheated their merchants. A range of informal institutional arrangements supported the operation of this multilateral reputation mechanism. At the heart of the coalition lay the mutual commitment to hire only agents that were members of the Maghribi traders' coalition, and to exclude dishonest agents from future relations with any merchant.[28]

This way, the commitment problem inherent in merchant–agent relations was surmounted in a self-enforcing manner, as an agent's expectation of future hiring was conditioned by his behaviour in past transactions. Close ties among members of the Maghribi group of traders created a network of information transmission that enabled merchants to monitor agents and make cheating known to all. Of course, this required a common definition of acts that constituted a case of cheating. The historical records suggest that most merchant–agent relations were not based on explicit contracts. Instead, the coalition used a set of cultural rules of behaviour as their "Merchant's Law" that specified cases in which the actions by an agent should be considered as cheating.[29] By solving both the

---

[27] Multilateral reputation mechanisms not only facilitated contract enforcement in merchant relations, they also allowed a multilateral response by all merchants to a ruler who had behaved opportunistically towards an individual merchant. Such multilateral action could consist, for instance, of a trade embargo that required the collective commitment of all merchants to withdraw their trade from the territory of the ruler who did not respect a merchant's rights. However, as Greif, Milgrom and Weingast (1994) note, prices rose during an embargo and so did the marginal returns from trade. The gains from breaking an embargo thus increased for the individual merchant and, as soon as they exceeded the long-term stream of returns from guild membership, threatened the sustainability of the embargo.

[28] To involve only coalition members in the management of long-distance trade under the condition was possible because of the widespread presence of Maghribi traders across Europe and the Middle East. In the eleventh century, Maghribi traders had emigrated from Tunisia to other trade centres in the Muslim world such as Spain, Sicily, Egypt and Palestine where they become integrated into the existing social structures of already well-established Jewish communities (Greif 1993).

[29] According to Greif (1993), the practise to rely on informal Merchant's Law, rather than on individual contracts, was less the consequence of the ineffectiveness of the formal legal and juridical system that prevailed in the eleventh century. More likely, this practice was due to the asymmetric information that characterised agency relations in long-distance trade and that made the proofing of an agent's wrongdoing before official courts difficult.

4.2 Alternative Institutions for Contract Enforcement

commitment and information problem which allowed them to operate a multilateral reputation mechanism, the Maghribi traders' coalition promoted efficiency in long-distance trade. Transaction costs were reduced by using the services of overseas agents, while the unified Merchant's Law, as a substitute for comprehensive formal contracts, reduced negotiation costs in merchant–agent relations.[30]

The circumstances which gave rise to the emergence of the pre-modern institutional framework that supported trade relations in Europe in the late medieval period exhibit interesting parallels with contemporary situations in low-income countries. Yet, examples of private contract enforcement institutions that support economic exchanges in the developing world are still among the less well investigated areas of empirical research in institutional and development economics.[31]

Jul-Larsen (1993) observed a community of migrant fishermen who belonged to the Popo tribe from Benin and had settled in the town of Pointe Noire in the Republic of Congo (formerly Congo-Brazzaville). Faced with repatriation and confiscations by the Congolese government in 1977, these apparently vulnerable Popo fishermen understood to use the power they had to protect their rights vis-à-vis the government if they organised their response collectively. Through the *Association des Ressorticants du Bénin (ARB)*, an association through which Popo people from Benin organise their interests in Congo, they called on all Popo fishermen to withdraw their fish from the local market, thereby causing a sever shortage of fish in Pointe Noire. Realising the cost of this, the Congolese government eventually revised its policy towards Popo community members, and the old situation was gradually restored. As this case demonstrates, the Popo fishermen were able to regain their community's right of access to the local waters by imposing costs on the government through a collective response to its transgressions. They thus effectively used a privately governed multilateral enforcement mechanism that was sustained by the internal coherence and integrity of their community and benefited from the coordinating role of the *ARB*.

---

[30] Further historical evidence of institutions that have been used to overcome commitment problems in trade is given by the analysis of agency-relations in Genoa during the twelfth and thirteenth century in Greif (1997). Furthermore, Greif (1994) conducted a comparative historical analysis of the trading institutions of Genoese traders (as part of the Latin world) and the Maghribi traders (which were active in the Muslim world). Milgrom, North and Weingast (1990) analysed the role of a private ordering institution (the "Law Merchant") in the Champagne fairs during the eleventh and thirteenth centuries. Similarly, Clay (1997) examines a reputation-based private-order institution that facilitated inter-merchant trade in California during the 1830s and 1840s.

[31] For a review of the literature on informal institutional arrangements that support economic activity in low-income countries see Platteau (2000).

4.3 Alternative Institutions for Property Rights Protection

The previous analysis has focussed on exchange as an important element of economic activity. Exchange, however, requires specialisation in production, and production requires investment. Legal uncertainty constrains incentives to invest if property rights in the asset and returns of an investment are insecure. Without effective protection of property rights, it may take less effort to steal a property than to create it. This is why the potential for theft and other property rights violations constitutes a strong disincentive to invest in the creation, accumulation and maintenance of property.

4.3.1 The Definition of Property Rights

An important issue that has to be addressed prior to a discussion of various forms of property rights protection is to ask how property rights can adequately be defined. The definition of property rights and their protection are two different, though related, problems, just as entering a contract and enforcing its mutually agreed obligations are two separate processes. If formal legal and juridical institutions are weak or absent, people are as much affected by the lack of a system of clearly defined and recognised property rights, as they are constrained by the absence of effective protection of private property by the state.

The state has a clear comparative advantage in defining property rights. The reason is that governments can reap territorial scale economies from their natural monopoly in defining property rights through a single, universally recognised system of (national) property law. But if such a system does not exist, or lacks universal legitimacy, the delineation of private property rights remains often subject to social conventions. The same informal mechanisms that assure cooperative behaviour in exchange relations among members of homogenous social groups are also capable of securing property rights within the boundaries of the group. However, property rights defined on the basis of such informal arrangements means that they are only defined *de facto* by possession, not *de jure* through formal legal title.

Hernando de Soto, whose Institute for Liberty and Democracy studied informal property arrangements in a wide range of developing countries, found that the legitimacy of all informally held property is based on collective understandings of how things are owned and how owners relate to each other. The rules that govern property rights relations in the informal economy are thus built from a consensus among people as to how their assets should be held, used, and exchanged (de Soto 2000). Such a "social contract", which comprises explicit obligations between members of a community or group, is characteristic for the governance of economic and social relations in the informal economy. Its rules are influenced by customs and socio-cultural traditions of the community to which it applies, and provide security for its member's property and economic activities.

The absence of a state-governed system for the formal establishment, definition and recognition of property rights has its own economic implications. If rights are not clearly defined, property cannot freely be moved and traded across large jurisdictions, and is less likely to be sold at an adequate price. Especially land obtains significantly lower prices if sold without legal title.[32] Furthermore, without an officially recognised proof of ownership, property, and in particular land, cannot be used as collateral for gaining access to credit. This is a main reason why in many low-income countries investments remain essentially a one-way stream from which no money flows back that could be reinvested in new productive activities. Other profitable uses of assets are as well prevented if ownership rights are not clearly assigned. For instance, owners of informally build houses are sometimes reluctant to offer them for rent, fearing that a tenant may try to assert a claim to it. A more basic fact by which unclear property rights constrain investment is that people may be less willing to invest in a property which they do not legally own. For instance, studies from Ghana and Nicaragua revealed that farmers invest up to 8% more in their land when their rights to it are secure (World Bank 2004).[33]

4.3.2 Sources of Property Rights Violations

Secure property rights are as fundamental to the operation of an economic system as the institutions that enable mutually beneficial exchange. A unifying theme that links the discussions on exchange relations and property rights is that of enforcement. Every exchange involves a transfer of property rights that needs to be enforced just as the contractual terms by which the transfer takes place require enforcement. It is therefore difficult to draw an analytical distinction between contract enforcement and the protection of property rights in exchange relations, since the effective enforcement of contractual obligations also implies that property rights must be honoured. This becomes evident if one considers that cheating in contractual relations always also involves a violation of rights to the property that has been the subject of exchange.

Cheating in contractual relations is but one of the many ways in which property rights can be violated. Most infringements on private property are actually caused by unilateral action. This raises some further issues that are different from those raised with respect to the economic governance of voluntary interactions between two or more parties. An act of theft is a single-person choice problem in

---

[32] Deininger (2003) found that, after being titled, the value of rural land increased in Brazil by 72%, in Indonesia by 43%, in the Philippines by 56%, and in Thailand by 81%.

[33] Further problems inherent to the definition of property rights arise with regard to property rights in natural resources such as forest, fisheries or mineral oil deposits. Problems concerning the delineation of property rights for such common pool resources have extensively been studied, among others, by Ostrom (1990), Ostrom et al. (1999) and Libecap (1994).

which the gains from stealing are balanced against the probability of detection and the cost of punishment. Correspondingly, the deterrence of theft and, if it fails, the detection and punishment of the thief, may be accomplished by unilateral action as well. Without assistance from the state's executive powers, property owners may try to do this directly by physically protecting their property, by hiring specialised private protectors, or by engaging in collective protection together with their neighbours or other forms of organised self-help. As the discussion in Chap. 3 has shown, the need for such private protective measures increase transaction costs, diminishes the returns from an investment, and thus hinders the expansion of economic activity to its efficient level. In the worst case, any surplus accumulated by individuals may not be reinvested at all in the local economy, but instead contributes to large-scale capital flight or emigration, which is indeed pervasive in many low-income countries with poor property rights environments.[34]

Sometimes the state itself, and its agents, can threaten the security of private property. The state's coercive power does not only enable him to enforce property rights; governments can equally misuse their power by expropriating privately owned wealth. Outright expropriation is only the most direct form of a state-led property rights violation. Often, the state infringes on private property indirectly through corruption, onerous regulation or progressively high taxation that leaves those liable no choice but to sell parts of their property in order to raise the means to comply (World Bank 2004, especially Chap. 4).[35] Finally, the state is, at least indirectly, involved in property rights violations that occur through damage of human, physical and social assets during armed conflicts and civil wars. Nothing disrupts private investment and economic development more than violent conflict: it destroys property, restricts the free movement of people and goods, diverts resources from productive into destructive uses, and consequently increases poverty in all its dimensions.

A final possibility for property rights violations arises if interdependencies among people cause the activity of one actor to inflict damage on someone else's property. If such negative externalities are not prevented by some kind of internalisation mechanism, compensation of damages will not occur unless clear liability rules are established and can be enforced. As Griffin (1991) notes, liability rules are as fundamental to a juridical system for settling value after a transaction has occurred, as property rules are to the operation of markets.

---

[34] Theft, predation and other forms of violent crime are actually among the highest-ranked impediments to private sector development. Investment climate surveys carried out by the World Bank in various low-income countries show, for example, that 37% of surveyed firms in Nigeria identify crime as a major or severe constraint on their operations, 50% in Zambia, 70% in Kenya, and as much as 80% in Guatemala (World Bank 2004).

[35] Among others, Olson (1993) and Shleifer and Vishny (1993) offer theories to explain the economic consequences of different manifestations of power abuses by the state.

4.3.3 Private Protection of Property Rights

Individual or collective private protection of property has traditionally been a main and inevitable strategy to address the consequences that arise from the inadequate protection of property rights by the state. As noted earlier, this can either be done though self-protection, like building fences, or by hiring the services of a private protector. Both options increase the cost of doing business, but the latter in particular involves some subtle decisions: A property owner will only buy the services of a private protector if his service fee does not exceed the discounted rate of future return (or utility) that he expects from the protected asset. A private protector will thus only be hired for high-valued (i.e. high-return) properties while owners of lower valued assets will resort to usually less effective self-help.[36] However, without the threat of sanctions, the private protector's honesty is not guaranteed. He faces himself the choice of whether he should earn a fee as private protector or turn into a predator and steal the property he is supposed to protect. He will tend to choose the latter if he considers the one-time gain from stealing higher than the discounted stream of fee income that he earns from his protection service.[37] Note, however, that theft is not a unilateral action anymore if it is committed by a protector who turned into a predator. In this case, the property owner and the predator are related to each other through the initial agreement on the supply of protection services. Because of this relationship, the potential predator has to balance the gains from theft against the risk for being punished plus the discounted future stream of income from the relation that he loses. Generally, the existence of any kind of relationship between a predator and a property owner, be it by mutual contract, repeated interaction, or social bond, may reduce the potential for property rights violations.

Similarly, inculcation to moral values or norms of reciprocity can be considered as a way to prevent theft. If a predator feels inclined to take the well-being of the property owner into account, this might change his balance of gains and costs from stealing. As the discussion in Sect. 4.1.1 has shown, the internalisation of moral norms and norms that induce reciprocity in individual relations may rule out opportunistic behaviour and can thus establish and sustain respect for property rights as well. While this effect is strongest among members of homogenous social groups which are bound by limited-group morality, the fact that people actually do not size every occasion for theft that arises also suggests that general morality is to a certain extent capable of preventing crime.

---

[36] As Gambretta (1993) notes, the protection of more valuable assets by private guards creates a negative externality for owners of lower-value properties, because in such cases predators will concentrate on lower-value assets, which are more likely to become a subject of theft as they are relatively easier to steal.

[37] Dixit (2004, Chap. 5) constructs a model of private for-profit protection that illustrates several choices by property owners, predators and protectors, and confirms some of the shortcomings of for-profit protection discussed above.

4.4 The Scope and Limits of Informal Enforcement Institutions

The above discussion made evident that economic activity is possible in the absence of formal law and enforcement institutions backed by the coercive power of the state. Following this observation to its logical conclusion makes clear that the authority of the state is but one possible means of contract and property rights enforcement needed to support economic exchange and investment. Economic relations can indeed also be governed by a variety of informal institutions and private arrangements that are able to substitute for much of the functions attributed to formal state law and courts. Yet, the question arises if, and under what conditions, this substitution enhances or constrains the efficiency and scope of production, exchange and investment. Although informal enforcement institutions may represent the best available alternative to formal institutions in the absence of the latter, they may not be sufficient to accommodate all potentially profitable business opportunities.

Against this background, the following subsections examine the relationship between informal enforcement and the scope and efficiency of exchange. It will be asked under what conditions informal modes of economic governance have relative advantages, and when they have limits. The discussion enters into a brief look at how private, self-enforcing arrangements can even facilitate economic activity in advanced countries, where they often co-exist with formal legal institutions and complement their functions in vital respects.

4.4.1 The Relationship Between Informal Enforcement and the Scope of Exchange

The effectiveness of informal enforcement institutions in supporting economic exchange and investment is a downward-sloping function of the size of the relevant economic space that they govern. The above discussion addressed several cases which show that the expansion of trader communities and their engagement into long-distance trade tends to be accompanied by a shift from bilateral reputation mechanisms to coordinated, multilateral enforcement systems and the engagement of private third parties. It is indeed observable that the relative effectiveness of norm- and relation-based enforcement arrangements decreases as the scale of economic transactions broadens and deepens. This suggests that economic development requires at some point the emergence of more complex formal institutions that help to sustain the expansion of markets.

Li (2003) offers a theoretical explanation for the relationship between informal enforcement and the scope of exchange. He recognises that setting up formal institutions requires high fixed costs but leads to low marginal costs of exchange, whereas informal institutions are associated with high marginal costs, but low initial set-up

4.4 The Scope and Limits of Informal Enforcement Institutions

costs. Exchange transactions that are subject to formal rules and third-party enforcement can largely rely on publicly available and verifiable information, can use explicit and standardised contracts, and thus reduce private search, negotiation and monitoring costs.[38] These transaction costs economies compare to the one-time cost of drafting, interpreting, and enforcing a unified system of contract and property law. In contrast, relation-based governance systems involve few fixed costs, as only minimum *ex ante* collective action is required to create them. Yet, they produce significant marginal costs that result from the need to build a long-term relationship with every additional exchange partner, to verify and monitor his behaviour, or otherwise to create trust and assure commitment. Moreover, any acquired information remains implicit, relation-specific and non-transferable, and can thus hardly be observed and verified by an external party. Consequently, the marginal costs associated with informal exchange relations cannot be reduced effectively by delegating enforcement and dispute resolution to an outside third party.[39]

However, this explanation is to some extent incomplete as it compares formal contracting solely with informal exchange through long-term relationships based on repeated interactions. In fact, the high marginal costs that Li attributes to relation-based contracting are likely to be much lower when exchange partners are homogenous with respect to their ethnic origin, religious belief or other attributes that make them share the same cultural values and social norms. In these cases, the information on features that all community members have in common represents shared local knowledge that is embedded in the group structure and thus available even before transaction partners enter into an exchange relationship. Moreover, the self-enforcing property of economic transactions governed by moral norms or other shared values makes them particularly efficient. The assertion that informal exchange relations are associated with high marginal costs is yet justified from the point on at which intra-group trade expands beyond the boundaries of the homogenous group. If new exchange partners cannot anymore be acquired from within the group, the marginal costs of an additional transaction that involves strangers will instantly rise.[40]

---

[38] Nevertheless, actual recourse to legal procedures and court action is not without cost and can sometimes be inefficient, for instance, if transaction values are small, or legally relevant information is difficult to recover.

[39] A formal demonstration of the limits of relation-based governance is offered in Dixit (2004, Chap. 3.3). Dixit constructs a game-theoretic model with which he tries to establish the highest attainable value for the gains from trade as the size of the self-governing community expands. This model is subject to the assumptions that cheating becomes more attractive the more distant the partner is located, and that the gains from trade increase exponentially with distance.

[40] Therefore, the marginal costs curve of informally governed transactions is by no means linear, but rather a positively sloped exponential function (or even a kinked curve with a high positive gradient after a linear interval that denotes the feasible intra-group transaction set).

4.4.2 Natural Limits of Private Governance Mechanisms

The analysis so far suggested that the relative advantages of informal modes of governance turn into their limits relative to formal governance structures as the division of labour deepens, and the scope of transactions expands. However, the limits of informal governance systems are not a function of the cost and scope of economic activity alone. There are yet also drawbacks of private governance mechanisms that exist independently of the scope of exchange. For instance, collectivist systems of reputation and trust-based governance that support economic activity within homogenous social groups segregate the economic space unless it is applicable as a governance mechanism also in inter-group relations. This segregation limits possible gains from specialisation, competition, and hence efficiency. Moreover, the segregation of exchange into separate groups, communities or networks may also have important distributional implications, as the benefits of relation-based exchange only accrue to the members of a specific group. Equal opportunities may also not be realised, even not within closed groups, because new members might be discriminated as they lack the reputation from a history of repeated successful exchanges. Relation-based contracting thus creates barriers to entry as entrepreneurs stick to established relationships rather than working with new, untested partners (Johnson et al. 2000). Finally, the concentration of business activity and productive resources on small, ethnically or religiously homogeneous groups raises the risk of social tensions or even expropriation by the government.[41]

In some cases, informal mechanisms of economic governance can provide incentives that even discourage the engagement in profitable business relations. One such case is family-based exchange. If economic transactions are restricted to relations with kin, strong egalitarian norms and a sense of family obligation may have a negative impact on people's impetus for personal achievement. Although such obligations act as an important form of insurance for people with a very low level of income, they may, in the same time, discourage investment and the expansion of economic activity.[42] Similar disincentives may be generated by social or

---

[41] The difficult process of land reform in southern African countries may be illustrative in this respect. Especially the recent experience in Zimbabwe, where the government initiated its controversial fast-track land reform programme in 2000, shows how the concentration of economic power on a relatively small group of ethnical Europeans has triggered violent conflict. While the case for land reform and redistribution in Zimbabwe is legitimate – given the white minority's privileged status as former colonial power – the way in which the government under President Robert Mugabe carried it out contributed to the loss of more than 400,000 domestic jobs, significant fall in agricultural production and export revenues, and directly caused the country's current economic and humanitarian disaster.

[42] In their analysis of the economic effects of family-based governance systems in a modernising society, Hoff and Sen (2006) ask if the "social contract" of mutual assistance that bounds members of the kin system actually represents a poverty trap when faced by an expanding economy. From a simple model of the individual and collective responses of kin group members to increased economic opportunities outside the group they show that network externalities in the migration decisions of kin members can lead to coordination problems and inefficient outcomes, and that kin groups often try to raise exit costs to preserve their status quo. While the authors find evidence for these patterns especially in African economies, they also acknowledge that the kin system was able to encourage entrepreneurship in other places like, for instance, East Asia.

religious norms that are capable of creating trust in economic relationships, but in the same time condemn certain business practices, such as trade for personal profit or money lending for interest, as socially undesirable.

4.4.3 Natural Advantages of Private Governance Mechanisms

Private governance based on morality, trust or reputation exhibits several features that give it a natural advantage over formal modes of economic governance. This suggests that private governance mechanisms can play an important role in complementing the functions of formal institutions besides their function as substitute for the state in the context of limited statehood.

A main advantage of private, self-enforcing exchange arrangements stems from the availability of nearly complete relation-specific information that is required for bilateral enforcement by the exchange partners. A formal third party can only enforce those elements of an agreement on which information is transferable to, and verifiable by a third party. Given bounded rationality, very few formal contracts are *ex ante* complete. In fact, the more aspects of a transaction are implicitly agreed, the smaller is the subset of contractual elements for which effective external enforcement and dispute resolution is possible. Thus, a large part of disputes among the partners to a transaction can only be resolved by relation-based governance, but not by rule-based governance. This point is very well reflected in the analysis on homogenous social groups by Backhaus (1980). He recognises that

> the more heterogeneous the population, and the more heterogeneous the object of their respective transactions and conflicts [...], the more conflict-relevant information is foregone during the process of abstraction and subsumption under formal rules. Decentralised procedures, adopted to specific social and local conditions, may integrate more information necessary for conflict resolution than can be integrated into a forensic procedure (*Ibid.*, p. 28).

Along similar lines does Cooter (1994) develop his argument that decentralised law is more efficient than centralised law the more societies advance and the more complex economic transactions become. He observes that modern economies have created many specialised business communities with their own internal norms and standards, and refers to the latter as the "new law merchant" in imitation of the medieval Law Merchant discussed in Milgrom, North and Weingast (1990). Although these informal community norms arise outside the body of state law, both governance systems interact in dynamic ways: The members of business communities need the authority of the state as ultimate backstop in the settlement of their disputes, whereas the state requires insider information from within the specialised communities to regulate their activities effectively. According to Cooter, the efficiency of state law depends on the extent in which lawmakers succeed in aligning formal law with the informal norms already practiced within communities and business networks. He proposes an approach for the adjudication of informal norms "from bottom to top", which is capable of combining the advantages of the state-governed legal and juridical system (namely the territorial scale economies present in the control of a large economic space by a single third-party enforcement power) with the information advantage inherent to the private governance mechanisms of homogenous groups. With this approach, Cooter not only recognises the natural advantage that private governance mechanisms have in coordinating the interactions of people within informal networks and groups, but also offers a methodology by which this advantage can possibly be preserved in the process of formalisation and subsumption of informal practices under state-governed law. This makes the approach clearly relevant also for the design of legal reform proposals in the context of low-income countries in which a large informal sector and strong reliance on relation-based modes of exchange dominate in economic life.

The widespread use of informal modes of contract enforcement and dispute resolution in advanced economies has first been analysed by Stuart Macaulay ([1963] 1992). He observed that few contractual disputes in business relationships in the United States are actually litigated through formal juridical institutions, and that most are settled without resorting to government-enforced laws. He points out that the parties to an exchange usually pay more attention to assure that they both understand the primary obligations on each side, than to plan for all conceivable contingencies. Thus, legally binding contracts are far more common in the creation of exchange relationships than in the adjustment of such relationships and the settlement of disputes. This explains why disputes are frequently settled without reference to the contract or potential legal sanctions, but rather through the mutual desire to continue a business relationship, through reference to the partners' reputation, or because the business partners know each other socially well. This is well illustrated by the responses that Macaulay received from surveys among American managers and lawyers. For instance, lawyers reckoned that businessmen often enter contracts without a minimum degree of advance planning and rather desire to "keep it simple and avoid red tape" (ibid., p. 269). They also frequently observed that "businessmen do not feel they have "a contract" – rather they have "an order". They speak of "cancelling the order" rather that "breaching a contract" (ibid., p. 273). A purchasing agent told: "if something comes up, you get the other man on the telephone and deal with the problem. You don't read legalistic contract clauses at each other if you ever want to do business again". Finally, a businessman reckoned: "You can settle every dispute if you keep the lawyers and accountants out of it. They just do not understand the give-and-take needed in business" (ibid., p. 273).

These statements display a healthy degree of ignorance towards the legal consequences of formal contracts and a strong preference for informal modes of enforcement and dispute resolution. But unlike in situations in which a functioning formal legal and juridical system does not exist, these private ordering mechanisms are not fully independent from formal law, as the latter always remains available as a last resort if informal enforcement fails. In the context of advanced economies, private governance mechanisms thus mostly operate in the shadow of formal law. It is the credible threat to resort to state-governed courts that creates commitment in private ordering relations and, in a seeming paradox, enables the involved parties to enforce their obligations informally without recourse to formal court order.

The observed attitudes and business practices in advanced economies imply a strong functional complementarity between informal and formal mechanisms of

4.4 The Scope and Limits of Informal Enforcement Institutions

economic governance. They also suggest that formal law is only inadequately equipped to govern economic relations in all their facets. In many instances, social norms, personal trust and reputation do constrain economic behaviour much more effectively in ways conductive to mutually beneficial exchange than written laws and courts alone can do. This is why private governance mechanisms can help to make the economic system run smoothly and at lower transaction costs in spite of the existence of a formal system of laws and enforcement institutions. This conclusion suggests that private governance arrangements play a continued role in supporting economic activity while countries develop beyond situations of weak or absent economic governance by the state. The dynamic interactions between informal and formal institutions in the process of economic development and institutional change represent an important new field of research that will be taken up again in the third part of the analysis.

Chapter 5
Informal Economic Activity

The previous chapters have dealt with important economic characteristics of poor countries. Each of them actually provides some explanation also for the large size of the informal sector in low-income countries. Exclusion from the merits of formal institution is a dimension of poverty that often makes the family, mutual assistance groups or other informal community networks the only source for obtaining a minimum level of social protection and livelihood security. Being denied access to official product and labour markets, moreover, means that poor people have to live from subsistence farming, unregistered homework, small-scale trade or from employment by informal firms. Informal economic activity is often a reaction of individuals and firms to the high transaction costs associated with entering the formal sector. For example, a substantial number of companies in Angola, Benin or Djibouti operate in the informal economy, as the legal registration of their activities would cost them more than twice their respective country's annual per capita income (World Bank and IFC 2008). Property titles are also mostly exchanged informally in countries such as Nigeria or Senegal where formal registration of property transactions costs more than 20% of the property value (ibid.). In other countries, property registers are not established at all, which means all property is, by default, possessed informally. The discussion in Chap. 4 has shown that wherever necessary formal institutions are absent or ineffective, people will invent informal alternatives or have to resort to traditional ways of organising social and economic life.

Although the previous chapter was concerned with the private governance mechanisms of economic activity outside the formal law, the purpose of this chapter is to study the manifestations and scale of informality in the private sectors of low-income countries. The focus will primarily be on the diverse forms in which informal firms manage to organise their business activities and interests, and on the economic implications of these informal modes of organising economic transactions for a country's development.

5.1 Defining and Measuring the Informal Economy

In the economic sector, informality includes all unreported, unregistered and hence unregulated economic activities by individuals, households or firms. Although informal economic activity takes place outside the law, it is not meant to include illegal actions of criminal nature such as drug trafficking, people smuggling, illegal gambling or money laundering. While these activities obviously represent a subset of the informal sector, the following analysis will concentrate on informal activities that can potentially also be found in the formal economy.[1]

The concept of the "informal sector" was first put on the development agenda in the 1970s by the International Labour Organization. It initially referred to survival and other unreported activities in peripheral segments of the economy (ILO 2002a). Over the years, a broader understanding of informality evolved, which acknowledges the following characteristics as additional elements of a definition of the informal economy in developing countries:

1. The dominance of unincorporated small-scale units which produce and distribute goods and services, consisting largely of independent, self-employed micro-entrepreneurs or home-workers (in urban areas), as well as of household enterprises and subsistence farmers (in rural areas).
2. Ease of entry into the informal sector as opposed to the administrative barriers of entering the official economy with regard to the formal processes of registration, licensing and inspection of enterprises.
3. A relatively low level of productivity as the result of limited specialisation, an insufficient deployment of capital, technology and skills, that can result in restrictions to growth and the realisation of scale economies.
4. Low and unstable incomes, low employment security, poor working conditions, and exclusion from official social security benefits of those employed in the informal economy.
5. No recognition under the law and hence no formal legal definition and enforcement of property and contract rights, combined with enhanced vulnerability to crime, predation, extortion, corruption and harassment by state authorities, as well as dependence on strategies of large domestic and foreign suppliers and/or purchasers.
6. Restrictions in access to public services and infrastructure and thus reliance on private, informal institutional arrangements for representation, information, exchange, protection of property, credit, training, and social security.

---

[1] The term informal economy is used here to indicate the conceptual whole of informal economic activity, spanning across both production and employment relationships. It is sometimes also called the "extralegal", "shadow", "unofficial", "unprotected", "underground", "parallel", "dual", "grey" or "black" economy. Note that the term "informal" in the sense that an activity or arrangement is outside the reach of formal law has a different connotation than its use in the later theoretical analysis where informal institutions denote people's culturally derived values, norms or mental models.

Informal economic activity can be found in virtually every sector of the economy. It is particularly widespread in repetitive and labour-intensive manufacturing activities including the production of garments, textiles, footwear, toys, furniture and electronics, as well as several other handicraft and artisan products. These sectors mostly represent key export industries, and it is often informal manufacturers who are at the bottom of global value chains that, further upstream, are often controlled by large importers and retailers from developed countries. Informal activities in the manufacturing sector are typically carried out in workshops and unlicensed factories or through industrial outworkers that is, home-based producers which are linked with larger enterprises through outsourcing or subcontracting arrangements.

The unlicensed operations of street vendors, which provide an example of informality in domestic trade and retail sectors, belong to the street scene of most cities in developing and transition countries. Cross (1998) attempted a conservative estimate of the different forms of street vending in Mexico City in the mid-1990s. Accordingly, there were a total of 121,738 stalls located on sidewalks and street corners, rotating markets, ambulatories and metro stations of Mexico City, not including temporary stalls operated by vendors during peak commercial seasons. An additional 293,000 street vending stands exist in the 43 other Mexican centres (de Soto 2000). In a report that synthesises findings from case studies on street vending in six African countries (Kenya, Cote d'Ivoire, Ghana, Zimbabwe, Uganda and South Africa), Mitullah (2004) documents some general features that characterise street vending and small-scale trade activities in Sub-Saharan Africa. Accordingly, the majority of street vendors are woman who engage mostly in retail activities and work on their own account. They generally have primary or lower levels of education, and most of the sampled traders report to engage in street vending for lack of other sources of income and employment. Some of them sell home-made products and processed food, while others obtain their wholesale supplies from their country's capital, its main port cities or from neighbouring countries. Most vendors work close to their living places either on streets, district markets, at bus stations or other central points with heavy pedestrian traffic, and some have an established clientele. Although street vendors, due to their informal nature, pay no taxes on the income they earn, some municipalities charge them dues or daily fees for the trading spaces they occupy.

The conditions that are common for informal street-vending activities also characterise informal economic activity in the services sector. Such activities include shoe polishing, hairdressing, barbering, photography, security services, commercial pay phone services, currency exchange, money lending, medical services, or repair services including garment, shoes, bicycles, cars, as well as watch and clock repairs. These services are either provided directly on the streets, at the client's location, or through small, unlicensed workshops. In the transport services sector of low-income countries, unauthorised busses, taxis, jitneys or rickshaws often represent the only means of urban public transportation. Finally, millions of poor people make their living as home-workers and farmers in the agricultural and dependent sectors. Women, in particular, are active in subsistence farming, as well as in the sale of home-made beer or other forms of processed food.

In the construction sector, informal economic activity ranges from the employment of unregistered workers on large building sites to unofficial do-it-yourself construction of own dwellings in informal squatter settlements. The Peruvian Institute of Liberty and Democracy found that throughout Latin America, six out of eight buildings have been built informally, and that 80% of all real estate is held outside the law (de Soto 2000). A famous example is Brazil's *favelas* – informal areas of large cities which provide for most of the supply of rental housing in the country's mega-cities. They were once built illegally by peasants from the North-East of Brazil who had been attracted by urban centres. There are no rent controls in the *favelas* and rents are paid in US dollars and based on privately enforced contracts. Before the *favelas* emerged, more than two-thirds of housing construction in Brazil was for rent. At the end of the 1990s, registered rentals constituted merely 3% of Brazil's official construction (ibid.). According to Perlman (2005), there are today 752 *favelas* in Rio de Janeiro alone, which are home to approximately 1.65 million inhabitants, and continue to grow much faster than the *asfaltos*, as locals call the city's formal settlements. Yet, in spite of the extralegal nature of rental agreements, property transactions, and land tenure arrangements, the *favelas* are not the slums or shanty towns as which they were once perceived. As Perlman reports, there are now many brick houses with indoor plumbing and electricity provided by private companies.[2] Very different conditions still prevail in other squatter settlements of African and Asian mega-cities. One of Asia's largest slums is Dharavi, covering 220 hectares near the airport of Mumbai, India, with poor-quality structures usually build of mud or brick and asbestos sheets and no sanitation. Nevertheless, Dharavi, as Mumbai's other extensive slum areas, hosts a thriving community of informal micro-entrepreneurs that run everything from potteries, metal and leather workshops to bakeries, and produce goods worth over 500 million US Dollars a year (The Economist 2005).

The informal economy does not just serve the private needs of poor people engaged in it; informal activities are in many ways also linked with the formal sector. Just as informal workers spend parts of their income in the formal economy, so do firms and households in the formal sector commission and consume informally produced goods and services. For instance, informal trade across borders is very common and a clear example of how the informal and formal economies are linked. South Africa, for instance, attracts a large number of temporary immigrants from neighbouring countries who purchase goods for resale in their home countries. Cross-border trading is also significant in West Africa, not only within the region, but also between west African countries and places such as Dubai and Hong Kong, China, where traders cheaply purchase manufactured goods for sale at home (ILO 2002a).

---

[2]This is partially due to an ambitious squatter settlement upgrading programme, the *Favela-Bairro*, which was started in the 1990s with funding from the Inter-American Development Bank and aimed at integrating the *favelas*, at least physically, into the surrounding urban neighbourhoods (Perlman 2005). That objective may, however, be undermined by recent plans by the city authorities to build walls around Rio's *favelas* that will effectively result in a segregation of residents of the *favelas* from the rest of Rio society (The Gringo Times 2009).

Linkages between formal and informal firms have specifically gained momentum in the context of international trade liberalisation and investment. In fact, the globalisation process is more and more claimed as an explanatory factor for the recent growth of informal economic activities in many developing countries (Carr and Chen 2002). In particular, it is argued that the impact of global competition encourages firms to shift formal wage workers into informal and unprotected employment arrangements. This means that production processes are being decentralised functionally and regionally into smaller, more flexible specialised production units, with many of them operating in the informal economy of developing or transition countries.

Global commodity or value-added chains provide a good example to illustrate this trend. Through global value chains, production and distribution processes are broken up into many geographically and operationally separated steps. The design of global value chains follows the strategic objective of leading production or retail companies to combine the comparative advantage of countries with the competitive advantage of firms. In many industries, the first and most labour-intensive step in these global production networks is performed in the informal economy of developing or transition countries. An illustrative example is the vertical disintegration of apparel chains in the fashion industry. As major retailers and brand companies have moved out of manufacturing to concentrate mostly on design, marketing and distribution of goods, they now sub-contract or outsource manufacturing activities to local firms and middlemen who again subcontract to own-account producers and home-workers. Another example is the production of fruits, vegetables, cut flowers and other horticultural products in Africa and Latin America, and increasingly in Asia as well. The global value chains for these non-traditional agricultural exports (NTAEs) are buyer-driven and controlled at the upper end by a few major supermarket chains in North America and Europe. At the lower end, however, most backward linkages, such as production, collection or pre-processing, are carried out informally. Similar structures are found with regard to the production and export of non-timber forest products (NTFPs) where millions of people individually and informally engage in the collection of medicinal plants, gum arabic, rattan, natural honey, mushrooms, neem, shea nuts, and other types of wild nuts and seeds which produce oils that can be used for cooking, skin care or medical purposes.

5.1.1 *The Size and Growth of the Informal Economy and How It Can Be Estimated*

The characteristics and economic implications of informal economic activity can be analysed either from the perspective of informally employed workers, or with a view to unofficial trade and production activities. Both perspectives are associated with different approaches to estimate the size of the informal economy: Employment-based approaches define and count the people employed in the informal economy, whereas output-based approaches measure the size of the informal economy in terms of the output generated by informal firms.

Early contributions to the development and application of the employment-based definition of the informal economy have been made by the International Labour Organization. It encouraged the compilation of data on employment in informal sector enterprises through national labour force surveys or special informal sector surveys, and worked towards an international, harmonised definition of employment in the informal economy.[3] However, to date, most available data still reflect individual countries' national definitions of informality, which may vary, among others, with respect to the criteria used to define the informal economy, the branches of economic activity covered (particularly with respect to the inclusion or exclusion of agricultural activities), the geographical coverage (urban and/or rural areas), and with regard to the reference period, as most statistical information on the informal economy is collected through surveys on an ad hoc rather than a regular basis. This means that survey-based methods cannot provide measures on the development and growth of the informal economy over a longer period of time. It also implies that international comparison of survey-based data is inherently difficult. The greatest advantage of using surveys for obtaining employment-based estimates is that they also provide detailed information about the structure, composition and types of employment in the informal sector. A more fundamental problem that concerns all direct methods of estimating the extent of informal economic activity or employment is that they have to rely on the respondents' willingness to cooperate. As unreported, informal activity is all about not being officially detected, survey data on informal work and production relationships are likely to underestimate the real scope of the problem.

Conversely, indirect methods for estimating the size of the informal economy avoid problems of underreporting by using indicators that indirectly reveal information about the extent of informal economic activities. These methods are commonly applied in conjunction with approaches that aim at estimating the size of the informal economy in terms of its contribution to national income or GDP, but are also used to estimate informal employment where survey-based data are incomplete.

In a survey of the relevant literature, Schneider and Enste (2000) identify, among others, the following indirect methods as the most commonly applied approaches for estimating the share of the informal economy in GNP:

1. *Discrepancy between national expenditure and income statistics*: This approach is based on the assumption that in the absence of any unreported economic activity, the income measure of (official) GNP in a country's national accounts should generally be equal to the expenditure measure of (official) GNP. If expenditure data exceed national income statistics in a given reference period, this difference

---

[3]To account for the increasing informalisation of employment relations in the formal sector, which results, among others, from a growing number of outsourcing and sub-contracting arrangements, the ILO recently complemented its measures of "employment in the informal sector" by a measure of "informal employment". Although the concept of "employment in the informal sector" includes all jobs in informal sector enterprises, "informal employment" is defined as comprising the total number of informal jobs, whether carried out in formal sector enterprises, informal sector enterprises, or households. So far, the ILO has compiled statistics mostly on employment in informal sector enterprises only (Hussmanns 2004).

could be used as indicator for the size of the informal economy. Unfortunately, national account data – in particular those from low-income countries – are usually incomplete and subject to various kinds of measurement errors, which lead to discrepancies between expenditure and income data that are actually not related to the real extent of unreported economic activity.

2. *Currency demand approach*: Various estimates for the size of the informal economy especially in OECD countries are derived from econometrically estimated functions of a country's currency demand over time. This approach assumes that informal economic transactions are based on cash-payments in order to remain invisible in the accounts of the parties to an exchange. Accordingly, the part of demand for currency that cannot be attributed to conventional determinants of the demand for money in cash is then used as indicator for the size of the informal economy. The underlying regression model relates the demand for currency to variables that capture conventional influencing factors for currency demand such as interest rates, changes in aggregate income or payment habits, as well to the average tax rate which is used as a proxy variable to capture changes in the size of the informal economy. Apart from the model's extensive empirical requirements, its theoretical specifications are problematic in at least two respects. First, the extent of informal economic activity is determined by many more factors than just a raising tax burden. The average tax rate is thus insufficient to approximate changes in the size of the informal economy, especially in a developing countries context. Second, cash payments are only one possible mode of settling transactions in the informal economy. The size of the informal economy might be larger than estimated by the model if, for instance, barter deals were considered as well.

3. *Physical input (electricity consumption) method*: The basic idea behind this indirect method is to use the consumption of a physical input factor, which is used in all informal and formal economic activity alike, as indicator for the size of informally generated output. In most cases, electric energy consumption is used as the relevant input factor as it is assumed to change proportionally with overall (formal and informal) economic activity. The difference between growth in official GDP and the growth of electricity consumption in a given time period then serves as a measure for the growth of the informal economy. For calculating the actual size of the informal sector from these relative measures, a given historical base value has to be known.[4] Limits on the reliability of estimates obtained from this method result from the fact that not all informal enterprises (especially in labour-intensive sectors) have similar energy consumption patterns as their competitors in the formal sector. Moreover, other sources of energy can be used instead of electricity. Finally, estimation errors may occur as the electricity/GDP elasticity is unlikely to be constant over time and across countries given the development of more energy-efficient production technologies.

4. *(Dynamic) multiple indicators, multiple causes model approach (MIMIC/DYMIMIC)*: This approach uses a statistical method that allows to estimate a directly unobservable

---

[4]This is done by choosing a base year in which the size of the informal economy is assumed to be low or zero.

variable (i.e. the size of the informal economy). A MIMIC model is composed of two parts: a measurement equation and a set of structural equations. The former relates the unobservable variable to a number of observable proxy variables (i.e. indicators that reflect changes in the size of the informal economy like, for instance, the number of cash transactions, or the labour force participation rate in the formal economy). The structural equations establish the correlation between exogenous explanatory variables (e.g. the tax rate, the regulatory burden or measures of tax morality) and the unobservable variable. Unlike the electricity demand and the physical input methods, which estimated the size of the informal economy through only a single indicator, the model approach explicitly considers the effects of multiple indicators on the size of the informal economy, and simultaneously accounts for multiple causes of informal economic activity. However, the multiple variables and indicators that the MIMIC model uses increase the risk that its variables are (nearly) multicollinearly related, with the result that its coefficient estimates change erratically. Moreover, as the MIMIC model provides only relative estimates, other methods have to be found to obtain absolute values for the size of the informal economy.

A lack of reliable data from direct, survey-based collection methods on informal employment in both the formal and informal sectors has led to the development of indirect methods also for estimating informal employment. The most common approach is the residual method, which draws on existing statistical data on the size of the total non-agricultural workforce and on the number of formal employees in the non-agricultural workforce. These data are usually available from population censuses, labour force surveys or other types of household surveys. From these data, an estimate on total informal employment (outside agriculture) can be obtained by subtracting the number of formal employees from the total non-agricultural workforce. This difference represents a residual estimate for the total informal employment in non-agricultural employment (ILO 2002b).

Table 5.1 presents estimates for the size of the informal economy for a selected number of developing countries. It contrasts measures of the informal sector as proportion of official GNP (output-based approach) with estimates on the share of employment in the informal sector (employment-based approach). The data on the size of the informal economy as percentages of GNP are shown for two different time periods to convey an impression also of the rate at which the informal sector changes. The estimates have been calculated by Schneider (2007) who uses a DYMIMIC model with variables obtained though the currency demand approach. The data on informal employment have been estimated by the International Labour Organization based on the residual method by using employment data from national censuses and labour force surveys. They are broken up into informally employed women and men to display gender-specific differences in informal employment.[5]

---

[5]Countries represented in the table have been selected because data on both output and employment-based calculations were available for close reference periods. Note that the selected estimates on informal employment draw on data that comprise urban and rural areas, but exclude non-market production and agricultural activities.

5.1 Defining and Measuring the Informal Economy

Table 5.1 The size of the informal economy (selected developing countries)

Country	Output-based approach Informal economy (as percentage of official GNP)[a]		Employment-based approach Informal employment (as percentage of non-agricultural employment)[b]			
	1999/2000	2002/2003	Year[c]	Total	Women	Men
North Africa						
Algeria	34.1	35.6	2000	43	41	43
Morocco	36.4	37.9	2000	45	47	44
Tunisia	38.4	39.9	2000	50	39	53
Egypt	35.1	36.9	2000	55	46	57
Sub-Saharan Africa						
Benin	47.3	49.1	1999	93	97	87
Chad	46.2	48.0	2000	74	95	60
Guinea	39.6	41.3	2000	72	87	66
Kenya	34.3	36.0	1999	72	83	59
South Africa	28.4	29.5	1999	51	58	44
Latin America						
Bolivia	67.1	58.3	1999	63	74	55
Brazil	39.8	42.3	1997	60	67	55
Chile	19.8	20.9	1997	36	44	31
Colombia	39.1	43.4	2000	38	44	34
Costa Rica	26.2	27.8	2000	44	48	42
El Salvador	46.3	48.3	2000	57	69	46
Guatemala	51.5	52.4	2000	56	69	47
Honduras	49.6	51.6	2000	58	65	74
Mexico	30.1	33.2	1999	55	55	54
Dominican Rep.	32.1	34.1	2000	48	50	47
Venezuela	33.6	36.7	2000	47	47	47

(continued)

Table 5.1 (continued)

Country	Output-based approach		Employment-based approach			
	Informal economy (as percentage of official GNP)[a]		Informal employment (as percentage of non-agricultural employment)[b]			
	1999/2000	2002/2003	Year[c]	Total	Women	Men
Asia						
India	23.1	25.6	2000	83	86	83
Indonesia	19.4	22.9	1995	78	77	78
Philippines	43.4	45.6	1995	72	73	71
Thailand	52.6	54.1	1995	51	54	49
Syria	19.3	21.6	2000	42	35	43

[a]*Source*: Schneider (2007, 2002)
[b]*Source*: ILO (2002b)
[c]*Latest* year in which labour force surveys or other types of household surveys have been conducted

Since informality in low-income countries is primarily a characteristic of small-scale enterprises and home-based producers of labour-intensive goods, its share of total employment should generally be larger than its share of gross national income. This is well reflected in the data despite the fact that the estimates on informal employment actually under-estimate the significance of the informal economy as they exclude informal employment in the agricultural sector. Because of such inconsistencies in the different estimation methods' underlying concepts of informality, the estimates on informal employment are not directly comparable with data on total informal output. In general, the widespread use of indirect methods to estimate the size of the informal economy instead of relying on directly observable data gave rise to controversial discussions on the economic rational and uses of informal economy estimates.[6]

The various attempts to measure the size and development of the informal economy are more in agreement about the fact that informality is a growing phenomenon around the world. The data provided by Schneider (2007) on informal economic activity as percentage of official GNP show an increase in the size of the informal economy for all observed developing and transition countries between 1999 and 2003.[7] According to the International Labour Organisation's Key Indicators of the Labour Market (ILO Bureau of Statistics 2003), the majority of new employment in recent years in developing and transition countries is informal. The increase is most significant in Africa where 93% of all additional jobs in urban areas in the 1990s have been created in the informal economy.[8]

5.2 Private Support Institutions for Informal Firms

The fact that the informal economy is not regulated by formal institutions and unprotected by official law does not mean that it operates in an institutional vacuum. The relations between informal firms, workers and customers are rather governed by their own extralegal norms and practices. These are supported and maintained by informal private arrangements based on mutual help and trust that facilitate trade and exchange, the protection and mobilisation of assets, and the transfer of technologies

---

[6] The interested reader may turn to *The Economic Journal*, Volume 109 of June 1999, which contains a series of contributions that discuss this controversy. See especially Dixon (1999) and Tanzi (1999).

[7] According to Schneider (2007), the size of the informal economy as percentage of official GNP increased between 1999 and 2003 on average from 33.9 to 41.2% in 24 African countries; from 34.2 to 41.5% in 17 Latin American countries; from 28.6 to 30.5% in 41 Asian countries; and from 31.5 to 37.9% in 23 transition economies. As these data denote percentages of official GNP, an obvious interpretation is that in all these regions, the informal economy grew at a higher rate than the official economy.

[8] See also Charmes (2000) who estimated a growth rate of (non-agricultural) informal employment between 1980 and 1990 for Sub-Saharan Africa of 6.7%, for North Africa of 4.6%, and for Asia of 10%.

and skills. Moreover, such private institutions also perform important social functions that were otherwise unavailable to those engaged in the informal economy. The foundations and underlying mechanisms of these privately governed institutions that support economic activity in the informal sector have been discussed in detail in Chap. 4. The purpose of this section is to look closer at the organisation and forms that these informal support institution take in low-income countries, as well as on their interactions with both the formal economy and the state.

Private support arrangements for informal economic activity are embedded in the social and economic structures of the groups, communities or networks that benefit from them. Depending on the kind of informal economic activity they support, and the functions they perform, these informal arrangements and organisations can take a variety of forms. They include small, sector-specific business associations, workers' cooperatives, marketing and supply cooperatives, private housing cooperatives and other member-owned self-help organisations, micro-entrepreneurial communities, transport federations, miners' claim clubs, residential boards, farming conventions or various village organisations.

A widespread form of organising self-support services in the informal economy is member-owned cooperatives. According to the definition adopted by the International Co-operative Alliance (ICA), the apex organisation that represents cooperatives worldwide, a cooperative is characterised by the "autonomous association of persons united voluntarily to meet their common economic, social and cultural needs and aspirations through a jointly owned and democratically controlled enterprise" (ICA 2009). A central feature of genuine cooperatives is that they are spontaneously created and owned by the members whose own needs and interests they serve.[9] Cooperatives exist in various forms and perform a wide range of economic and social functions for their members. The two main cooperative forms that can be distinguished are client-owned cooperatives and workers' cooperatives. Most member-owned self-help organisations in low-income countries that support informal sector activities can be classified in either of these forms.[10]

Client-owned cooperatives are voluntary associations of individual enterprises or households that aim at lowering production costs or the cost of living through bulk purchases of raw materials or food. Moreover, they are often used by their members to jointly organise the marketing and trade of their own products. Client-owned

---

[9] Cooperatives were once also common in Africa among the countries which experienced periods of socialist governments (e.g. Madagascar, Ethiopia, Sudan, Tanzania, Zambia and Mozambique). However, these cooperatives hardly displayed any of the characteristics of genuine cooperatives defined above. They were rather used as instruments to collectivise the ownership of production factors, or as a means to control the production and marketing of vital crops. This unfruitful history of cooperatives in some developing countries implicates that outside efforts to empower the poor through various forms of cooperative self-help are sometimes still met with suspicion.

[10] A more detailed review of cooperative forms, their origins, advantages, as well as related case studies, can be found in Schwettmann (1997) and Birchall (2003), on whose findings this discussion draws. See also Mitullah (2004) for a discussion on self-support organisations of small-scale traders and street vendors in Africa.

cooperatives are particularly common in the agricultural sector, but are also used by traders, street vendors and craftsmen to increase their bargaining power on markets. An illustrative case of a client-owned cooperative is the "Kampala Shoe Shiners Cooperative" through which more than 3,000 shoe shiners in the Ugandan capital jointly organise support services for their operations. Originally created as an informal savings and credit association to enable its members to finance extraordinary expenditures for equipment or rents, the shoe shiners gradually began to also organise other activities jointly through the cooperative. Among others, they equipped all members with standardised desks and initiated other measures to improve their professional appearance. They were even planning to establish a small manufacturing unit for shoe polish and brushes (Schwettmann 1997).

Savings and credit cooperatives represent a particular form of client-owned self-help organisations. They have developed from, and function like rotating savings and credit associations, which have a long tradition in developing countries and are known, for instance, as *Chit* funds in India, *Hui* in Taiwan, *Tontines* in Senegal or *Kye* in South Korea. Under their rules of operation, a group of members meets periodically to contribute small sums into a common fund that is allocated to one group member on a rotating basis. As members of credit and savings cooperatives usually know each other well, they can use peer monitoring to reduce the risk of unilateral default. The principles of peer monitoring and joint liability of group members for loan repayment have also inspired the micro-finance revolution. In fact, the business model of Grameen Bank, which has been discussed in Sect. 4.2.2 of Chap. 4, is based on the idea of group lending.[11]

Although client-owned cooperatives promote cooperation among individual enterprises to realise economies of scale, the members of workers' cooperatives are both workers and employers of their jointly owned enterprise. Workers' cooperatives are formed as joint production units to achieve economies of scope through the pooling of their members' capital and the diversification of their skills. They are particularly common as handicrafts and small industrial cooperatives. Moreover, the principles of workers' cooperatives are sometimes also adopted to organise and manage horizontal networks of micro-entrepreneurs who are active in the same industry and use the same production facility or jointly operate common support services like, for instance, net control stations used by groups of independent taxi drivers.

---

[11] Membership in a savings and credit cooperative is but one important way for poor people to obtain the financial resources necessary for engaging in productive businesses. Another source of finance accessible to informal firms is to borrow from informal moneylenders, relatives and friends. However, these loans are usually very small and have high interest rates and short repayment periods. They are therefore only suited to finance the short-term working capital needs of informal enterprises and home-based producers. An increasingly important source of investment funding not only for informal firms in low-income countries are workers' remittances. The volume of these transfers of migrants to their home countries has significantly grown in recent years. According to the World Bank's latest estimates, remittance inflows to developing countries have reached 328 billion US Dollars in 2008, making remittances the largest source of private capital for many low-income countries (Ratha et al. 2009).

A well-documented example of an informal business association that applies cooperative principles in the provision of a wide range of support services is the Self-Employed Women's Association (SEWA) in India. Founded in 1972, it is the oldest trade union of women who work in the informal economy. Today, SEWA has a membership of over 250,000 self-employed women and women engaged in home-based work, street vending and casual work. They benefit from a wide range of financial, health and childcare services, as well as training and the representation of their interest towards formal state institutions and international development agencies. SEWA is also pioneering a marketing infrastructure for informally manufactured products to connect its members with local and international markets, and helps to increase their bargaining power on markets and as participants in global commodity chains (Carr and Chen 2002; and Chen, Jhabvala and Nanavaty, 2004).[12]

The example of SEWA shows that, apart from their industry-specific functions, cooperatives play an important role in the organisation and representation of their members' interests towards public authorities or large companies that control relevant market segments as large vendors or purchasers. In that way, they can establish vital links between the informal and formal economy, and may eventually also be instrumental in facilitating the formalisation of informal firms. This function of bridging between the informal and formal sector is particularly effective where cooperative societies of informal firms are formally registered.

5.3 The Role and Implications of Informality for Economic Development

As discussed in Chap. 4, a common characteristic of privately governed institutional arrangements is that they enable transactions at "arms length", while their underlying norms and cultural values alone cannot support the expansion of economic activity into impersonal modes of exchange. This implies that economic transactions within the informal sector, or between informal firms and their formal business partners, are either restricted to simple and instantaneous modes of exchange, or can only be carried out with partners that are linked together by some kind of private governance mechanism. Voluntary associations among informal entrepreneurs can provide them with an enhanced degree of protection, security and bargaining power. However they cannot substitute for the functions that a well-functioning formal system of legal, economic and social institutions offers.

Supposed that the option to formally register a business exists, the decision to enter the formal economy is a function of both the relative limits of informal modes of organising economic activity, and the quality of state-governed support institutions in

---

[12] SEWA also served as a model for the Self-Employed Women's Union (SEWU) in South Africa, as well as for women's associations and trade unions in several other developing countries.

the formal sector relative to their informal equivalents. This leaves policymakers with two alternative strategies for dealing with the informal economy. They can either increase the cost of staying informal by fighting informal economic activity and oppressing the operation of alternative forms of organisation in the informal sector. Or, a government may lower the entry barriers into the formal economy by improving the legal, political and institutional environment for private businesses. Yet another position that many governments in low-income countries sadly adopt is complete ignorance towards the needs of the people that make their living in the informal sector. A common excuse is that because they are informal they do not officially exist and are thus by definition excluded from public institutions and official support. Thereby, governments decline responsibility for sometimes more than half the population of their jurisdictions (Table 5.1). For instance, between 600,000 and 1.2 million people are estimated to live in Kibera, arguably Africa's largest and poorest slum, located on Nairobi's south side. They represent a third to a half of the city's population, but the government provides them with neither basic services such as paving, running water, sanitation or lighting, nor with title deeds to the land (The Economist 2007b).

Given the role and magnitude of informal economic activity in low-income countries, its impact on economic development cannot be ignored. The policies and strategies that are adopted towards the informal sector, however, differ widely in their forms depending on their underlying interpretations of the causes and consequences of informality, as well as the state of a country's development. The purpose of this section is to present some of the seemingly contrasting views on the informal economy, and to discuss their implications for the choice of policies towards the informal sector.

5.3.1 *Different Interpretations of Informal Economic Activity and the Merits of Formalisation*

Whether informal economic activity has overall a positive or negative effect on a country's development is still a matter of debate. Controversies over the social desirability of integrating informal activities into the formal sector, as well as over the best ways to achieve this formalisation, often stem from different explanations for the existence of the informal economy. Accordingly, three main perspectives are distinguished in the literature.

First, it is argued that people engage in informal economic activity primarily to avoid taxes and regulatory obligations.[13] Adherents to this view stress the informal economy's negative welfare effects from eroding the government's tax base, from the lack of public control over their activities, or from the unfair competition for formal firms that informal enterprises create due to their potential cost advantages.

---

[13] See, for instance, Schneider (2007, 2002), and Schneider and Enste (2000).

This interpretation tends to implicate a hostile approach towards informality, and regards better enforcement of existing laws and recourse to criminal procedures as appropriate strategies for curbing informal economic activity.[14]

An opposite view recognises the positive functions of the informal sector as a low-cost mode of operation particularly for small and microenterprises, and hence as an important source of employment, income and mutual support especially for the poorest parts of the population. Adherents to this view thus tolerate the informal economy as a response to poorly performing formal institutions, unemployment, poverty, population growth, rural–urban migrations, civil conflict or political crises. They support policies towards the integration of informal activities into the official economy primarily for the sake of improving the productivity and working conditions of those engaged in the informal sector. The beneficial character of informal activities is often highlighted by international development institutions with a strong focus on poverty reduction.[15]

A more elaborate interpretation of informality emphasises structural barriers to entry into the formal economy as the main cause for the existence and development of the informal economy.[16] Such barriers are prevalent especially in low-income countries and arise as a consequence of the poor performance of legal and juridical institutions combined with high levels of bureaucratic corruption that often leave people with little choice but to resort to the informal sector. This view highlights the merits of formalisation both for those engaged in the informal sector, and for the economy as a whole. Accordingly, formalisation leads to better protection of property rights, opens access to formal infrastructure services and credit, and thereby allows once informal entrepreneurs to expand their businesses and hence to contribute to economic growth. Corresponding policies recommended focus mainly on the removal of structural barriers to legality through institutional reform and the implementation of good economic policies.

Although the latter view is widely accepted in the development literature, it also involves some of the most difficult policy challenges. Institutional and policy

---

[14] A most extreme case of a heavy-handed intervention against informal economic activities is Robert Mugabe's infamous 2005 "Operation Murambatsvina" (meaning "Restore Order"), in which the government ordered the destruction of tens of thousands of unregistered shanty dwellings, informal traders' markets and street stalls in urban townships across the country. The implementation of this policy left an estimated 700,000 people homeless or deprived of their livelihood, and adversely affected some 2.4 million additional people (Freedom House 2009).

[15] For instance, in a statement on the characteristics of the informal sector, the scientific Advisory Council of the German Ministry for Economic Cooperation and Development (BMZ) recommends policies to promote the informal economy in anticipation of its positive contributions for the development of poor countries (BMZ 1999). A more balanced view has been adopted by the International Labour Organization, which acknowledges the informal sector as a "convenient, low-cost way of creating employment", but emphasises that its promotion must orient at the objective to "eliminate progressively the worst aspects of exploitation and inhuman working conditions in the sector" (International Labour Office 1991, p. 58).

[16] This view is advanced, among others, by Friedman et al. (2000), Johnson et al. (2000) and Marcouiller and Young (1995).

reforms are difficult to achieve in the short-run. Those active in the informal sector, however, have to experience sensible changes in the formal business environment that can convince them to formalise their activities. As Galal (2005) notes, entrepreneurs decide to stay informal if they perceive the total costs of entering, operating and eventually exiting the formal sector as greater than the potential benefits from formalising their activities. Institutional reforms in the formal sector thus have to accomplish a shift in the balance of costs and benefits from informality in favour of formalisation in order to provide informal entrepreneurs with appropriate incentives to leave the informal economy. The problem with this approach is that the private benefits of informality are often underestimated. It is a common misconception to equate the benefits of informality with only the cost that informal firms avoid from operating outside the official economy. The informal arrangements and support institutions that have evolved in the informal economy actually provide benefits for those active in the informal sector too. These long-practiced informal institutional arrangements thus create incentives for individuals and groups to work towards their maintenance. The persistence of informal institutional patterns through time can be seen as a kind of institutional path dependency. In consequence, choices for or against formalisation are often influenced by deep-seated cultural beliefs, customs and conventions that underpin informal institutions.[17] Against this background, policies towards the formalisation of informal economic activities are unlikely to succeed if they only concentrate on efforts to lower the relative costs of entry, operation and exit associated with the official economy. Instead, a main objective of any strategy towards the formalisation of informal economic activity must be to reform the existing legal system in such a way that those active in the informal sector can recognise the formal law as legitimate and commensurate to their customary practices. This requires an approach to legal reform that seeks to align formal law with the informal practices, norms and institutional arrangements that have a long tradition in governing economic relations in low-income countries.[18]

The various interpretations of the informal economy have to be evaluated against the background of different developmental states of the formal economy. In advanced economies, where market institutions and regulatory systems function effectively, evasion from taxation and social security obligations can indeed be seen as a primary motivation for hiding economic operations before the law. In these contexts, the social costs of informality certainly outweigh the private benefits and justify policies to curb informal economic activity through better enforcement of existing laws. In the context of low-income countries, however, tax evasion rather plays a minor role in the decision to operate informally. Here, informal businesses

---

[17] The dynamic interrelations between informal institutions and formal institutional change are just beginning to be explored. See, for instance, North (2005) as well as Sects. 8.2.2 and 13.2.2.
[18] An interesting approach for aligning formal law with informal business practices is offered by Cooter (1994).

and workers are actually "taxed" by the cost of undercapitalisation, limited access to infrastructure and market institutions, poor working conditions and the cost of hiding their activities from official authorities.

Informality in developing countries is more appropriately explained by factors that relate to the performance characteristics of the formal economy.[19] The problem that a county's legal and juridical system discriminates against large parts of the population cannot be solved by more stringent enforcement of existing laws. Nor can informality be taken as an excuse by governments for not servicing those engaged in it. Instead, legal reforms are required that grant those in the informal sector access to legality. A first important step for policymakers in low-income countries is to recognise the social benefits that can stem from informal economic activity. The more difficult question that then arises is how the potential of the informal economy can be harnessed for overall economic development by integrating informal firms into the formal economy.[20] This should be a key priority for policymakers and development institutions, as all other efforts at promoting trade and investment in low-income countries will remain infective if they do not reach out to the major parts of the population that operates outside the law.

---

[19]The relation between the effectiveness of the formal legal system and the size of the informal sector is confirmed by findings from a new cross-country database on the contribution of small- and medium-sized enterprises (SME) to total employment and GDP in both the formal and informal sectors. According to these data, the contribution of SMEs to GDP is roughly the same in low- and high-income countries, whereas about three quarters of all SMEs in low-income countries operate in the informal economy; this proportion reverses in high-income countries where less than one quarter of all SME activity is unregistered (World Bank 2004; and Ayyagari et al. 2003).

[20]De Soto (2000) provides evidence on how large this potential actually is.

Part II
Development Economics: The Past 70 Years

Trying to understand the process of growth and development has always been a major concern of economists. From the Physiocrats through the Classical School to neoclassical economics, and from old to new institutional theory, economists have been concerned with problems of economic development, motivated by the desire to understand the process of economic growth and structural change, and the mechanisms through which it may lead to an increase in living standards. However, it was only in the late 1940s that development economics emerged as an own sub-discipline of economics.[1] Its specific purpose was to study the economies of less developed countries, most of which were, at that time, just about to gain independence from their colonial rulers.

At the same time when development theory emerged as a specific branch of economics, the publication of Paul A. Samuelson's *Foundations* in 1947[2] marked a watershed in the method and scope of general economic analysis. Thereafter, the neoclassical paradigm became, and up to now still is, the dominant mode of thought in economics.[3] Both developments were quite independent of one another,[4] but as it should become apparent soon, the more influence the neoclassical paradigm gained in mainstream economics, the more territory it also claimed from the field of development research.

The early pioneers of development economics were still relatively successful in defending their new sub-discipline against the influences of mainstream neoclassical economics. They tried to identify, mostly at the macro-level, persistent structural

---

[1] Some (e.g. Kanbur 2005) date the birth of modern development economics even further back to the publication of Allyn Young's classic paper on "Increasing Returns and Economic Progress" in 1928 (*The Economic Journal*, Vol. 38, pp. 527–542).

[2] Samuelson Paul A. (1947): *Foundations of Economic Analysis*. Cambridge: Harvard University Press.

[3] Neoclassical economics actually dated from the development of marginal utility theory in William Stanley Jevons's *Theory of Political Economy* (1871), Carl Menger's *Principles of Economics* (1871), and Léon Walras's *Elements of Pure Economics* (1874). But at their times, neoclassical theory has neither been the single dominant paradigm in economics, nor has it had the degree of formalisation that characterised neoclassical economics since Samuelson.

[4] According to Meier (2005), Samuelson referred to problems arising in developing countries at only three points in his entire book.

imbalances and gaps which they thought would keep less developed countries stuck in a vicious cycle of poverty. But their reliance on the state as a main source of investment and planner of their country's industrialisation resulted in price distortions and misallocations of resources in many developing economies. This brought them increasingly under the criticism of neoclassical economists whose main concern was to promote the efficient use of resources in developing countries. The focus in development economics thus shifted to market-based solutions and the role of the price mechanism as main allocative device. On the methodological level, the absorption of development economics by neoclassical theory meant that theories based on the realities of advanced economies were generalised and extended to also explain the economic phenomena in developing countries. But it turned out that the theories and market-based policies that worked well in advanced economies failed to achieve their intended outcomes in developing economies, given these countries' immature markets and lack of market-supporting institutions. This led to an increasing emphasis on market imperfections and on the role of institutions in the development process that was further driven by theoretical advances made in modern institutional and information economics.

The evolution of development economics marks in no way an even path of continuous progress. Development theory and policy as practiced since the second half of the twentieth century rather describes a process of trial and error in which new discourses often emerged as the result of lessons from failure that were then again challenged by the next disappointment. In this process, old theories have been extended by new explanatory factors that were considered significant in light of the limited effectiveness of development strategies based on previous generations of development theories and models. Also the meaning of economic development underwent changing interpretations, evolving from measures of a country's industrialisation and growth in aggregate output, over income per capita growth and poverty alleviation, to concepts like sustainable development, human development, freedom, equality, and even happiness.

In retrospect, three generations of development economists can be distinguished, of which each had established its own development theories and associated policy conclusions. The following chapters will be structured according to the division of the evolution of development economics into the phases of these three generations: namely the generation of early pioneers of development economics (Chap. 6), the generation of neoclassical development economists (Chap. 7), and the third generation which applied the framework of modern institutional economics to the study of problems of less developed countries (Chap. 8). The central questions that arise from this interpretative review are, first, to what extent these three, regarding their aims, methods and philosophy diverse generations were able to explain economic reality in low-income countries; and second, how relevant their theoretical findings have been for the design and implementation of effective growth-igniting policies in these countries. Finding answers to these questions will be attempted in Chap. 9. Its purpose is to draw lessons and conclusions from the review of past development theories and policies, and to identify both missing elements in the existing analytical framework, as well as new research priorities for a prospective fourth generation of development economists.

Chapter 6
The First Generation of Development Economists

The vision of the first generation of development economists about the purpose of their young subject was quite promising. They aspired towards an economic sub-discipline that applied new methods and propositions to establish relevant theories about economic development in the then so-called Third World. In their view, both neoclassical and Keynesian economics were inappropriate for analysing the economic characteristics that set developing countries apart from advanced economies. The price system determined through supply and demand on markets, a central element of neoclassical analysis, was considered less relevant as markets in developing countries were fragmented, imperfect or even non-existent. Moreover, the interest of early development economists was much more in studying structural changes in the economy rather than in analysing the effect of incremental changes in variables on economic decisions and outcomes as common to marginal analysis in the neoclassical tradition.

Keynesian analysis was as well considered inapplicable to less developed countries, among others, because their high rates of unemployment were not seen as a result of a Keynesian cyclical under-utilisation of capital, but rather as the consequence of a limited capacity of poor economies to save and to accumulate capital. In spite of this, Hirschman (1981a) points to the instrumental role of the Keynesian Revolution in the rise of development economics as a separate economic sub-discipline by noting that "the claim of development economics to stand as a separate body of economic analysis and policy-derived intellectual legitimacy and nurture from the prior success and parallel features of the Keynesian Revolution" (ibid., p. 7). The early development economists did in fact view orthodox economics as applicable to only the "special case" of advanced market economies in which the neoclassical equilibrium conditions prevailed, just as the Keynesians confined the applicability of neoclassical economics to the "special case" of full employment. Both claimed the need for a different system of theoretical propositions and policy prescriptions for circumstances that deviated from these "special cases". Another parallel feature with Keynesian economics was to use the special conditions identified in developing countries to justify interventionist policies in the form of public investment planning and foreign aid. There was, indeed, a widespread feeling among early development economists that Keynesian principles of macroeconomic management of the economy by governments were principally considered to be a feasible option for developing countries too.[1]

Even though early development economists were united in their aspiration for a specific body of theory expressively aimed at explaining economic development outside the industrialised countries of Europe and North America, they actually arrived at quite different hypotheses and models about the causes and consequences of underdevelopment. Among the diversity of approaches, two main groups of early development economists can roughly be distinguished: Firstly, the modernisation theorists, who shared a rather optimistic view about achieving economic progress in developing countries by assuming that they could generally follow the same path of development as Western economies did in the course of their industrialisation. They contributed to the case for establishing development economics as separate discipline by focusing on particular economic characteristics of developing countries that distinguished them from advanced economies like, for instance, rural underemployment as in Lewis' dual sector model.

The second group of early development economists, broadly summarised as structuralists, saw a main factor for explaining the underdevelopment in the South in the policies by industrialised countries of the North, and in the structure of North-South economic relations. They attributed differences between developed and developing countries especially to the fact that the development paths of latecomers differed from that of already industrialised countries due to the latter's influence on the former.

While early development economists can be credited for rejecting the "monoeconomics claim" (Hirschman 1981a) of traditional economics by challenging the universal validity of its theorems and assumptions, they mostly regarded developing countries as a homogenous group that differed from advanced economies in a number of specific economic characteristics or structures common to all of them. By building up development economics on the basis of the construct of the "typical underdeveloped country", they recognised important structural differences between advanced and developing countries, but did not fully consider the implications of the context-specificity of development problems, and the related fact that similar policy prescriptions can differ markedly in their results across different historical, cultural and political contexts in developing countries. It is for this reason that early development economists also tended to believe that concentrating efforts at raising national incomes of developing countries would implicate beneficial effects in the political, social and cultural realms as well. But as the histories of many developing countries in the years after their independence from colonial rule have shown, the early successes in economic development were often followed by retrogressions in these other areas.

---

[1] For further reference on the affinity of early development economics with Keynesian economics see Seers (1963).

6.1 Modernisation Theories

The early development theories, which also influenced the early policies adopted by the young Bretton Woods institutions (i.e. the World Bank and the IMF) and Western governments towards the (Non-Soviet) developing world, did not come up to the initial vision of creating an entirely new body of thought that was more realistic and relevant for the problems of less developed countries. Instead, the discourse remained close to the traditional framework of economic analysis. The early development theories were inherited from classical growth economics with its emphasis on capital accumulation, population and (later) technology as the main explanatory factors for development. Development, the dependent variable, was largely interpreted as growth in aggregate output. Development problems were approached by identifying missing components, or gaps, from comparisons of development histories of advanced economies with the conditions of underdeveloped countries. As the latter were abundant in labour, the major constraint to their development was seen in their lack of capital, which in turn resulted from a "savings gap". The early modernisation theories can be described as the view that development is a virtuous circle driven by external economies. Accordingly, underdeveloped countries that are lacking the capital for realising economies of scale in the industrial sector remain stuck in a trap of low productivity. This view provided a powerful case for public investment planning and foreign aid as a way of breaking out of this trap.

6.1.1 Paul Rosenstein–Rodan: Industrialisation and the "Big Push"

The idea that modernisation could lead to a self-reinforcement of growth through the realisation of scale economies, and the argument for coordinated investment as a means to get the industrialisation process started at a sufficiently large scale, was clearly expressed in 1943 in a paper by Paul Rosenstein–Rodan (1902–1985) on the problems of industrialisation in Eastern and South-Eastern Europe. In their paper they proposed to simultaneously plan the creation of several complementary industries in developing countries. They argued that the complementarity of different industries would ensure that each industry could sell its products to firms in other, complementary sectors of the system. The industrialisation of many sectors simultaneously was expected to create substantial external economies as compared to a system of independent investment decisions where each firm had to carry individually not only the cost of uncertainty about whether their products would find a market, but also the cost of investing in the necessary infrastructure and training of its workforce. As, however, individual firms were considered unable to coordinate their investment decisions on a large scale, the state was given a role in carrying out the investment plan.

Underlying the proposal of a large-scale planned industrialisation, or "big push" as Rosenstein–Rodan called it, were two key assumptions that are present in most early development theories: The assumption of a positive interaction between market size and economies of scale, embodied in the assertion that new industries must be established at a sufficiently large scale and in complementary branches to raise the level of exchange between them; and the assumption of dualism, which saw developing countries characterised by an excess supply of unskilled labour in the traditional agrarian sector, which could more productively be employed in combination with capital in the modern, industrial sector. On the latter assumption, Rosenstein–Rodan stated that

> [l]abour must either be transported towards capital (emigration), or capital must be transported towards labour (industrialisation). From the point of view of maximising the world income, the difference between these two ways is one of the transport costs only. [As emigration] cannot be considered feasible on a large scale, [a] very considerable part of the task will have to be solved by industrialisation. (Rosenstein-Rodan, 1943, p. 202)

From this, they draw the conclusion that a "big push" in investment, funded through loans guaranteed by advanced countries, was the best way to create an industrial sector sufficiently large to absorb the "agrarian excess population" of developing countries.

6.1.2 Arthur Lewis: The Dual Sector Model

The assumption of rural underemployment in developing countries was central also to Nobel laureate Arthur Lewis' (1915–1991) dual sector model, which he presented in his article on "Economic Development with Unlimited Supplies of Labour" (1954). For Lewis, a main economic characteristic of low-income countries was the co-existence of two separate economies: A large traditional sector composed of subsistence farming, handicraft workers and petty traders, and a small capitalist sector composed of mines, plantations, manufacturing companies and large-scale transport providers. The traditional sector was characterised by an unlimited supply of unskilled workers and low labour productivity,[2] whereas in the capitalist economy, enterprises hired labour at a money wage and resold their output for a profit, which was then assumed would be reinvested in the creation of new capital. The purpose of the dual sector model was to explain economic development as an interaction process between the traditional and the capitalist sector. When the capitalist sector expanded, it could draw from an unlimited supply of labour from the subsistence sector, provided that wages in the capitalist sector were higher than

---

[2]The low labour productivity in the traditional sector was explained by the unlimited availability of labour vis-à-vis a limited amount of land that can be cultivated, and the fact that no capital can be formed through savings from subsistence farming in the traditional sector. The marginal product of an additional farmer was therefore assumed to be zero.

subsistence earnings. This was assumed to be the case because the utilisation of unskilled labour with capital raised labour productivity in the capitalist sector above the productivity of labour in the traditional sector. In this model, development was described as a process in which a growing capitalist sector absorbs more and more labour from the traditional sector at constant wages until the traditional low-productivity sector withers away.[3]

Lewis identified a lack of capital as the major constraint to development, as it was assumed that only through the process of capital accumulation could the surplus labour be absorbed into the more productive capitalist sector. For this conclusion to hold, it was crucial to further assume that labour was available at a constant wage rate, so that the expansion of the capitalist sector was associated with a raising share of profits in national income, and that capitalists reinvested parts of these profits in the domestic capitalist sector. The empirical basis from which Lewis drew these assumptions were provided by his studies of the industrial revolution in Great Britain in the late eighteenth and early nineteenth centuries, in which industrial wages had indeed been nearly constant. However, Great Britain's industrialisation was driven by new inventions in the techniques and modes of production and took place under the rule of law, secure property rights and the preservation of personal liberty. The question of how a capitalist sector could emerge in the absence of such an enabling environment remained secondary in Lewis' analysis. Instead, much hope was placed in the power of economic planning by the state.

6.1.3 Ragnar Nurkse: Balanced Growth, Capital Formation and the Primacy of Domestic Action

The argument that only investment in a number of different complementary industries could create the kind of mutual demand needed for economic development was reinforced by the Estonian economist Ragnar Nurkse (1907–1959). He went, however, beyond Rosenstein–Rodan in that he saw capital formation in low-income countries not only as a matter of capital supply, but attributed parts of the problem

---

[3] It has to be noted that the dual economy models of Lewis and other early modernisation theorists exhibited a rather naïve view of pre-modern societies. As a result, they largely ignored, for instance, the social implications of moving vast numbers of workers from a rural subsistence economy to an urban industrialised sector. These sectors differ not only in the prevailing wage rate but they can also be considered as representing two distinct economic styles: One in which economic activity is embedded in traditional societal life, and the other where societal life is subordinated to economic market criteria. At about the same time, but largely unnoticed by early modernization theorists, did Karl Polanyi ([1944] 2001) warn of the dangers of the disintegration of social relations that this move entailed. The social consequences of the transformations postulated in early modernisation theories may actually be as forceful as to reduce the postulated effects of an elastic labour supply to insignificance. See Part III on the concept of economic styles, and especially Sect. 13.2.1 for a further discussion of Polanyi's work.

also to the conditions that determine the demand for productive capital. In his main work, *The Problems of Capital Formation in Underdeveloped Countries* (Nurkse 1953), he identified the small size of domestic markets as the main obstacle to the development of low-income countries, which limited opportunities for profitable expansion of domestic industries. For Nurkse, "the main trouble [...] is not that countries are too small but that they are too poor to provide markets for local industries" (ibid., 1953, p. 19). He thus defined market size not in terms of physical area or the number of a country's inhabitants, but in terms of domestic purchasing power. Given that low demand on markets made it unprofitable for each industry to expand individually, Nurkse concluded that all industries had to grow simultaneously in order to create the mutual demand that made an expansion of supply productive for all producers. From this, he developed his theory of balanced growth, in which he suggested that a coordinated expansion of different industries at the same rate of growth was an appropriate means for enlarging domestic markets and in turn for increasing the inducement to invest.[4] At the same time, the theory emphasises the need for growth of output in different sectors to be consistent with the growth of demand for different goods as income rises.

A main aspect of Nurkse's work is his reasoning in terms of circular and multi-causal relationships of the forces that tend to act and react upon each other in way that can lead to processes of self-sustained growth, but that can also keep a poor country in a state of poverty. Such a vicious circle of poverty is present where low incomes on the demand side are combined with low productivity on the supply side. More specifically, Nurkse explained the low level of capital accumulation in developing countries by people's small capacity to save due to their low level of real income, which resulted from their lack of capital which in turn kept their labour productivity low.[5] A similar vicious circle can emerge at the firm level if low incomes lead to a small buying power on domestic markets, which in turn discourages firms from investing in the expansion of their production. The low level of capital again explains the low productivity of labour and hence the low level of real incomes.[6]

---

[4] Balanced growth is just one strategy to deal with the negative consequences of narrow markets. Another strategy to broaden an industry's markets would be to expand industries with a comparative advantage into foreign markets. Nurkse did not object to export-led growth, but was rather pessimistic about international trade and thus gave priority to achieving balanced growth through the simultaneous expansion of mutually supportive domestic industries and markets (Nurkse [1957] 1961, pp. 244, 241).

[5] A country's domestic capacity to save (and hence its ability to accumulate capital) was assumed to be further restrained when poor people obtain knowledge of consumption patterns in advanced economies. According to Nurkse (1952 and 1953), such international demonstration effects raise poor peoples' propensity to consume, and hence further discourage saving and investment activity.

[6] In its most extreme form, Nurkse summed up the effect of the vicious circle of poverty in this 1952 Commemoration Lecture in Cairo by the tautologous proposition that "a country is poor because it is poor" (Nurkse 1953, p. 4).

Of contemporary relevance is yet another aspect of Nurkse's pioneering contributions to development economics.[7] Unlike many modernisation theorists who thought that the capital gap in developing countries resulting from their low level of domestic saving capacity could be filled with foreign capital inflows, Nurkse cautioned that the "effectiveness [of international aid and investment] depends on domestic action; only with strong domestic policies directed to this end is there any assurance that it will go wholly into added [capital] accumulation rather than consumption" (Nurkse 1953, p. 140). Without naming it, Nurkse thereby aptly raises the issue of good governance as a precondition for effective development assistance, a claim which is currently an essential element in the debate on aid effectiveness as well.[8] Good governance in Nurkse's view means strong domestic administrative capacity that enables developing countries to effectively absorb international aid, as well as policies that encourage domestic saving as a complement to foreign capital inflows. But unlike the long-standing practice of international financing institutions which hoped to achieve good governance from the outside by attaching it as a condition to their policy-based loans, Nurkse stressed the need for domestic action prior to the inflow of foreign capital. This is aptly expressed in this statement that "capital is made at home" (ibid., p. 141).[9]

Nurkse placed the same emphasis on local capacity also with regard to the implementation of his proposed strategy of balanced growth. Like Rosenstein-Rodan, Nurkse considered planned investments by the state as an appropriate instrument for achieving balanced growth in a number of different industries, but he made state intervention dependent on the specific circumstances of a country and, in particular, on the capacity of its government to effectively carry out its role as investor (ibid., p. 16).

Nurkse's pragmatic view on the role of the state is typical for the approach he followed in analysing economic phenomena. As Drechsler (2007) points out, Nurkse's work was strongly geared towards realism and a focus on what is "factually given" (Nurkse 1935, p. 7). Just as he recognised that economic phenomena have multiple causes, he also realised that development policies may have multiple effects, and that sometimes the unintended side-effects of a policy may significantly interfere with its stated goals. Nurkse thus always maintained a focus on the real, rather than the supposed effects of a development programme or policy.

---

[7] See also Drechsler (2007) and Kattel et al. (2009) for a discussion of the timely nature of Nurkse's work.

[8] See Sect. 8.4 below on the more recent discourse on good governance in developing countries.

[9] In spite of his strong emphasis on capital formation, Nurkse saw capital as a necessary but not as a sufficient condition of progress (1953, p. 1). He equally recognised the importance of attitudes, political conditions and historical events, but left these noneconomic aspects largely outside the scope of his analysis.

6.1.4 The Analysis of Typical Growth Paths by Clark, Kuznets, Rostow and Gerschenkron

Among modernisation theorists, a group of early development economists applied a historical perspective on the analysis of development processes. They assumed that currently underdeveloped countries are merely at an earlier stage than advanced economies in what they considered a linear historical progress of development. From this view, it seemed obvious that lessons for developing countries could be learned from the historical experience of advanced Western economies' transition to modernity. Their main approach was the long-term comparative analysis of development processes across a wide range of countries. Exemplary for this approach was Colin Clark's historical cross-country comparisons of real products with which he sought to establish a historical relation between capital accumulation and economic growth (Clark 1957). Furthermore, he did several international comparisons of agricultural output per worker, by which he tried to demonstrate that improvements in agricultural productivity were another necessary precondition for industrial development (Clark and Haswell 1964). A similar approach was followed by Simon Kuznets in his 1966 study "Economic Growth and Income Inequality" where he analysed the trend of inequality across countries over time, and suggested that inequality in income distribution increased during the early rapid phase of economic growth and subsequently moved towards equality, thus tracing an inverted U-shape known as the "Kuznets curve" (Kuznets 1966).

More directly related to the conditions of developing countries were the historical growth models of Walt W. Rostow (1916–2003) and Alexander Gerschenkron (1904–1978). They attempted to capture stylised facts about development from the historical analysis and comparison of typical growth paths of developed and developing countries. Rostow studied the process of economic development in the context of the dynamic evolution of whole societies in both their economic and noneconomic dimensions.[10] His aim was to devise a dynamic theory of production, which required "a systematic way of breaking through the aggregates which we have inherited from Keynesian income analysis in order to grip dynamic forces at work in the particular sectors on which the growth depends" (Rostow 1952).

The idea that growth and increasing technological sophistication in some leading sectors was a powerful engine of economic transformation in other sectors, and ultimately of growth in aggregate income, led Rostow to the development of his stages of growth, also known as the "Rostowian take-off model" (Rostow 1960). He used a society's capacity to absorb modern technology as a criterion to distinguish between five stages through which economies had to pass on their way to modernity.

---

[10]Rostow placed particular emphasis on the role of politics in the early phases of modernisation, and argued that the nationalism in developing countries that emerged in reaction to the intrusion from more advanced economies was a more powerful motivating force in the transition from traditional to modern societies than the profit motive (Rostow 1984).

These stages were: traditional society, the precondition for takeoff, the takeoff itself, the drive to maturity and the stage of high mass consumption. In this classification, the critical stage was, obviously, the takeoff, which, according to Rostow, required as necessary preconditions a substantial rise in the rate of productive investment, the development of a fast-growing manufacturing sector and the emergence of a supporting political, social and institutional framework.

Gerschenkron's "backwardness model" represents another important historical model of economic growth. In his 1962 book *Economic Backwardness in Historical Perspective* (Gerschenkron 1962) he examines, in 14 separate essays, the history of industrialisation in Europe and compares the differences in the development of selected countries. He rejected the idea of linear stages of growth, which presupposed that more backward countries follow the development path of advanced economies. Instead, he found that the development of backward countries, by the very virtue of their backwardness relative to more advanced countries, differed fundamentally from advanced economies' historical paths of development. Gerschenkron argued that relative backwardness creates a tension between the promise of economic development as achieved elsewhere, and the continuity of stagnation. Such a tension takes political form and motivates institutional innovation, which functions as appropriate substitute for the absent preconditions for growth.[11]

6.2 Structuralist Approaches to Development Economics

While to modernisation theorists, underdevelopment reflected a stage in a country's development to industrialisation, other early development economists attributed the economic conditions in poor countries primarily to the structure of international relations between developing and advanced economies. These "structuralist" development economists thus opposed the belief that underdeveloped countries could follow the same path to prosperity as already industrialised countries. Instead, they emphasised the structural differences between developing and advanced economies by acknowledging that different rules and principles apply to different economic conditions. On account of this, the structuralists went even further than modernisation theorists in countersteering conventional neoclassical "monoeconomics", which saw economics as a body of universal principles applicable to all countries and at all times. It is yet important to note that structuralist approaches to development economics were not conceived by its adherents in opposition to early modernisation theories. The structuralists also acknowledged the dualistic economic structure of developing countries, and equally emphasised a rise in the rate of capital formation as a main development policy priority. They were more divided with

---

[11] The recognition of the role of politics in economic development is notable in the works of both Gerschenkron and Rostow. See also footnote 10 above.

modernisation theorists over issues of policy, though. For instance, the structuralists were sceptical about the mutual benefits of free trade, and instead advocated protectionist measures to shield developing countries from the impact of structural imbalances identified in North–South trade. As regards monetary policy, the cause of rising inflation in many Latin American countries was not seen in excess demand (the monetarist explanation advanced by the IMF) but in particular structural supply-side constraints that emerged in the process of development.

In the 1950s and 1960s, the structuralists' perspective became influential at the policy level especially through its adherents' service in influential capacities at various UN agencies. Gunnar Myrdal, for instance, was the first Executive Secretary of the United Nations Economic Commission for Europe (UNECE) from 1947 until 1957, while Raúl Prebisch was the first Executive Secretary of the United Nations Economic Commission for Latin America (UN ECLA), and later became the first General Secretary of the United Nations Conference on Trade and Development (UNCTAD) after the organisation's foundation in 1965. Hans W. Singer helped to set up the United Nations Department of Economic and Social Affairs (UN DESA), and was instrumental in initiating the United Nations World Food Programme (WFP), the United Nations Development Programme (UNDP), the African Development Bank, and in changing the United Nations International Children's Emergency Fund (UNICEF) from an emergency fund into an organisation concerned with promoting the long-term interests of children. He also guided the creation of the Special United Nations Fund for Economic Development (SUNFED), a concessionary loan fund for the least developed countries which could not afford market interest rates. SUNFED later formed the basis for the creation of the International Development Association (IDA), the soft-lending arm of the World Bank Group.

6.2.1 Albert O. Hirschman: The Strategy of Unbalanced Growth

Albert Otto Hirschman is one of the early economists who clearly stressed the need for country-specific analyses of development problems. In his 1958 *Strategy of Economic Development*, he digressed from the application of general prescriptions for economic development, and insisted that development problems should be analysed on a case-by-case basis, exploiting indigenous resources and structures to achieve context-specific solutions. His interest was in uncovering the "hidden rationality" of seemingly idiosyncratic but functioning elements and processes of developing countries' realities, and to exploit these indigenous solutions for the design of context-specific development policies.[12] Based thereon, he presented his famous

---

[12] Hirschman's conviction that economic processes in developing countries are often characterised by seemingly irrational or "wrong-way-around" sequences grew out of several field studies he did in Latin America. For instance, Hirschman observed in Argentina that a large poor but well-organised community of families occupied previously idle land in Quilmes at the outskirts of Buenos Aires. They built on it exceptionally solid houses from wood, brink and cement, even

linkages concept as an alternative to the idea that development could be achieved by a planned "big push" industrialisation effort. Hirschman's proposition was that industrialisation in developing countries is a process of sequential rather than simultaneous investment decisions, in which development is accelerated through the promotion of industries and projects with strong forward and backward linkage effects.[13] Backward linkages of an investment also lead to new investment in input-supplying companies. Forward linkages generate additional new investment in downstream industries, which use the supplying industry's product as an input. Instead of an *ex ante* plan of balanced investments in a number of complementary industries as postulated in Nurkse's theory of balanced growth, Hirschman argued for a strategy of unbalanced growth that focused on the individual decision-making of entrepreneurs in both the private and public sectors, who were assumed to respond in an unbalanced way to investment opportunities generated by the existence of forward and backward linkages with complementary industries.

The linkage concept also allowed for a more nuanced analysis of the structure of developing countries' export industries. While other structuralists like Singer and Prebisch argued that developing countries' dependence on the export of primary goods established a structural tendency for their terms of trade to deteriorate in their exchanges with industrialised countries, Hirschman saw these effects as dependent on the kind of primary goods a developing country exports. What matters, in his view, is the presence of linkage effects in a particular primary export industry, that is, its potential to generate investments in down- and upstream industries. Therefore, very different growth paths can be traced out by developing countries exporting, say, copper as opposed to countries the main export commodity of which is, for instance, coffee.

The linkage concept has been widely invoked in development economics as a useful analytical tool for studying the sequence of industrial development. But the far more fundamental theme in Hirschman's work – his exploration of "hidden rationalities" and "wrong way around" sequences in economic realities of developing countries – remained largely unheard by succeeding generations of development economists and practitioners. Only now, as the shortcomings from implementing universal policy prescriptions in developing countries abound, are development

---

though they had no formal title to the land. While the conventional wisdom is that secure land titles are a precondition for people to be willing to invest in the construction and maintenance of their houses, these squatter families argued that the more solid and respectably built the houses are, the less likely it is that the authorities will send bulldozers to demolish the whole new settlement, and the more likely it will instead become that people are eventually granted official titles to the land (Hirschman 1984a). Another such "wrong way around" sequence that Hirschman describes is that certain attitudes and beliefs, that are believed to be conductive to economic progress, are actually acquired "on the job" in the course of the development process. In this respect, Hirschman (1984b) mentions how narrow latitude in standards of performance (a task has to be performed just right) brings pressures for efficiency, quality performance, good maintenance habits etc. and thus substitutes for a pre-existing performance attitude or actually creates it.

[13] For later refinements of his approach see Hirschman (1981b, especially Chaps. 3–5; and 1984b).

economists gradually realising that their preoccupation with the obvious elements of poor countries' realities made them blind of indigenous factors, which tend to vary considerably across different contexts.

6.2.2 Gunnar Myrdal: Development as a Cumulative Process of Circular Causation

Another dissenter from mainstream neoclassical analysis was Karl Gunnar Myrdal (1898–1987). He can be seen as a structuralist development economist on grounds of his deep concern about raising economic inequalities between industrialised and developing countries, and his resulting interest in the structures and processes that underlie these inequalities.

In his 1957 *Economic Theory and Under-Developed Regions*, Myrdal already argued against the belief by the neoclassical mainstream that economic processes generally tend to develop towards an equilibrium outcome. Neoclassical equilibrium analysis implies that changes of some economic factors call forth countervailing reactions in the system that may ultimately result in a state of balance between these forces. Myrdal objected to this analysis for its consideration of interactions between only economic variables. He maintained that if applied to the theoretical analysis of development problems, the neoclassical equilibrium assumption would break down because it abstracts from exactly those noneconomic factors of the realities of developing countries which often react to changes of economic factors in a disequilibrating way. By taking changes in both the relevant economic and noneconomic factors into account, Myrdal realised that "the essence of a social problem is that it concerns a complex of interlocking, circular and cumulative changes" (Myrdal 1957, p. 16). By circular causation he meant a process in which "a change in any one [variable] induces the others to change in such a way that these secondary changes support the first change, with similar tertiary effects upon the variables first affected, and so on" (ibid., p. 17). Because a change in a single factor tends to change all the other factors in the same direction, this circular causal relationship results in a cumulative development. This process can be either positive or negative. The circular causation of a negative cumulative process is described by the notion of the vicious circle of poverty. But, in the same way, a particular exogenous influence can also set in motion a process in which circular forces cumulate in an upward spiral of development. Like most development economists of his time, Myrdal believed that such an external push could came from a government-executed development plan. Specifically, he required the government "to prepare and enforce a general economic plan, containing a system of purposefully applied controls and impulses to get development started and keep it going" (ibid., p. 80). In order to lower economic inequalities, this plan had, moreover, to "increase the strength of the spread effects of the development impulses as between regions and between occupations" (ibid., p. 81). As in Nurkse's theory of balanced growth, Myrdal advocated planned investment in different industries, and emphasised the need for simultaneous engagement by the state in areas such as infrastructure, health and education.[14] But unlike other early development economists in the structuralist tradition, Myrdal's contributions had less direct influence on the development policies and strategies of his time. On the relevance of this research for policy formulation, he noted that

> [t]he more we know about the way in which the different factors are inter-related – what effects a primary change of each factor will have on all the other factors, and when – the better we shall be able to establish how to maximise the effects of a given policy effort designed to move and change the social system. (Ibid., p. 20).

Of relevance beyond his time remain in particular Myrdal's analytical efforts to understand and explain the mechanisms behind development and social change. With his hypothesis that a social change is a cumulative process because of circular causation he provides not only a framework for analysing the causes and consequences of poverty. To him, the principle of cumulation also promised to result in development outcomes of much greater magnitude than the efforts and costs of the initial reform itself. Unanswered, however, still remains the related question of how to ignite economic development in places where it did not previously occur.

6.2.3 Hans W. Singer: The International Distribution of Gains from Trade and Investment

Like Myrdal did also Hans Wolfgang Singer (1910–2006) become a pioneer in development economics[15] mainly due to his research of the interdependencies between developing and existing industrialised economies. Singer was trained by Arthur Spiethoff and Joseph Schumpeter at Bonn before he became a scholar of John Maynard Keynes. From Spiethoff he learnt about the importance of considering the historical context in which economic development takes place. From Schumpeter, he acquired a lasting interest in problems of technical progress and its effects on long-run trends in economic development. Keynes, however, had the deepest influence on Singer's structuralist orientation by showing that the economic rules that apply to conditions of unemployment are not the same as those applicable to the classical economics of full employment. Singer expanded this view that different rules and principles apply to different economic conditions into the field of development economics.

---

[14] Myrdal was well aware of the limits and problems of state planning, and noted that the state may, especially at the beginning of the development process, itself be in the hands of social groups that have an interest in preventing the traditional status quo (Myrdal 1957).

[15] According to *Pioneers in Development* by Meier and Seers (1984). The other pioneers in development included in that volume are Peter T. Bauer, Colin Clark, Albert O. Hirschman, Arthur Lewis, Gunnar Myrdal, Paul Rosenstein–Rodan, Raúl Prebisch, Walt Rostow and Jan Tinbergen.

He shaped the structuralist approach to development economics by highlighting that economic development in Latin America, Asia and Africa was constrained by specific structural economic problems that distinguished these countries' development from the path that advanced countries had taken in their transition from agrarian to industrialised economies. A particular class of structural problems, to which Singer devoted much of his research, is problems that resulted from the fact that poor countries attempt to emerge from poverty in the presence of a powerful group of already industrialised economies. The interrelations between developing and advanced countries, and the distribution of gains from these interrelations, were his principal area of study.

From analysing the patterns of trade between industrialised and less developed countries, Singer observed that developing countries mostly exported primary goods to advanced economies, while their main imports from industrialised countries consisted of manufactured goods. Furthermore, he found that, in the long run, the price of primary goods tended to decline relative to that of manufactured goods – an unfortunate process for the less developed, primary goods producing countries because this meant that their export prices rose less quickly than the prices they had to pay for imported manufactured goods.

Singer formulated his thesis about the long-term deterioration of poor countries' terms of trade in opposition to the widely held view that foreign trade was particularly instrumental for less developed countries in raising their productivity and standards of living as it was believed to accelerate the use of more capital-intensive methods of production, as well as the spread of knowledge and modern technology. Singer cautioned that developing countries' export industries in the primary goods sector had mostly been established as foreign direct investments and were thus foreign-owned. Although they were geographically located in developing countries, these industries were not part of the internal economic structure of their host countries, because both outputs and profits from them were returned to the foreign investors' home countries (Singer 1950).[16] Singer argued that the benefits from this specialisation of developing countries on the export of food and raw materials to industrialised countries not only accrued mostly to the latter, but also diverted resources away from other productive uses that could offer a larger scope for technical progress and the development of local markets in developing countries.

Singer found the main explanation for his thesis about the negative effects of international trade and investment on developing countries in their terms of trade. From analysing the patterns of trade between industrialised and less developed countries, Singer observed that, in the long run, the prices of primary goods tended to decline relative to those of manufactured goods. This meant for the less developed, primary goods producing countries that their export prices increased less

---

[16] Note that this proposition related to foreign investment in export-oriented raw material and food industries. The development effects of foreign direct investment are more likely to be positive if the investment is made in the manufacturing sector with the purpose to primarily service the local market of the host country.

quickly than the prices that they had to pay for imported manufactured goods. According to Singer, these changes could not be explained by productivity changes in the manufactured goods sector relative to that in the primary goods sector, but rather by the way in which the productivity gains from technical progress are distributed between produces and consumers in both these sectors. He assumed that, in the case of manufactured commodities, these gains accrue to producers mainly in the form of higher incomes, whereas in the case of primary goods, they are more often distributed to consumers in form of lower prices. If producers and consumers were part of the same economy, these differences would only affect the internal distribution of income within that economy. Because, however, raw materials produced in developing countries are consumed in industrialised economies where also the incomes from the production of manufactured goods are earned, the gains from technical progress are disproportionately distributed in favour of industrialised countries as they benefit from both, lower prices for primary goods, and higher incomes in their domestic manufacturing sectors.

Singer identified additional divergences in the effects of technical progress on incomes in the manufacturing and primary goods industries respectively, which he used to further support his thesis about the long-term deterioration of developing countries' terms of trade. He argued that producers of manufactured commodities actually benefit twice from technical progress, firstly through higher domestic incomes, and secondly through increased demand for domestic manufactured goods as a result of the income rise. Conversely, technical progress in the primary goods sector of developing countries also results in lower prices for these goods, but this price decrease have lower effects on demand for these goods due to the low price elasticity of demand for food and raw materials. Finally, technical progress in the manufacturing sector of developed countries often means a reduction in the amount of raw materials used per unit of output – an effect that, according to Singer, further aggravates the structural tendency for the terms of trade of developing countries to deteriorate in their exchanges with industrialised countries.[17]

Singer had developed his thesis about the long-term deterioration of less developed countries' terms of trade during his early years at the UN, and presented it first at the annual meeting of the American Economic Association in 1949 in a contribution on "The Gains and Losses from Trade and Investment in Under-Developed Countries".[18] In his later work, Singer revisited the problem of distribution of the gains from trade and investment by putting more emphasis on relations between types of countries rather than types of commodities. In his original contribution, the power relationships between developing and industrialised countries had been analysed only in terms of the effects of foreign direct investment by industrialised

---

[17] This effect could hardly be offset by the effect from higher incomes in advanced countries, as the demand for primary goods was generally not very sensitive to changes in real incomes.

[18] This paper was published in 1950 under the title "The Distribution of Gains between Investing and Borrowing Countries" (Singer 1950), and later led to the pairing of Singer's name with that of Raúl Prebisch in the designation of their contribution as the Prebisch–Singer thesis.

countries in the primary goods industries of developing countries. Later, Singer identified divergences in technological power as the root course of imbalance between poor and rich countries. He recognised that industrialisation and the diversification of export industries in developing countries were not sufficient to countervail the uneven distribution of the gains from trade and investment, but that the major task lies in breaking up the research and development monopoly that follows from advanced countries' technological leadership.[19]

6.2.4 Raú Prebisch: Import Substitution as Strategy for Development

At roughly the same time as Singer, though independently of him, had also Raúl Prebisch (1901–1986) sought to explain the unequal contributions of trade and technological advance to the national incomes of less developed and industrialised countries. As an Argentinean, and Executive Secretary from 1950 until 1963 of the United Nations Economic Commission for Latin America (UN ECLA, or CEPAL), he had particularly great influence on the formulation of policies for developing countries in Latin America. Contrary to the free trade paradigm which assumed positive welfare effects for all countries participating in the international division of labour, Prebisch argued that Latin America's lack of economic progress was primarily caused by its structurally disadvantaged position in the system of international trade. Prebisch captured the unequal distribution of the gains from trade and technology in his "centre-periphery model", according to which the industrialised countries at the centre of the international system of trade not only keep the benefits from the use of new technologies in their own economies, but are also in a favourable position to obtain a share of the gains from technological progress in the less developed countries at the periphery of the global system of trade (Prebisch 1950).

Prebisch gave two main explanations for the structural disadvantage of less developed countries: First, price reductions are avoided in the countries of the centre because their markets are characterised by imperfect competition, while strong competition among primary goods producers in the less developed periphery reduces the prices of their goods. His second explanation has been that the income elasticity of demand is higher for industrial than for primary goods, that is, an increase in incomes raises demand for goods exported by industrialised countries more than it raises demand for primary exports of developing countries. Both explanations imply a decline in the terms of trade of the countries at the periphery of the global trade system.

This explanation was essentially the same as that of Singer, and has since become known as the Prebisch-Singer thesis. It strongly inspired a new school of dependency theorists that emerged, especially in Latin America, in reaction to the

---

[19] See Singer (1971, 1984).

6.2 Structuralist Approaches to Development Economics

liberal free trade paradigm, and ascribed their countries' underdevelopment primarily to the existence of an unequal, exploitative relationship between industrialised and less developed countries. While the Prebisch-Singer has empirically never fully been proven, and was thus less relevant for the projection of empirical trends in the terms of trade, it had great impact by inspiring the national development strategies of Latin American and other developing countries in the 1950s and 1960s.[20]

In view of the limitations of developing countries' primary export activities, and their restricted possibilities for increasing export activities in the manufacturing sectors, a main policy conclusion that emerged from the analyses of Prebisch and Singer was to expand the production of agricultural and manufactured goods for domestic consumption. This required shielding developing countries through protective measures against commodity imports from advanced countries in order to allow domestic manufacturing industries to grow and become internationally competitive. Such a policy of import-substituting industrialisation was considered to help correct the unfavourable terms of trade for developing countries that were assumed to result from the low income elasticity of demand for imports of primary products by the centres, compared with the high income elasticity of demand at the periphery for manufacturers from the centres. Especially Prebisch argued that protectionism at the centres would aggravate these discrepancies in demand elasticity, while at the periphery it could correct them (Prebisch 1984). Besides its effects on developing countries' terms of trade, the pursuit of industrialisation through import substitution was used to support several related economic policy objectives as well: First, it was conjectured that protective tariffs on manufacturing will initially raise the domestic price of manufactured goods, giving both foreign and local entrepreneurs an incentive to invest in the sector. Second, provided that a country's internal market is sufficiently large, economies of scale in production and competition in the domestic manufacturing sector will eventually lower domestic prices to the point at which they are internationally competitive and no protective tariffs are required anymore.

The policy conclusions from the Prebisch-Singer thesis were well received by policymakers in developing countries. Especially countries in Latin America like Argentina, Brazil, Chile, Columbia, Mexico and Uruguay adopted import substitution policies between the 1950s and 1960s with some success.[21] Their economies

---

[20] Nevertheless, the Prebisch–Singer thesis was never established as part of core trade theory. However, the widely used concept of "immiserising growth" can clearly be related back to the work of Prebisch and Singer. In trade theory, "immiserising growth" refers to a situation in which growth in a poor country would actually be self-defeating if it was biased towards growth in exports which worsened the exporting country's terms of trade so much that it would be worse off than if it had not grown at all. The concept of "immiserising growth" was first emphasised under this name in 1958 by Jagdish Bhagwati.

[21] The particular popularity in Latin America of import-substitution schemes with protective tariffs had also historical reasons. Latin America had been affected more than any other developing region in the world by the negative consequences of the Great Depression of the 1930s. At the beginning of the twentieth century, Latin American economies depended heavily on the export of just a few primary goods (wool was the main export good of Argentina and Uruguay, silver that of Bolivia and Mexico, copper that of Chile, coffee that of Brazil and Venezuela, saltpetre that of

grew at hitherto unprecedented rates, and this growth was mainly fuelled by a disproportionately high increase in domestic manufacturing activity. However, most Latin American countries also serve as cases to illustrate the limitations of protective tariffs behind the import-substitution schemes. As mentioned above, the size of the internal market was crucial for the development of a competitive national manufacturing industry. In Latin America, this condition was attempted to attain by both national policies that aimed at raising demand through higher and more equally distributed household incomes, and efforts to increase the size of the internal market through regional integration.[22] Another limitation of import substitution arose from the neglect of Latin America's export industries. With the protection of the domestic manufacturing sectors, resources were diverted away from existing primary export industries. As world market prices for primary goods rose in the wake of the Korean War, Latin American countries benefited less from this development than their export potential would have allowed them to. Moreover, import-substituting industrialisation in Latin America was pursued at the cost of an early diversification of exports into manufactured goods. The neglect of export industries combined with high demand for capital goods and industrial inputs by the domestic manufacturing sector also created current account deficits and contributed to the region's foreign debt build-up. This way, new international dependencies abounded from policies that had originally been put in place to countervail Latin America's dependence on the industrialised world.

An important reason why Latin American countries got "locked" into the perpetuation of protective trade policies relates to the central role assigned to the state in the planning and implementation of Latin America's import-substituting industrialisation. Public agents decided not only about the target industries that were protected under the import substitution schemes, the state itself invested heavily into these strategic sectors. In consequence, during the period of import substitution, Latin American countries experienced a steep rise of the public sector share in GDP. Moreover, industrial production was concentrated in the countries' urban centres at the expense of agricultural production in rural areas.[23] These structural

---

Columbia and sugar that of Peru). With the economic downturn in the industrialised countries, demand and hence prices for primary goods dropped sharply. Without export revenues to finance their manufacturing imports, and no domestic manufacturing industry to absorb the loss of economic activity in the export industries, primary goods exporting countries in Latin America were driven into their hitherto worst economic and social crisis.

[22] The two main trade agreements among Latin American countries that date back to the time in which import substitution policies were pursued are the Central American Common Market (CACM or Mercado Común Centroamericano, MCCA), agreed between five Central American countries in 1960; and the Andean Community of Nations (Comunidad Andina de Naciones, CAN), a trade agreement between Bolivia, Colombia, Ecuador, Peru and Venezuela (which left the organisation in 2006) that came into existence with the signing of the Cartagena Agreement in 1969.

[23] For instance, in 1970, half of Mexico's industrial production took place in Mexico City alone.

characteristics required for continued trade protection and contributed to the persistence of high tariff barriers in most of Latin America.

The negative consequences of import substitution strategies pursued in Latin America became evident in the 1970s when inefficiencies in the manufacturing sector held the level of domestic consumer prices high, while a growing informal sector further decreased public revenues. High budget and trade deficits led to unsustainably high levels of inflation and overvalued currencies, which further precluded the development of a non-traditional export sector, while agricultural activity was tied down by price controls, import licensing and other restrictions. Ultimately, a collapse in output and massive devaluations of domestic currencies brought the era of import-substituting industrialisation in Latin America to a provisional end, and invited free market reforms in many countries which lasted until the international debt crisis in 1982.

The Latin American experience with import substitution policies has often been taken as clear proof of the ineffectiveness of import-substituting industrialisation as a development strategy. But this evaluation fails to recognise the potential of import substitution schemes as a strictly temporary instrument for allowing countries to catch up in a world of uneven progress.[24] Among the countries which have used this instrument wisely are East Asian economies like Taiwan, South Korea or Singapore, which employed labour-intensive import substitution successfully as a temporary economic policy to create the conditions for their subsequent pursuit of export led growth strategies.

Another, much older example for the successful pursuit of import-substituting industrialisation is the German *Zollverein*, which helped Germany in the nineteenth century not only to expand its domestic manufacturing sector under conditions of relative protection from British imports, but also to overcome the country's political and economic fragmentation. Credited with masterminding the *Zollverein* is the German economist Friedrich List. His work displays a surprising relevance and topicality also for present discourses in development economics and shall thus be devoted a brief mention in the next section.[25]

---

[24] The recent expansion of trade between China and African countries has stirred new interest in the questions of whether and how relatively less developed African economies can and should protect their domestic industries from the massive influx of cheap manufactured goods and textiles that are supposed to undermine their own attempts at building a domestic manufacturing industry.

[25] Reinert (2007) shows that from the Italian Renaissance to the present day, economic policies of the type proposed by Friedrich List have been a "mandatory passage point" for all successful national traditions out of poverty. In the same vein as List did also the American Treasury Secretary Alexander Hamilton propose measures to protect America from Britain's manufacturing might in the late eighteenth and early nineteenth century. In his 1791 "Report on the Subject of Manufactures", he dissented from free-trade doctrines of the classical liberal economists and recommended the government to shelter and promote American industry through its infancy until it was strong enough to compete with the British manufacturing sector. In his 1841 *National System of Political Economy*, List does not refer to Hamilton, however.

6.2.5 Excursus: Friedrich List and the German Zollverein

The surprising correspondence between the writings of Singer and Prebisch, and that of Friedrich List (1789–1846) shall justify a brief excursus into that latter's ideas and policy conclusions. List, a forerunner of the German Historical School, paid special attention to identifying stages in economic development, and acknowledged that all results from economic research are valid only for a specific set of national and historical circumstances. In his days, the world was divided into Great Britain that had advanced to a stage of economic supremacy and the countries of continental Europe, Russia and North America that were still at a stage of economic emergence. For List, the understanding of each of these stages required a discrete economic theory.[26] He considered the "cosmopolitan" theory by Adam Smith with its idea of free trade and competition under laissez-faire conditions as valid for countries at the developmental stage of Great Britain.[27] But for continental Europe in general, and the German states in particular, he envisaged an economic theory that focussed on possible ways and means for building a national manufacturing sector in the face of an already existing and dominant British manufacturing industry that, at his time, exported most of its output to continental Europe and its overseas colonies in exchange for their raw materials.

Like Singer and Prebisch, List expressed very clearly the detrimental effects of free trade among countries that differed in their stage of development. Regarding the free trade paradigm of classical economists he contended that

> [t]he school fails to perceive that under a system of perfectly free competition with more advanced manufacturing nations, a nation which is less advanced than those, although well fitted for manufacturing, can never attain to a perfectly developed manufacturing power of its own, nor to perfect national independence, without protective duties. (List [1841] 1959, p. 279).

And he further remarked with regard to the monetary effects of free trade among countries at different stages of development that

> [e]xperience has proved repeatedly (and especially in Russia and North America) that in agricultural nations, whose manufacturing market is exposed to the free competition of a nation which has attained manufacturing supremacy, the value of the importation of manufactured goods exceeds frequently to an enormous extent the value of the agricultural products which are exported, and that thereby at times suddenly an extraordinary exportation of precious metals is occasioned, whereby the economy of the agricultural nation,

---

[26] This is a distinctive proposition of the German Historical School of Economics. It will be taken up in more detail in Chap. 12 again.

[27] Besides that, List shared with the English classical school the recognition of the important contribution of manufacturing to a country's development – much in contrast to the Physiocrats' view of the pre-eminent position of agriculture in economic development that prevailed in continental Europe at that time.

especially if its internal interchange is chiefly based on paper circulation, falls into confusion, and national calamities are the result (List [1841] 1959, p. 246).

For the scattered coalition of individual states that made up Germany in the early nineteenth century, List's main advice was the creation of a single internal market, the blueprint for which he presented in 1841 in his main work *The National System of Political Economy*. List envisioned the economic integration among German states as a first step towards a continental alliance of all emerging economies in Europe.[28] In Germany, this common domestic market was realised in 1834 with the creation of the German *Zollverein* (German Customs Union), a free trade agreement between the German states that, at the same time, established a temporary regime of import tariffs on manufacturing commodities and colonial products from Great Britain. List's recommendations for the policies of the *Zollverein* included in particular (1) to build a complete network of ship and railway transport, which presupposed the future integration of the coastal regions (especially Belgium and Holland) into the customs union; (2) to import all required colonial products directly from tropical countries in exchange for their own manufactured goods – which essentially implied a preference for trade with independent overseas territories like the West Indies (the Caribbean) as well as North and South America and (3) to increase protective duties only as much as domestic capital, technical abilities, and entrepreneurial spirit were increasing or were being attracted from abroad. This condition was meant to ensure that trade is restricted only to the extent in which a country is able to process the surplus of raw materials that it had previously exchanged for imported manufactured good (ibid.).

In all his writings, List was looking upon protection as a strictly transitional phase that would be followed by free trade once a country had passed from an emerging to an advanced stage of development. Similarly, he generally condemned permanent state subsidies to certain industries and found them justified only as "temporary means of encouragement, namely, where the slumbering spirit of enterprise of a nation merely requires stimulus and assistance in the first period of its revival, in order to evoke in it a powerful and lasting production and an export trade to countries which themselves do not possess flourishing manufactures" (ibid. p. 278).

While List devised many ideas that later reappeared in the structuralists' contributions to development economics, his focus remained largely on the relations between emerging and advanced European economies. He was less decided in his views about the effects that international trade had on the raw material-supplying colonial regions, that is, today's emerging countries of the South. He tended to see

---

[28] While in his *National System of Political Economy* this continental alliance is clearly defined in opposition to the British Empire, List's later writings suggest a change in his view towards closer alignment of Germany with Great Britain.

them benefiting from their role in the international division of labour as the scale of world trade increased:

> If thus the countries of the torrid zone produce enormously greater quantities of colonial goods than before, they will supply themselves with the means of taking from the countries of the temperate zone much larger quantities of manufactured goods; and from the larger sale of manufactured goods, the manufacturers will be enabled to consume larger quantities of colonial goods. In consequence of this increased production, and increase of the means of exchange, the commercial intercourse between farmers of the torrid zone and the manufacturers of the temperate zone, i.e. the great commerce of the world, will increase in future in a far larger proportion than it has done in the course of the last century (Ibid. p. 242–243).

6.2.6 Peter T. Bauer: A Class of His Own

The subdivision of the early development economists' rich and varied contributions into particular theoretical stands is always beset by a certain degree of vagueness. In the case of Lord Peter T. Bauer (1915–2002), the attribution of his work to a particular school seems almost futile. He was an outstanding but singular exponent of development economics. As Armatya Sen (2000) puts it, Bauer is in a class of his own.

In *The Economics of Under-Developed Countries* (1957, together with Basil S. Yamey), Bauer recognises not only structural differences between advanced and underdeveloped countries, but especially also highlights the great range of internal regional differences within the developing world, and warned of the dangers of theoretical generalisation:

> There are no special economic theories or methods of analysis fashioned uniquely for the study of the under-developed world. But while the tools of analysis are of wide relevance, in a study of under-developed countries the situations to which they must be applied vary greatly. [...] The Economist, although equipped with versatile general-purpose tools, must proceed with caution both in the way in which he uses them and in the identification of the relevant data in a situation or problem to which he is applying them (Bauer and Yamey 1957, p. 8).

In raising topics that are characteristic for the economic landscape in developing countries, Bauer adopted a focus on microeconomic rather than macroeconomic phenomena.[29] He was perhaps the first economist to recognise the structures and important functions of informal economic activity in low-income countries. For instance, he carefully analysed the importance of individual effort by small landowners in course of the transition from communal to individual land tenure, or by

---

[29] The approach of basing his analysis on careful and direct observation of conditions in the developing world certainly owes much to Bauer's field experiences in former Malaya (now West Malaysia) and former British West Africa (now Nigeria, Ghana, Sierra Leone and the Gambia) in the 1940s where he was active as representative of a London-based merchant house and for conducting studies on the local rubber industry.

internal traders in transforming a subsistence economy into an exchange economy.[30] For Bauer, economic development depended largely on "human qualities and aptitudes, on social and political institutions, which derive from these, on historical experience and also on natural resources and on various other factors" (ibid., p. 11). His proposition was that if these factors are favourable, capital will be generated locally or attracted from abroad without the need for state-executed investment plans or foreign aid.

What sets Bauer most apart from the first generation of development economists is his strong dissent with their policy conclusions. He was highly sceptical about the effectiveness of both, attempts at industrialising developing countries through large-scale investment plans and the provision of foreign aid. He also argued against the case for planned public investments to encourage balanced growth by the simultaneous promotion of a group of selected interrelated branches of manufacturing industry. If the coordinated investment into complementary industries was indeed economically viable, the information to private investors about available business opportunities would suffice, according to Bauer, to establish balanced growth without a state-led plan. Furthermore, he rejected the alleged responsibility of advanced Western economies for poor countries' underdevelopment, and the trade pessimism the structuralists deduced from it, by pointing out that the countries least exposed to the Western economies are also among the world's least developed economies.

As a libertarian, Bauer's dissent with assigning the state a leading role in the development process also made him an indefatigable opponent of the notion of developing countries being stuck in a vicious circle of poverty, which was used as an argument in favour of state-led investment planning, and had been invoked to justify international development aid. He refuted the vicious circle thesis by arguing that if it were true, no country or individual would have ever been able to rise from poverty, and warned that "[i]f the thesis of the vicious circle were valid, the conclusion would be simple, irresistible and meaningful. But once it is recognised that it is invalid, no such simple conclusion is possible" (Bauer 1965, p. 11).[31] But by disproving the vicious circle thesis in an attempt to defy state-led investment planning and foreign aid as associated policy responses, Bauer failed to recognise both, the origin of vicious circles in diminishing returns that often characterise poor countries' natural resource-based activities, and the potential for virtous circles that emanate from synergies between manufacturing activities that lead to increasing returns to investment.[32]

---

[30] For further discussion see Sect. 2.1.1 above.

[31] Elsewhere (Bauer 2000, p. 6), he called the idea of the vicious circle of poverty "a major lapse in modern development economics" and argued that "if the notion of the vicious circle of poverty were valid, mankind would still be living in the Old Stone Age".

[32] See Reinert (1996) who discovers a clear understanding of the effects of diminishing and increasing returns to scale on economic development already in the writings of Antonio Serra and John Stuard Mill.

Bauer's critique may sound familiar to many second generation development economists who invoked concepts central to neoclassical economics such as allocative efficiency, market-based competition, appropriate incentives, sound money and economic openness in trade against the contributions by members of the first generation of development economists. Bauer, however, raised his doubts much earlier and well before the adverse economic and political consequences of the first generation's policy recommendations cleared the way for a neoclassical resurgence in development economics.[33]

---

[33] This does not make Bauer an early exponent of the second generation of development economists, though. He also followed development policies in the neoclassical tradition with a critical eye and warned, for instance, against the adverse effects of linking foreign aid to government policies.

Chapter 7
The Second Generation: Return to the Mainstream

7.1 Neoclassical Development Economics

While early development economists had placed great confidence in state-led development planning, they had been less mindful of problems of implementation and political governance. Consequently, many of the early development policies had produced uneven results and distortions in the economic systems of developing countries. This was a main reason why in the late 1960s, the first generation's development theories were increasingly challenged by mainstream neoclassical economists who focused on government failure and price distortions as main reasons for the lack of progress in the developing world. The early development economists had seen problems of underdevelopment primarily as structural in nature and thus not amenable to price and income changes. The neoclassical economists instead argued that this view produced policies which violated fundamental principles of neoclassical theory and thus resulted in a misallocation of resources. Policy-induced price distortions prevailed, for instance, in the labour market, where relatively high wages for unskilled labour did not correspond with conditions of "unlimited" supply of labour. Conversely, in the capital market, real interest rates were considered too low in view of an undersupply of capital in developing countries. And given large current account deficits, especially in countries which had pursued import-substitution policies, the consequent foreign exchange shortages were not adequately reflected in their prevailing exchange rates, which were mostly overvalued.

In light of these economic problems that many developing countries faced after a phase of state intervention and protectionism, the focus on the price mechanism and allocative efficiency, as well as on related neoclassical concepts like market-based competition, appropriate incentives, sound money, or open economies, seemed justified. The trouble was that this focus was introduced in development economics along with a set of general assumptions and premises of neoclassical theory that reflected economic realities in advanced economies rather than the specific contexts that determined allocative choices in developing countries. These assumptions, upon which neoclassical economics rests in its original approach, expect that individual actors operate rationally, seek to maximise their individual utility or profit, and make choices on the basis of full and relevant information. Even when the neoclassical approach was later gradually refined, among others, by incorporating theories of imperfect competition and asymmetric information, the observed behaviour of known phenomena in advanced economies continued to provide the premises from which its theoretical conclusions were inferred.

The general approach by the second generation of development economists was to take rich countries as the model at which research on developing countries was oriented. Behind this approach stood the belief that industrialised economies provided a clear example of a development path that was, in principle, also open to the developing world. Theories and assumptions developed to explain economic phenomena of advanced economies were thus generalised and extended to developing countries. The universal application of these theories to contexts of both developed and developing economies was also favoured by the generality of the tools and assumptions of neoclassical economics, which claimed validity in all times and places. This provided not only a convenient shortcut around more context-specific research, but also allowed for the formulation and mathematical treatment of the economic models that relied upon a limited set of measurable explanatory variables.[1]

The formalisation in the analysis of the economies of developing countries was also favoured by the advancement of quantitative techniques and the better availability of cross-country statistical data.[2] This made it possible to develop and to mathematically test formal models of economic growth and development. It also raised the expected standard of rigour in economic thinking which was quite different from the visionary and qualitative style of early development economists. As Krugman (1994) notes, the increasing formalisation in development economics delivers a methodological explanation for the fact that concepts like increasing returns to scale, market-size externalities and circular causation, that were so central to the explanation of the development process in the formative years of the sub-discipline, were largely abstracted away from the models of neoclassical development economists because they were, at that time, difficult to formalise with available modelling techniques. This methodological reason for the demise of early development theories was, of course, reinforced by the ideological differences

---

[1] In this view, this subchapter's title "Neoclassical Development Economics" must seem contradictory, as the application of neoclassical analysis for the study of developing countries actually meant the absorption of development economics as a separate sub-discipline of economics by the neoclassical mainstream. It did not, however, weaken the interest of economists and development institutions in finding solutions for the problems of developing countries. These solutions, and the theories from which they were drawn, represent what is referred to as neoclassical development economics in this section.

[2] For instance, the International Comparison Program (ICP), which provides historical purchasing power parity (PPP) data for a wide range of countries, began in 1968 with a small project by Irving B. Kravis, Alan Heston, and Robert Summers and is by now one of the world's largest statistical initiatives (see also footnote 23 above). Also in 1968, the United Nations also began to systematically collect national accounts statistics, and the World Bank published its World Development Indicators on an annual basis since 1978 together with its World Development Reports (Meier 2005).

between the first and second generation of development economists: Neither would the early pioneers (especially those in the structuralist tradition) have probably been willing to switch from their narrative, qualitative style to the formal approach acclaimed by neoclassical economists, not even if available modelling techniques had allowed them to do so; nor had neoclassical development economist at first any particular interest in searching ways to model market structures characterised by scale economies, as their presence indicated a market distortion from the perspective of their standard model of the perfectly competitive economy.

The second generation's emphasis on the efficiency of resource use and their focus on "getting the prices right" was accompanied by a shift of attention from macro- to microeconomic foundations underlying the development process. The interest was not anymore primarily in studying the effect of, say, investment and capital accumulation on growth, but rather in the extent to which an economic regime, and its associated economic policies, were conducive to the achievement of an efficient allocation and use of resources. The market mechanism was, in fact, seen as the regime that satisfied this condition best, and was thus believed to be capable of coordinating the changes needed for igniting and sustaining economic growth.

Beyond the microeconomic focus of neoclassical development economics, growth theory was increasingly called upon to gain an understanding of processes at the macroeconomic level. Modern growth theory had evolved independently from development economics in the 1940s with the first formalised growth models developed by Roy Harrod in 1939 and Evsey Domar in 1946.[3] While these Keynesian growth models were devised primarily with the advanced industrialised countries in mind, they found an early practical application in the planning exercises for developing countries. But it was with the second generation of development economics that modern growth theory became an inherent part of the analytical framework for studying the economic development of poor countries.

A landmark contribution to the modelling of long-run economic growth within the framework of neoclassical economics is the exogenous growth model of Robert Solow. In his "A Contribution to the Theory of Economic Growth" in 1956, and subsequent papers, Solow extended the Harrod–Domar model by relaxing the assumption that production takes place under conditions of fixed proportions (meaning that labour cannot be substituted for capital), which had led to the Harrod–Domar conclusion that growth is proportionate to investment, and that investment is hence the main source of growth. Solow arrived at the conclusion that

---

[3] Due to their formal correspondence, both growth models became collectively known as the Harrod-Domar model, which states that a country's rate of growth is determined by its propensity to save (which determines investment) and the capital-output ratio (which indicates the productivity of capital). A main conclusion from this Keynesian growth model is that the economy does not naturally find a full-employment, stable growth rate, but that its rate of growth can be raised by economic policies that increase investment or saving, as well as by using capital more efficiently through technological advances.

not investment but technological change (determined exogenously) determines growth in the long run. His explanation was that growth in output per worker cannot be sustained through investment in capital (i.e. machinery) because, in his model, capital is subject to diminishing returns. He further assumed that labour is in fixed supply so that the elasticity of labour supply cannot offset the effects on growth of diminishing returns to capital. Therefore, only a more productive use of the existing stock of labour through technological progress can help a country to sustain a constant rate of growth in production per worker.

It is interesting to see that the assumption of a fixed stock of labour, that made technological progress the only source of long-term growth per worker in the Solow model, was intentionally relaxed in the models of early development economists as they considered it not to fit into a framework for the analysis of developing countries. Lewis, for instance, build his dual sector model on the assumption of an unlimited supply of labour, which in turn led him to the conclusion that investment, and hence capital, are the main determinants of growth in poor countries. Although Solow originally applied his model for explaining economic growth over time in the United States, and never maintained that his theory is applicable also to less developed economies, it became the standard model of growth for neoclassical development economists. They argued that increasing the capital stock per worker through investment can be a temporary source of growth in the transition from a low to a higher level of capital. In the long run, however, neoclassical economists assumed the effect of investment on growth to disappear as diminishing returns to capital set in. A key prediction of neoclassical growth theory is, in fact, that an economy will converge towards a steady state (its long-run equilibrium) at which output per worker grows at only the rate of technological change. Applied to explaining the growth experiences of developing countries, this prediction suggested that the income levels of poor countries would tend to catch up with, or converge towards, the income levels of rich countries. While this prediction found some empirical support for countries that had already converged towards a high level of income, it failed to explain existing cross-country differences in income between rich and poor countries: Neither did international finance capital flow to poor countries because of their predicted high returns to scarce capital; nor was there any sign of convergence between low- and high-income countries over time.[4]

The recognition that the Solow prediction applied to developing countries had failed was followed by a resurgence of theoretical interest in growth in the 1980s that can be traced to the work of Paul Romer (1986) and Robert Lucas (1988). They tried to explain growth by factors determined within the model without having to rely exogenously on technological progress as an explanation of long-term growth.

---

[4]In response to the fact that poor countries tended to grow slowly despite their postulated high marginal return to investment, neoclassical development economists acknowledged that factors like subsistence consumption constraints or imperfect international capital markets could interfere with the results predicted by the Solow growth model. In this context, they argued that foreign aid could accelerate growth rates in the transition to a steady state.

For this purpose, they had to abandon the assumption of diminishing returns to capital (and constant returns to scale for labour and capital combined). Whereas Romer identified externalities generated by investments into new technologies through R&D as a source of increasing returns to capital that made self-sustained growth possible, Lucas developed a model of growth in which investment in physical capital and output growth are driven by the accumulation of human capital.[5] These endogenous growth models are less concerned with steady-state growth, and more with the factors that explain why some economies grow faster than others.[6]

With endogenous growth theory, may of the ideas central to early development economists like increasing returns associated with both internal economies of scale in industrial production, and technological externalities, as well as an elastic supply of labour in the early stages of development, reappeared in development economics albeit now in more formalised exposition.[7] This convergence in ideas and explanations of growth notwithstanding, differences in economic methodology between the first and second generation of development economists prevailed, with crucial implications for development policy and assistance.

7.2 Methodological Considerations

The above discussed changes that characterise the neoclassical resurgence in development economics, namely the application of universal behavioural assumptions, the high degree of abstraction and formalisation of economic models, the shift of attention from the macro-level to the foundation of models on microeconomic principles, and the shift in the perspective from short-run to a long-run decision making, are all changes that basically relate to issues of methodology in development research. Many of the retrospectively misleading implications of the application of neoclassical theory for the explanation of economic phenomena in low-income countries can indeed be related to their underlying method of research. Some methodological considerations are therefore warranted to better understand the outcomes and policy conclusions from the neoclassical era in development economics.

---

[5] An augmented Solow growth model that includes accumulation of human as well as physical capital has also been used by Mankiw et al. (1992) to understand international differences in income per capita.

[6] See Section 8.3 below for a discussion of the voluminous body of empirical literature that emerged since the work of Romer and Lucas that examines correlations of growth with "deeper" determinants of economic performance such as geography and institutions.

[7] See Ros (2005) for an analysis of the relevance of the first generation of development economists for modern growth theory. Ros argues that early development economists actually offer a more promising path away from the neoclassical model of growth than contemporary contributions to endogenous growth theory.

The scientific method to comprehend and predict real phenomena in neoclassical economics is to logically deduct their behaviour from other known phenomena. This requires a logical structure, which in neoclassical economics frequently takes the form of a mathematical model, but which can also consist of a verbal description of objects and their properties and interrelations, a graphical illustration as common to many game-theoretic models, or any other form that satisfies the rules of logic. But a logical structure alone does not make for an economic theory. It merely provides a system to organise factual observations, to classify them in categories and to define these. Thereby, the logical structure is instrumental to facilitate the researcher's understanding of real phenomena, and helps him to evaluate their relevance for explaining a set of concrete problems. Alfred Marshall referred to the logical structure of a theory as its "language", designed to promote "systematic and organised methods of reasoning" (Marshall 1925 [1885], p. 164).

According to Milton Friedman, who clearly shaped the methodological underpinnings of the neoclassical paradigm, this language element of economic theory has no substantive content; it represents a set of tautologies, which are true by definition, as they are based on real observations (Friedman 1953). If a theory is to be able to predict the consequences of action, it has to entail substantive hypotheses and assumptions as well. Hypotheses provide theoretical explanations or predictions of the behaviour of a particular class of phenomena. Assumptions are necessary to extract from the complex circumstances of reality those elements which are considered crucial for the class of phenomena to be explained. Hypotheses can be tested against the facts, that is, by comparison of their predictions with experience.[8] As long as the evidence from experience confirms the predictions, a hypothesis remains valid. Conversely, a hypothesis is refuted if its predictions are contradicted by experience. In economic science, however, the evidence is almost never complete. This is why hypotheses can only be "confirmed", and never fully "proven", by factual evidence. Unlike tautologies, predictions from hypotheses must therefore never be taken as truths, but rather as statements of probability or tendency about the behaviour of a real phenomenon (ibid.). Friedman was very intent on pointing out that the validity of a theory should be judged on the basis of the accuracy of its predictions and never on the basis of the conformity of its assumptions to reality. He compellingly argued against the view that a theoretical hypothesis should be rejected if its underlying assumptions were found to be unrealistic. For Friedman, the relevant question about the assumptions of a theory was not that they are descriptively "realistic", but whether they are sufficiently good approximations for the purpose at hand (ibid., p. 15).

This view has yet to be distinguished from situations in which assumptions fail to account for elements of reality upon which the explanation of a particular phenomenon is crucially dependent. Situations like this arise when established theories

---

[8]See Section 9.2.2 for a discussion of why the role of empirical research in theoretic analysis should actually be twofold: empirical data is vital for testing the validity of hypotheses, but empirical data from observations of the relevant reality is equally important as a basis for the construction of meaningful hypotheses.

are generalised and extended to circumstances that differ from those, for which they had originally been formulated. In this case, Friedman argues that the assumptions are false not in the sense that they are inaccurate descriptive representations of a relevant segment of reality, but because they no longer bear any significant relation to reality under the new circumstances. Therefore, the assumptions are false because the theory does not hold under the new circumstances. Friedman's concern was to emphasise that this is very different from concluding that the theory is invalid because its assumptions were found to be false – a conclusion which, according to him, has been a frequent source of the erroneous belief that a theory can be tested by its assumptions.[9] Despite these insights, it had been exactly those fallacies against which Friedman advised, to which the second generation of development economists fell victim. By applying neoclassical theory to the contexts of low-income countries, they carried with them all those assumptions which represented approximations of the realities of advanced countries, but which bore no significant relation to the realities of developing countries.

How does neoclassical theory reach from assumptions to its relevant variables? As the primary aim of neoclassical theory is to predict, rather than merely to explain economic behaviour, it requires that all relevant determinants of an economic phenomenon have to be objectively measurable and subjectable to formal treatment in mathematical models. The methodological approach of neoclassical economics therefore mostly relies on the use of aggregate variables. For instance, in the neoclassical treatment of equilibrium analysis, the subjectively determined choices by individual actors are made objectively measurable by assuming *ex post* that the plans of all individuals are known in form of aggregate demand or supply schedules. This method is founded on the assumption of methodological individualism, which forms an essential part of modern neoclassical economics and implies that all economic phenomena can be ultimately explained by aggregating over the behaviour of individuals.[10] Applied to the study of low-income countries, this method may easily issue into a misleading picture of economic activity. For instance, aggregating over the measurable (i.e. monetary) part of poor households consumption expenditures may give an adequate impression of their spending power on markets, but seriously understates their real consumption patterns which also result from informal, non-market transactions such as the value of their own subsistence production, intra-family services, or in-kind contributions from local community groups. Similarly, as noted in Sect. 2.1.1 earlier, poor people do make

---

[9] For Friedman, the only acceptable test of the validity of a theoretical hypothesis was comparison of its prediction with the evidence. But the predictions from a theory the assumptions of which are false may be contradicted by the evidence exactly for that reason. Thus, as Friedman acknowledges, "the two supposedly independent tests reduce to one test" (ibid. p. 15)

[10] The term methodological individualism was first used by Schumpeter in his 1908 work *Das Wesen und der Hauptinhalt der theoretischen Nationalökonomie* (Leipzig: Duncker and Humblot) with reference to Max Weber, who had introduced the doctrine as a methodological precept for the social sciences in the first chapter of his *Economy and Society* (Berkeley: University of California Press, [1922] 1978).

substantial investments, for instance, by clearing and improving fallow land, by constructing their own dwellings, or by the breeding of livestock. But these forms of capital formation involve almost no monetary expenditure and are therefore ignored in official statistics, as well as in the specification of modes of development theories in the neoclassical tradition. Yet, for the understanding of economic activity in low-income countries, they are highly significant both quantitatively and qualitatively.

Over and above its reliance on aggregate variables, the methodological approach of neoclassical economics is characterised by analysing these variables subject to several *ceteris paribus* conditions (lat. for all other influencing factors held constant). This allows the partial analysis of a specific causal relationship by intentionally ignoring the influence of all other independent variables on the dependent variable (i.e. by holding all the other relevant factors constant). The *ceteris paribus* condition is thus essential for both the predictive purpose of neoclassical theory, as well as for its formalisation in mathematical models. However, the methodologically correct use of the *ceteris paribus* clause, as a way to isolate the effects of a particular variable from a complex reality, requires that only those variables are assumed to be constant which are independent of a theory's explanatory (i.e. independent) variables. This type of analysis thus fits squarely within the view, most prominently advanced by Myrdal (1957), that social and economic processes in low-income countries are determined by a complex of interlocking, circular and cumulative changes.[11] Moreover, economic realities in low-income countries are strongly influenced by noneconomic factors belonging to the realm of informal behavioural norms or non-market economic interactions which in turn are in no way independent of changes in conventional economic variables.[12]

The above types of methodological problem have in fact already been noticeable in classical economics. An instructive account of these problems and their implications is provided in Joseph A. Schumpeter's methodological criticism of David Ricardo's classical works. In his *History of Economic Analysis*, Schumpeter called Ricardo's approach to economic inquiry the "Ricardian Vice" and set forth that

> [h]is interest was in the clear-cut result of direct, practical significance. In order to get this, he cut that general system to pieces, bundled up as large parts of it as possible, and put them in cold storage – so that as many things as possible should be frozen and "given". He then piled one simplifying assumption upon another until, having really settled everything by these assumptions, he set up simple one-way relations so that, in the end, the desired results emerged almost as tautologies (Schumpeter 1954, pp. 472–473).

---

[11] The causal ambiguity that may result from this type of research method has serious implications for the practical value of theoretical findings for policymaking. For a further discussion of these implications see Sect. 9.2.1 below.

[12] The implications of omitting significant explanatory variables from the analysis of economic phenomena in low-income countries are further discussed in Sect. 9.2.2 below.

7.3 Neoclassical Welfare Economics and Methods of Project Appraisal

The second generation of development economists' fondness for market-based reforms notwithstanding, these reforms had ultimately to be implemented by governments. To ensure that public decision-making led to the efficient allocation of scarce resources and to the maximisation of economic welfare, several techniques and efficiency criteria were invoked to guide the choice of policies and the appraisal of associated development projects. A good illustration of the methods of public project appraisal as practiced since the late 1970s is social cost–benefit analysis, a technique firmly rooted in the utilitarian tradition of neoclassical welfare economics. The following discussion is intended to give a glimpse of the operational difficulties and ideological controversies that accompany the application of neoclassical techniques to non-market decision-making on development policies and projects.

7.3.1 Social Cost: Benefit Analysis

Noble Laureate Jan Tinbergen was among the first economists to develop and recommend social cost–benefit analysis as a technique for improving decision-making processes in development planning (Tinbergen 1967). In 1969, Ian Little and James Mirrlees wrote their *Manual of Industrial Project Analysis in Development Countries* for the OECD, a study related to the work of Tinbergen. Important contributions have also been provided by Amartya Sen, Partha Daspypta and Stephen Marglin in their research on social cost–benefit analyses on behalf of the United Nations Industrial Development Organization (Daspypta et al. 1972). Among the many more neoclassical economists who shaped the methods of public project evaluation, Arnold Harberger, Edward Mishan and Maurice Scott deserve mention.

In most general terms, social cost–benefit analysis is an appraisal tool by which the social desirability of undertaking a public project is assessed. Specifically, its purpose is to allow public decision-makers to arrive at informed choices about alternative plans of how specific social objectives are to be implemented. It is thus as much a tool for project selection, as it is a technique for project appraisal and evaluation. In this context, a project is referred to as any public action that involves the move from a given social state to another. The scope of the analysis is hence a very broad one, ranging from particular public investment decisions (public expenditure projects) to the undertaking of any proposed change in public regulatory policy. Since all such projects pursue social objectives, and are to be judged in terms of changes in social welfare (i.e. economic welfare accruing to society as a whole), it is not sufficient to account for their private costs and benefits alone, as it would be the case if private investment decisions were concerned. Instead, all kinds of external effects, which are usually not reflected in market prices, have to be enumerated as well. In other cases, market prices may be distorted, which makes them equally useless for valuing the social costs and benefits of a proposed project. To accommodate these valuation problems, Little and Mirrlees (1969) proposed the use of "accounting prices" or "shadow prices" to value all effects that accrue to society from the implementation of a project in terms of an objectively measurable unit of account. In social cost–benefit analysis, shadow prices are instrumental for both the adjustment of (price-distorted) market items and the valuation of non-market items.

7.3.2 Shadow Pricing

In cases where market prices are distorted, for instance due to taxation, subsidies or equivalent distortions resulting from foreign exchange, trade and labour policies, the purpose of shadow pricing is to correct a project's financial inflows and outflows by those amounts that actually represent a mere transfer of wealth on the level of society as a whole.[13] Furthermore, shadow prices are used where price distortions stem from market imperfections that result in prices well above marginal cost.[14] A practical procedure given by Little and Mirrlees (1969) for adjusting existing market prices in ways to reflect a project's social implications is to value a project's inputs and outputs at world prices (or more strictly, in terms of border prices), in order to eliminate the effects of imperfections in the domestic price system on the outcome of a social cost–benefit analysis. This approach is straightforward if applied to the valuation of tradeable goods, but is excessively complicated when a project also involves non-tradeable goods such as services, construction work or water and electricity supply. A variant of this approach that has widely been recognised and adopted by both project practitioners and researchers was to choose a *numéraire* as an invariant unit of account for expressing shadow prices that is applicable to both tradeable and nontradeable goods. If all cost and benefit items are expressed in terms of such a common yardstick, it is assumed that the flaws of an economy's domestic price system can be bypassed. Little and Mirrlees (1969) suggested treating foreign exchange as such an invariant unit of account. Shadow prices will then coincide with the border price of a unit of a specific commodity after its conversion into units of foreign currency at the official exchange rate.

A second area where shadow pricing was considered relevant concerns cases in which market prices do not capture the full impact that a transaction had on the level

---

[13] For instance, an *ad valorem* tax on project inputs is an internal transfer within the public sector as it is a debit from the public project's accounts, but at the same time enters the public tax authority's accounts as a credit. From a social cost accounting point of view, the tax value hence cancels out, with no cost to society.

[14] Suppose, for instance, that a project input is produced by a monopolist. Then the implicit loss in consumer surplus is offset by an extra gain earned by factors. Unless one accounts for potential distributional implications, the effect on social cost pattern is zero, which implies that monopoly rents should be deducted from the relevant input's market price to obtain its shadow value (Scott 1990).

of society as a whole, that is, where a project generates externalities or spill-over effects that are not accounted for in market prices. As social costs are made up by the sum of private and external costs (or benefits, respectively), all project-related external effects have to be identified, valued and offset against their respective cost- or benefit-position in order to obtain their shadow value. Finally, a related need to compute shadow prices for the conduct of social cost–benefit analyses emerges when a project's inputs or outputs are not marketed at all. In such circumstances, shadow prices are understood as means to reflect the scarcity of a specific project resource. Environmentally related project outcomes are an area where shadow prices were applied in this sense. Since environmental goods have no production costs that could be used to approximate their value, the analyst has to compute their shadow price from people's expected marginal utilities of consumption of that particular environmental good. Especially the measurement of non-marketed goods on a monetary scale requires the design of some kind of "artificial market" where preferences for these items are stated in analogy to the formation of prices of marketed goods. The valuation methods that have been designed for this purpose intend to derive consumers' preferences either from direct preference statements (contingent valuation methods), or indirectly from their behaviour in dealing with non-marketed goods or effects (revealed preference methods).

7.3.3 *Time Discounting*

Divergences between privately determined market prices and their social implications abound not only with regard to commodity and factor prices, but also concerning their values over time. Since a project's effects accrue over an extended period of time, but have for reasons of effective project selection to be comparable with alternative plans at a single point in time, future costs and benefits have to be discounted at an appropriately chosen social rate of time discount. Discounting of future costs and benefits implies that future items are given less weight than current ones. In the case of a private investment project, the income from that project will usually be discounted by using the prevailing market interest rate (or the rate of return on a safe alternative investment) to arrive at the present value of its benefits, which can then be measured against the costs. This may not be so regarding the future benefits and costs of a public investment. Several approaches have been developed to determine social discount rates, including reference rates such as the social cost of capital, or the social rate of time preference in consumption. As the expected future benefits of a project, and thus its social desirability relative to alternative courses of action, depend sensibly on its rate of time discount, the choice of the discount rate was, and still is, a matter of intense debate.[15]

---

[15] A recent case in point, that also illustrates how deeply techniques based on neoclassical welfare economics are still entrenched in contemporary development thinking, is the Copenhagen Consensus. This project consists of a panel of eight distinguished economists who gathered in 2004 to answer the question "how to spend 50 billion US-Dollars to make the world a better place"

7.3.4 Choice of the Time Horizon

Controversial debates abound not only on the value of the discount rate, but also with regard to the choice of the appropriate time horizon over which project-induced social costs and benefits have to be accounted for. Irrespective of a project's limited period of operation, it may well live on through various kinds of multiplier effects by which the project's main impact indirectly also affects the welfare of society in the more distant future, let alone that of future generations. This question about the time period considered in the appraisal process, as the choice of the rate of time discount applied over that period, has particular implications for the intertemporal and intergenerational distribution of welfare. Sen (1979), who strongly favours the recognition of future generations in social cost–benefit analysis, argued that benefits to future generations also yield utility to individuals today and will hence lower the disutility resulting from a sacrifice in present consumption, that is, it lowers the social time preference rate and in turn increases the present value of future benefits.

A long time horizon, however, also makes social cost–benefit calculations increasingly susceptible to unanticipated changes in the project environment. Nothing can be known, for instance, about people's preferences and tastes, or the technologies available in distant times. But judgements about economic welfare are meaningful only under the assumption of constant preferences. Therefore, the longer a project's life span, the less reliable are the results obtained under its present assumptions. Additional problems abound if time horizons are chosen across generations, as this requires judgements about the intergenerational distribution of income, which are often inspired by ethical considerations along with economic ones (The Economist 1999).[16]

(Lomborg 2006). Their evaluation resulted in highest priority for projects with a relatively short time horizon, such as measures to prevent the spread of HIV/AIDS, policies to reduce malnutrition and hunger, trade liberalisation, and the controlling and treating of malaria. Poorly ranked were instead long-term challenges such as addressing climate change. These results have widely been criticised especially with regard to the discounting methods used. Not only is it problematic to compare projects with very different time horizons, the Copenhagen Consensus panel also applied different discount rates to different projects (e.g. a discount rate of 5% for actions against climate change, but a rate of only 3% for fighting HIV/AIDS), which of course affected the rank a project gained.

[16] A related issue of relevance for the economic appraisal of public projects is the treatment of the risks of whether a projected benefit actually accrues to society (in technical terms expressed by the variance of projected values around their mean). Accounting for risky outcomes has the effect that such outcomes have to be valued at less than their expected risk-free value. This either happens directly through the choice of a discount rate that then includes a risk premium, or indirectly by provisioning for risk and uncertainties, which then increases the cost of a project.

7.3.5 Implications of Neoclassical Welfare Economics

These and other limitations of social cost–benefit analysis mirror the problems that abounded in theory. Welfare economists have led long and controversial debates about appropriate approaches and criteria for making judgements about the desirability of alternative social arrangements. The neoclassical approach of adding all individual's net benefits up to a single metric rests upon the assumption that social welfare is an additive cardinal function of individual utilities. This requires the additional assumption that preference are exogenously given and stable, individuals have interpersonally comparable utility functions, and it is possible to construct a social welfare function from aggregating over all individual utility functions. Only on the basis of these assumptions is it possible to express the net benefit of a project to society by a single objective metric.

A very important implication of the theoretical assumptions that underlie the method of social cost–benefit analysis is that it focuses on achieving allocative efficiency, leaving concerns for the distribution of income outside the scope of the appraisal process.[17] The reason is that if a project's outcomes are quantifiable in some unit of account, then, given decreasing marginal utility of money, one extra unit of the project's benefits to the poor should be given a larger weight than the same unit in the hands of a rich person. If applied this way, projects the benefits of which flow primarily to the poor shall be favoured in the project selection process. Many economists, such as Harberger (1978), Mishan (1976) and Musgrave (1969), argued against the pursuit of redistributive objectives as part of the selection and appraisal process of development projects, and instead suggested a sequential approach. This means that social cost–benefit analysis is supposed to be limited on the pursuit of allocative objectives (i.e. the maximisation of total output), while the arrangement of an equitable distribution of the gains is left to separate distributional policies.[18]

If, however, the objective is to achieve both allocative and distributive efficiency, or if, for other reasons, the notion of cardinal utility is rejected, then ordinal welfare criteria such as the Pareto criterion provide alternative decision rules. The Pareto criterion, and other criteria derived from it, is defined in terms of ordinal utility

---

[17] In fact, until the late 1980s, the notion was widespread that achieving a high rate of growth of overall income through promoting the accumulation of capital by the rich and most productive parts of society would eventually "trickle down" to all parts of society through job creation and increased economic opportunities, and would thus indirectly also benefit the poor.

[18] Some attempts to accommodate redistributional concerns in the design of social cost-benefit analyses were developed, for instance, by Ray (1984). He proposed to distinguish only a few income levels and to apply progressive weights on them (i.e. the lower the income the greater the weights). A weight of unity is then proposed to be given to the income level that corresponds to the national level of income per head. As an alternative approach, he suggested giving the same weights to all income groups except those with the lowest level of income.

alone, a property that explicitly circumvents the postulate of interpersonal comparisons of utility and instead only indicates the social desirability of one project, or social state, relative to an alternative course of action. It can thus only rank, but not objectively measure, the social desirability of alternative project or policy options. Pareto optimality prevails if a change in a social arrangement, or a reallocation of resources, makes at least one individual better off without making any other individual worse off. The Pareto welfare criterion is also satisfied if those who gain from a change are able to actually compensate those who incur a loss under the new regime. That way, the Pareto criterion combines two propositions in one principle: an allocative one (represented by a project's effects on the social product), as well as a distributional one (represented by the compensation of net losers by net gainers). Further welfare criteria have been developed that differ specifically in their approaches towards the problem of income distribution. An overview of these criteria is given in Box 7.1.

Box 7.1 Welfare criteria from Ordinal Utility Theory

Pareto welfare criterion: A Pareto improvement takes place when a social rearrangement makes some better off without making anyone worse off. This can be illustrated graphically as done in Figure (a). The diagram is in ordinal utility space; the curves (U and U') are loci of points that indicate different levels of economic welfare (or real income), while different points on the same curve indicate distinct ways of distributing the given welfare between the two individuals (or groups), A and B, the utility of which is shown on the respective axes of the diagram. The curves are called utility possibility curves, sometimes also compensation curves or redistribution curves. In Figure (a), only a move from point Q_1 to point Q_2 is Pareto optimal (where $U < U'$). Moves to points such as Q_3 or Q_4 are not, because they make only one of the two individuals better off while leaving the other worse off.

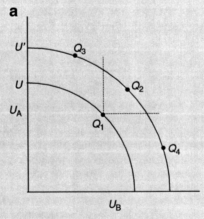

(a) Pareto welfare criterion and Kaldor–Hicks criterion

Box 7.1 (continued)

Hicks–Kaldor criterion: Because the Pareto criterion is constrained to changes in social arrangements where no one is made worse off, Nicholas Kaldor and John Richard Hicks, independently, suggested that economic welfare is also increased at points such as Q_3 and Q_4 relative to Q_1 [in Figure (a)] if those who gain from the change could (costless, as they assume) compensate those who lose from it and would still be better off relative to the initial position. Only if compensations are actually made, is an actual Pareto improvement attained. If not, the move is describes as a potential Pareto improvement. Those who favour the use of the Hicks–Kaldor criterion for project evaluation restrict the appraisal process on allocative considerations while leaving the question of how to distribute a project's benefits to the political decision-making process.

Scitovsky criterion: According to Tibor Scitovsky it is possible that a move from one social arrangement to another [say, from Q_1 to Q_2 in Figure (b) is characterised by a potential Pareto improvement, but that the reverse move (i.e. from Q_2 to Q_1) satisfies the same criterion. The reason why this apparent contradiction may arise is essentially that there might be a significantly different distribution of income (or utility) after the change that, if regarded as the new status quo, would make a move back to the initial position (i.e. Q_1) desirable by the same criterion. Scitovsky therefore proposed a double criterion that requires, in a first step, that any move from a position should pass the Hicks–Kaldor test (i.e. that the net gains to one group exceed the net losses to the other), and must, in a second step, fail that test for the reverse move.

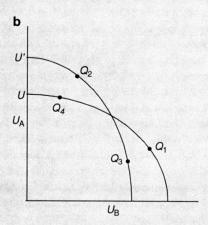

(b) Scitovsky criterion and Little criterion

Little criterion: Little (1957 and 1979) intended to reconciles real world judgements with theoretical analysis by separating allocative and distributional judgements and then combining them in a dual criterion. His criterion says that a change is desirable if it would result in a good redistribution of wealth and if the potential losers could not profitably bribe the potential gainers to oppose that change. According to Little, a move from Q_1 to Q_2 [in Figure (b)] would involve a good redistribution of wealth if a point such as Q_4 (attained through lump sum transfers, i.e. a redistributive movement along the initial utility possibility curve) would be preferable to Q_1. If the Little criterion is applied for project selection purposes, judgements about a project's social desirability rest upon its effects on economic welfare, that is, on both allocative and distributive considerations.

Sources: Mishan (1976); Little (1957, 1979); Cullis and Jones (1992).

7.4 Development Policies and the "Washington Consensus"

At the policy level, the neoclassical treatment of development problems implied that professional thinking about strategies for development was much occupied with the search for universal, all-purpose remedies for the problems of low-income countries. The convergence of views on these remedies was indeed so high that a consensus emerged about a set of policy reforms that were considered most contributive to economic growth in less developed countries. Initially conceived as a guide for international programmes by the Washington-based institutions, especially the World Bank and the IMF, to assist the development of Latin America, these consensus policies were soon extended to other developing countries as well by development economists both inside and outside Washington. In its original version, this Washington Consensus combined macroeconomic stabilisation measures with policies aimed at changing the structure of the economy in order to achieve a more efficient allocation and use of resources. Williamson (1990) defines the Washington Consensus policies as pursuing the following priorities: Privatisation; deregulation; trade liberalisation; a competitive exchange rate; liberalisation of inflows of foreign direct investment; interest rate liberalisation; tax reform towards lower marginal rates and a broader tax base; fiscal discipline; redirection of public expenditure priorities toward fields such as primary health care, primary education and infrastructure; and secure property rights. In fact, as Rodrik (2006) points out, the actual Washington Consensus policies went much farther in their neoliberalist and market-fundamentalist stance than what Williamson had anticipated from the vantage point of the late 1980s. This holds true in particular for financial liberalisation, the deregulation of international capital flows, and the mass privatisation of state-owned enterprises in Latin America and Eastern Europe.[19]

---

[19] Sharp and prolonged declines in output in Eastern Europe, and costly financial crises in Mexico (1994), East Asia (1997), Brazil (1998), the Russian Federation (1998), Turkey (2000), and Argentina (2002) were among the unexpected results of these policies.

The main instrument for implementing these priorities in developing countries was policy-based lending, either in the form of macroeconomic stabilisation packages, or through structural adjustment loans. The rationale behind both was to make the disbursement of development loans contingent upon the implementation of certain predetermined policy reforms by the recipient governments. These conditionalities comprised commitments to, among others, balancing the government budget through liberalisation of prices, privatisation of state-owned enterprises, cutting of subsidies and other government spending; the introduction of restrictive monetary policies to curb inflation; or liberalisation of foreign trade and exchange rate regimes through abolishment of export and import licences, quantitative restrictions and tariffs.

Conditionality (i.e. the provision of aid in return for explicit negotiated commitments to policy reform) was thought to provide sufficient incentives to recipient governments to embark on policy change that they had otherwise been unwilling or unable to implement on their own. But apart from the fact that these incentives proved to be very short-lived, the main problem with aid conditionality was that it had been used by Western governments and financing institutions as a means to "buy" reforms from developing countries, which the donors then consequentially "owned" (Collier 2002). There was little scope for the use of local knowledge and participation of recipient countries in the choice of policies that donors demanded in return for their loans or grants. Furthermore, aid conditionalities were lacking the incentive-compatibility that would have been necessary to encourage a national consensus on all levels of society towards social change and sustainable development. The disillusioning lesson from such policy-based aid was that the countries, especially in East and South Asia, which had indeed seen spectacular growth and social progress in the 1990s, had hardly followed any recognisable economic model advocated by international financing institutions.

Chapter 8
The Third Generation: Institutional Turn and the "New Development Economics"

Till today, the policies of the Washington Consensus, just as their neoclassical foundations, are still a vital part of development economics. Since the late 1990s, there was, however, a growing recognition that economic policy reforms will remain ineffective if they are not complemented by a similar effort to improve a country's underlying institutional environment. For instance, trade liberalisation requires, among other things, effective fiscal institutions that are able to compensate for lost trade revenue. Capital markets, an efficient banking system, or labour market institutions that can reduce transitional unemployment are just some of the institutional preconditions for the effective implementation of mass privatisation programmes. Nobel Laureate Douglass C. North was among the first to caution that free markets do not in themselves mean efficient markets, as the latter require a well-specified legal system with effective enforcement mechanisms and a set of attitudes towards contracting and trading that would encourage people to engage in trade and production at low costs (North 1986).

The new stance over the Washington Consensus has aptly been summarised by Fukuyama (2002, p. 24) in a paper in which he introduces the concept of social capital to the agenda of development economics:

> The failure of the Washington Consensus was one of omission, rather than of policy. Privatization of inefficient nationalized assets, reduction of trade and investment barriers, phasing out of subsidies that distort market prices, industry deregulation, and market integration into the global economy are all unexceptionable policies that, in the long run, are necessary for economic growth. Any rethinking of the development problem should not reject these policies as long-run objectives. The problem with the Washington consensus was not that it was misdirected, but rather that it was incomplete. One of the ways in which it was incomplete was its failure to take account of institutional and cultural factors. [...] What we have learned over the past decade, then, is not that liberalization does not work, but that economic policy by itself is not sufficient to induce development.

This conclusion has stimulated numerous attempts at incorporating proposals for institution-building and so called "second-generation" reforms into the original consensus. Although these moves towards a Post-Washington Consensus broadened the set of relevant areas of intervention, they unintentionally abided by the idea that the diverse problems of less developed economies could be remedied by a one-size-fits-all consensus on policy reforms.

The transition experience of former communist countries in Eastern Europe provided a particular lesson that further stimulated research on the institutional determinants of development. The lesson was that the transition to a market economy required more than dismantling old institutions and reassigning their functions to the market. Instead, it became clear that markets required the building of a system of supporting institutions that secured property rights, enabled the enforcement of contracts, regulated externalities, stabilised the business environment, and provided a minimum level of social security.

The institutional turn in development economics thus went farther than the first attempts at devising a Post-Washington Consensus. In particular, the discipline gained much from the application of findings from the New Institutional Economics to the study of development problems. At the same time, modifications and extensions to neoclassical framework, such as the imperfect information paradigm, raised the prospect of making the assumptions of neoclassical theory more appropriate for the study of economic realities in low-income countries. The question is if this "New Development Economics" already represents the needed paradigm shift in development economics away from neoclassical theory.

8.1 Imperfect Information and the "New Development Economics"

Already in 1986 did Joseph Stiglitz publish an article titled "The New Development Economics" in which he applied his findings from past research on the similarities and differences between less and more developed economies, and in particular his imperfect information paradigm, to study the organisation of the rural sector in low-income countries (Stiglitz 1986). His approach consisted of five main assumptions: (i) individuals in low-income countries are rational; (ii) information is costly (which implies that individuals may behave very differently from what would be expected if they had full information); (iii) institutions change in reaction to changes in information and other transaction costs; (iv) with imperfect information, and hence incomplete markets, the economy is constrained Pareto inefficient (meaning that scope for Pareto improvements exist); and (v) such a Pareto improvement can potentially be brought about by the government if it has sufficient knowledge about the structure of the economy, if it has the same information as private agents, and if Pareto efficiency is the main objective of government policies.

Based on this general framework, Stiglitz formulated a theory of rural organisation with specific emphasis on sharecropping as a prevalent form of rural organisation in less developed countries.[1] Under the assumption of full information, sharecropping (i.e. the working of land the worker does not own in return for a predetermined

---

[1] See also the analysis of alternative institutions for contract enforcement in low-income countries in Sect. 4.2.

share of the output) must be considered an inefficient institution; the alternatives of wage employment or renting of the land provide potentially more efficient modes of organising relations between (landless) farmers and landowners. By contrast, if imperfect information is assumed, several incentive problems become apparent which provide a plausible explanation for the persistence of sharecropping relative to alternative arrangements in rural areas of low-income countries. Imperfect information implies that wage employment involves monitoring costs for the landowner if he wants to ensure that the worker has an incentive to work. Renting arrangements solve the incentive problem, but involve enforcement costs for the landlord if the worker cannot pay his rent, and may as well be unattractive for risk-averse workers as they have to pay the landlord even if they harvest less than the value of the rent. Sharecropping, instead, solves both kinds of problems as the calculation of the rent as a share of the worker's crops involves a risk-sharing mechanism that solves the incentive problems that characterise the alternative modes of rural organisation.

The sharecropping example represents just one example of how the assumption of imperfect information raises issues like incentive, motivation, and monitoring problems which lead to markedly different results, and would remain unexplained by neoclassical economics in its traditional form. This conclusion reflects a broader direction in the work of Stiglitz, which characterises his contributions to development economics, and which he described in his Nobel lecture as follows:

> My first visits to the developing world [...] made an indelible impression on me. Models of perfect markets, as badly flawed as they might seem for Europe or America, seemed truly inappropriate for these countries. While many of the key assumptions that went into the competitive equilibrium model seemed not to fit these economies well, I was particularly struck by the imperfections of information, the absence of markets, and the pervasiveness and persistence of seemingly dysfunctional institutions, such as sharecropping. [...] There was a massive discrepancy between the models we had been taught and what I saw (Stiglitz 2002, p. 460).

There is considerable overlap between the Stiglitzian new development economics and recent contributions that apply the theoretical framework of the New Institutional Economics to the study of less developed countries. But Stiglitz would probably disagree if his imperfect information paradigm was treated as a complete subset of the New Institutional Economics. For instance, he did not regard information costs as conceptionally equivalent to transaction costs. He rather saw an extra explanatory value from accounting for the cost of information for the understanding of a wide range of persistent market failures and incentive problems, such as adverse selection, moral hazard problems, coordination failures, problems relating to the distribution of income, or poverty traps. As information economics provides a structure for explaining these otherwise unexplained phenomena, it goes beyond and extends traditional neoclassical theory. But that information economics replaces the neoclassical paradigm, as Stiglitz (2002) claims, is questioned. Ravi Kanbur, in a comment at the conference for Joe Stiglitz's 60th birthday noted that "there is one aspect of the [neoclassical] textbook model that has been central to the Stiglitzian paradigm, and is therefore also central to modern development economics. This is the assumption that individuals behave according to the textbook axioms of rational choice" (Kanbur 2002, p. 1).

Together with other contributions on imperfect competition, imperfect markets, incomplete contracts, or bounded rationality, the imperfect information paradigm is part of a wider effort to broaden the scope and explanatory power of the neoclassical framework for the study of less developed countries. This very motivation has also given rise to the resurgence of institutional explanations of economic development and the application of findings from the New Institutional Economics on problems of low-income countries.

8.2 The New Institutional Economics and Development

According to North (1992), the New Institutional Economics is an attempt to incorporate a theory of institutions into orthodox economics. It builds on, modifies, and extends neoclassical economics to permit it to hold under a broader range of different institutional structures. It maintains the fundamental assumption of scarcity, which implicates competition. But it dilutes the assumption of instrumental rationality which says that individual agents act perfectly rationally and on the basis of perfect information and foresight. Rationality is kept as a behavioural assumption, but in modern institutional theory, rational choices are not just determined by economic factors alone, but also bound by the constraints of an individual's institutional environment, which implies additional consideration of social, ethical, political cultural and historical influences on an individual's decision field. Furthermore, institutional theory sees individuals as members of communities, firms and other organisations, rather than as the *homo economicus* who autonomously maximises his utility. Correspondingly, institutional economics focuses on the relation or transaction between two or more individuals as its unit of analysis, rather than on just the individual alone (Bromley 2003).[2] Most importantly, however, new institutional theory abandons the assumptions of a frictionless, transaction cost free world which is precisely what made neoclassical economics an institution-free theory (North 1992).

Within this framework, institutions are defined as formal political, social, and legal rules (as codified, among others, in constitutions, statute law, common law, and other regulations, as well as their respective enforcement mechanisms), and the informal constraints that are derived from people's attitudes, mental models and ideologies, and that find expression in the norms, values and conventions to which they feel bound.

---

[2]This relates to the question of whether the New Institutional Economics adheres to the precept of methodological individualism. If the unit on analysis in modern institutional theory is the transaction between two or more individuals, methodological individualism, in a narrow sense, would not persist. Yet, North seems to disagree when he states that "institutions are a creation of human beings, they evolve and are altered by human beings, hence our theory must begin with the individual" (North 1990, p. 5).

Together, formal and informal institutions provide the incentive structure of an economy which governs all political, economic, and social interactions (North 1990).

Modern institutional theory is in two ways particularly significant for development economics. First, by introducing transaction costs as a main explanatory variable, institutional theory can contributes to the understanding of how different modes of governance and organisation of economic activity emerge within a given institutional environment. Second, the New Institutional Economics induces development economists to think of development as a dynamic process of institutional change, and provides them with a framework for understanding how institutions, both formal and informal, change over time.[3]

8.2.1 The Concept of Transaction Costs in Institutional Theory

The concept of transaction costs is central to understanding how individuals organise their interactions within a given institutional setting. Under conditions of scarcity, competition leads individuals to organise their interactions in ways that lower the costs associated with their transactions.[4] This, in turn, allows them to find for every type of production or exchange the least transaction cost intensive mode of governance. As discussed in Chap. 3 above, the cost associated with economic transactions, together with the technology employed, influence the level of production costs and hence the productivity of an economy. Moreover, transaction costs also determine the degree of specialisation in an economy, as the division of labour is only possible if there is exchange, and the lower the cost of exchange is, the more specialisation will be possible.

An important insight for development economists, which arises from the discussion of transaction costs, is that each distinctive institutional structure that arises from a particular pattern of transaction costs supports its own generic modes of governance and organisation of economic activity. Very specific and diverse forms of organising economic activity may therefore evolve in different country contexts as a result of their prevailing transaction costs pattern. A further important implication of the transaction cost characteristics of low-income countries is that they compel development economists and policymakers to think in terms of second-best settings. For instance, the transaction costs to developing countries from exporting to foreign markets are often a greater hindrance to trade than are tariff and capital controls. Trade-related transaction costs may thus seriously affect the outcome of

---

[3] By remaining tied to neoclassical economics, the New Institutional Economics is yet not as successful in explaining the dynamic process of institutional change as its predecessor, the old institutional economics of Veblen and Commons has already been more than a century ago. See Sect. 12.4 on their contributions to institutional theory.

[4] The view of institutions as efficient solutions to problems of organisation in a competitive framework has in particular been advanced by Williamson (1975, 1979, 1990). See also Chap. 3.

any trade liberalisation policy as these costs cannot be eliminated even under a fully liberalised trade regime. Therefore, broad generalisations and recourse to universal economic principles, as common to the second generation of development economists, must issue into ambiguous conclusions and misleading policy advice if applied without recognition of the second-best responses to positive transaction costs that characterise economic activity in low-income countries.

8.2.2 The Process of Institutional Change

Another reason why institutional theory is important for the study of economic development is the framework it provides for the analysis of institutional change. According to the New Institutional Economics,[5] institutions are shaped by the interaction of individuals under conditions of scarcity. Competition not only induces them to economise transaction costs within a given institutional setting, it also gives them incentives to acquire new knowledge through learning in order to improve the efficiency of their organisation relative to that of their rivals. In this case, institutional change happens as an endogenous process. But institutional change can also be the result of external influences, like technological change or other events, deliberate or accidental, that change relative prices and thus incentives. Here too, learning is a fundamental source of institutional change, this time induced through the need to adapt to the new circumstances.[6] In both cases, new skills and knowledge are not only associated with a change in formal institutions, they also shape perceptions about opportunities (and hence choices). Perceptions that determine individual choices are derived from the subjective models people have to interpret and process the information they receive. According to Denzau and North (1994), these shared mental models and ideologies represent informal institutions that people construct to make sense out of the world around them. They reflect people's learning experiences and knowledge of the world. The acquisition of new knowledge through learning can thus incrementally alter informal institutions. Because different cultural backgrounds result in different perceptions of reality, and hence in different choices, the economic system will not necessarily have to move towards a single stable equilibrium. Instead, multiple equilibria may occur. This approach to choice, which borrows major insights from cognitive science, contrasts with rational choice models of neoclassical economics in that the latter assume perfect information and thus make the distinction between

---

[5] See especially North (1990, 1992, 1995a). Menard and Shirley (2008) provide a good overview of the New Institutional Economics literature.

[6] The ability of societies to adapt to altered conditions can be described by the concept of adaptive efficiency (North 1995a). Unlike allocative efficiency, which is a static concept valid only within a given set of institutions, adaptive efficiency can serve as a criterion to evaluate an economy's performance in terms of the flexibility of its institutions to adjust to evolving technological, social, political and demographic changes or shocks to the system.

the real world and the individual's culturally-determined perception of it irrelevant.[7]

A further property of institutional change is that it is typically assumed to be incremental, and path-dependent because people have invested into their relationships and organisations under the existing institutional matrix, and have acquired skills and knowledge consistent with it. Path dependency suggests that the investments made into the existing set of institutions constrain choices about the form of future institutions. North (1995b, 2005) believes that the informal constraints from norms and conventions that have deep-seated cultural antecedents are an important source of path dependency. This property of institutional change is often interpreted as being an impediment to deliberate institutional reform. While this consequence of path-dependency is likely with regard to attempts at transplanting a formal institution from more advanced countries into the contexts of low-income countries, institutional reform may still succeed if it is knowledgeable about prevailing mental models and traditions, and incorporates local knowledge and existing informal structures into the design of institutional reforms.[8]

8.2.3 Institution-Building and Policy Reform

The dynamics involved in the evolution and change of institutions suggest that institutional change is ultimately driven by endogenous forces. How then can developing countries be assisted in this process from the outside? Exogenous changes through deliberate policy reforms do have the potential to alter the transaction cost structure of an economy and hence the organisation of interactions within the existing institutional environment. Formal institutions can also be built or changed by deliberate action, for instance, through the passing of new laws in the process of legal reforms. But although such external influences can create new or altered opportunities for individuals and organisations within the existing incentive structure of an economy, they will only translate into lasting institutional change (and hence development) if people's perceptions about these opportunities induce them to learn and acquire new knowledge that is consistent with the new institutional structure. This brings informal institutions into play. These culturally-derived values and norms of behaviour are outside the influence of any externally-imposed institutional reform programme. Yet, they are pivotal for the ultimate success of any such programme – through their influence of individual behaviour and perceptions, and also through their legitimising function for the (new) institutional structure.[9]

---

[7]The implications of considering cultural influences on economic behaviour are further discussed in Sect. 13.1.4.

[8]This argument will further be developed in Sect. 13.2.2.

[9]In this context, North (1984) also refers to informal institutions as the "ideological superstructure" of a society, an expression which has, albeit in a different context, already been used by Karl Marx in his critique of morality.

The limits that informal institutions impose on attempts to deliberately change a country's institutional environment by means of externally-imposed reform policies can be illustrated by way of the following example. Suppose a developing country wishes to implement, with assistance from a foreign aid agency, a regulatory reform programme aimed at lowering the domestic cost of doing business. In line with institutional theory, the causal chain is expected to run from a decrease in transaction costs that opens opportunities for a more efficient organisation of economic activity, which in turn results in raised productivity and investment, and ultimately in an increase in the overall performance of the economy. However, for the expected transaction cost economies to materialise, firms must perceive the new institutional arrangement as an opportunity from which they derive an incentive to invest in the reorganisation of their activities. If they have reason to perceive the new institutional setting as inferior to, or incompatible with the existing one – for instance because most companies operate in the informal sector and are thus not directly affected by changes in the formal regulatory framework – then the proposed reform may not translate into lasting institutional change. Path-dependency can also be an issue. For instance, if firms that operate in the informal sector have invested over generations into alternative informal arrangements,[10] they may prefer to maintain these arrangements rather than to venture to formalise their businesses in order to benefit from the improved formal business environment as a result of the regulatory reform programme.

The example shows how policy outcomes depend on factors internal to the incentive structure of an economy that can hardly be controlled by outside policy-makers. This said, it has to be noted that business regulation is an area where individual perceptions, and hence the behaviour of firms, tend to be far easier to predict than in areas where individual behaviour is more responsive to culture, ideology or other informal constraints. This may, for instance, be the case with regard to reforms in the health system of low-income countries, where cultural beliefs about certain diseases or treatment practices by traditional healers may prevent people from visiting formal health care centres or clinics. Similarly, any reform programme that aims at formalising property rights in assets such as land may be perceived as illegitimate if it colludes with people's collective understandings of how informally held property is possessed, used and exchanged.

In spite of advances at the theoretical level, this understanding of the deep determinants of institutional change is not yet fully reflected in the way in which policymakers and development organisations tend to think about institutions and institutional change. Similarly, most attempts at integrating an institutional theory into development economics are still based on a much narrower definition of institutions than that advanced by North. Not surprisingly, what mostly remains unconsidered are the

---

[10]Note that the term "informal" in connection with economic arrangements and activities in the informal sector is meant in a narrower sense here than the concept of informal institutions of the previous analysis. In the present context, "informal" refers to the extralegal nature of an arrangement in the sense that it is outside the reach of formal law.

informal, culturally-derived constraints on people's choice sets, as this is the part of institutional theory that is the furthest removed from the assumptions of standard neoclassical theory.[11] Narrower (and easier to grasp) definitions of institutions that focus on specific organisational entities, procedural devices, laws and regulatory frameworks are therefore mostly used. Corresponding institutional studies mainly evaluate a country's institutions by the degree of property rights protection, the degree to which laws and regulations are fairly applied, or the extent of corruption. Much of the recent research into the institutional determinants of economic development has actually adopted such narrow definitions, not at least because this made it easier to operationalise institutions in the econometric models of the growing empirical literature on institutions and economic growth.

8.3 Empirical Literature on Institutions and Growth

The third generation of development economists added the quality of a country's institutions to the list of potentially significant determinants of growth. First attempts at applying the theoretical framework of the New Institutional Economics to problems of economic development in low-income countries were published in the early 1990s,[12] followed by critical assessments of the Washington Consensus from an institutional perspective.[13] But the largest part of the literature on the role of institutions in economic development emerged at the turn of the millennium when international donor agencies began to endorse the plea for "getting the institutions right" in their development policies and programmes.[14] These programmes received, and continue to receive, their academic support largely from a burgeoning empirical literature on the relationship between the quality of institutions and long-term growth.[15]

---

[11] Note that these culturally-derived influences on economic behaviour can only be analysed in a meaningful way if research is tied to context. The enormous range of possible cultural adaptations to similar economic situations implies not only that the informal influences on individual choices and institutional change vary with the decision-maker's cultural background, but also that, for this very reason, a given stimulus for institutional change can lead to very different, context-specific outcomes. The argument in favour of context-specific analysis in development economics is further developed in Sect. 9.2. For a further discussion of the influences of cultural factors on economic outcomes in low-income countries see Sect. 13.2.1.

[12] See, for instance, Nabli and Nugent (1986, 1989), Bardhan (1989), North (1995a), and Olson (1996).

[13] See, for instance, Borner (1998), Burki and Perry (1998), and Zattler (2004).

[14] The World Bank devoted its 2002 World Development Report to the subject of institution-building for growth and poverty reduction (World Bank 2001b). The IMF made growth and institutions the subject of its flagship publication, the World Economic Outlook, in 2003 (IMF 2003).

[15] Bardhan (2005) observes that nearly 90% of the papers presented in Development Seminars in the U.S. are now mainly empirical.

Among the early contributions that heralded the institutions-cum-growth literature in both its intent and method were two papers by Stephen Knack and Philip Keefer. Building on earlier contributions to neoclassical growth theory,[16] Knack and Keefer (1995) analysed empirically the influence of institutions on economic performance by using indices comprised of data from evaluations of contract enforceability, the rule of law, and the risk of expropriation as proxies for the security of property rights and hence the quality of a country's institutions. By including these measures of the institutional environment in cross-country growth regressions, they found a strong correlation between the quality of a country's institutions that protect property rights and its growth and convergence to US income levels. Moreover, their results implied that more direct institutional indicators account much better for the influence of institutions on economic growth and investment than the use of indirect variables for the approximation of property rights like indicators of political and civil liberties. The authors reached similar results in a related paper (Knack and Keefer 1997a) in which they employed an extended set of institutional measures (the previous indicators plus the pervasiveness of corruption) to confirm that the ability of poor countries to catch up is largely explained by the quality of their institutions, and not – as the neoclassical convergence thesis purports – by the fact that poor countries grow faster than rich ones due to technological advances and the diminishing returns to capital in the latter. They concluded that weakly performing institutions actually reduce investment and the ability of poor countries to absorb modern technologies from rich countries, which is why they are actually falling behind instead of catching up.

The problem with cross-country regressions, like those performed by Knack and Keefer, is that the resultant high correlation between institutional variables and economic performance does not say anything about the causal relationship between institutions and growth. Besides the original hypothesis that institutions cause growth, it may as well be possible that better institutions are the result of economic progress as institutional change requires time and resources that rich countries may just better afford to invest.[17] This problem of reverse or two-way causality has been addressed in a study by Acemoglu et al. (2001a) who propose settler mortality during the time of colonisation as an instrumental variable for current institutions that accounts for

---

[16] Especially Barro and Sala-i-Martin (1992), and Mankiw et al. (1992). For a further discussion of neoclassical growth theory see Sect. 7.1.

[17] This problem besets as well many other assertions of causality in development economics that will be further discussed in Sect. 9.2.1. In econometric terms, the problem is one of endogeneity of explanatory variables which occurs when the independent and dependent variables in a regression model are jointly determined, i.e. when they affect each other in such a way that the direction of causal effects between them is ambiguous. Endogeneity means that the independent variable is correlated with the error term in a regression model (i.e. $Cov(x,) \neq 0$), which has the effect that the coefficients in an OLS regression are biased and inconsistent. The usual solution to this problem, the use of an instrumental variable instead of an OLS regressor, is an accurate one from an econometric standpoint, but tends to be conceptionally problematic as the theoretical link between the instrument and the independent variable that it replaces is often vague and seldom credible.

the effects of a country's institutional environment on economic performance without being itself correlated with the regressand (i.e. economic growth). This choice of the instrument rests upon the authors' premise that Europeans had build lasting institutions only in those colonies in which local conditions allowed them to settle, while they set up "extractive institutions" (which imply weaker institutions today) in countries with a high prevalence of deadly diseases or other factors that led to high settler mortality. From applying this instrumental variable approach, the authors found strong evidence in support of the positive influence that good institutions have on a country's economic performance.[18]

The primacy of institutions as driver of economic growth received further support by Easterly and Levine (2003) who showed that policy reforms, such as those promoted through the Washington Consensus, did not exert any independent effect on long-term economic performance once the quality of institutions is controlled for in the regression. Moreover, they proved that a country's endowments, like its geographic location, ecological conditions, natural resources, or the prevalence of diseases, have no direct effect on growth, but influence a country's economic performance indirectly through their effects on domestic institutions. Acemoglu et al. (2001b) as well as Rodrik et al. (2002) had come to similar conclusions, while authors of an emerging second stream of literature maintained that both institutions and geographic factors such as resource endowments are critical for explaining a country's economic performance over time.[19]

With the reliance on applied econometrics in the institutions-cum-growth literature, the third generation of development economists entered a strongly empirical phase, after the concentration on theory by its predecessors. This is in part a result of the improvement and easier availability of detailed cross-country and household-level data, as well as advances in the tools of applied econometrics. It is, however, also a reflection of an effort to increase the policy-relevance of development research. But can this truly be achieved by a flood of cross-country regressions? As Rodrik (2007) points out, the recent empirical literature actually tells us very little about how the institutional determinants of economic growth are to be attained. In other words, knowing that institutions matter does not yet give policy-makers and working professionals in developing countries and at international aid agencies the kind of operational guidance they need to devise effective development strategies and programmes. On the operational level, knowledge of causal relations is required, whereas regression analyses yields correlations between factors which do not automatically prove causation. Especially where problems of

---

[18] An alternative approach, which allows for a larger sample of countries, is the use of instruments based on language use, namely, the fraction of the population that speaks English or other European languages (see, for instance, IMF 2003). However, Glaeser et al. (2004), who revisit the institutions-cum-growth literature, find that most indicators of institutional quality used to establish the proposition that institutions cause growth are constructed to be conceptually unsuitable for that purpose. Moreover, Glaeser et al. show that some of the instrumental variable techniques used in the literature are flawed.

[19] See, for instance, Gallup et al. (1999), Henderson et al. (2000), and Sachs (2003).

two-way causality abound, reality may be, as Basu (2005) notes, the reverse of what is being claimed.[20]

Moreover, recent empirical analyses have typically considered quantifiable variables for the outcomes or performance of a country's institutional environment as measures of institutions. These include, among others, the perception of corruption, indicators for the independence of the media, or the level of education of civil servants (as measures for the effectiveness and accountability of the government); the time and cost involved in carrying out various business activities (as a measure for regulatory burdens); or perceptions of the incidence of crime, the effectiveness and predictability of the judiciary, and the enforceability of contracts (as measures for the rule of law). However, all these performance indicators say nothing about how well performing institutions can be designed. Even worse, evidence abounds that the measured institutional functions, such as the enforcement of contracts or the protection of property rights, can be achieved through markedly different, context-specific institutional forms.[21]

Finally, the fact that economists' current views on development are mostly based on empirical facts derived from multiple regressions means that only those factors of a country's institutional environment are being considered, for which measurable data or indicators are available. Thereby, potentially important parts of the institutional environment, which reach beyond the quantifiable parts of formal institutions' performance characteristics, tend to be omitted from the analysis. Not considered are especially cultural factors as reflected in people's intrinsic motivations, ideologies and informal norms, which influence individual behaviour and hence economic outcomes as much as the quality of the formal institutions that regulate their interactions.[22]

8.4 The Good Governance Agenda

With the turn to institutional explanations of economic development, attention has also shifted back to the governance of state institutions. This development is most prominently reflected in the recent discourse on good governance by

---

[20] Basu even maintains that "causality lies in the eyes of the beholder" (2005, p. 36), with which he means that economists are often so used to thinking in terms of causality that they see causal relation even if they do not exist. For a detailed discussion on the implications of reverse causality problems for the policy-relevance of development theories see Sect. 9.2.1.

[21] See, for instance, Rodrik (2007). Empirical evidence for this supposition is provided in Part I (especially Chaps. 3 and 4). The implications of context-specificity for development research and policymaking are further discussed in Sect. 9.2.

[22] Note that even if all relevant factors could be expressed in quantifiable data, the attempt to endogenise all of them in empirical analyses would lead to impossible infinite regressions. Retreat to partial analyses does hardly solve this problem as those variables of the institutional environment that are held constant are still likely to be determinants of the dependent variable, and may, at the same time, be correlated with the model's endogenous variables.

development institutions (see, for instance, World Bank 2007; DFID 2006; European Commission 2003). The focus on governance – i.e. on the way in which the government exercises its power in the management of a country's economic and social resources – maintains the second generation of development economists' emphasis of government failures, while being supported and reinforced by the third generation's empirical contributions on institutions and growth. But whereas the second generation of development economists concentrated in their dealing with government failure almost exclusively on reducing the role of the state and broadening the influence of markets, the third generation recognised the state as fundamental for ensuring the proper functioning of the market.[23] This rising emphasis on institutions, and in particular on the role of the state in the development process, has eventually also given rise to the now widely adopted focus on good governance.

In the current discourse, governance appears as an open-ended concept. It is variantly approximated either broadly by the degree of liberty, justice and democracy in a society (e.g. Sen 1999), or more narrowly by measures of political accountability, state capacity and the rule of law.[24] Especially with regard to the latter definition, governance is inextricably linked to the performance of a country's political, legal, and economic institutions. In consequence, the wide endorsement of the positive correlation between institutions and economic growth is purported to apply to the interactions between governance and growth as well. But while the historical evidence suggests that this holds true in the long run, the fact that countries like China, Vietnam, Cambodia, or Russia rank low on many governance measures despite their rapid growth appears to contradict this view, at least for the short run.

What the governance agenda contributes to the evolution of development economics is that it brings to the fore a set of political and legal factors that are crucial for understanding development processes in low-income countries, and that have previously been largely presupposed in economic analyses. It has thus broadened the scope of development economics and fosters interdisciplinary exchange with the legal, political, and historical sciences. Its methodology and approaches to policymaking are, however, that of previous generations of development economists and practitioners. Accordingly, good governance is evaluated against a universal set of indicators, like the World Bank's worldwide governance measures (Kaufmann et al. 2007), or its comparative data on the cost of doing business (World Bank and

---

[23] For instance, the World Bank devoted its 1997 World Development Report to the theme "The State in a Changing World" (World Bank 1997).

[24] The most comprehensive attempt at measuring governance more narrowly defined is the World Bank's Worldwide Governance Indicators project. It gathers data on more than 60 indicators that are based on several hundred individual variables measuring perceptions of governance covering 212 countries and territories. The dimensions of governance measured by aggregate governance indicators include voice and accountability, political stability and absence of violence, government effectiveness, regulatory quality, rule of law, and control of corruption.

IFC 2008), which are then used to determine reform priorities.[25] However, as these indicators only measure outcomes, they convey no information on the context-specific political and legal arrangements that bring them about, and therefore provide little guidance on how to improve the attributes of governance that are captured by the indicators.

In this respect, the near-exclusive focus of the good governance agenda on the performance of formal state institutions is not helpful either, as it disregards the many alternative modes of governance that can emerge as second-best responses to dysfunctional public sector institutions. As the analysis in Chaps. 4 and 5 has shown, these informal institutional arrangements, and their governance structures, often serve as functional equivalents to state governance if it is weak or absent, and thus can help on a certain scale to alleviate the constraints that poor state governance imposes on economic activity. The danger of setting reform priorities according to a country's rank on a list of predefined governance indicators is that policies may not be targeted at the problems that represent a country's most significant constraints to growth.

---

[25] According to Bandura (2008), the performance of national governments is continuously being assessed and ranked against more than 175 composite indices, many of which measure attributes of governance like, for instance, the United Nations Economic Commission for Africa's African Governance Indicators, the Bertelsmann Transformation Index, the Corruption Perceptions Index by Transparency International, the World Bank's Country Policy and Institutional Assessment and the International Development Association's Country Performance Ratings, the Fraser Institute's Economic Freedom of the Word Index, the Index of Economic Freedom by the Heritage Foundation and the *Wall Street Journal*, the Millennium Challenge Account country rankings by the U.S. Government Millennium Challenge Corporation, PriceWaterhouseCoopers' Opacity Index, or Deutsche Bank's Stability Index.

Chapter 9
Conclusions from the Past and the Agenda for a New Generation of Development Economics

9.1 The Challenge of Igniting Growth in Low-Income Countries

After three generations of changing paradigms, development economists know more today about the deep determinants of economic development than at any time before. This knowledge has helped to devise policies and programmes that contributed to the promotion of economic and human development in many parts of the world. But in almost all of these cases, internationally assisted development policies complemented already existing, home-grown development processes. In no case have development economists been able to devise programmes or policies that succeeded in *igniting* previously inexistent processes of sustained, broad-based growth.[1] Of course, such economic miracles did happen in the last decades, most notably in East and South Asia, and have helped there to significantly lower the proportion of people that live in extreme poverty. But, again, these sustained growth accelerations were mostly driven by indigenous factors and unorthodox development strategies that dissented from the prevailing paradigms in the development literature.

For development economists, the question of how to ignite self-sustained growth in low-income countries remains an unresolved challenge, the relevance of which is sadly proven by the many countries that are as poor today as they were more than 60 years ago. This challenge defines the current frontier of development economics

---

[1] Evidence for this statement is implicitly provided by a number of influential studies on the effectiveness of international aid (see, e.g. World Bank 1998; Burnside and Dollar 2000). By concluding that aid does work, but only in countries that have good economic policies and institutions, these studies actually admit that development assistance cannot ignite growth-promoting policies, but can only support existing policy reform processes that are driven by strong government ownership on the part of the recipient country. This is a notable implication of the studies' conclusions. For their detailed discussion see Sect. 9.2.1.

to which this book intends to contribute.² How can this be done? At first, it requires to understand the scale and scope of the problem. Igniting processes of broad-based growth is a challenge that largely applies to low-income countries, specifically if they are identified not only through their low levels of per capita income at a single point in time, but especially by the persistence of low levels of income as the result of the absence of prolonged growth accelerations. Moreover, the scope of the challenge of igniting growth in low-income countries is defined by the nature of the growth that is to be achieved. Here, quality matters besides quantity, i.e. the challenge goes beyond achieving high growth rates from a few large-scale investments by the government or foreign investors that mostly happen in the extractives sector. Especially in weak governance environments, few spill-over effects on other spheres of the economy and the population at large can be expected from this type of growth.³ The growth that is needed in low-income countries has rather to be endogenously generated through the realisation of economic opportunities by broad parts of the population in a diverse range of occupations. This type of growth is considered of high quality in the sense that it directly and proportionally contributes to poverty reduction.⁴

Having defined the scope of the problem, another necessary step in confronting the challenge of igniting growth in low-income countries is to understand the context to which this challenge applies. It became obvious from this study's descriptive account of poor countries' economic characteristics in Part I of this study that their economic conditions and structures differ markedly from that of more advanced economies, and that they themselves represent a diverse group of countries. Every policy or programme that aims at encouraging change in low-income countries must hence be bound to these

---

²Accepting this challenge requires realising that igniting economic growth in low-income countries and sustaining existing growth dynamics in more advanced developing countries are two different enterprises which require differentiated policy agendas. Moreover, it has to be noted that igniting growth, as understood here, is a long-term process that involves the formation of an institutional environment that provides the preconditions and incentives for economic activity to grow on a broad base beyond subsistence levels.

³In the last decade, many African low-income countries south of the Sahara have experienced hitherto unknown rates of economic growth. But in very few of them has this growth actually been of a sustained nature and resulted from economic activity in diverse fields of the economy and with broad participation of the poor. Instead, according to the World Bank's African Development Indicators (World Bank 2008), growth was highest in oil-exporting low-income countries like Equatorial Guinea (30.8% average GDP growth per year in the period 1996–2005), Chad (9%), Angola (8.5%), Sudan (6.3%), Nigeria (4.3%) and the Democratic Republic of Congo (3.4%). This implies that in many of these countries, the challenge of igniting broad-based, sustained growth represents a challenge in spite of their positive aggregate growth rates.

⁴The notion of high quality growth has entered the rhetoric at international development institutions in the last decade, meaning mostly economic growth that brings lasting employment gains and poverty reduction, provides greater equality of income through broader access, especially for women, to markets, education and finance and protects the environment. It has frequently been invoked as an important objective of development policy, with very little mention of how it is to be achieved, though. For further reference on the quality dimensions of growth, see Barro (2002) and World Bank (2000); and for a summary of the discussion on pro-poor growth, see Ravallion (2004b), and Lopez (2005).

countries' specific contexts. Conversely, neglect of the distinctive characteristics of low-income countries may lead to an incomplete or even misleading picture of economic activity in low-income countries. This, by and large, describes what happened to previous generations of development economists. Confronting their conclusions and findings with insights from the descriptive analysis of low-income countries' economic realities can provide important lessons in the search for more relevant, context-specific solutions to the problem of persistent poverty and unfavourable conditions for self-sustained growth.

This will be attempted in the remainder of this chapter by synthesising the lessons from the foregoing review of contributions to development economics over the past 70 years into a number of key conclusions that set out the research agenda of a new generation of development economists. An overarching conclusion, discussed in Sect. 9.2, is that the influencing factors of economic life in low-income countries tend to be highly context specific. An important implication from this conclusion is that successful development policies require context-specific solutions (Sect. 9.2.1). This, in turn, has ramifications for the choice of research methods in development economics (Sect. 9.2.2). Besides conclusions that concern approaches to development policymaking and the methodology of development research, bureaucratic failures in the implementation of development measures are identified in Sect. 9.3 as further reasons for the limited effectiveness of development policies in low-income countries. A summary of all key lessons and conclusions at the methodological, policy and operational levels is presented in Sect. 9.4.

9.2 Why Context Matters

Development economics has been advanced by some of the most able economists[5] and provides a field of application for many of the most seminal contributions to economic theory.[6] Given this scholarly track record, why has the discipline's policy

---

[5] The economists whose contributions to development economics earned them a Noble Prize are Jan Tinbergen, Noble Laureate in Economics in 1969; Simon Kuznets in 1971; Gunnar Myrdal in 1974; Arthur Lewis in 1979; James Mirrlees in 1996; Amartya Sen in 1998 and Joseph Stiglitz in 2001.

[6] Noble-Prize-winning research in economics that has fruitfully been applied to the study of problems of developing countries include Friedrich von Hayek's analysis of the interdependence of economic, social and institutional phenomena (1973 Noble Prize in Economics); Herbert Simon's research into the decision-making process within economic organisations (1978); George Stigler's studies of industrial structures, functioning of markets and causes and effects of public regulation (1982); James M. Buchanan's development of the contractual and constitutional bases for the theory of economic and political decision-making (1986); Robert Solow's contributions to the theory of economic growth (1987); Ronald Coase's clarification of the significance of transaction costs and property rights for the institutional structure of an economy (1991); Gary Becker's extension of the domain of microeconomic analysis to a wide range of human behaviour and interaction, including non-market behaviour (1992) and Douglass North's renewal of research in economic history to explain economic and institutional change (1993).

impact on low-income countries been so sobering in the past? The lessons and conclusions from the foregoing analysis of development theories and policies suggest that this situation can in large parts be attributed to a combination of methodological problems and omissions in the theoretical explanation of low-income countries' realities. In particular, ignorance of important indigenous elements of their economic systems has led to the illusive belief that economic development can be analysed irrespective of a country's specific historical, cultural and geographical contexts.

Each generation of development economists emphasised a particular set of explanatory factors for development and related policy objectives, which they each associated with a particular policy reform design. For instance, the early modernisation theorists broadly emphasised physical capital formation as a primary objective of development policy and favoured state-led industrial planning as the way to achieve it. The second generation of development economists associated their focus on markets to a large extent with price liberalisation policies. More recently, development economists came to acknowledge the role of institutions in the development process, but tend to relate every function that institutions perform in an economy to a single universal institutional form.[7]

The expectation of development economists and policy advisors that universal policy prescriptions and institutional blueprints would provide a good recipe for getting growth started in low-income countries rests upon the implicit belief that economic development could be achieved by assisting poor countries in doing what rich countries did on their way to prosperity. Accordingly, realities in developing countries were, and still are, explained by inference from theories and models that had originally been derived from observations of economic life in advanced economies, just as most policy advice was and is inspired by lessons from the experiences of developed nations.[8]

But the more the histories of developing countries actually differ from Western development paths, the more likely they are to fail in adopting the economic institutions of more advanced countries. As has become evident from the discussion in Part I, the functions and principles that enable economic activity in low-income countries are actually supported by a plurality of institutional forms that are quite distinct from those of Western economies and vary markedly with different local constraints and structures. This is confirmed through research by Rodrik (2007, p. 15) who points out that "there is no unique correspondence between the *functions* that good institutions perform and the *form* that such institutions take". He asserts that, for this reason, policymakers have considerable room for finding solutions and institutional designs that fit in with local structures and are sensitive to local constraints and

---

[7] For instance, the function of legal and juridical institutions to ensure compliance in contractual relations is often thought to correspond exclusively with the institutional form of a state-backed system of formal laws and public courts.

[8] See Sect. 9.2.2 for a detailed discussion of the methodological problems with this approach and their implications for development policy.

opportunities.[9] This conclusion not only contradicts the conventional approach of associating a certain reform objective with one exclusive "best practice" policy instrument or institutional design. The plurality of solutions to given development problems also explains why the same policy may work well in one country, while it fails in another. And it finds further support in the fact that today's economically most successful developing countries are those that actually followed very diverse, indigenous development strategies that often deviated substantially from Western experts' policy prescriptions.[10]

A first insight from confronting past development policies with the economic reality of low-income countries is thus that the development objectives which enjoy a broad consensus today are confronted by a multitude of ways of implementation. Knowledge about the kind of changes that are desirable in low-income countries is only a necessary condition for successful reform. As a sufficient condition, effective reforms require additional knowledge about how to implement a planned change in the specific contexts of low-income countries. The purpose of development economics thus cannot be confined to identifying and testing the factors that determine economic development in general, and from these to derive universal policy prescriptions. Good development economics has, above all, to start with identifying and analysing these factors in the specific context of each concerned country or groups of similarly structured countries. Context-specific analysis adds to the identification of certain general first-order principles that any economic system should accommodate (such as the undistorted supply of physical capital, labour and land; effective provision of education and reliable infrastructure services; secure property rights and the rule of law and sound macroeconomic management) information about their relative priority for a country's development and their interaction with local factors such as initial conditions, attitudes towards change, indigenous informal arrangements or other second-best conditions arising from a country's specific constraints and structures.[11] Only a combination of general theoretical analysis with profound knowledge about the context-specific

---

[9] Determining the goodness of fit of a policy of institutional design with local circumstances requires understanding the dynamic interplay between the economic system and the social, political and cultural spheres of life. It is in the latter where people's mental models, traditions and customs are shaped. These informal institutions ultimately decide about the compatibility, and hence effectiveness, of an imported institutional design or policy reform. See Sect. 13.2.1 for a detailed discussion of this argument.

[10] For a collection of country studies that discuss such unconventional but successful development strategies, see Rodrik (2003).

[11] It is relevant here to recall from Sect. 6.2.1 that a similar view had already been adopted by Albert O. Hirschman in the 1950s. He was interested in uncovering the "hidden rationality" of seemingly odd, irrational or reprehensible social behaviour that determines development outcomes in low income countries, and aspired to exploit these countries' indigenous resources and structures for the design of context-specific development policies. Hirschman thus pioneered an approach the time of which had yet to come. At his time, however, development economics evolved into the opposite direction and became, with the second generation's neoclassical turn, increasingly preoccupied with the obvious, i.e., with the visible and measurable characteristics of developing countries.

conditions in low-income countries will enable development economists to grasp the character of their economic realities, and to understand the direction of its causal relationships. Only on the basis of such an understanding will development economists be able to arrive at theoretical conclusions that offer real operational guidance to policymakers in low-income countries.

9.2.1 Operational Guidance to Policymakers: An Often Neglected Objective of Development Research

Development economics has from its beginning been a policy-oriented subject. Given the conspicuous poverty and backwardness of many regions in the world after World War II, the motivating question behind the emergence of development economics as a separate field of scientific investigation was to find out how the pace and quality of the development process in the world's poorest countries could be accelerated. However, as the subject evolved, scientific elegance prevailed over practical relevance, with the effect that development economists arrived at a growing number of general propositions about the impact of a large variety of explanatory factors on growth and economic development, but at the same time provided very little operational guidance to policymakers who sought to improve the performance of developing economies.

The standard method to empirically test theoretical propositions in development economics is to specify a linear regression model with the growth rate of per capita income (or any other performance indicator for economic development) as dependent variable, and a diverse selection of factors as independent variable, the respective effect of which on growth development economists seek to explain.[12] The data to run such growth regressions are usually obtained from national account statistics or household surveys of a representative sample of countries. If these cross-country growth regressions turn out individually or jointly significant estimation coefficients (implying a high individual or joint correlation between the respective explanatory variables and growth), the regressors of the model, say, the savings rate, the primary schools enrolment ratio, the degree of openness of the economy, or indicators for the quality of a country's institutional environment, are each confidently inferred as significant causes of growth and recommended as objectives of growth-promoting policies.

---

[12] Regression analysis is applied to estimate economic relations since the 1930s. Early examples include the study of demand for agricultural products by Schultz (1938) or the pioneering monograph on statistical testing of business cycle theories by Tinbergen (1939). Albeit the scepticism especially voiced by Keynes (1939) in the Keynes–Tinbergen debate, the use of econometric methods in empirical development research has risen continuously, partly because of the increasing formalisation of theoretical research in development economics, and in part also due to improvements in the quantity and quality of statistical data from developing countries. Today, cross-country regressions are the method of choice for almost all of the empirical literature on institutions and growth (see Sect. 8.3).

But the results from regression analyses do actually only reveal that a statistically significant correlation exists between, say, trade liberalisation and the quality of a country's institutions on the one side, and economic growth on the other or between growth and poverty reduction (in each of these cases, the identified correlation is actually mostly positive).[13] What they do not reveal is the true direction of causation between the studied variables, which is exactly the kind of information that would be needed to use the findings of a theory for purposes of prediction and policy advice. Instead, the direction of causation is usually anticipated ex ante in the specification of the regression model or in the hypotheses and assumptions of the theory from which the model derives. The more these assumptions and hypotheses bear significant relation to the real context of the phenomena that they are supposed to explain, the more reliable their imputed causality relations tend to be.

Unfortunately, in development economics more attention has often been paid to the empirical testing of theories than to empirical research that precedes the formulation of theories. If, however, theoretical hypotheses about the behaviour of phenomena in low-income countries bear little relation to these countries' actual realities and are instead deduced from mathematical or intuitive logic, it is well possible that the causality imputed in the regression models is in reality the reverse of what is being claimed. Such reverse causality problems frequently beset assertions of cause-and-effect relationships in development economics. As discussed in Sect. 8.3, it is, for instance, far from certain that good institutions cause growth, as it can as well be that the quality of institutions improves while economic activity becomes more diversified, and the division of labour deepens in the course of a country's development. Similarly, trade openness may not necessarily accelerate growth; it is equally possible that growth encourages policymakers to lower trade barriers once domestic export industries have become internationally competitive. The same applies to the widely adopted assumption that underdevelopment is caused by a shortage of capital, while a low savings and investment rate can actually be as much a symptom of underdevelopment as it is claimed to be a cause of it.

A case in point is the influential World Bank assessment of the effectiveness of foreign aid (World Bank 1998), which is based on Dollar and Pritchett (1998) and makes heavy use of the results from an earlier paper by Burnside and Dollar (2000) that later appeared in the *American Economic Review*. Its authors use cross-country regression analysis to assess the impact of foreign aid on growth and conclude that aid results in faster growth when an economy is open, has stable prices and pursues prudent fiscal policies. But they miss to address that it could as well be possible that faster growth attracts more foreign aid as donors are keen to back a country's existing growth path. Specifically, their study is infested with the problem that neither policies nor foreign aid can seriously be considered as exogenous: Not only is it

---

[13] Studies that use cross-country econometric analysis to test the empirical relationship between growth and trade openness include Dollar and Kraay (2004);Lopez (2005) and Yanikkaya (2003). For a discussion of the empirical literature on growth and institutions, see Sect. 8.3. Dollar and Kraay (2002), Cord et al. (2004) and Kraay (2006) use cross-country growth regressions to assess the empirical relationship between growth and poverty reduction.

highly problematic in growth regressions to treat policies that have systematically been used by governments to promote economic growth as random.[14] Also aid and the quality of policies are in many cases correlated. As this endogeneity of explanatory variables (i.e. the problem of reverse causality) produces highly biased results in OLS regressions, the authors are forced to make highly restrictive assumptions on the behaviour of their variables and the choice of corresponding instruments in order to preserve the consistency of their results.[15]

In spite of the tentative and fragile nature of the empirical results reported by Burnside and Dollar, they had a surprisingly strong impact on international development policymaking. Not only have they been used to prove the case for development aid in influential World Bank reports, they also informed the rationale behind George W. Bush's Millennium Challenge Corporation (MCC), as well as the 2002 Monterrey Consensus. Both initiatives aim at increasing the amount of foreign aid, while at the same time intend to allocate it more selectively to benefit countries with good policies and institutions in the first place.[16] It is certainly true that there is a strong theoretical presumption in favour of the intuitive argument that aid is used more effectively by countries with good institutions and policies rather than buy those with poor governance and a high level of corruption. But from the Burnside–Dollar study and related empirical work, it is far from clear which policies and institutions actually matter, how they impact on the effectiveness of aid and how aid precisely influences economic growth. On such operationally important issues, the regression results provide no reliable and unambiguous guidance.[17]

---

[14] Rodrik (2005) discusses the implications of regressing economic growth on policy variables. He notes that in these cases, problems of reverse causality (or endogeneity) are bound to happen as the policy variable is an integral part of the null hypothesis that is being tested and thus cannot be treated as if it were exogenous or random. He concludes that in such a setting, any interpretations of the results from cross-country growth regressions must lead policymakers astray.

[15] Many further methodological problems challenge the robustness and reliability of the study's findings. For instance, the results become untenable after adding four more years to the sample, or after the use of more plausible measures of aid and policies (see Easterly et al. 2003; The Economist 2007c). Similar points of critique were raised in an evaluation of the World Bank's in-house research commissioned by the bank to a group of top academic economists chaired by Angus Deaton of Princeton University (Banerjee et al. 2006). Further critical reviews of the Burnside/Dollar and Collier/Dollar aid allocation models can be found in Beynon (1999, 2003).

[16] The Monterrey Consensus was the outcome of the 2002 United Nations International Conference on Financing for Development, in which over 50 Heads of State and 200 ministers pledged, among others, to increase their official development assistance to developing countries. The Consensus codified officially the call for effectiveness of foreign aid. The Millennium Challenge Corporation, announced by George W. Bush in 2002, was set up in 2004 as a new mechanism for granting up to 5 billion US dollars per year in additional US bilateral aid to well-governed developing countries. Eligible countries are selected on the basis of a number of independent policy indicators.

[17] For further critical reviews of the empirical growth literature, see Temple (1999), Glaeser et al. (2004) and Easterly (2005), as well as Sect. 8.3. Technical limitations of using cross-country regressions in explaining economic growth are discussed in Rodríguez (2007).

Besides these rather technical problems, development economists are confronted with the more fundamental challenge that it is generally hard, and sometimes even impossible, to identify in the economic realities of low-income countries relations that reveal a clear-cut direction of causality. Whereas this possibility was still well articulated by some first-generation development economists, it has much lesser been recognised from their time on. Gunnar Myrdal, for instance, considered the determination of economic development as a complex of interlocking, circular relations and cumulative changes. Other early development economists, like Ragnar Nurkse, availed themselves of the notions of vicious or virtuous circles to describe the possibility of two-way causality of economic relationships in poor countries.[18] Again, where such circular or two-way relationships of causality are at work, the described problems with using standard growth regressions for empirical testing abound; in fact they are even present when it comes to decide clearly and without ambiguity which factors constitute dependent and which explanatory variables of a model. Albert O. Hirschman offers yet another reason for being cautious with causality assumptions deduced from mathematical or intuitive logic. Observing the realities of Latin American countries, he discovered that many economic processes are organised in ways that, when looked at from a (Western) commonsense point of view, represent "wrong way around" development sequences.[19] Where economic realities are indeed reflected by such inverted sequences, conventional cause-and-effect assumptions would have to be turned upside down, making the unambiguous determination of causality relations an even more difficult task.

A key implication of the causal ambiguity, by which many theoretical conclusions in development economics are affected, is the limited operational value of research findings for development policymaking. Policymakers need to know the direction of the variables' causal relationship in order to tackle a problem at its origin, rather than to direct efforts at mitigating its effects.[20] For example, a recurring policy recommendation, drawn especially from early gap theories or more recent applications of institutional theory in development economics, is that growth can be pushed through the provision of undersupplied resources such as capital, infrastructure or deliberately designed institutions. But these strategies represent valid options only if the direction of causality indeed runs from the provision of these undersupplied resources to growth. However, policymakers will have to pursue markedly different development strategies if the underprovision of capital,

---

[18] See Sect. 6.2 for a detailed discussion of their contributions to development economics.

[19] See Hirschman (1994) and Sect. 6.2.1 (especially footnote 13) above.

[20] Clear cause-and-effect relations are also an indispensable precondition for the planning, implementation and evaluation of development assistance measures. For this purpose, development institutions often apply the so-called Logical Framework approach, a project management tool that involves identifying strategic elements (inputs, outputs, outcomes and impact) and their causal relations, together with performance indicators, as well as risks and assumptions that may influence project results. Without clear guidance as to the direction of causality between relevant objectives and the intervention strategy, as well as the causal chain of individual factors and conditions that need to be addressed, development projects cannot be planned and implemented in a meaningful way.

infrastructure services or institutions is instead the result of a lack of demand for them, given poor countries' low levels of economic activity.[21] Growth would then rather have to be understood as a consequence of various pull factors originating, for instance, from developments on neighbouring markets, as the linkages concept by Hirschman implies, or from changes in a country's terms of trade as suggested by development economists in the structuralist tradition.[22]

These examples illustrate the difficulty for policymakers to extract operationally relevant information from research findings that fail to unambiguously relate the consequences or effects of a phenomenon to its real causes. Moreover, as discussed in the previous section, these causes tend to vary widely with different local conditions and thus also make available policy options highly context specific. In consequence, the policy advice inferred from general development theories often represents just one out of many alternative options including sometimes even reverse courses of action. Disregard for context-specific factors often results from generalising too broadly about the explanatory factors of development. It is this remoteness of development theories from low-income countries' diverse realities that also makes theoretical findings often inconclusive regarding the direction of their established causality relations. These problems relate, at their core, to the issues of methodology in development research, and in particular to questions about the right sequence and balance between empirical and theoretical analysis in development economics, with which the next section will be concerned.

9.2.2 The Balance and Sequence of Empirical and Theoretical Analysis in Development Economics

The foregoing conclusion suggests that as development economics has increasingly become an empirical discipline, it has at the same time forfeited much of its operational value for policymakers. This may seem a somewhat odd statement, because

---

[21] This possibility had first been considered by Ragnar Nurkse (see Sect. 6.1.3).

[22] Similar examples can be found in almost all areas of development policy. For instance, the theoretical finding that high growth correlates positively with a high exposure to international trade does convey little policy-relevant information per se. What policymakers are actually interested to know is if they can expect an economy to grow if they abolish import restrictions or if they may instead be better advised to strengthen the competitiveness of its domestic industry, for instance, through investments in the education system that increases labour productivity and in turn enables domestic firms to increase production and exports. Another example is the theoretical finding that good institutions matter for growth. In order to translate this conclusion into effective development policies, additional knowledge is needed, for instance, on how high quality institutions evolve in a specific country context or on how to determine appropriate institutional forms and governance structures that a policy should promote to increase their long-term effectiveness and legitimacy. Finally, the empirical evidence on the link between economic growth and poverty reduction provides relatively little operational guidance as to how effective growth strategies can be designed that create the means and incentives for the poor to contribute to, and benefit from, economic growth.

the very idea of empirical research should be to ensure the practical relevance of theoretical findings. The problem is that in development economics, empirical research is almost entirely used for the subsequent testing of preconceived theoretical models and rarely done prior to their formulation. This is, in principle, a perfectly allowable approach and common to all research that follows a deductive reasoning method. This approach involves the logical inference of theoretical conclusions from other known regularities stated in the form of premises.[23] It provides an elegant way of reducing the complexity of reality by way of isolating abstraction and generalisation, thus saving the researcher from the need to find particular explanations for every contextually essential instance. Moreover, this reductionist approach makes theoretical models more susceptible to formal mathematical treatment, which is particularly important for their subsequent empirical testing with the tools of regression analysis and other statistical methods.

But at the same time, the deductive method confines the researcher to consider only a narrow range of general explanatory factors of a given economic phenomenon. Applied to the theoretical analysis of low-income countries, deductive conclusions tend to exclude particularly the manifold noneconomic influences on the economic behaviour of individuals and groups, which have their origin in the institutional framework of their customs, ethical norms and culture, and may differ markedly across regions and countries. As discussed above, these context-specific factors are highly significant for the understanding of economic life in low-income countries. At the same time, they are difficult to uncover from the outside. Since research in development economics was, and still is, primarily carried out in advanced countries, these context-specific factors tend to be hidden from the view of the remote researcher's eye. Conclusions about the behaviour of economic phenomena in low-income countries have instead often been deducted from the researcher's generalised knowledge about real phenomena observed in advanced countries. In the past 70 years, most development theories have in fact sought to explain the causes of underdevelopment through theories and models constructed from the historical experience of industrialised countries. For instance, they were based, implicitly or explicitly, on assumptions of the existence of various kinds of gaps in the endowment of underdeveloped economies, on missing markets and market-supporting institutions or a lack of free enterprise and competition – all of which had once also been crucial elements in explaining the transition of Western countries from agrarian to modern industrialised economies. But this preoccupation with Western models of development has made development economists often for the many idiosyncratic institutional forms that have evolved in low-income countries as functional substitutes in response to their lack of the conditions that had played a crucial role in the development of Western economies. A fallacy here is to assume that only because Western experts are part of societies that accomplished this transition to modernity, they would also know how to lead poor

---

[23] Premises represent general laws about the expected behaviour of individuals or groups (e.g. the postulates of rationality or the efficiency rule), as well as assumptions about the conditions under which they interact (e.g. the available production technologies or the constraints that economic actors face).

societies to a sustained path of prosperity. Unfortunately, also leaders in developing countries themselves tend to fall victim to this fallacy by regarding the Western advisors' universal policy prescriptions as superior, modern and more sophisticated relative to the learning from their own experience, even though their indigenous knowledge has often proven to be more effective than the Western expert's advice.[24]

Especially when development economics became increasingly neoclassical in its assumptions did the deductive method advance as the method of choice for the study of low-income countries. As discussed in Sect. 7.2, applying neoclassical theory to the contexts of low-income countries meant that development economics embodied most assumptions that represented approximations of economic realities in advanced countries, while exploratory data analysis as a preliminary stage of research for verifying their consistence with the specific contexts of low-income countries was kept at a minimum. In accordance with this method, the primary concern of research was to ensure that deductive conclusions were valid in the sense that they are logically consistent with the premises, rather than that they were reliable in the sense that their premises are consistent with the facts. As a result, development theories were not only confined to a narrow range of general economic variables, but they also became more likely to incur various kinds of reverse causality and omitted variables problems, because in the new context, the significance and relevance of the adopted premises and assumptions was no longer certain.

A major implication of the conclusions from the present methodological discussion is, again, that when theoretical models fail to account for significant explanatory variables of the phenomena which they are supposed to predict, they can also easily issue into misleading policy recommendations. The history of development policy failures in low-income countries is, indeed, as much one of omissions and ignorance of factors on which economic phenomena in these countries crucially depend, as it is a history of failure from adopting inappropriate approaches to reform. Those who recognise the implications of deductive reasoning for the policy relevance of research results often argue that general theoretical findings need to be adapted by means of sound judgement, common sense or intuition in order to render them more context specific, and hence more policy relevant. A case in point is

---

[24] Such self-deprecatory attitudes have already been noted by Hirschman (1961), and are more recently also contended by African leaders themselves. For instance, the Asantehene Otumfuo Osei Tutu II, traditional king of the Ashanti in Ghana, urged Africans in a speech at the Third German-African Forum on November 3, 2007 to realise the importance of their tradition in addressing their situation, and continued that "[w]e have allowed ourselves to be persuaded that there is nothing good in our tradition. As a consequence, we have almost jettisoned our tradition and culture, thinking that everything African is bad and everything foreign is good." [quoted from Kumi (2007)]. A similar attitude can also be observed with regard to the research orientation of economists from developing countries. Instead of taking advantage of their familiarity with the reality of their home countries, they often turn towards the pursuit of economics as a science of universal laws in order to meet the high standards of formal rigour and innovative use of econometric methods that is still demanded by most international top journals. On the dualist structures that are evolving in many African societies as a consequence of the juxtaposition of traditional and modern influences, see Sect. 13.2.1.

9.2 Why Context Matters

the following note by Srinivasan (2000, p. 269) in a retrospective comment on the Washington Consensus:

> Simple and abstract theory [...] and its highly restrictive econometric specification cannot deliver policy conclusions that can be directly applied to the situation of any given economy at a particular time. To advise on policy requires sound judgment on the part of the advisor – judgment that goes beyond findings for theoretical and econometric models.

A very different way of rendering theoretical findings in development economics more context sensitive and policy relevant is to base the formulation of development theories on sound empirical foundations from the outset. Empirical description as a preliminary stage of research would not only help to tie the formulation of development theories closer to the specific contexts to which they apply, but it would, in consequence, also increase the predictive power of theoretical findings, and hence their relevance and guidance for policymaking. It follows as a logical conclusion from the above discussion that this advantage comes at the expense of a narrowing of the theory's external validity in contexts that differ significantly from the reality from which the empirical groundwork of the theory has been drawn.

The logical process of deriving theoretical hypotheses and conclusions from such a preliminary stage of empirical research involves inductive reasoning, which means the researcher comes to conclusions about the whole on the basis of observations of particular instances. The inductive method is distinguished from deductive reasoning not only by inverting the sequence of empirical and theoretical stages of research, but it also differs in the kind of empirical research it involves. Specifically, inductive reasoning requires the observational and explorative generation of data within the relevant context of a given phenomenon, rather than the application of statistical and mathematical methods to the empirical estimation of isolated economic relationships. In effect, theoretical conclusions from inductive reasoning represent overarching but yet context- and time-conditioned explanations of the probable behaviour of a phenomenon. They cannot, however, claim the general validity of conclusions from deductive reasoning that arises from their logical consistence with the premises.

This emphasis on empirical research prior to the formulation of theoretical hypotheses and models does not mean, however, that empirical analysis should prevail over the aim to arrive at logically reasoned conclusions. Exploratory data analysis can rather aid the formulation of theories by empirically describing a given phenomenon's characteristics, by identifying empirical regularities or patterns the relations among which need to be explained by the theory and by specifying the nature of the assumptions that a theory can make without gross violation to the empirical patterns.[25] In relation to that, it is important to note that the inductive and deductive approaches should not be regarded as competing methods of research. They rather complement each other if combined in a research agenda that begins with careful and direct observation aimed at an empirical description of a given phenomenon,

---

[25] For a recent deliberation on the role of explorative data analysis in the process of theory formation in development economics, see Mookherjee (2005).

moves on to the formulation of related theoretical propositions and hypotheses, then uses empirical data analysis to test these hypotheses, then modifies or replaces previous theories if suggested by the data in order to finally use the least unsuccessful theory from the standpoint of empirical verification for purposes of prediction and policy advice.

The additional explanatory value of theoretical findings that are informed by explorative data from low-income countries may, of course, not render policymaking entirely devoid of the need for sound judgement and the researcher's use of intuition. But in this case, judgement and intuition are more likely to be informed by a qualitative understanding of low-income countries' realities that goes beyond explanations inferred from quantitative data alone. This method has the prospect of uncovering the deeper causes behind a given economic phenomenon, which are irreducible only to numbers and symbols in that they also account for relevant noneconomic variables like the motives and attitudes of human agents who brought a certain phenomenon into being.

The challenge of perceiving economic reality in low-income countries as it really is, rather than on the basis of the researcher's subjective concept of the world as he sees it from his often remote perspective, had already been noted by Schumpeter (1954, p. 34), who cautions in a comment on the special nature of "economic laws" that

> [...] whenever we attempt to interpret human attitudes, especially attitudes of people far removed from us in time or culture, we risk misunderstanding them not only if we crudely substitute our own attitudes for theirs, but also if we do our best to penetrate into the working of their minds. All this is made much worse than it would be otherwise by the fact that the analyzing observer himself is the product of a given social environment – and of his particular location in this environment – that conditions him to see certain things, rather than others, and to see them in a certain light. This brings us up to the problem of ideological bias in economic analysis.

The possibility for a Western-centred bias (or Eurocentrism) in development economics can also be explained on the basis of findings from the sociology of knowledge according to which reality is perceived differently in different societies of the world (Berger and Luckmann 1966).[26] Applying these findings to the practice of development policy and assistance, Werner (2003) points out that

> For the people living in an African slum, drinking water means something different from what it does for an academic's family in Cologne, and the perception of freedom of a nomad in the Sahel zone is different from that of a middle-class voter in a small German town.

This discussion amounts to conclude that a return to inductive reasoning in development economics would help to restore its policy relevance and bring the field closer to achieving its original purpose of explaining and predicting economic phenomena in the distinct contexts of developing countries. Besides, such an approach could broaden the spectrum of available policy interventions. It offers possibilities

---

[26]See also Sect. 13.1.4.

to complement what already exists instead of blindly supplanting indigenous structures and arrangements in low-income countries with the formal institutions of a modern market economy. Interestingly, the reliance on inductive reasoning in development economics is nothing entirely new. The approach had been pursued by a few early development economists such as Gunnar Myrdal and Albert O. Hirschman who preceded the formulation of their theories with a detailed exploratory analysis of relevant economic phenomena in developing countries, as well as by Walt W. Rostow and Alexander Gerschenkron who aimed at extracting operational lessons for development policy from the historical analysis of typical growth paths. The first and methodologically most advanced application and defence of the inductive method in economics has, however, even earlier roots in the contributions by members of the Historical School, the relevance and use of which for modern development economics will be evaluated more closely in Chaps. 11 and 12. Albeit without reference to the intellectual heritage of these earlier empiricists are inductive conclusions based on findings from empirical observations of the realities of low-income countries regaining new influence in development economics. Examples include Stiglitz's (1986) pioneering work on agricultural contracts in developing countries, as well as a growing number of explorative studies on various forms of indigenous market and non-market institutions in low-income countries.[27] The very recent debate, and related new approaches and analytical techniques in development economics that head into a similar direction, will be surveyed in Chap. 10.[28]

9.3 The Danger of Bureaucratic Failure in the Administration of Development Assistance

The discussion has so far revolved around methodological issues and derived policy approaches in development economics and their implications for the effectiveness of development theories and policies. But even the best applicable theory or most relevant policy recommendation will have an only effective in igniting and sustaining economic growth in low-income countries if the structures and instruments through which they are implemented fail. While development economists have long been occupied with tackling market and government failures in low-income countries, they have paid less attention to bureaucratic failure at the level of the Western system of granting and managing foreign aid. Interest in this issue rose in the 1990s when growing recognition of the mixed record of international assistance to developing

---

[27] See, for instance, Besley (1995) and Fafchamps (2003, 2004). For a discussion of these and related contributions, see Chaps. 4 and 5.

[28] Inductive research is actually also the favoured method of scientific inquiry by many authors of genuine African culture. Tévoédjrè (1978), for instance, calls for a rethinking of the economy along inductive lines.

countries led to a broad debate on the effectiveness of development assistance.[29] In a broader sense, this aid effectiveness debate stretches across both questions relating to the right choice of development policies and goals, as well as to the relative success of different implementation arrangements in bringing about a targeted change in a country or to the life of a specific beneficiary group. By contrast, the concept of bureaucratic failure shall be invoked here as to refer specifically to the delivery mechanisms of foreign aid, and to the organisation, governance and incentive structures that characterise the international aid system. This subsection thus concerns the delivery of policy solutions and related assistance programmes, whereas policy and programme failures that stem from flaws in the specification of policy objectives and approaches were dealt with in the previous discussion of the implications of theoretical and methodological issues in development economics at the policy level.

The distinction between bureaucratic and policy failure follows the approach by William S. Peirce (1981), who defines bureaucratic failure in relation to the implementation of a goal that is legislated or otherwise mandated by politicians to an administrative body or agency. If the agency does not achieve the goal, a failure has occurred either in the design of the respective programme or in its implementation. Only the latter constitutes a bureaucratic failure, while the former relates to problems with the adopted policy approach or strategy.[30] Within these bounds, bureaucratic failure in the administration and implementation of development assistance can be attributed to the incentive structure at various levels of the aid system that influence individual behaviour of bureaucrats at both the donor and recipient side. Such incentives can either result from the design of particular development policies, plans or strategies, or may be associated with the organisation, governance structures and operational rules of the international aid system.

While a detailed discussion of all likely factors that contribute to bureaucratic failure in the delivery of development assistance would exceed the scope of this analysis, some stylised facts shall be presented here that characterise frequent problems of the present system of granting foreign aid to low-income countries. The purpose of this section is especially to evaluate if and how the structures, approaches and mechanisms at the level of development assistance and policy implementation

---

[29] The growing body of the aid effectiveness literature ranges from historical assessments of the effectiveness of development assistance (e.g. Tarp 2000; Easterly 2001; Goldin et al. 2002) over econometric analyses of the effects of aid on growth and poverty reduction (e.g. World Bank 1998; Burnside and Dollar 2000; Collier and Dollar 2004) to in-house evaluations by development institutions of the effectiveness of their own projects and programmes (e.g. the *Annual Reviews of Development Effectiveness* by the World Bank's Independent Evaluation Group or the *Development Effectiveness Reports* by the UNDP Evaluation Office).

[30] In his study, Peirce formulates a large number of hypotheses about the causes of bureaucratic failure which he illustrates by means of 11 case studies that deal with various instances of bureaucratic failures at the level of the US federal government. In spite of his focus on the United States, several aspects of his work, as well as the conceptual framework of the study, are useful and applicable also to the analysis of the institutional and behavioural determinants of bureaucratic failure in the foreign aid system.

have themselves undermined the effectiveness of efforts to assist low-income countries in igniting processes of economic growth and in improving the long-term performance of their economies.

9.3.1 Problems of Accountability and Feedback

Unlike in any other field of national policy, public spending on development assistance is not in the first place intended to benefit those who provide the necessary revenues to the government. This separation of taxpayers from beneficiaries of foreign development assistance is an important structural characteristic of the international aid system from which many of its problems originate. A first consequence is that Western governments try to reap immediate benefits for their own country from providing assistance to developing countries. For instance, to assure that aid money ends up where it came from, Western governments provided, and to a lesser extent still provide, development assistance on the condition that it is spend on goods or services produced in the donor country.[31] One consequence for developing countries of such tying of aid is higher project costs due to limited competition in the procurement of goods and services.[32] More importantly, however, tied aid inhibits the growth of local suppliers in developing countries and instead promotes the import of goods and services that are often ill-fitted to local needs and circumstances.

Another consequence of Western governments trying to justify the benefits of development policies and interventions to their domestic taxpayers is to set the priorities of development policies on areas that enjoy broad public approval in the donor country. Despite that Western citizens have generally very little knowledge of the actual needs and circumstances of people in developing countries, they may still feel that something has urgently to be done about world poverty. As Easterly (2006) notes, the Western public is more willing to approve the provision of massive amounts of foreign aid if it is backed by bold pledges towards cutting poverty in half by 2015 (United Nations General Assembly 2000) or the promise of the end of poverty (Sachs 2005), even if such goals are not connected to the reality of recipient countries. Although this situation represents primarily a failure in the design of development policies, it also favours bureaucratic failures if these goals turn out as too ambitious to be implemented by the administration. According to

---

[31] According to the 2007 OECD Development Cooperation Report (OECD DAC 2008), the proportion of financial aid from Western donors recorded as untied increased from 42.5% in 2002 to 53.0% in 2006 (the remaining share accounts for tied aid or aid those status is not reported). Despite the increasing untying of aid, the report also notes that the latest figures suggest that a large proportion of contracts financed from untied aid are still going to suppliers in donor countries.
[32] The OECD estimates that tying aid to specific commodities and services, or to procurement in a specific country or region, increases development project costs by as much as 20–30% (Jepma 1991).

Peirce (1981), failure is particularly likely if the final outputs of programmes that promote such ambitious goals are difficult to measure, if the achievement of goals is outside the control of an agency or if meeting the goal requires an agency to engage in many diverse areas of activity simultaneously.

A related but even more momentous consequence of the separation of taxpayers from beneficiaries in development assistance is the lack of accountability and feedback in the provision of foreign aid. While citizens in a representative democracy can vote their government out of office if they are dissatisfied with the way it spends their taxes, recipients of foreign aid have no such feedback mechanism on their disposal. Lack of feedback from beneficiaries makes bureaucratic failure more likely because it deprives aid agencies from crucial information about the real impact of their development interventions, as well as of the true needs of local beneficiaries. In this case, mistakes are more likely to be repeated while learning from experience and the scope for improving ongoing programmes and the allocation of assistance across partners are limited.[33]

Lack of feedback about the impact of development assistance interventions also limits the accountability of donors for the effectiveness and sustainability of their programmes, because in the absence of clear and verifiable results, it is difficult to compare what an agency is doing with what it is supposed to do. Accountability is even further weakened if multiple donors share the responsibility for development outcomes, which happens if they are collectively engaged in a programme as co-financing partners, or in the case of multilateral development assistance.

9.3.2 Adverse Behaviour of Aid Bureaucrats

Another way in which aid agencies can fail to achieve their intended goals is through adverse behaviour of bureaucrats and agents along the chain of aid delivery. The analysis of organisational decision-making from a behavioural perspective goes back to Herbert A. Simon's seminal work on administrative behaviour (Simon 1947). Accordingly, bureaucratic failure may occur as a consequence of individual decisions that are inefficient against the background of an organisation's purpose and objectives.

---

[33] In order to mitigate theses sources of bureaucratic failure, aid agencies increasingly aim at obtaining feedback from independent evaluations of their projects and programmes. These evaluations often take the form of programme assessments including organisational reviews and process monitoring, which cannot estimate the magnitude of effects of an intervention with clear causation. Causal analyses that help to understand the relative role of alternative interventions require assessing the counterfactual (i.e., the situation of a target group without the intervention). This is inherently difficult and adequate approaches are just about to be developed and tested. For a discussion of some of these new techniques see Sect. 10.4.

9.3 The Danger of Bureaucratic Failure in the Administration of Development Assistance

In the context of development assistance, an example of how internal incentive structures at development agencies can induce aid bureaucrats to behave in ways that undermine the agency's organisational goals is the resistance or slow adaptation of aid agency staff to change. Information problems due to limited feedback that development agencies obtain from the beneficiaries of their assistance are often aggravated by the fact that bureaucrats at aid agencies are slow in adapting to changes in policy approaches and aid instruments that result from lessons gained through such feedback. In spite of the rhetoric about new strategies for development or a "new" development economics, neoclassical thinking is still very much alive at the level of project implementation. For instance, Rodrik (2006) reports how difficult it is to bring the implications from a recent World Bank review of the growth experience of developing countries in the 1990s[34] to bear on the Bank's country operational work. The review actually recommends that the World Bank should apply more context-specific approaches to policy reform, while the projects it actually implements still reflect to a large extent the Washington Consensus-type of reforms.[35] Moreover, many of the newer and promising development approaches and theories cut across disciplines. Economists, who by far dominate the development field, will thus be required to cooperate with psychologists, sociologists, anthropologists and historians. Unfortunately, the skill mix at international development agencies does not yet allow for such interdisciplinary cooperation. Finally, technical staff specialised in old-fashioned areas may lobby for the continuation of projects in their areas of expertise. This pressure for continuity creates strong impediments to the application of new development paradigms and innovative implementation approaches.[36]

There are many other instances where personal goals are in conflict with organisational ones and hence make bureaucratic failure in the administration of development assistance more likely. Collier (2002), for instance, notes that staff at donor organisations has strong incentives to keep lending – even in environment of low recipient government ownership or limited absorption capacity – both to prevent default on previous loans and to maintain the flow of project work which underpins their jobs.

---

[34] See Sect. 10.1.

[35] Uphoff and Combs (2001) provide two interesting case studies which demonstrate how "paradigm blockages" can obstruct the view on efficient but by the standard of the prevailing paradigm seemingly impossible solutions. In one case, they report of unrecognised opportunities for alternative growing techniques of rice in Madagascar which depart from international best practice but produce even higher crop yields in the Madagascan context. In another case they discuss how childhood rickets going unseen as a disease in Bangladesh because conventional wisdom stipulates that rickets does not occur in the tropics.

[36] The slow adaptability of the World Bank and other aid agencies to new development approaches has already more than two decades ago been noted by Ascher (1983) who found that employees at the Bank are much more guided in their decision-making by their ideologies and professional role models than by the political agreements that set out the institution's goals and strategies.

9.3.3 Informational and Motivational Problems Associated with the Provision of Aid

Bureaucratic failure is not confined to the individual behaviour of bureaucrats at aid agencies alone. The implementation of development policies and assistance programmes can equally fail because the presence of foreign donors may create perverse incentives for intermediaries and beneficiaries at the recipient side. In such cases, bureaucratic failure at the operational level is linked to processes at the policy level of decision-making, as well as at the level of the rules according to which international development cooperation is organised and governed. The incentive structures at these levels need to be aligned with local incentives at the operational level if the goals of development assistance are to be achieved.

The most comprehensive analysis of the relationship between incentives, foreign aid and the effectiveness and sustainability of development outcomes has been conducted by a research team lead by Elinor Ostrom of the Workshop in Political Theory and Policy Analysis at Indiana University on behalf of the Swedish International Development Cooperation Agency (Ostrom et al. 2002).[37] To study the incentives in the development system, the authors have developed an illustration (see Fig. 9.1) that

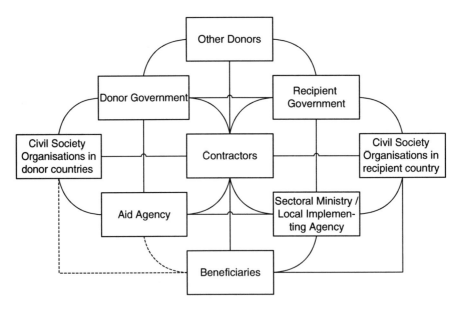

Fig. 9.1 Actors and linkages in the International Aid System. *Source*: Adapted from Ostrom et al. (2002)

---

[37] See also Kremer (2002) who extends the focus on the role of institutions and incentives on development outcomes to the design of development assistance. Easterly (2001) makes the argument that foreign aid doesn't work because it doesn't take into account the fact that people respond to incentives. For further elaborations on his arguments, see Sect. 10.2.

features the relationships between all major actors of development cooperation and the way in which they are linked across organisations and national boundaries.

Exploring the relationships between the actors in development cooperation elucidates a variety of incentive problems that can lead to bureaucratic failure at the operational level, for instance:[38]

1. *Principal–agent problems*: In many situations, there is great asymmetry in the bargaining power and information between donor and recipient governments. If a recipient is weak because he lacks administrative capacity or is dependent on aid, he may not prioritise his needs and instead accept (as agent) any development plan that a strong donor (as principal) presents to him. This principal–agent relationship may result in bureaucratic failure as the efforts of the recipient are difficult to monitor and his incentives are likely to differ from those of the donor. Moreover, the asymmetric information that is associated with principal–agent problems can lead to unproductive outcomes when the donor is missing local information about some of the actions he could take or about the real effects of his actions on their outcomes.

2. *Moral hazard problems*: Asymmetric information may also create unproductive incentives for recipients to act in ways that incur costs they do not have to bear. The availability of aid creates a moral hazard, since it may shield incompetent recipient governments from the consequences of their actions, discourage reform efforts and weaken their incentives to search for alternative sources of revenue.

3. *Samaritan's dilemma*: Like in the case of moral hazards, foreign aid can alter incentives that recipients face in ways that undermine its effectiveness. Once recipients recognise that the amount of the aid they receive varies inversely with the amount they earn on their own, they will have an incentive to reduce their own efforts so as to obtain larger contributions from international donors.[39] For instance, many donors have relied on financing gap models in determining the amount of aid they grant. But such models have given recipients an incentive to increase the financing gap by favouring consumption over saving.[40]

4. *Missing or weak formal institutions*: As shown in Part I of the analysis, actors in low-income countries can seldom build trusting relations on the basis of effective state-backed contract enforcement and property-rights regimes. Instead, they have to rely on alternative modes of governance that can differ markedly from those common in donor countries. In effect, the operational rules of Western aid agencies are often incompatible with local rules in use. While local actors may be used to deal with members of social groups, communities and networks

---

[38] The following examples are drawn in part from Ostrom et al. (2002).

[39] The "Samaritan's Dilemma" has earlier been analysed by Buchanan (1975). For an application of the dilemma in a study on the effectiveness of development assistance, see Pedersen (2001).

[40] A further problem associated with the Samaritan's Dilemma and the ability of recipients to reallocate resources to other uses (i.e., the problem of the fungibility of aid) is that recipients are more likely to become dependent on aid.

which they trust on the basis of common values, conventions or cultural beliefs, Western donors strictly oppose relation-based contracting for fear of favourism, rent-seeking and corruption. Implementing their own operational rules, however, requires strong donor involvement and control over the process, which is in conflict with efforts towards greater local ownership in development aid.

5. *Corruption*: A related source of bureaucratic failure that can undermine the effectiveness of development assistance is corruption. The more widely discussed manifestation of corruption is the embezzlement of public assets by political leaders especially in developing countries, as well as the influence of political decisions by powerful groups or individuals through private payments to public official and politicians (state capture). Less in the spotlight is administrative corruption at the level of development institutions or local implementing agencies. Here, corruption occurs through the misuse of the aid bureaucracy for personal or political gain. Reducing administrative corruption requires understanding and changing the internal incentive structures at implementing agencies in both the donor and recipient countries. For instance, adequate wages, a credible organisational culture or open and transparent decision-making processes all help to reduce the motivational problems that can lead to corruption at the operational level.[41]

The linkages between actors in the development aid system shown in Fig. 9.1 also illustrate well the above discussed problems of feedback and accountability in development cooperation. It becomes obvious that the weakest link in the system actually is the link with beneficiaries. Donor governments and aid agencies are only indirectly linked to beneficiaries through the recipient's implementing bodies as well as through contractors or consultants who are engaged by the donor to assist the recipient in implementation. Especially the central position of the latter may lead to considerable information asymmetries that have important implications for aid sustainability. For instance, the engagement of contractors deprives donors from valuable information that they would need for the evaluation of projects and the design of future interventions. In many cases, contractors have the closest and most regular contact with beneficiaries in the recipient countries. Yet, they are only temporarily engaged for the duration of a project and are thus rarely in a position to feedback their experiences in the process of design and delivery of future interventions. Moreover, the principal–agent relationship that characterises the linkage between contractors and donors often discourages contractors from using their knowledge about beneficiaries in the interest of the latter, as they often regard the aid agency (their principal), and not the recipient, as owner of the project. One conclusion of the study by Ostrom et al. (2002, p. 160) is that external contractors and consultants often face incentives to maximise their efforts on tasks they think will please the Western donor or aid agency in order to maintain their reputation and increase the prospect of future reemployment.

---

[41] For a more detailed discussion of the problem of corruption in both donor and recipient countries, see Shleifer and Vishny (1993, 1998), Hancock (1998), Johnson et al. (1998), Klitgaard (1988) and Wade (1982).

To sum up, it can be concluded that the presence of a foreign donor in a recipient country alters existing incentives in both intended and unintended ways. Bureaucratic failure is particularly likely if the incentive structures at the operational and policy levels of the international aid system are insufficiently aligned with local incentives and power configurations. Often, the donor enters a recipient country with the objective to change existing institutions, policies or rules. Such changes are rarely neutral in their effects on the allocation of resources. Instead, the involvement of foreign donors in domestic institutional and policy reform changes perceived benefits and costs of existing and potential policies and institutions for different actors. It is thus necessary to understand what societal actors, with what interests, are affected by the intended institutional change: who benefits and who loses from current institutional arrangements, and who would benefit and lose from the changes. Although a socially desirable reform makes many people better off at the expense of only a few, the support of the winners is often more difficult to mobilise than the opposition by the losers. This is because potential benefits of reform are usually more uncertain than potential costs. Moreover, beneficiaries of reform are usually numerous, dispersed, poor, uninformed and unorganised, while potential losers tend to be concentrated and well organised. The technically optimal design of an intended policy reform or institutional change therefore may need to be adjusted in order to become compatible with the existing incentive structure (Burki and Perry 1998).

9.4 Summary of Conclusions from the Review of Development Economics

In the following, the main results from the preceding appraisal of development thinking and its influence on development policy over the past 70 years will be restated in a number of guiding principles. These statements summarise the main lessons and conclusions from past experiences, and highlight areas for future research. As such, they are intended to guide development research and policy into new directions with a view to arrive at a deeper understanding of economic realities in low-income countries, and to better enable policymakers and development experts to master the challenge of igniting and sustaining processes of broad-based growth in today's poorest economies.

1. Development economics is the branch of economics that studies economic phenomena in the specific contexts of developing countries. These countries tend to differ markedly in their economic characteristics from advanced economies, and even among one another. Their distinct characteristics arise out of their specific cultural, political and historical legacies, which influence the evolution of their institutions and hence the way in which economic relations are organised and governed.
2. Development theories must reflect the specific contexts of developing countries in their assumptions and premises. Inference from economic theories and models

that are derived from observed realities in advanced economies, or from the researcher's subjective concept of the world as he sees it from a remote perspective, can instead be highly misleading if applied to the contexts of developing countries.
3. The differences between developing and advanced countries are particularly significant in the case of low-income countries, which represent the poorest and least developed economies, most of which are located in Africa south of the Sahara. In these countries, structural constraints to private economic activity are particularly high. Consequently, low-income countries have hitherto rarely experienced any significant and sustained growth accelerations. The first and foremost challenge of development policy in these countries is to ignite processes of sustainable, broad-based growth. It involves identifying the binding constraints to economic activity in specific cultural and historical contexts of low-income countries.
4. The distinct characteristics of low-income countries not only require development theories to be contingent upon these countries' specific contexts. They also imply that no common policy solutions exist to similar problems that emerge in different local settings. The economic functions and principles that are essential for economic activity in low-income countries to evolve are actually supported by a diversity of institutional designs, which are quite distinct from those of advanced economies and can vary markedly with different local constraints and structures. A related conclusion is that the objectives of development policy that enjoy a broad consensus today are confronted with a multitude of ways of implementation.
5. Development economics is a policy-oriented subject. It should be pursued like an applied field of research with the objective to provide clear operational guidance to policymakers. This implies an emphasis on relevance above elegance and formal rigour. It requires economists to think more in terms of second-best settings by paying greater regard to how policies interact with informal institutional arrangements and indigenous modes of organising economic activity that arise from the constraints economic actors face in an environment of persistent poverty, high transaction costs, incomplete markets and weak governance of formal state institutions. Broad generalisations inspired by first-best models of the economy and recourse to universal economic principles alone cannot inform effective policies in such a setting. Nor will policies succeed if they seek only to foster convergence towards a unique, predetermined set of best-practice institutional forms.
6. To accommodate the need for greater context specificity and policy relevance of development theories, a research methodology is required that starts from the facts, and not from a set of general principles and axioms. It involves arriving at theoretical explanations by inductive reasoning, i.e. by a logical process that begins with the observation of specific empirical circumstances, and derives from these overarching but yet context- and time-conditioned conclusions.

9.4 Summary of Conclusions from the Review of Development Economics

7. The quality of empirical research that is required for scientific induction is quite different from the aggregate statistical data needed for the econometric analysis and testing of isolated economic relationships across different countries and contexts, on which development economists have relied for a long time. The inductive method demands for careful explorative and observational research and rigorous country analytic work to uncover the essential characteristics and causal relationships of economic life in low-income countries.
8. Context-specific determinants of development defy universal generalisations. Theoretical findings based on aggregate data from a cross-section of diverse countries are likely to ignore exactly the kind of context-specific information that is crucial for effective policy advice. Even though development theories that followed this approach were able to explain how different factors relate to one another, they tended to remain inconclusive about the direction of causation in the relationships. Such causal ambiguity has limited the possibilities of policymakers to extract from the theoretical findings and models operational guidance for the design and implementation of growth-igniting policies in low-income countries.
9. Bureaucratic failures in the implementation of growth-igniting policies in low-income countries within the framework of international development cooperation can further undermine the effectiveness of these policies. The involvement of foreign donors in domestic institutional and policy reform almost always changes local incentives as well as perceived benefits and costs of existing and potential policies and institutions. Development assistance is most successful if the incentive it provides are compatible with incentive structures at the level of local intermediaries and beneficiaries. Such an approach requires information about indigenous institutional structure and arrangements, as well as about the involved actor's motives, interests and expectations.
10. Development economists have achieved much in identifying and explaining the determinants of growth and development, but their findings did not always provide the kind of policy-relevant information needed to implement effective measures towards igniting and sustaining growth in low-income countries. At the theoretical level, the key to improving the policy relevance of development theories lies in the choice of appropriate analytical techniques and methods of research. At the policy level, success will be decided by the approaches taken to reform. And in the area of development assistance, the effectiveness and sustainability of aid will depend in the first place on the incentive compatibility of delivery mechanisms and implementation arrangements. Increasing the amount of official development assistance and choosing the right funding priorities are necessary, but no sufficient concerns.

Part III
In Search of an Analytical Framework for the Study of Low-Income Countries: The Style-Economic Approach

This part takes the conclusions from the historical review of the contributions from three generations of development economists as point of departure for the search of an analytical framework that accommodates the demands for a more context-sensitive approach to development research and policy advice. The purpose is to outline, in an admittedly preliminary fashion, a research methodology that makes the interrelations between economic, cultural and historical influences in the development process accessible to economic analysis. This is thought to be of essence for uncovering contextual characteristics of countries or societies, and is therefore considered instrumental also for understanding the distinct, context-specific elements of economic life in low-income countries.

The book is not singular in this effort, though. In the last decade, serious attempts have been made at devising new research methods and techniques that allow for deeper and more relevant analysis of economic life in poor countries. These attempts, to a large extent, have been motivated by evidence from recent policy evaluations that revealed a wide variation in the impact of similar policy prescriptions across different contexts, and led to an increasing recognition of the conclusion that effective solutions to common development problems tend to be context-specific. The analysis in this part will start with a closer look at these emerging new contributions to development economics (Chap. 10). This will be done by assessing the present state of research in modern development economics, as well as with the purpose to identify possible links with the contextual approach that shall be advanced in the remainder of this part.

Surprisingly enough, the problem of context-specificity had once already been fully recognised by members of the Historical School of Economics, whose contributions shaped the economic mainstream in much of continental Europe from at least eighteenth until the early twentieth century. Its members practised contextual economics in that they recognised the time-conditioned nature of economic processes, as well as their dynamic interrelationship with noneconomic, namely cultural factors. Their empirical–historical approach, which involved establishing theoretical conclusions inductively from observation, was distinctly different from the classical economics of David Ricardo and John Stuart Mill that dominated economic research in the Anglo–Saxon world. Albeit members of the Historical School were often criticised for never actually arriving with their empirical–historical method at the stage of theory formulation, they provide ample resources for modern development economists: First, through their attempts at a methodological modification of economics into a science of reality that necessarily also embraces cultural and institutional elements of economic life; and second, through their aspiration for a historical instead of a general theory of economic development.

Unfortunately, the contributions by the Historical School disappeared from the research agendas in the mid-twentieth century just at the time when development economics emerged as an own economic sub-discipline that studied the economies of less developed countries. The more development economics became neoclassical in its assumptions, the more did the importance to consider economic phenomena in their specific historical and geographical context, which was so central to the research programme of the Historical School, escape the view of development economists. It was only when their universal policy prescriptions proved to be highly variant in their results across different contexts, that historical, institutional and cultural factors were rediscovered as explanatory factors of economic outcomes. And while the context-specificity of development paths and strategies has long, though often only tacitly, been reckoned by those development practitioners who have been working extended periods in the field and in close contact with the local population, it is now gradually regaining attention in economic research as well.

Both the relevance and intellectual oblivion of the Historical School's scientific method and concepts warrant an attempt at their rediscovery for modern development economics. This shall be done in the last three chapter of this part. A focus will be on the "younger" and "youngest" Historical Schools of the early twentieth century and their methodological and conceptual contributions, while the economic policy activism regarding the problems of their time, which especially the "younger" Historical School under Gustav Schmoller was famous but also criticised for, will largely remain outside the scope of the discussion. Besides an assessment of the relevance of the historical–empirical method of research, a particular focus will be on the concept of the "economic style", which epitomises the contextual approach to economics by the Historical School. Following the German economists' historical method, the concept of economic styles rests upon the assumption that most economic processes are conditioned by the historical and institutional context in which they take place. The idea is to model these context-specific characteristics of an economic system as elements of a discrete economic style, which delineates the space within which appropriate assumptions and generalisations about the behaviour of economic phenomena can be made. As it is often historical and culturally derived factors that determine people's economic preferences, attitudes and choices, and as these tend to account for the most significant differences across countries and societies, the concept of economic styles is in particular useful as a tool for modelling the influence of cultural factors on economic behaviour and outcomes. Given the misleading conclusions that instead the use of an abstract and timeless notion of culture frequently produced, economists usually display a healthy degree of scepticism towards any recourse to cultural explanations in economic analyses. As the discussion in this part hopes to show, the conceptualisation of cultural influences on economic life as time- and context-conditioned occurrences of attributes of an economy provides an analytically sound alternative.

Chapter 10
Emerging New Directions in Development Economics

In what direction does development economics head? How are the conclusions from the historical review of development economics shaping current development thinking? Are development economists on the point of devising the methods and techniques to uncover and explain the specific constraints and opportunities that characterise economic activity in low-income countries? This chapter attempts to give some tentative answers to these questions by discussing several recent contributions and trends in the development literature that are emerging out of their authors' interpretation of the widely varying results of hitherto practiced methods and approaches to development theory and policy. Many of these contributions can in fact be viewed as first signs for the advent of a fourth generation of development economists.

The main purpose of an emerging new generation of development economics should not be to search for even further panaceas for growth, but rather to complement the available knowledge about multiple determinants of growth and development with appropriate methods of researching these determinants in the specific contexts of low-income countries, and to devise effective approaches for the design and implementation of related policy solutions. Indeed, one of the implications of the conclusions from past experiences is that any new paradigm in development economics will have to focus more than anything else on questions of *how* to do arrive at relevant theoretical conclusions and effective policy advice, rather than on the question of *what* to do, which centres around a growing list of principle themes in the development literature and related options in development policy.

10.1 Confessions of Humility and Ignorance

A good indicator to establish which direction mainstream thinking in development economics may take is to look at what the World Bank does.[1] In this respect, a recent report in which the Bank reviews the growth experience of developing countries in the 1990s, evaluates the effects of its own growth-promoting policies, and tries to interpret the reasons for the wide variation of these effects from expected results (World Bank 2005) stands out. In the preface to the report, Gobind Nankani[2] writes:

> The central message of this volume is then that there is no unique universal set of rules. Sustained growth depends on key functions that need to be fulfilled over time: accumulation of physical and human capital, efficiency in the allocation of resources, adoption of technology, and the sharing of the benefits of growth. Which of these functions is the most critical at any given point in time, and hence which policies will need to [be] introduced, which institutions will need to be created for these functions to be fulfilled, and in which sequence, varies depending on initial conditions and the legacy of history. Thus we need to get away from formulae and the search for elusive "best practices," and rely on deeper economic analysis to identify the binding constraints on growth. The choice of specific policy and institutional reforms should flow from these growth diagnostics. This much more targeted approach requires recognizing country specificities, and calls for more economic, institutional, and social analysis and rigor rather than a formulaic approach to policymaking. [...] To mainstream this approach to the formulation of growth strategies needs persistent efforts and willingness to experiment. The new perspectives also have implications for behavior – in particular the need for more humility. And, last but not least, they highlight the need for a better understanding of noneconomic factors – history, culture, and politics – in economic growth processes (Ibid, pp. xii–xiii).

This note captures many of the demands on a new generation of development economists that follow from the preceding analysis: the recognition that effective solutions to common development problems tend to be context specific; the plea for new techniques that allow for deeper and more relevant economic analysis of low-income countries' distinct characteristics; and the need to consider a broader set of factors, both economic and noneconomic ones, in the explanation of economic phenomena. For an institution like the World Bank, these are ground-breaking conclusions. They are not without controversy, though: just as the World Bank reflected on its growth-promoting policies in the 1990s, the IMF published a paper in which it reviews the outcomes of the Washington Consensus policies on growth in Latin America – and comes to strikingly different conclusions (Singh et al. 2005).[3] In this paper, the authors

---

[1] Of the almost 10,000 people that the World Bank employs, nearly 100 are development economists who work full-time with the Bank's Development Economics Vice Presidency. Apart from them, many more do research at the Bank's thematic networks and regional units, at its Independent Evaluation Group, and at the World Bank Institute.

[2] At the time the report was produced, Gobind Nankani, a Ghanaian native, was Vice President and Head of the World Bank's Poverty Reduction and Economic Management Network. He oversaw the report which was written by a team led by Roberto Zagha. Members of that team were J. Edgardo Campos, James Hanson, Ann Harrison, Philip Keefer, Ioannis Kessides, Sarwar Lateef, Peter Montiel, Lant Pritchett, S. Ramachandran, Luis Serven, Oleksiy Shvets and Helena Tang.

[3] For a review of both the World Bank report and the IMF paper see Rodrik (2006).

identify policy imbalances, the lack of policy resilience, and the need for more sustained institutional reforms as the main reasons for the disappointing results of the Washington Consensus policies in Latin America. The authors thus abide by the second generation of development economists' approach to universal policy reforms, albeit in an augmented fashion.[4]

Another recent report that aims at pushing the frontiers of understanding of growth is the final document of the Commission on Growth and Development (2008). In this commission, 21 leading practitioners and policymakers chaired by Nobel-Laureate A. Michael Spence have reviewed, over a period of 2 years, the current state of science in a variety of areas relevant for economic growth and development to find answers to the question of how developing countries can achieve high, sustainable and inclusive growth. In particular, the Commission assessed the causes, consequences and internal dynamics of economic growth in 13 fast and sustainably growing developing economies with a view to draw conclusions from their experiences for today's low-income countries.[5] An apparently straightforward but far-reaching conclusion from the report, which is reflected in many of its recommendations, is that poor countries differ markedly from rich and mature economies. Not only are low-income countries lacking many of the institutions that allow markets to function, they also differ in the way in which their economies respond to policy reforms. The authors of the report thus recognise the difficulty to replicate successful growth experiences, and recommend an experimental or pilot approach to development policymaking in order to identify, from a menu of options, those interventions that prove to be most effective in a particular country context. Moreover, and similar to the findings from the review by the World Bank of its growth policies in the 1990s, the Growth Report concludes that while there is a broad consensus about the conditions and strategies that foster growth, the way to achieve these varies greatly from setting to setting.

The valuable progress that the Growth Report makes in departing from the wholesale approach to policy reforms of the Washington Consensus, as well as the lessons that the World Bank derives from its review, are much in the spirit of Harvard University professor Dani Rodrik's work.[6] Among contemporary development economists, he comes very close to what can be considered an exponent of a prospective fourth generation of development economists. The motivation behind much of his work is to resolve the paradox that development is working in countries like China and India, while development policy as advocated by bilateral and

---

[4] Not only are Washington-based institutions everything but in consensus about prospective approaches to development policy, the World Bank study obviously didn't met everyone's approval even within the Bank: In November 2006, Gobind Nankani resigned after 30 years in service at the World Bank, becoming the "latest casualty in President Paul Wolfowitz's management shake-up" (Reuters 2006).

[5] These economies that grew at an average annual rate of 7% or more for 25 years or longer in the post-war period are Botswana, Brazil, China, Hong Kong (China), Indonesia, Japan, South Korea, Malaysia, Malta, Oman, Singapore, Taiwan (China) and Thailand.

[6] Rodrik contributed to both the work of the Growth Commission, as well as to the preparation of the World Bank's *Economic Growth in the 1990s* review. Moreover, he is teaching in an executive programme that the Center for International Development at Harvard University runs for economists at the World Bank.

multilateral development institutions is not. Rodrik criticises the "laundry-list" approach to policy reform behind the Washington Consensus that tries to simultaneously achieve as many objectives as possible from a predefined list of universal policy prescriptions. Instead, he argues for a strategic approach of sequential interventions that focus on only one or very few areas of reform that have the greatest impact on unlocking a country's growth potential. Rodrik refers to these areas as the "binding constraints" to growth and proposed (together with Hausmann and Velasco) a framework for diagnosing these biggest hurdles to growth in the specific economic environment of any given country (Hausmann et al. 2008).[7] A key theme in the writings of Rodrik is that policy prescriptions have to be contingent upon a country's specific context, i.e. its initial conditions, endowments, history and administrative capacity. By that, and by recognising that effective institutional outcomes do not map into unique institutional designs, he compellingly reveals the futility of efforts to search for universal empirical regularities that link specific institutional rules to economic outcomes (Rodrik 2007).

10.2 Planners vs. Searchers

Inspiration for a fourth generation of development economists also comes from New York University economist William Easterly. His focus is primarily on the design and implementation methods of international development assistance. In his *The Elusive Quest for Growth* (Easterly 2001), he presents a historical review of the solutions offered by Western experts and aid agencies to the development problems of low-income countries, and shows for each of these solutions how they failed to give people the right incentives to respond in the intended ways. In his later book *The White Man's Burden*, Easterly (2006) interprets this failure to apply basic economic principles to the practical implementation of development objectives as the consequence of a "Planner's approach" to policymaking and aid delivery. Planners, according to Easterly, believe in big plans to solve the big problem of world poverty. Yet, they fail to consider the near impossibility of implementing their vision of the transformation of poor societies from the outside by means of international development assistance. He contrasts the Planners' approach with the mentality of "Searchers". Development economists who work as Searchers get close to the people, find out through ground-level explorations what is feasible, and concentrate on piecemeal improvements in response to concrete needs. Easterly presents his sharp division of the development community into Planners and Searchers as follows:

> In foreign aid, Planners announce good intentions but don't motivate anyone to carry them out; Searchers find things that work and get some reward. Planners raise expectations but take no responsibility for meeting them; Searchers accept responsibility for their actions.

---

[7] This growth diagnostics approach is discussed in more detail in Sect. 10.4.

10.2 Planners vs. Searchers

> Planners determine what to supply; Searchers find out what is in demand. Planners apply global blueprints; Searchers adapt to local conditions. Planners at the top lack knowledge of the bottom; Searchers find out what the reality is at the bottom. Planners never hear whether the planned got what it needed; Searchers find out whether the customer is satisfied. [...] A Planner thinks he already knows the answers; he thinks of poverty as a technical engineering problem that his answers will solve. A Searcher admits he doesn't know the answer in advance; he believes that poverty is a complicated tangle of political, social, historical, institutional, and technological factors. A Searcher hopes to find answers to individual problems only by trial and error experimentation. A Planner believes outsiders know enough to impose solutions. A Searcher believes only insiders have enough knowledge to find solutions, and that most solutions must be homegrown (Ibid, p. 6).

Its provocative and highly stylised account notwithstanding, the opposing characteristics of Planners and Searchers mirror well the differences in methodology that distinguish mainstream development economists from a prospective fourth generation that seeks to accommodate the lessons from past experiences. Among these conclusions, the emphasis on context-specific answers to common development problems corresponds with the Searcher's consideration of local knowledge and preference for homegrown solutions; the operational guidance required from development research is reflected in the Searchers' demand-driven action as well as their appreciation of a larger variety of relevant endogenous factors; and the Searchers' bottom-up approach echoes the need for greater reliance on inductive reasoning in development economics that is informed by careful observation of the realities of low-income countries prior to the formulation of development theories. Finally, Easterly's praise of Searchers leads him to favour a sequential approach to reform as opposed to an implementation strategy that aims at doing everything at once – just as Rodrik urges to concentrate reform on the areas of the economy where the binding constraints to growth lie.

The Planners-versus-Searchers divide also highlights the important role of accountability and feedback (or lack thereof) in the delivery of international development assistance.[8] Searches only work if knowledge about local needs and of the actual impact of an intervention is made available through some kind of feedback mechanism that gives intended target groups a voice in the design and delivery of assistance programmes. But donors and policymakers do not have much incentive to listen to such feedback unless they can be held accountable for the success or failure of their programmes.[9]

Easterly invokes the market model as an ideal for feedback and accountability (customers provide feedback through their buying decisions, whereas produces take responsibility for meeting customer expectations). But while taking the market mechanism as an inspiration for the Searcher's approach, Easterly does not offer markets as solution to the problems of low-income countries. Instead, he acknowledges the difficulty to make markets work in countries that lack properly governed

---

[8] See also Sect. 9.3.

[9] Even though both accountability and feedback are highly desirable, the challenge lies in eliciting information from the poor about their real preferences in light of the fact that they often lack possibilities to convert their needs into a market demand.

state institutions that guarantee economic freedom in production and exchange activities as well as the security of property rights. These market-creating institutions emerge from a complex of interlocking social norms and customs that are often hidden from the view of the outsiders; much less can they be built from the outside through universal free-market reforms. As discussed in Part I, an important characteristic of countries that evolve from subsistence to market economies is the formation of diverse institutional arrangements that perform, to some degree, equivalent functions as market-creating and market-supporting institutions. They thus permit trade and implicit contracts between parties before there are formal property titles, uncorrupted courts, or regulatory and supervisory agencies. Easterly recognises these institutional arrangements as "bottom-up" solutions to the absence of possibilities for efficient rule-based exchange on markets. These indigenous institutions can in fact be viewed as the result of poor peoples' own searches for functioning modes of governance of their economic relations. In most cases, they provide a solution to just one particular problem in one particular setting. But given their alignment to the specific conditions of the context in which they evolve, these indigenous solutions frequently prove to be more effective than any large-scale development plan.[10]

There are indeed many more examples for development measures that can be considered as the invention of Searchers in the sense that they were found from ground-level exploration of the conditions and needs of poor people. A well-known example is Grameen Bank of Bangladesh with which its founder Muhammad Yunus pioneered the micro-lending movement. During the Bangladesh famine of 1974, Yunus, then an economics professor at Chittagong University, realised how little economic theory had to offer to explain the famine, and decided to study the real lives of the poor in a nearby village. From this perspective of a Searcher, he identified the lack of formal micro-credit services to the poor as the binding constraint to their escape from poverty, which eventually led him to demonstrate that the poor are bankable and that lending to them on a commercial basis is practicable and even profitable.[11] In his autobiography, Yunus (Yunus and Jolis 1999, p. 5) notes:

> By attempting to equip the students with a bird's eye view, traditional universities had created an enormous distance between students and the reality of life. When you can hold the world in your palm [...] you do not realize that when looking from such a great

---

[10] Other recent voices of disenchantment with the results of international development assistance include Calderisi (2006), and Moyo (2009). Both are focussing on aid to Africa. Like Easterly, Calderisi, a former World Bank Country Director for Central Africa, sees no benefit in calls for increasing the amount of aid to Africa. In light of his view that Africa's problems were too often self-imposed by incompetent and corrupt heads of state, he even recommends cutting foreign aid to African governments in favour of direct support to promising private initiatives, multi-country projects, and political backing of the few governments that are credibly committed to fighting poverty. Zambian-born economist Moyo offers an African perspective on the problem of aid that leads her to very similar conclusions, though. Specifically, she provokes by maintaining that aid is no longer part of the potential solution to African ills, but has become part of the problem itself. For further critical reading on international aid see Hancock (1998).

[11] On the economic rationale behind group lending as practiced by the Grameen Bank see Sect. 4.2.2.

distance, everything becomes blurred, and that you end up imagining rather than really seeing things. I opted for what I called the 'worm's view'. I thought that I should rather look at things at close range and I would see them sharply. If I found some barrier along the way, like a worm, I would go around it, and that way I would certainly achieve my aim and accomplish something [...]. This idea of providing small-scale yet real help, not just theory, to at least one living person gave me enormous strength.

In spite of such evidence, the Planner's mentality is still present in current thinking at development institutions and in academic research. A prominent example is the United Nations Millennium Project headed by Jeffrey Sachs, the underlying approach of which Easterly so fiercely controverts in his *The White Man's Burden*.[12] Based on the premise that the world community today has at its disposal the technologies, policies, financial resources, as well as the courage and compassion to achieve the Millennium Development Goals (MDGs), Sachs and his team have presented a needs assessment and calculation of the cost of attaining the MDGs (UN Millennium Project 2005).[13] This plan includes the recommendation for large-scale coordinated investments in human capital, public infrastructure, and agricultural technologies that are reminiscent of the early modernisation theorists' "big push" approaches to economic transformation in developing countries. With regard to achieving the MDGs in south of the Sahara Africa, Sachs and his team presume the continent to be caught in a poverty trap from which it can only escape through a substantial increase in foreign aid.[14]

A first step towards implementing the findings of the UN Millennium Project are the Millennium Villages through which communities of selected villages across Africa are empowered and provided with the necessary resources to implement a basket of development interventions. The central hypothesis underlying the Millennium Village project is that the whole of the intervention is greater than the sum of its parts. It suggests, for instance, that the impact of an educational intervention is limited if children are malnourished or affected by diseases, and that therefore a programme to lift multiple constraints at the same time will have a disproportionately high impact. The idea behind this strategy is very different from the approach presented by Rodrik (2007), who recommends concentrating development interventions on the binding constraints to development in any given setting. However, it has to be noted that Rodrik's approach refers to growth promoting policies at the macroeconomic level, while the Millennium villages feature a new approach for fighting poverty at the programme level.

The Millennium Project adds to the MDGs (as the widely accepted consensus on the objectives of international development policy) a plan of *what* to do to

---

[12] The Millennium Project was commissioned by the United Nations Secretary-General in 2002 as an independent advisory body to recommend a concrete action plan for the world to achieve the Millennium Development Goals. As of 2007, the Millennium Project secretariat has been integrated into the United Nations Development Program (UNDP).

[13] For a presentation of the MDGs, see Table 2.1 in Sect. 2.2.

[14] See also Sachs et al. (2004), and Sachs (2005) for similar proposals.

achieve these objectives. But it fails to offer an answer to the question of *how* the proposed interventions can effectively be implemented in low-income countries. Even the approach piloted with the Millennium Villages is much more focussed on resources than on issues relating to the organisation and governance of delivery mechanisms. For instance, the Sachs report recommends the mass distribution of free insecticide-treated bed-nets, and presents the associated costs of doing so as a part of the financial commitment which supposedly buys the world a two-thirds lowered under-five mortality rate, and a reversal of the incidence of malaria. However, a crucial assumption for this link between spending and results to work is that the targeted populations respond to the intervention in the desired manner. This means that they must actually use the freely distributed bed-nets for purposes of malaria prevention rather than as wedding gowns or fishing-nets. But whether or not people respond in a desired manner to the incentives that a development measure provides depends on how sensibly local conditions are accounted for in the design of related policies and implementation arrangements. It is here where a new generation of development economists will have to contribute operational guidance and innovative new thoughts which Sachs and the Millennium Project fail to deliver.

This brief review of current streams in development thinking – both unconventional ones that head into new directions, as well as ones that intensify past practices – suggest that development economists are far away from a consensus about the way ahead, and in particular about how best to confront the challenge of igniting growth in low-income countries. Nonetheless, new thinking in development economics like that by Rodrik and Easterly, as well as advancements in economics and neighbouring disciplines, are inspiring further academic research and experimentation with new approaches at the level of both development theory and policy. Above these new directions in development economics, concepts like increasing returns to scale, market-size externalities, linkage effects, or circular causation that were so central to the explanation of the development process in the formative years of the sub-discipline, are as well worth revisiting.[15]

10.3 Behavioural Development Economics

The interpretation of lessons from past development theory and policy is not the only source of inspiration for a fourth generation of development economists. New directions in development research are also influenced by advancements in economics and neighbouring disciplines that can help development economists to draw nearer to a broader and more relevant set of behavioural assumptions for the study of economic activity in low-income countries. First such attempts originated from applications of the rational choice model to contexts where information is expensive

---

[15] See Sect. 6.2 on these contributions.

10.3 Behavioural Development Economics

(e.g. Stigler 1961) and imperfect (e.g. Stiglitz 1985; and Sect. 8.1), where transaction costs and the structure of property rights matter (e.g. Williamson 1979; De Alessi 1983; and Sects. 8.2.1 and 3.1), and where decisions have to be made under risk and uncertainty (e.g. Kahneman and Tvesky 1979; as well as Sect. 2.1.4 and Chap. 4). Moreover, conventional definitions of rationality have been challenged by new developments in behavioural economics (e.g. Simon 1987 and Becker 1976), and the testing of systematic deviations from the standard rationality assumption with the methods of game theory and experimental economics (e.g. Smith 1962; Selten 1988; as well as Fehr and Schmidt 2000).

While all these contributions share the intent to enrich neoclassical models of individual behaviour, they deal differently with the challenge their findings pose to the standard axioms of rational choice theory. On one side of the spectrum are contributions that aim at extending neoclassical models of rational choice by departing from one or more of its underlying assumptions. By assuming external constraints that place bounds on the behaviour of otherwise fully rational and self-interested individuals, these contributions leave the basic edifice of neoclassical economics intact. For instance, bounded rationality, a central concept in behavioural economics, explains deviations from conventional behavioural assumptions by limited cognitive abilities that constrain intendedly rational behaviour (Simon 1947). As a further example, Becker (1984) has argued in his study of the family that altruism is still another facet of utility maximisation in that people derive utility from the well-being of others. He thereby demonstrated that seemingly altruistic (or at least reciprocal) aspects of human behaviour are consistent with individual utility maximisation and hence still constitute rational behaviour. The argument common to these contributions is that not all behaviour, which fails to meet the ideal hypothetical situation of standard neoclassical theory, must necessarily be irrational.

Insights from contributions that remain firmly grounded in the rational choice framework of neoclassical economics have to a large degree already been integrated into development research by the third generation of development economists.[16] They require further reconsideration with regard to some fundamental methodological questions they pose. First, it has to be asked if the newly recognised constraints from, say, limited information, knowledge or cognitive capacities actually fit into the standard neoclassical framework. At present, most economists continue analysing the "hybrid" models, which result from modifying and extending the assumptions of the rational choice model, in the same orthodox manner as before. For instance, as Furubotn and Richter (1997, p. 227) note, it is not unusual to find in such hybrid models that the individual decision maker is assumed to be perfectly informed about some matters while, at the same time, completely ignorant of others. Inconsistent model structures are also likely if findings from behavioural economics about the influence of moral norms or reputation on individual choices are introduced into new models without simultaneously relaxing, among others, the neoclassical assumption

---

[16] See especially Sect. 8.1 on contributions that model the consequences of imperfect information, and Sect. 8.2.1 on those that integrate positive transaction costs in development theory.

of given individual preference functions. Similarly, with the assumption of positive transaction costs, institutions have been introduced into economic analysis as an efficient response by individuals who seek to economise on the cost of their transactions. But this focus on allocative efficiency makes the analysis incomplete if it does not also account for the many noneconomic factors that influence the evolution of institutions. Finally, it has to be asked if models that take into account the behavioural consequences of norms and values within families, communities or social networks can still adhere to the precept of methodological individualism which regards individuals as autonomous maximises.[17]

On the other side of the spectrum are recent advancements in behavioural economics that integrate insights from psychology to enrich models of individual choice, as well as empirical findings from experimental economics that are apparently inconsistent with even the extended versions of the rational choice model. Nevertheless, these contributions show particular promise for the study of economic behaviour in low-income countries as they allow evaluating a broader set of behavioural assumptions that better account especially for noneconomic (i.e. cultural, psychological or historical) influences on individual decision making. Their application to the study of low-income countries can thus help to significantly broaden the scope of development economics beyond the influence that applications of information economics and institutional theory have had on current development research. But unlike these earlier extensions of standard rational choice theory, advances in behavioural economics and new methods of experimental research are much less well integrated into modern development economics yet.[18] Applying these methods to the analysis of economic phenomena in low-income countries will thus have to become an important area on the research agenda of a fourth generation of development economists.

First such attempts have generated intriguing results. For instance, recent empirical evidence from field experiments by Duflo et al. (2007, 2008), who studied the economic behaviour of small-scale peasant farmers in Western Kenya, suggest that the failure of these farmers to adopt new technologies cannot be explained by low expected rates of return, and only to a lesser extent by external constraints such as insufficient capacity to absorb new technologies. Instead, the field trials revealed that profitable investment decisions are not being made because of internal constraints to solve an underlying optimisation problem (i.e. to do the necessary saving needed for later financing of the investment). In the field experiments that generated these results, the authors tried to understand why most small-scale peasant farmers in the studied region do not use fertilisers for maize in spite of evidence for their high rates

---

[17]See also Furubotn's (2001) critical assessment of institutional extensions to the theory of the firm. He maintains that the procedure of constructing models with ill-matched assumptions drawn from the disparate neoclassical and neoinstitutional universes precludes economists from maintaining a consistent analytical viewpoint.

[18]Initial attempts at integrating insights from behavioural and experimental research into modern development economics include, for instance, Kanbur (2003); Mullainathan (2007); and Cardenas and Carpenter (2008). See also Sect. 10.4 on applications of new experimental methods for empirical research in development economics and impact evaluations of development policies.

of return – an observation that apparently contradicts the assumption that peasant farmers are rational profit maximisers. They found that the farmers did not know that the return to fertiliser use is sensitive to how it is used. But even after they were told how to use the fertiliser, most of them still did not use any fertiliser in the following season. The majority of farmers explained that they do not have the money to buy fertiliser, which was unconvincing as they had a return from their yield from the previous season, and even a small amount of it saved and invested in fertiliser during the next planting season would have been very profitable. Only when the farmers were given the opportunity to buy fertiliser immediately after harvest time against the promise to get it delivered in the planting season did the use of fertiliser go up. These findings suggest that peasant farmers face some kind of internal constraint that prevented them from doing the necessary saving on their own as would have been predicted by rational choice-based theories. Results of this kind pose a formidable challenge for future development research.[19] They not only seem to bring into question the empirical validity of basic axioms of economics, but they can also hardly be understood with the help of existing theories (Duflo 2006).[20]

10.4 Trends at the Level of Research Methods and Analytical Techniques

The nature of theoretical conclusions and the relevance of research findings for policymakers crucially depend on the scientific methods and analytical techniques that development economists employ. As the discussion in Chap. 9 suggested, it is at this level where innovative change is likely to have the greatest impact on the validity and policy relevance of results from future research. In this section, newer developments at the level of the methods and analytical tools for empirical research on low-income countries will be reviewed. In particular, the focus is on those new methods and techniques which, in view of the conclusions from past practices, are expected to lead to theoretical conclusions that feature both, sensitivity to local contexts, and operational guidance for policymakers.

Many of these new methods for empirical research in development economics are arising from the motivation to overcome the limits of regression analysis discussed in Sect. 9.2.2. But this motivation has not only driven the search for alternative methods and approaches, but theeconomists that are fond of regression analysis have also themselves acknowledged its limitations, and responded with a voluminous literature that attempts at addressing the problems associated with growth regressions

---

[19] For an attempt to master this challenge see Part III, especially Sect. 13.1.4.
[20] Apart from the finding of apparently irrational behaviour from field experiments, the assumption of economic rationality is also called into question by behavioural evidence from recent laboratory experiments, especially where complex decision situations are concerned (see, for instance, Fehr and Rockenbach 2003).

by increasing the sophistication in the use of econometric techniques even further. Such refined techniques include, for instance, longitudinal panels to control for unobserved heterogeneity, or the more careful selection of instrumental variables to minimise errors resulting from endogenous regressors and reverse causality problems.[21] Moreover, much effort is being directed at increasing the quantity and quality of statistical data sets from developing countries in order to gain an improved basis for the measurement of variablesThere obviously is still a strong tendency towards abiding by the use of econometric methods since the elegance of their results, and the mathematical precision of their findings fit in so neatly with the highly formal standards of conventional development economics.

But these contributions only cursorily address the methodological problem associated with the use of cross-national regressions in development research. Mere refinements in econometric techniques and statistical data sets cannot solve the more fundamental problem that very little explorative empirical research is still done prior to the formulation of hypotheses and the specification of econometric models that are used for their subsequent empirical verification. It is not without reason that the alternative methods presented in the following have originated from their authors' healthy scepticism towards the presumptive, *ex ante* knowledge about economic problems and conditions in low-income countries that so often informs the formulation of models and assumptions in development research. Their common purpose is, indeed, to generate new knowledge that is relevant to the specific contexts to which the theoretical conclusions and policy recommendations that are based on it shall apply.

This does not mean, however, that these new techniques are intended to replace cross-national econometrics. They shall rather be used in a complementary fashion to advance the understanding about economic realities of specific countries and thereby help to generate novel and more context-sensitive hypotheses and theoretical conclusions. But in spite of that, econometric methods can remain an important tool for their subsequent testing, given the availability of relevant statistical data.

10.4.1 Analytic Narratives

The analytic narratives method[22] uses narrative techniques for the detailed and textured account of economic processes, specific institutions or problems and puzzles that occur in the context of a particular time and place. These narratives are

---

[21] Mookherjee (2005, p. 4331) says about these new econometric contributions that "[r]esearch papers tend to get evaluated almost exclusively in terms of their success in combating the econometric problems, often to the exclusion of the importance of the context or issues addressed by the analysis, the imaginativeness of the underlying hypotheses formulated or tested, or the importance of the findings from a wider standpoint."

[22] On the question whether analytic narratives are indeed a method or rather an approach, see Bates et al. (2000). As they are presented here, analytic narratives clearly describe a method for empirical research.

analytic in that they use explicit and logical lines of reasoning to provide a model of a complex phenomenon, and to theorise about the relationships among the actors, institutions and structures that are constituent parts of that phenomenon. Levi (2004, p. 208) describes the steps involved in assembling an analytic narrative as follows:

> Analytic narratives involve choosing a problem or puzzle, then building a model to explicate the logic of the explanation and to elucidate the key decision points and possibilities, and finally evaluating the model through comparative statics and the testable implications the model generates.

Narratives as a form of reasoning have long been employed in scientific research. They are particularly common in the historical sciences. The application of analytic narratives as a method of research in development economics is quite novel, though.[23] This is despite the fact that this method is, for several reasons, particularly suited to study economic phenomena in low-income countries[24]:

First, analytic narratives offer explanatory accounts of phenomena and processes within the specific institutional context in which they occur and, at the same time, highlight important interactions between these specific country circumstances and influences from the external environment. For instance, the country analytic narratives collected in Rodrik (2003) explore the respective roles of microeconomic and macroeconomic policies, initial conditions, the institutional arrangements that arise from these, as well as other country specific historical, technological, geographic and political factors. As such, they enable development economists to find answers to selected growth puzzles not previously explained by the empirical literature on growth.

Second, analytic narratives provide information required for causal assessments, which is crucial especially in situations where temporal sequencing, particular events, and path dependence must be taken into account (Mahoney 1999). By allowing for clear causal inferences, they also address the reverse causality problems that may arise in econometric analyses, and thus help to arrive at a better understanding about the direction of causal relationships in the realities of low-income countries.

---

[23]Country case studies have also been a main analytical tool of the first generation of development economists. But they used them rather as result of a lack of reliable statistical data from developing countries, and were often too quick in generalising observations from one country to the whole group of developing economies.

[24]A compilation of recent contributions that each applies the analytic narratives approach to answer a specific growth puzzle in a developing country is provided by Rodrik (2003). Among others, the studies in the volume try to unravel the driving forces behind the exceptional growth experiences of China, India, Botswana and Mauritius, as well as the patterns that can help to better understand earlier growth accelerations in Brazil, Mexico, Venezuela and Indonesia. Of interest to development economists is as well the analytic narratives project (Bates et al. 1998), which synthesises the approach in a number of essays that combine historical and comparative research with rational choice models in order to explain the formation and change of specific institutions in particular times and places. Also multilateral development banks are discovering analytic narratives as a method to complement statistical estimates and indicators with a more profound understanding of their underlying causes and deeper determinants (see, for instance, Anderson 2009).

Third, analytic narratives can provide important insights, especially when the specificity of a phenomenon does not allow for accumulating the kind of empirical data required for good statistical analysis. The same applies to situations where either the phenomenon itself or the period under study is not amenable to quantitative research as it is the case, for instance, in small-N research (Levi 2004, p. 210f).

From a methodological point of view, analytical narratives produce exactly that kind of explorative empirical information that is needed for arriving at theoretical conclusions through a process of inductive reasoning. They are particularly useful for empirical description of the relevant phenomenon prior to the formulation of relevant theories. A logical consequence of the context-conditioned nature of empirical data generated by analytic narratives is, however, that the findings obtained by this method are of limited portability into other, differently structured contexts. But this apparent limitation may also be seen as a safeguard that prevents economists from generalising their findings too broadly across different places and times.

10.4.2 Growth Diagnostics

While analytic narratives describe a scientific method of empirical research, growth diagnostics represent a new approach to economic reform. But both share an emphasis on context and the diversity of possible growth strategies, and thus can complement one another in fruitful ways. As the discussion will show, the growth diagnostics framework offers an approach to policymaking that is a lot more flexible than the best-practice approach adopted by the second generation of development economists, as well as the approach to policy design by those third generation development economists who inform their policy prescriptions by cross-country benchmarking of data on the quality and performance of a country's institutions.

The growth diagnostics approach has been developed by Ricardo Hausmann, Dani Rodrik and Andrés Velasco of Harvard University (2008) in response to their rejection of what they call a "laundry-list" approach to policy reform that was so common in the era of the Washington Consensus. This approach meant to simultaneously achieve as many policy objectives as possible without paying due regard to a country's specific circumstances, which, as the authors argue, has often led policymakers to start with reforms that were not crucial to their country's growth potential.[25] Growth diagnostics are, instead, a tool that can help policymakers to focus their reform efforts on those areas of the economy where the "binding constraints" on economic activity are. Growth diagnostics thus provide a framework for designing a growth strategy that adopts a sequential approach to reform by focusing on only one or very few areas of intervention that have the greatest impact on unlocking a country's growth potential. Moreover, as the focus is primarily on an economy's short-term constraints, the growth diagnostics framework is

---

[25] See Sect. 10.1.

10.4 Trends at the Level of Research Methods and Analytical Techniques

particularly suited to support attempts at igniting growth and identifying constraints that inevitably emerge as an economy expands (Hausmann et al. 2006).

The growth diagnostics exercise offers a decision tree methodology that can help to identify relevant binding constraints to a country's growth. As an example, Fig. 10.1 displays a basic taxonomy of possible causes of the problem of low levels of private investment in a low-income country. By following the decision tree, possible explanations of the problem can sequentially be ruled out until the key constraint to private investment is identified. This process starts by asking what keeps investment low (inadequate returns to investment or inadequate access to finance). If it is, for instance, a case of low returns, the question is whether that is due to insufficient investment in complementary factors of production (such as human capital or infrastructure) or due to poor access to imported technologies. If, instead, the cause of the problem is rather one of high financing costs, the binding constraint to low levels of private investment should be sought on either domestic or external financial markets (Hausmann et al. 2008). It has to be emphasised that such an assessment of individual causes along the decision tree is inherently country- and time-specific and needs to be informed by rigorous country analytic work.[26]

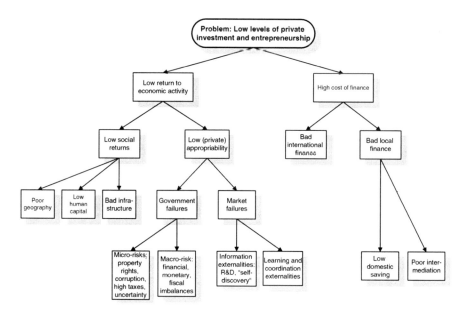

Fig. 10.1 The growth diagnostics methodology. *Source*: adapted from Hausmann et al. (2008)

---

[26]Hausmann and Rodrik (2005) apply the growth diagnostics approach to El Salvador to identify its greatest obstacles to growth and to explain why the country did not perform well despite adopting almost every possible reform from the Washington Consensus policy list after its civil war in the 1980s. The South African National Treasury recently appointed an international advisory panel to perform growth diagnostic assessment of the South African economy and to help it identify the binding constraints to shared growth (Hausmann 2008).

10.4.3 Experimental Methods

What growth diagnostics can achieve at the level of macroeconomic policies is attempted through experimental methods at the microeconomic level. In particular, experimental techniques can be useful to evaluate a wide range of development programmes targeted to individuals or local communities (such as projects in the area of sanitation, local government reform, education, or health). Unlike analytic narratives, experiments are not in the first place a method of explorative or observational empirical research that informs theoretical hypotheses prior to their formulation, but rather a tool for impact evaluation. This is because experimental methods require that a concrete project, as well as related hypotheses about its underlying cause–effect relationships, already exist before the method can be applied. Nevertheless, new insights obtained from experimental evaluations about the causal links between a project measure and the outcome of interest can still offer strong priors for any subsequent theoretical treatment of the problem in question.

The most commonly used experimental methods for the evaluation of development outcomes are randomised trials or, where the conditions permit, natural experiments (i.e. experiments involving the comparison of groups whose variants of interest arise naturally).[27] Randomised experiments that are used for impact evaluation try to answer an essential counterfactual question: how would individuals who participated in a programme have fared in the absence of the programme? Or, how would those, who were not exposed to the programme, have fared in the presence of the programme? Because, at a given point in time, nobody can be observed to be both exposed or not exposed to a programme; the idea behind randomised trials is to compare an individual, or group of individuals, that are affected by a development measure with a similarly structured group that lives in the same context but without any exposure to the effects of the evaluated programme.[28] In the language of experimental research, the first group is called the treatment group, while the other is known as the control or comparison group. A good comparison group should be fully isolated from the effects of the programme and should not differ from the treatment group in any respect other than the effect of the programme. If that is not assured, any pre-existing differences between the two groups will inevitably be captured together with the effects of the programme and thus distort the evaluation results. Such a so-called selection bias can be avoided through the randomisation of the evaluation. This is done by selecting the treatment and comparison groups randomly from a potential population of

---

[27] The following discussion on randomised experiments in development research draws on Duflo and Kremer (2005).

[28] The alternative strategy to observe the same group before and after their exposure to the programme (which is usually done by performing a baseline and a follow-up survey of the beneficiaries) would in most cases yield biased and hence unreliable estimates about the impact of the programme, because the results will also capture the effect of any other changes in the environment of the observed group that occurred in the interim.

10.4 Trends at the Level of Research Methods and Analytical Techniques

participants (such as individuals, communities, schools, or classrooms). For instance, Kremer (2003) shows how randomised evaluations work to estimate programme effects and provide lessons for policymakers in the case of programmes intended to increase school participation, provide educational inputs, and reform the education system.[29]

Randomised trials only work if their evaluation strategy (i.e. the identification of treatment and control groups) is integrated into the implementation design of the programme concerned. For instance, the method is often used in the framework of pilot projects that can then be scaled up if their effectiveness is confirmed by the results of the randomised evaluation. Moreover, randomised phasing in programmes allows impact evaluations with an experimental design to be performed simultaneously with programme implementation. An example that follows this approach is a project by a Dutch NGO that was evaluated by Miguel and Kremer (2003). The project distributed deworming drugs to schoolchildren in Busia district in Western Kenya where over 90% of the children were infected with intestinal worms that caused listlessness and malnutrition. The project was phased in the deworming programme for over 3 years. In the first phase, phase I schools (the treatment group) were compared to phase II and III schools (the comparison groups). In the second phase, phase I and II schools as treatment groups were compared to phase III schools as the comparison group. From this experiment, Miguel and Kremer were able to identify a positive effect of deworming drugs on school attendance, but found no effect of deworming education on worm infection rates.

The advantage of experimental evidence is that it clearly, and without ambiguity, identifies causal links between the policy or treatment in question and the outcome of interest. Technically, this means that experimental results have strong internal validity. But their results are only valid within the confines of the experiment, implying that their external validity is relatively weak. Generalisations to other contexts or settings are only possible if repetitions of the experiments in these contexts yield similar results. Just as results from cross-country regressions are frequently contested for their lack of internal validity (on grounds of their often inconclusive identification of the direction of causality between dependent and independent variables), the results from randomised experiments can also be contested for their lack of external validity (on grounds of the limited portability of their results to other contexts). While internal validity decides about the operational guidance that policymakers can extract from empirical results, external validity determines how this guidance can be used for informing policies that shall apply to a broader population of interest, or other countries and contexts. By inferring

---

[29] For more examples of pioneering research on development and poverty based on randomised trials see the work done in and around the Abdul Latif Jameel Poverty Action Lab (J-PAL), which was founded in 2003 by Abhijit Banerjee, Esther Duflo and Sendhil Mullainathan at the Massachusetts Institute of Technology (http://www.povertyactionlab.org). A good review of the recent literature on randomised trials, and a discussion of the strengths and limitations of the experimental approach to development economics, is provided by Banerjee and Duflo (2008).

theoretical conclusions from experimental evidence, development economists face the same basic question that is involved in every exercise of theoretical abstraction and generalisation: they have to decide whether a particular context is sufficiently similar to the context from where the empirical data and results were drawn. This is very similar to the old and controversial problem of determining the applicability of a theory by asking whether its assumptions are sufficiently good approximations of the reality they are supposed to explain.[30]

But for all that, randomised experiments certainly represent a major step forward for development economists in refining the methodology of their research. This is not only because randomised experiments are less ambiguous in their determination of causal relationships than other methods of empirical research, but also because experimental methods play to the claim for more modest, manageable, and sequential policy interventions because the method works best as a tool for rigorous evaluation of programmes that are small and the effects of which are confined to a specific context.

Rodrik (2008) offers yet another reason for being optimistic about the gradual appreciation of experimental methods in development economics. He sees considerable commonalities between the experimental approach that development economist apply in their study of microeconomic interventions, and the experimental character of identifying a country's binding (macroeconomic) constraints to growth within the framework of growth diagnostics.[31] For him, this means that both micro- and macro-development economists are moving towards the adoption of the same pragmatic, experimental, and contextual mindset when trying to find out what policies work in low-income countries. It is this convergence at the methodological level that marks, for Rodrik, the advent of a New Development Economics.

---

[30] For a detailed discussion of this problem, see Sect. 7.2.

[31] As Rodrik (2008) notes, the best known example for the successful application policy experimentation as a strategy for discovery of what works is China's experience with experimental gradualism. Among the policy experiments that underpin China's economic success are, for instance, the household responsibility system, dual-track pricing, township and village enterprises, and special economic zones. For a detailed discussion of China's experience at economic reform, see Heilmann (2008) and Qian (2003).

Chapter 11
German Historical Economics as Development Economics

The tradition of the Historical School of Economics reaches back to the end of the 30 Years' War which was fought between 1618 and 1648 mainly on the territory of today's Germany. It left the country in a state of devastation and had considerably depleted its productive resources.[1] The task of the German public administration was thus one of reconstruction and directed towards a gradual catch-up with the German states' wealthier neighbours – a theme that also motivated much of the later writings by members of the Historical School and made them a genuine part of the development literature, albeit one from the perspective of a backward nation.[2]

But this does not in itself explain the relevance of the Historical School for modern development economics. It is a characteristic trait of the writings in the historical tradition that none of their solutions were meant to be immediately transferable into other contexts. Nor is it supposed that the problems of their time were identical to the challenges that today's low-income countries face. The true relevance of the German Historical School instead lies in the scientific method that its members developed and applied in their study of problems of economic development, and in the epistemological value of the concepts they formed.

The main purpose of this chapter is therefore to lay down the research methodology of the German Historical School, with a special emphasis on the writings by its younger exponents, and to propose it as an alternative to the prevailing deductive method in development research.

---

[1] In some areas, the war and war-related famines had cost the lives of up to 70% of the civilian population. The Swedish armies alone destroyed 2,000 castles, 18,000 villages and 1,500 towns in the German states, representing one-third of all German urban areas (Trueman 2008).

[2] One frequently encounters in early historical writings the idea of Germany as a *verspätete Nation* (a laggard nation) compared to the rest of Europe (Reinert 2005).

11.1 Scope and Scientific Method of the German Historical School

The early methodological principles of the German Historical School were laid down by Wilhelm Roscher (1817–1894).[3] In his 1843 *Grundriß zu Vorlesungen über die Staatswissenschaft nach Geschichtlicher Methode* (Outline of Lectures on Political Economy According to the Historical Method), he criticised the abstract character of classical economics, which had, since Ricardo, increasingly relied on purely deductive reasoning. He instead proposed a return to more evidence-based research and the use of historical-empirical data. Moreover, he argued for the historical method as contributive to a positive rather than normative science. Bruno Hildebrand (1812–1878), another member of the "older" Historical School, was particularly critical of classical theories' timeless and static character, and wanted to transform political economy into a theory of laws of the economic development of nations (Hildebrand 1848). In about the same period, Karl Knies (1821–1898) adopted an even more radical standpoint in his *Die Politische Ökonomie vom Standpunkt der Geschichtlichen Methode* (Political Economy from the Standpoint of the Historical Method 1853) where he went as far as to deny the existence of economic laws of whatever kind, including Hildebrand's developmental laws (Lane and Riemersma 1953).[4]

An elaborated treatment of the methodological tenets of the Historical School is offered by Gustav von Schmoller (1838–1917), a member of the "younger" Historical School, in his *Grundriß der Allgemeinen Volkswirtschaftslehre* (1923a, especially Introduction III-4), which will be discussed here in more detail and in place of similar contributions by other members of the school. For Schmoller, the aim of economics as a science was to design a detailed picture of the (national) economy – a compendium of all economic phenomena in their specific historic and geographic context. To achieve this aim, he proposed a three-step approach that provided a formal structure to economic research in the historical tradition. Accordingly, the economist has first to correctly observe economic phenomena across time and space, secondly to define and classify them according to their similarities and distinguishing features, and

---

[3] The contributions by Roscher and members of the early Historical School were again foreshadowed by cameralistic science (*Cameralwissenschaft*) which had its origin in the German cameralistic system: From the end of the middle ages, most German countries kept an institution called the Council (*Kammer*) which was concerned with the administration of justice and the regulation of private enterprises. The knowledge necessary for these council officials, which found no place in the lectures on law, was treated in a special discipline, the cameralistic science. It was Frederick William I., himself a clever cameralist, and author of the masterly financial system of Prussia, who took the important step of founding in 1,727 special chairs of economy and cameralistic science at Halle and Frankfurt/Oder. The later chairs in political economy in Germany were formed out of these schools of cameralists, while in England, Scotland and Italy, political economy had its origin mainly in the study of questions of finance and foreign commerce (Roscher 1878, p. 96f).

[4] For recent discussions of the Historical School, see Backhaus (2005), Reinert (2005) and Shionoya (2001).

finally to find typical forms and regularities that enable him to explain causal relationships (Schmoller 1923a, p. 101).[5]

According to Schmoller, correct scientific observation of economic phenomena means that repeated observations by the same or different observers will lead to the same results. This in turn requires that the process of observation must be free from any subjective influence or personal opinion. The observation shall have "objective validity, exhaustive precision, and extensive completeness" (Ibid, p. 102).[6] To achieve this, any observed phenomena must be analysed in the context of the larger system of related phenomena, and be compared with theses in order to identify similarities and differences.

According to Schmoller, the purpose of scientific description is to attain a more general picture of the economy through the observation of particular economic phenomena. This is done by comparing the observations with known phenomena and by describing these with the aid of existing notions and concepts. The description of economic phenomena involves processes of concept formation (*Begriffsbildung*) whenever established concepts and notions are insufficient to express the characteristic core of an observed phenomenon. Accordingly, the formation of new concepts means establishing the most defining features and significant characteristics of a phenomenon. Furthermore, it represents a way of classifying economic phenomena according to a specific research question or interest.

The last step in Schmoller's research programme finally requires the economist to arrive at insights about causal relations among the observed factors. This is the most important and, for two main reasons, also the most difficult task: First, the economist has only limited knowledge about the remote past that would enable him to infer future events from historic developments. The second complication stems from the fact that all economic phenomena are twofold conditioned: First, through material (i.e. physical, technical or natural) factors, and secondly, through mental (i.e. psychological, moral, cultural or political) influences (Ibid, p. 108). Schmoller argued against the belief that either class of factors follows from the other. For instance, a society's culture cannot primarily be explained by prevailing climate conditions or other natural circumstances, just as cultural factors deliver no complete explanation for differences in production technologies. Schmoller not only emphasised the pivotal role of psychological factors and ethical value orientations in the humanities in general, and in economics in particular, he also stressed that these factors introduce a degree of complexity into the

---

[5] Elsewhere (Schmoller 1923a, p. 77), Schmoller breaks down and extends these three tasks of the economist (observation, classification and explanation) into seven criteria that any economic inquiry has to satisfy: (1) to describe and define economic phenomena; (2) to draw up an appropriate picture of them with the aid of scientific notions and concepts; (3) to comprehend the phenomena both as a coherent whole as well as a part of the entire social life; (4) to explain particular elements from their causes; (5) to recognise the historical course of economic developments; (6) to predict the future where possible; and (7) to give policy recommendations that will help to shape future developments in an desirable manner (cf. also Backhaus 1989, p. 39 ff).

[6] In the German original, this quote reads as follows: "*Die Beobachtung soll objektive Gültigkeit, erschöpfende Genauigkeit [und] extensive Vollständigkeit besitzen*".

explanation of economic phenomena that inherently limits the scope for precise prediction and the possibility to establish simple, one-way relations of causality (Ibid, p. 109). Because psychological influences on economic outcomes are inherently difficult to quantify, real economic laws that describe stable and measurable relations of causality between observable factors are almost impossible to attain (Ibid, p. 110). However, this conclusion did not lead Schmoller to discard the quest for identifying causal relationships and building economic theories from them. His purpose was rather to make the theorist aware of the fact that economic phenomena involve complex chains of interrelated causes that each require consideration in their specific historical and cultural context, and that each individual consideration entails the employment of a different scientific approach and the application of concepts from different fields of knowledge.

Schmoller's "methodological pluralism" (Backhaus 1989) clearly features an interdisciplinary approach to the explanation of economic phenomena in which economic inquiry is complemented by the methods and concepts from natural science, psychology, and history. Moreover, his research programme reflects an inherently inductivist perspective on science. Accordingly, theories are developed by a logical process that starts with the observation of specific empirical facts, and derives from these overarching principles about the behaviour of a phenomenon by generalising from the specific instances. Schmoller brings the inductive nature of his approach to the point when he states that "[t]he most general is always the most complicated and therefore also the most uncertain; we approach [our subject matter] from the detailed facts" (Schmoller 1923a, p. 110).[7]

During the famous "dispute over methods" (*Methodenstreit*) between proponents of the Historical School (led by Schmoller) and members of the Austrian School of Economics (notably Carl Menger) about the "right" method of research, Schmoller vigorously defended the historical-inductive approach against the neoclassical Austrians' abstract and deductive method.[8] Yet, Schmoller never opposed theoretical deduction as such. He in fact acknowledged that every field of research strives to become, over time, a deductive science (Ibid, p. 111). Thereby, he clearly values the deductive approach as an appropriate method for any science that has reached a certain level of advancement in the sense that sufficient regularities and laws about the studied phenomena are already known, which then permit the deduction of explanations for unknown phenomena from these truths. However, in view of the

---

[7]In the German original, this quote reads as follows: "*Das Allgemeinste bleibt als das Komplizierteste stets das Unsicherste, vom Einzelnen ausgehend dringen wir vor*".

[8]The *Methodenstreit* emerged when Schmoller wrote in his *Jahrbuch* a highly critical review of Carl Menger's *Untersuchungen über die Methode der Sozialwissenschaften und der Politischen Ökonomie insbesondere*, a book on economic methodology that was published in 1883. Menger replied in a pamphlet entitled *Die Irrtümer des Historismus in der Deutschen Nationalökonomie* (The Errors of Historicism in the German Political Economy) in 1884. A series of further papers followed which brought some clarification of logical backgrounds but, as Schumpeter put it, constituted a "history of wasted energies, which could have been put to better use" (Schumpeter 1954, p. 814).

"confusing complications of phenomena" (Ibid, p. 111) which, according to Schmoller, still dominate in the field of economics, much inductive reasoning based on the careful observation of empirical facts is needed before economics can become a deductive science. In his own works, however, Schmoller never passed the point where he felt sufficiently certain about the determinants of all economic phenomena that would have allowed him to employ theoretical deduction as his main method of research. It is this conclusion that explains why Schmoller never derived a general theory from the rich historical and empirical material that he produced.

A related aspect of the controversy over the relative importance of inductive and deductive reasoning in economics relates to determining the acceptable degree of abstraction and generalisation from observed reality. Schmoller actually acknowledged that scientific observation relies on abstraction in that it isolates a single process from the "chaos of phenomena" in order to analyse it separately (Ibid,p. 102). But he also explained why the analysis of economic phenomena warrants a cautious approach towards abstraction: Unlike in the natural sciences, where the researcher is able to manipulate and isolate – through experimentation – the factors that cause a particular effect, economic processes rely on a multitude of complex and interrelated physical, psychological and cultural factors that are very difficult to observe and to quantify in isolation. In striking correspondence with what Schumpeter (1954, p. 472f) would later call the "Ricardian Vice" in economics,[9] Schmoller (Ibid, p. 103) wrote:

> The in itself justified procedure to dissolve an investigated process into smallest pieces, to observe each piece apart from each other, and to assemble a final result only from these observations is possible only under particularly favourable and rare circumstances.[10]

Consequently, Schmoller was particularly hesitant with regard to any form of abstraction, just as he distrusted theoretical deduction as a method for establishing causality in the explanation of economic phenomena.

A plausible interpretation of the true differences between the Historical School and the neoclassical Austrians is given by Shionoya (1989). He asserts that the *Methodenstreit* is actually a name misconception as it was not a debate over method but one over the scope of economic inquiry. Schmoller was interested in individual phenomena in their specific historical and geographical contexts and thus considered, besides material aspects, also a wide range of psychological, ethical and historical factors as relevant for their explanation. By contrast, the members of the Austrian School dealt with isolated economic phenomena which they sought to explain by economic factors alone and through the application of general economic principles and laws of universal validity. Their reliance on deductive-abstract reasoning thus followed from the narrow scope of their research programme. For Schmoller, theoretical deduction had to be an ill-suited method given his efforts to

---

[9] Compare Sect. 7.2.

[10] In the German original, this quote reads as follows: "*Die an sich berechtigte Vorschrift, einen zu untersuchenden Vorgang in seine kleinsten Teile aufzulösen, jeden für sich zu beobachten und aus diesen Beobachtungen erst in Gesamtergebnis zusammenzusetzen, ist nur unter besonders günstigen Umständen restlos durchzuführen*".

study all facets of an economic phenomenon – not just its quantifiable economic ones, but also its historical and ethical dimensions.

The interpretation of the *Methodenstreit* as a debate over the scope of economic inquiry actually offers a possibility to resolve the dispute. Schumpeter tries to do this when he classifies Schmoller as a historically minded sociologist (Schumpeter 1954, p. 812), and elsewhere (Schumpeter 1926) distinguishes Schmoller's research programme from that of the Austrian School by assigning it to the field of economic sociology, which actually is surprisingly akin to the research programme of modern institutional economics. The frequently voiced assertion that, soon after his death, Schmoller's work lost its significance for economic science does indeed mainly stem from the fact that younger disciplines like economic history and sociology have taken up and further developed his results,[11] while the scope of mainstream economics narrowed substantially under the increasing influence of the neoclassical paradigm.

Viewed from today's vantage point, it even seems accurate to assert that the Historical and Austrian Schools of Economics actually shared more common ground in terms of their scope and ideas about the determinants of individual economic behaviour, than both did with mainstream neoclassical economics as practiced from the 1940s on. This will be illustrated in a brief excursus into the Austrian School's contributions to marginal utility theory.[12] Carl Menger and, independent but almost simultaneously also William Jevons and Léon Walras, based the explanation of value on utility.[13] Menger realised that in choosing between different goods, consumers decide for the one that they consider to bring the highest marginal utility to them. This view rejected the hypothesis of the English Classical School of Adam Smith and David Ricardo according to which exchange value is unilaterally determined by the cost of production, specifically by the amount of labour embodied in a commodity.[14]

Menger acknowledged that values (or prices) of goods are subjectively determined by their relative marginal utilities to consumers, but his theory remained an objective one because he thought these values should be worked out in a market interaction process where they represented an objectively measurable cost. It was left to later members of the Austrian School, notably Ludwig von Mises and Friedrich von Hayek to develop a subjectivist theory that moved beyond the limits that the neoclassical description of equilibrium between marginal cost and marginal utility had imposed

---

[11] Hennis (1987), for instance, found extensive evidence for the deep roots of Max Weber's economic sociology in the work of the German Historical School.

[12] The following discussion is based on Altmann (1999).

[13] Jevons' *Theory of Political Economy* and Menger's *Grundsätze der Volkswirschaftslehre* both appeared in 1871. Walras began to publish his contributions to marginal utility theory in 1874 in his *Elements of Pure Economics*.

[14] This change in approach towards marginal utility theory as a subjective science came at the expense of a loss in objective, predictive content, however. The failed realisation of this should later result in much confusion when it came to the practical application of marginal utility theory on policy issues such as the restoration of optimal equilibrium conditions though non-market decision-making in response to "market failures" (Buchanan 1969).

on it by assuming an idealised market interaction process in which all individuals behave economically.[15] Their contention was that this idealised concept of equilibrium has a meaning only if applied to the actions of a single individual, because he is the only instance to which all "data" relevant for his choices are given (Hayek 1937). But since an individual's data are subjective in the sense that they are the result of his individual knowledge and anticipations, they apply only to this particular individual's own plans. In consequence, equilibrium at the level of society as a whole would require that all actors pursued compatible plans, which would mean that they all possessed the same subjective data – a proposition that appears duly unsound as it lacks empirical content.[16]

With their subjectivist methodology, the members of the Austrian School actually acknowledge that individual economic behaviour is determined by unquantifiable subjective knowledge, influenced also by psychological and ethical factors. In this sense, the propositions and assumptions of the Austrian School of Economics were much closer to those of the Historical School than both schools were willing to admit.

---

[15]The central features of the subjectivist methodology are laid down by Ludwig von Mises in his *Grundprobleme der Nationalökonomik* (Jena: Gustav Fischer Verlag 1933), and in Hayek (1937).

[16]Hayek (1937) further notes that, supposed there was such a social equilibrium, this would be stable only as long as all individual actors were in their individual behavioural equilibrium. The preservation of the latter in turn required every single individual's subjective knowledge to be the "correct" one for achieving his personal plan.

Chapter 12
From Stage Theories to the Concept of Economic Styles

The relevance of the Historical School for modern development economics arises not only from its members' methodological contributions, but also from the research findings and concepts that emerged from applying this methodology on problems of economic development. A particularly notable example is the attempts to identify typical development paths and stages of economic development. This research entered into the development of the concept of the economic system by Werner Sombart, who devised it as an analytical tool to distinguish alternative ways of organising economic life from an historical perspective. Sombart's economic systems finally served Arthur Spiethoff as the basis for the formulation of his concept of economic styles, which, as will be shown in Chap. 13, embraces in a single concept all demands on a theoretical framework for the study of today's low-income countries.

12.1 Stage Theories and the Idea of Economic Systems

The emphasis by members of the Historical School on historically conditioned, context-specific explanations for economic phenomena was closely connected with attempts to develop criteria by which the characteristics of economic life in different historical periods could systematically be ordered and distinguished.[1]

12.1.1 Historical Stage Theories

One of first attempts of this kind was made by Friedrich List (1789–1846) who identified five stages of economic development, which he differentiated by their respective development states of production. The stages he found ranged from a wild state over herding and agriculture to agricultural processing and trade. Bruno Hildebrand (1812–1878) discarded List's production-based criteria. Instead,

---

[1] For a more comprehensive review and critique of the older stage theories see Sombart (1925, pp. 6–14), and Spiethoff (1932, pp. 901–910).

he proposed to classify historical stages of economic development by their characteristic form of exchange (*Merkmal der Umsatzform*), and attributed barter exchange to the stage of a "natural economy", transactions based on the exchange of money to a "monetised economy", and credit-based exchange to a "credit economy". A treatment of economic stages that builds, in part, on List's stage theory is that of Gustav von Schönberg (1839–1908), who proposed the deployment and combination of the factors labour, natural resources, and capital in the production of goods as basic criteria to distinguish discrete historical types of economic activity. Accordingly, he identified six types which include the hunter, fisher, nomadic, agriculture, trade and commerce, and industrial economy (Schönberg 1869).

Gustav von Schmoller (1838–1917) also considered the course of economic history as a sequence of stages of economic development and defined as his distinguishing criterion the kind of interrelation between economic life and the main social and political institutions of a time. He distinguished between the "household economy" (*Hauswirtschaft*) in which economic activity is dominated by subsistence farming and in which the family represents the main social institution; the "town economy" (*Stadtwirtschaft*), characterised by independent corporate activity and the town-markets as its main institution; the "territorial economy" (*Territorialwirtschaft*), governed by feudal order that shaped the organisation of economic activity in (Western) Europe from the fourteenth until the eighteenth century; the "national economy" (*Volkswirtschaft*) in which the first modern private corporations emerged under the influence of the mercantilist system; and finally the "global economy" (*Weltwirtschaft*), which emerged from the globalisation of economic relations between Western powers and their overseas colonies. A remarkable element in Schmoller's stage theory is his emphasis on the political organisation of the people as the driving force behind economic development. He asserts that the main reason for the rise and fall of nations is to be found in the political-constitutional organisation of society – an insight that economists are gradually starting to recollect from studies on the institutional determinants of economic growth (see Sect. 8.2).[2]

For Karl Bücher (1847–1930), the idea of different stages of development was primarily a methodological device to discover regularities in economic development processes, although he never actually formulated an associated theory of development. Bücher was looking for a standard of comparison which would not presuppose the existence of markets and certain forms of exchange at all times, and established the distance between consumer and producer (*Länge des Absatzweges*) as his criterion to distinguish three stages of economic development: The closed "household economy" of antiquity in which production and consumption was bound to the household without any specialisation and exchange; the "town economy" of the later Middle Ages, in which produced goods were directly exchanged with final consumers; and the modern "national economy" in which goods had to circulate through several stages of production before they reached the final consumer (Bücher 1893).

---

[2]For Schmoller's historical stage theory see Schmoller (1884), as well as Schmoller (1923a, b). See also Schefold (1989, p. 91ff).

12.1.2 Werner Sombart and the Concept of Economic Systems

The thinking about stages of economic development by members of the Historical School was substantially refined by Werner Sombart (1863–1941).[3] He found the earlier stage theories untenable because they were, in his view, too mechanistic and even stood, especially in the case of Bücher, in conflict with historical realities.[4] Moreover, he argued that forms of economic life cannot possibly be characterised by a single analytical criterion alone. Sombart was searching for a concept by which the essence of economic life in a particular epoch could be expressed. His objective was to formulate specific theories for each historically discrete economic period. These historically discrete periods are distinguished by the "prevalent motivations (*Motivreihen*) which are the prime determinants of economic life in a particular epoch" (Sombart 1916). Sombart therefore replaced the idea of stages by the concept of the "economic system" (*Wirtschaftssystem*) and noted that there are as many economic systems as there are meaningful alternative ways to organise economic life. For him, the concept of the economic system was an analytical tool – an "ideal type" that describes the specific character of the economic order in a particular historical period. It is a mental construct which can be inferred objectively from its real manifestation in the actual economic constitutions that govern the organisation of economic activity in a specific epoch.[5]

---

[3] See, for instance, Sombart (1925).

[4] Sombart rejected Karl Bücher's theory by noting that the distance between producer and consumer had actually not varied much over the different periods of economic life (for the full argument see Sombart, 1925).

[5] The definition and use of "ideal types" in economics can be traced back to Max Weber (1904). Ideal types, in Weber's sense, represent deliberate mental constructs ("utopias") formed by the scientist to understand the essential properties of his subject of research. They are obtained by a one-sided exaggeration of one or more characteristics which are unified into a single picture that is, however, never to be found empirically in the real world. Although the ideal type is a model or construct, it differs from the abstract models of pure (or general) theory that are encountered particularly in the natural sciences. While the latter arrive at generalisations by isolating a few phenomena from observed reality, Weber's ideal types describe an ideal picture with which the scientist can compare time-conditioned historical situations and institutional patterns. Redlich (1970) proposed that the idea of real types can be expressed as models by reduction, while ideal types represent models by construction. For the exact or natural sciences, the formulation of abstract models is often their main objective of research. In the social sciences, however, ideal types are means, not ends, of the investigation. As Lane and Riemersma (1953) note, the conceptualisation by Sombart of his economic systems as "ideal types" does not exactly correspond with the use of ideal types in Weber's sense, as Sombart did not develop his economic systems purely as mental constructs, but with reference to concrete empirical evidence from historical situations in Europe in both medieval and modern times. As will be further discussed in Sect. 12.2.1, Spiethoff also used ideal type models in Sombart's sense, but furthermore proposed the notion of "real types" to define models that represent the totality of all essential and uniform pattern of a specific historical (i.e. time-conditioned) reality (see Spiethoff 1948, p. 571; and Spiethoff, 1953 for an English translation by Fritz Redlich).

Sombart defined an economic system as having three constituent elements that together describe the totality of economic conduct in a particular epoch.[6] These elements, or system-building components, were (i) the economic spirit as expressed in the thoughts, attitudes and ethos that motivate or constrain economic behaviour (*Geist, Wirtschaftsgesinnung*); (ii) the norms and their enforcement systems that determine the organisation of economic activity (*Form, Regelung, Organisation*); and (iii) the techniques applied to meet economic ends (*Technik*).[7] According to Sombart, this idea of the economic system meets all the demands that the scientist must make on a concept by which different epochs of economic life are to be distinguished: It is, firstly, comprehensive enough to allow for inclusion of all relevant aspects of economic life while, secondly, it is specific enough to capture the essential characteristics of economic life in a particular historical period, and, thirdly, it is general enough to be applicable to all conceivable economic constitutions throughout history (Sombart 1925).

In order to distinguish between different economic systems, Sombart formulated for each of the three constituent elements of economic systems several characteristics or attributes (see Table 12.1). Different occurrences of these characteristics denote different economic systems, just as different parameter values are associated with different structures of an economic model. Unlike the earlier stage theorists who were interested in a single typical characteristic by which the development of stages could best be described, Sombart chose categories that stand in a causal relation with the patterns of economic life (or institutional set-ups) of a specific economic system.

12.2 Spiethoff's Concept of the Economic Style

A conceptual difference between Sombart's "economic system" and earlier stage theories was that Sombart described his economic systems by elements and attributes that were not directly derived from historical experience, whereas the stage theorists chose different historical occurrences of a single characteristic of economic life as their criterion to distinguish between different stages of economic development. However, also Sombart used his concept to distinguish between different stages of

---

[6] Sombart (1925, p. 30) defined as an epoch a historical period during which a specific economic system is realised, that is, during which economic life displays specific characteristic patterns that correspond with the attributes of a particular economic system.

[7] Schmoller, as well as Karl Marx, had already used organisation and technique, respectively, as parameters to distinguish between different economic periods. The specific contribution that Sombart made was the introduction of the economic spirit as a further defining element (Lane and Riemersma 1953).

12.2 Spiethoff's Concept of the Economic Style

Table 12.1 Elements and characteristics of economic systems according to Sombart

Elements	Attributes of elements	Occurrences of attributes
Economic spirit (*Geist, Wirtschaftsgesinnung*)	Motivation for economic activity	Satisfaction of natural wants – earning of (money-) income
	Attitude towards the choice of means	Traditionalism – rationalism
	Attitude of economic agents towards each other	Solidarity – individualism
Forms of organisation and governance of economic life (*Form, Regelung, Organisation*)	Degree of regulation of economic behaviour	Restriction (normativism) – freedom (naturalism)
	Place and mode of organisation of entrepreneurial decision-making	Private economy – public economy
	Constitution of private economic activity	Democracy – aristocracy
	Degree of specialisation and division of labour	Compactness (in-house production) – looseness (professional specialisation)
	Organisation of production	Subsistence economy (production for use) – exchange economy (prod. for the market)
	Corporate governance and organisation	Individual enterprises – social enterprises
Techniques (*Technik, Verfahren*)	Origin of technological advance	Empirical – scientific
	Pace of technological progress	Stationary – revolutionary
	Basis of techniques	Organic – nonorganic (mechanical, inorganic)

Source: Sombart (1925), Spiethoff (1932)

development – or historical epochs – and thus finally pursued a similar objective as earlier stage theorists did before him.[8]

Arthur Spiethoff (1873–1957), a student of Schmoller, still considered Sombart's concept of economic systems as the "hitherto most complete enterprise on which alone his own contributions could be built" (Spiethoff 1932, p. 915). Like Sombart, he used a multiplicity of attributes or characteristics for the determination of different historical (i.e. time-conditioned) patterns of economic life. But he also modified Sombart's concept of economic systems in some important respects. First, he augmented Sombart's schema by refining existing categories and adding new ones to it (see Table 12.2). Secondly, he asserted that this augmented schema of characteristics described economic styles rather than economic systems. Finally, he stressed the openness of his concept by noting that the elements which he selected

---

[8] Sombart actually identified as the historically most important economic systems in Europe (i) the early subsistence economy, (ii) the crafts and (iii) capitalism.

Table 12.2 Basic elements and characteristics of economic styles according to Spiethoff

Elements	Attributes of elements	Occurrences of attributes
Economic spirit (*Wirtschaftsgeist*)	Ethical and moral motivations: leading ideas and convictions to which people subscribe and which guide their actions (*Sittliche Zweckeinstellung*)	Striving for either economic success; the common good; or the greatest possible individual happiness
	Spiritual motivation for engagement in economic activity (*Seelische Antriebe zum wirtschaftlichen Handeln*)	Fear of punishment; altruism; sense of duty; sense of honour; pursuit of economic advantage; striving for power (motivations can be directed towards satisfaction of natural wants or earning of income)
	Mental attitude (*Geistige Einstellung*)	Habitual attitude; or revolving attitude
Natural and technical basis (*Natürliche und technische Grundlagen*)	Population density (*Bevölkerungsdichte*)	
	Natural migration (*natürliche Bevölkerungsbewegungen*)	No; slow; moderate; or growing movement
	Production with or without specialisation (*Güterherstellung ohne und mit Arbeitsteilung*)	
	Intellectual or manual work; combined or separated (*Geistige oder Handarbeit vereint oder geteilt*)	
	Organic or mechanic realisation of technological advance (*Organische oder anorganisch-mechanische Durchführung der Technik*)	
Constitution of society (*Gesellschaftsverfassung*)	Size of economically active part of society (*Größe des wirtschaftlichen Gesellschaftskreises*)	
	Social cohesion (*Gesellschaftliches Verbundensein*)	Kinship; coercion; contractual relation
	Division of labour within society, and composition of society (*Gesellschaftliche Arbeitsteilung*)	

(continued)

12.2 Spiethoff's Concept of the Economic Style

Table 12.2 (continued)

Elements	Attributes of elements	Occurrences of attributes
Economic constitution (forms of organisation and governance of economic activity) (*Wirtschaftsverfassung*)	Property rights regime (*Eigentumsverfassung*)	Private property; state-ownership; or collective ownership
	Constitution of private production (*Verfassung der Gütererzeugung*)	Subsistence; planned economy; or market economy
	Distributional rules (*Verteilungsverfassung*)	General (basic) income; regulated special income; altruism
	Labour constitution (*Arbeitsverfassung*)	Cooperative, forced; or contracted
Economic process (*Wirtschaftslauf*)	Nature of progression of economic development (*Wirtschaftslauf*)	Steady state (static); progressive; cyclical fluctuation (dynamic)

Source: Spiethoff (1932, p. 916f)

to characterise a particular economic style are not predetermined but instead open to improvement on the basis of new observations or circumstances.[9]

Spiethoff's contributions differ from earlier concepts in yet another important point. He actually did not consider economic styles primarily as an instrument to classify historic (i.e. past) periods into successive stages of economic development. His interest was rather to devise a theoretical concept by which any form of independent patterns of economic life could be distinguished (Spiethoff 1932). This implies that Spiethoff did not follow the idea of earlier stage theorists that the development from one stage to another meant progress in the material as well as in the moral and spiritual sense. For him, each economic style described a picture of reality for which he intended to find appropriate theories. He wrote:

> For every style, a general economic theory is possible. Each theory is a genuine theory with general validity for explaining the reality that corresponds with a particular economic style. But the theory is applicable only to its particular style, not beyond it, not for the entirety of economic life, not for that of all times (Ibid, p. 893)[10]

---

[9] In an inquiry into the economic style of Eastern European transition economies, Backhaus (1997) avails himself of the open nature of Spiethoff's concept by adding three new categories to it: First, the social constitution (*Sozialverfassung*) as a central element of the modern welfare state; second, the fiscal constitution (*Steuerverfassung*) which is closely associated with the social constitution; and finally, the international order and global governance structure (*internationale Verankerung in Bündnissen und Vertragswerken*) as a third new and nowadays increasingly significant category.

[10] In the German original, Spiethoff writes:

> "Für jeden [...] Stil ist eine Allgemeine Volkswirtschaftslehre möglich. Für ihn hat sie Allgemeingültigkeit, für ihn ist sie eine echte Theorie. Aber sie gilt nur für ihren eigenen Stil, nicht darüber hinaus, nicht für alles Wirtschaftsleben, nicht für das aller Zeiten".

12.2.1 Methodological and Theoretical Foundations of Spiethoff's Economic Styles

The starting point of Spiethoff's work was given by his sense of dissatisfaction with the limited theoretical manifestation of the fact-based analysis by members of the Historical School, and their consequent loss of influence since the beginning of the twentieth century vis-à-vis the Anglo-American neoclassics. Spiethoff regarded Schmoller's aim to free economics from false abstractions and to replace its general theories by a new theoretical approach, that he stated in his *Grundriß* (Schmoller 1932a,b), as unattained, and concluded that "[Schmoller's] empirical inquiry does not cohere into a new theory" (Spiethoff 1938, p. 28).[11] While Spiethoff continued the Historical School's quest for a solid foundation of economic research into historical, context-specific evidence, he also had a vital interest in integrating the historical approach with the methods of pure economic theory.[12]

As mentioned before, Spiethoff aimed at associating each economic style model with a separate, style-specific theory. For this purpose, he distinguished four types of theories: Pure economic theory (*reine Theorie*) and economic gestalt theory (*anschauliche Theorie*)[13] on the one hand, as well as historical and nonhistorical theory on the other. The distinction between the former two roughly corresponds with the differences between deductive and inductive reasoning, whereas the applicability of either historical or nonhistorical theory depends on whether theory is used to explain time-conditioned institutions and patterns, or phenomena that show invariable uniformities and are not subject to change in time.

These relations between the four theoretical approaches to economic analysis that Spiethoff differentiated are illustrated in Fig. 12.1. As can be seen, nonhistorical pure theory and economic gestalt theory are mutually exclusive. Economic gestalt theory is historical theory by its very nature, while nonhistorical theories are by definition pure theories. Spiethoff speaks of "historical" pure theory if the methodology of pure theory is applied, for heuristic purposes, to the isolated analysis of relations

---

[11] In the German original, the complete quote reads: "*Ein neues Verfahren in der Auswertung der alten Theorie ist es, aber keine neue Theorie*". Spiethoff, a pupil of Schmoller, was his long-time assistant and later editor of *Schmollers Jahrbuch*. He was closely involved into Schmoller's work at the *Grundriß*, and was later both friend and advisor to Schmoller's wife Lucie, who finalised the publication of the second and fully revised edition of the *Grundriß* in 1923.

[12] A concrete example for this is Spiethoff's important work in business cycle theory (Spiethoff 1925), on which he based his later book *Die Wirtschaftlichen Wechsellagen: Aufschwung, Krise, Stockung* (Tübingen: Mohr 1955).

[13] Fritz Redlich, in his translation of texts by Spiethoff, considered "economic gestalt theory" the best conceivable translation of *anschauliche Theorie* as the method creates theories by isolating the gestalt of economic and social systems. Others have found still further translations. Among these are "empirical-realistic theory", "concrete theory", "historical-concrete theory", "observational theory", "essential-intrinsic theory" (E. Salin), "realistic theory" (Hero Möller) and "all-round sociological theory" (H. W. Singer). The German name "*anschauliche Theorie*" was first coined by Edgar Salin in a review article of Sombart's *Der Moderne Kapitalismus* (Salin 1927).

12.2 Spiethoff's Concept of the Economic Style

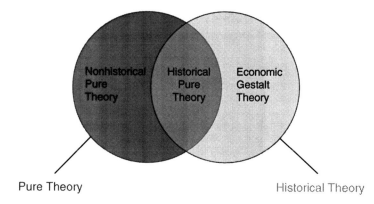

Fig. 12.1 Different approaches to economic analysis

between concrete, time-conditioned phenomena. This case is illustrated by the area where both pure theory and historical theory shade into one another. As will be discussed in more detail below, it is historical pure theory from which ideal type models originate. Real types, by contrast, are tools of economic gestalt theory.[14]

Before Spiethoff, the main poles, which had also been subject to the *Methodenstreit* in economics, were the methods of pure theory on the one side, and that of historical theory on the other. Unlike earlier exponents of the Historical School, Spiethoff was not interested in dismissing any of these contrasting types of theories, but instead argued in favour of a method of economic analysis in which abstract and historical theory interpenetrate. The fact that Spiethoff found it quite permissible to apply the method of pure theory to the study of historical (i.e. time-conditioned) phenomena is documented particularly well by the historical pure theory type of economic analysis, in which pure theory and historical theory overlap. Its method involves deriving from a real type model, which reflects a historical reality, a more abstract ideal type model, which is constructed from isolated elements of reality that are logically deducible from certain premises. Spiethoff (1953) emphasised the usefulness of this procedure as a heuristic device or means of investigation.

12.2.1.1 Pure Theory vs. Economic Gestalt Theory

Spiethoff was intent on clarifying the scope and applicability of each type of theory, as well as their respective significance for analysing the elements of distinct economic styles. Accordingly, he distinguished pure economic theory and economic

---

[14]A third approach that Spiethoff (1952) describes in his original discussion is economic history. The approach of economic history is concerned with unique historical cases that are not susceptible to theoretical treatment because they display no regularities.

gestalt theory by the method of abstraction and isolation which they use. Spiethoff (in a translation by Fritz Redlich) described the method and scope of pure theory as follows:

> Pure theory emphasises the isolation of specific phenomena and their relations to other isolated and specific phenomena; other relations which may also exist are disregarded. It is interested in isolated phenomena, not in the innumerable concatenations that in reality link them together. Attention is focused upon specific phenomena and relations, selected with the aid of a given frame of reference and manipulated for research purposes without regard for their location in a "total" situation. This may even lead to the study of phenomena that have not been observed but are merely assumed; in this case the object of research is an arbitrary or nonempirical model. Pure theory starts from data that have an axiomatic character, and conclusions are reached by a process of logical deduction: the student draws conclusions about effects by taking given data as causes. As a matter of principle, in the strictest version of pure theory, conclusions are reached without any control through comparison with reality. [...] The value which the results have for the explanation of economic reality depends on the way the problems are posed and upon the fruitfulness of the underlying assumptions (Spiethoff 1953, p. 445)

Pure theory thus isolates phenomena for the purpose of studying specific relations that have been defined in advance. This means, it selects its variables to suit a preconceived theoretical system. Spiethoff calls this approach to economic modelling arbitrary in the sense that it dispenses with a prior empirical analysis of the realities that a given theoretical model is supposed to explain. The method of pure economic theory is in fact very much akin to the way in which modern development economists in the neoclassical tradition generate their models and hypotheses.

Economic gestalt theory, by contrast, aims at studying economic phenomena in closest possible approximation to observable reality. Yet, its purpose is not to deal with reality as a whole. Instead, economic gestalt theory involves generalisations in that it isolates from a complex reality all essential[15] and uniform[16] relations that affect the behaviour of a given phenomenon. But unlike pure theory, it does not select these relations in advance, but identifies them in a process of induction based on data which it obtains through prior empirical research. According to Spiethoff (1953, p. 445), the ultimate purpose of economic gestalt theory is to "arrive at discrete species (*arteigene Formen*) of phenomena whose characteristics are the data from which it starts".[17] From this, it follows that both types of theory differ in the way and spirit in which they make use of abstraction and isolation: Pure theory isolates phenomena for the purpose of studying specific relationships that the

---

[15]Essential are those phenomena which appear to be causes or conditions of the phenomenon under investigation, or at least indicative for these causes and conditions (Spiethoff 1953, p. 446).

[16]As theories are built to explain regularities in economic life, Spiethoff rightly notes that only factors that uniformly affect a phenomenon of interest are susceptible to theoretical treatment.

[17]Elsewhere, Spiethoff (1948) described the methodology of economic gestalt theory as follows: The scientist first establishes the object and scope of analysis in a "system of meaning" (*Sinneszusammenhang*). By a process of inductive reasoning, he then sets out to delimit unique phenomena and selects those of their characteristics which, in relation to that system of meaning, are regular and essential. That way, economic gestalt theory finally arrives at a generalising presentation of the uniformities of a discrete species of phenomena.

12.2 Spiethoff's Concept of the Economic Style

researcher wishes to explore according to a preconceived model. Economic gestalt theory, by contrast, aims at isolating everything what is essential in relation to a given phenomenon in order to study particular relationships.

12.2.1.2 "Real Type" and "Ideal Type" Models

These different methodologies produce, of course, also different types of economic models. Accordingly, ideal types result from applying the method of abstraction of pure theory, whereas real types are arrived at by the method of economic gestalt theory. The theoretical status of the concept of economic style is located in the sphere of economic gestalt theory, because an economic style, by definition, describes characteristic patterns of economic life in a specific region and time. For this very reason, the specification of an individual economic style with the means of economic gestalt theory constitutes a real type model.

Real types had been proposed by Spiethoff as models that abstract essential elements from a complex reality, as opposed to Weber's and Sombart's ideal types which represent deliberate mental constructs formed by the scientist to picture the quintessence of a phenomenon.[18] The conceptualisation of Spiethoff's economic styles as real types points to a further important methodological difference between his concept and that of Sombart: Although Sombart constructed his economic systems in reference to real historical data, he conceived his scheme as an application of the ideal-typical approach. Spiethoff's economic styles, however, do not necessarily have logical unity or represent constructed "exaggerations" (*Steigerungen*) of certain aspects of economic life that are not necessarily to be found in it. Their internal coherence rather depends on the unity of economic forms and attitudes prevailing in a given period and place.

Ideal types are an appropriate approach especially to categorise and understand individual-historical phenomena that describe past patterns of economic life. Because the kind of observable data that are essential for the purpose of building economic styles as real types are lacking in historical descriptions and analyses, the researcher has to rely on an ideal-typical picture of past realities to states of economic life in former times. By contrast, real types are guided by the purpose to build, as much as possible, a complete picture of all essential causal elements to be found in given real context. In fact, the distinction between ideal and real types also reveals something about the research interests of Sombart and Spiethoff, respectively. Sombart followed the ideal-typical approach because his interest was primarily in differentiating between economic systems that characterised economic reality in different historical epochs. On the other hand, Spiethoff's confidence in real type models indicates that

---

[18] For example, the *homo economicus* can be regarded as an ideal type model of man in that it originates in the scientist's mind by exaggeration of certain elements in observed reality, but still remains a synthetic construction that has no necessary counterpart in real life. For a further definition and distinction between ideal and real types, see footnote 5.

his research interest was also and particularly concentrated on contemporary economic phenomena that can be investigated on the basis of real, observable data.

12.2.1.3 Historical vs. Nonhistorical Theory

There is considerable overlap between the definitions of pure and economic gestalt theory on the one hand, and historical and nonhistorical theory on the other. As indicated in the above scheme (Fig. 12.1), economic gestalt theory is a category of historical theory, whereas nonhistorical theory is necessarily pure theory. Yet, both pairs of opposites are worth exploring separately as they differ in the criteria according to which their different character is distinguished. As has been said, the characteristic difference between pure theory and economic gestalt theory lies in the degree and specific way in which they engage in theoretical abstraction. The difference between historical and nonhistorical theory, on the contrary, is defined by the nature of the phenomena for the analysis of which they are adequate theory. Both types are mutually exclusive in their scope of application: Historical theory deals with phenomena that are time-conditioned in the sense that they do not exist at all times and in all places in a uniform way, but are subject to change over time. By contrast, all phenomena that show no variation in time or across different places are the subject matter of nonhistorical theory. As a matter of fact, it leads to generalisations that represent statements of universal validity, and its conclusions are applicable regardless of an observed phenomenon's historical, cultural or geographical context.[19]

Of course, the choice of a theory that is considered appropriate for explaining a particular phenomenon depend on how and to what degree the researcher is willing to abstract from context-specific influences that shape the historical character of a given phenomenon. The more he is interested (in the spirit of economic gestalt theory) to consider the greatest possible variety of essential and uniform influences that he observes in reality, the more variations in the behaviour of a given phenomena will he find across time and space, and the more appropriate will the application of a historical theory appear to him. On the other side, if the researcher believes he can capture the crucial characteristics of a phenomenon by considering only a few significant influences in isolation (according to the methodology of pure theory), he will be more likely to opt for a nonhistorical approach. The art in making these choices lies in understanding a given phenomenon in such a way that one is able to determine its real character, as well as the forces that brought it into being and drive its behaviour.

In this respect, it is important to consider a distinction that is often made in German social sciences between "explaining" (*Erklären*) and "understanding"(*Verstehen*):

---

[19]It has to be emphasised that "historical" (*geschichtlich*) does not imply that a theory deals only with the past. In fact, the German word "*geschichtlich*", as Spiethoff uses it, has wider connotations than in the English usage in that it denotes all temporary (i.e. time-bound) economic conditions, even if they may appear, at first sight, nonhistorical. Elsewhere (Spiethoff 1932, p. 922), he differentiates between *bedingte* (conditioned) and *unbedingte* or *zeitlose* (unconditioned or timeless) theory to denote the same distinction as between historical and nonhistorical theory.

12.2 Spiethoff's Concept of the Economic Style

A phenomenon is "explained" by using abstraction (as commonly done in nonhistorical pure theory) to show its relationships with other phenomena, while it is "understood" by uncovering the motives of human agents who brought it into existence. The latter can only be achieved by a historical theory as the motives of agents are subject to change over time, and may markedly differ across different local contexts.[20] As Reinert (2005) notes, *Verstehen* describes a type of understanding that is irreducible only to numbers and symbols. This approach has its origins in the *geisteswissenschaftliche Methode* advanced in the philosophical writings of Wilhelm Dilthey (1833–1911) – especially in Dilthey (1883). It was applied in economics most prominently in the works of Weber, Sombart and Spiethoff. In this context, Schefold (2002, p. 128) refers to it as *Verstehende Nationalökonomie* the nature and purpose of which he describes as follows:

> [...] the *"Verstehende Nationalökonomie"* (intuitive economics) of Weber, Sombart and Spiethoff [...] represented an attempt to describe the specificity of economic forms prevailing in a given period and area in terms of economic styles in order to overcome the idea of linear progress and of an incessant evolution towards "higher" forms. Development was not denied, but the economic forms encountered in the past or on other continents were to be regarded not as primitive precursors of modern economy, backward in technique, rationality and institutions, but as specific formations, to be characterised in positive terms, by showing how prevailing mentalities, economic organisation, methods of production and the social and cultural life fitted together.

The relevance of Spiethoff's contributions for the contemporary analysis of economic phenomena in low-income countries does not only lie in the idea of modelling context-specific institutional patterns and phenomena as elements of a particular economic style. The concept of economic styles is also relevant because it coheres with a theoretical analysis that goes beyond most earlier attempts at building historical theories of economic development.

Spiethoff's work in defining different types of theories, and in clarifying their use in economic analysis, reflects his fundamental concern to find a synthesis between pure and historical theory, and to show that fruitful cooperation between their respective scientific methods is possible in that historical theory uses models of pure theory as heuristic tools. Accordingly, with his concept of economic styles, he emphasised the context-specific and time-conditioned nature of economic phenomena, but he does so without denying the existence of certain perpetual truths expressed by universal, timeless laws in economic analysis. That Spiethoff is today reckoned as one of the few members of the German Historical School who made a substantial impact on mainstream economics may indeed be owed to the fact that he succeeded in integrating historical-inductive with abstract-deductive methods of research, and thereby contributed towards relieving the tension between history and theory in economic analysis.

---

[20]Elsewhere (1953), Spiethoff differentiates between objective causality (*Sachkausalität*) and motivational causality (*Motivkausalität*). The former relates to phenomena that are "explained" by objective factors that caused them. Through the latter kind of causality, phenomena are "understood" as expressions of the specific motives that govern individual choices.

12.3 The Concept of Economic Styles in the Literature Since Spiethoff

12.3.1 Evaluation and Critique by Eucken

One of the most critical and profound surveys of Spiethoff's contributions is that by Walter Eucken (1950a,b).[21] A student at the time when the Historical School dominated the teaching of economics at German universities, he turned, unsatisfied by their aims and method of historical research, to economic theory and became the foremost opponent of the Historical School among German economists (Lutz 1950). But unlike Menger, who, in the *Methodenstreit*, questioned the scientific relevance and method of historical research in economics altogether, Eucken clearly felt that an approach integrating both historical and theoretical research was needed to understand and explain economic reality and its relationships. He actually considered the search for a synthesis between individual-historical and general-theoretical approaches the foremost challenge in all economic analysis, which economists have to master if they are to understand the course of economic life. Eucken referred to this challenge as the "Great Antinomy" of economics, the core question behind which he posed as follows:

> The economist has to see economic events as part of a particular individual-historical situation if he is to do justice to the real world. He must see them also as presenting a general-theoretical problem if the relationships of the real world are not to escape him. How can he combine these two views? (Eucken 1950b, p. 41).

Eucken continued by noting that "if [the economist] does only the one or only the other, he is out of touch with the real world" (Ibid, p. 41). This brings to the point the reason that Eucken gave to explain the failure of all previous schools of economics in overcoming the tension between history and theory. Accordingly, classical and early neoclassical economics failed because their theoretical solutions did not fit the existing historical variety of economic life. By contrast, the Historical School failed, in Eucken's view, to explain the course of the economic process, because its member's preoccupation with the collection of real facts made them unable to understand the relations between them, and to advance from the facts to theory. Eucken thus used the degree by which economists recognised and succeeded in overcoming the Great Antinomy as the standard by which he judged the contributions of both the historical and classical schools of economics.

But for this very reason, it must astonish that Eucken fully counted Spiethoff's work on economic styles into his vigorous critique of the aim and method of earlier contributions to the Historical School. Although Spiethoff conceptualised his economic styles as models of historical theory, he clearly valued pure theory as a necessary heuristic device for the isolated analysis of relations between concrete,

---

[21] Much of his critique of the historical method in general, and Spiethoff's concept of economic styles, is laid down in Eucken (1950). Supplementary readings include Eucken (1938, 1940).

time-conditioned phenomena. Thereby, Spiethoff advanced far in achieving a synthesis between descriptive-historical and general-theoretical research. Eucken did, in fact, acknowledge the perception of the Great Antinomy in all contributions that sought to divide the course of history into separate stages or styles of development, and aimed at explaining them by individual, time-conditioned theories. But it was for this procedure that Eucken rejected the contributions by Spiethoff and all earlier stage theorists. Specifically, he argued that by dividing the course of history into discrete series or phases of development, economists illegitimately divorce economic events from the rest of the historical process, and thus loose sight of the course of history and the evolution of different economic systems.

It is yet unfortunate that Eucken framed his critique of the concept of economic styles into the broader context of his repudiation of earlier stage theories. Their original purpose was indeed to identify, in the course of history, discrete periods of economic development, and to explain them by constructing cross-sections of economic life for each of them. Based on a discussion of the ancient "household economy", the medieval "town economy", and capitalism as discrete historical stages in Europe's economic development, Eucken criticises this approach an "unhistorical oversimplification" (Ibid, pp. 91 and 328, n21). But in that he extended his critique on stages and styles in equal measure, and at the same time restricted his notion of economic styles on their application as a tool for research in economic history, Eucken appears not to have fully recognised the concept's benefit as a framework for the analysis of contemporary economic reality in its respective historical, geographical and cultural contexts.

Instead of stages or styles, Eucken considered the system of an economy or economic order (*Wirtschaftsordnung*) as the only appropriate criterion by which different patterns of economic life can be understood and distinguished in a meaningful way. According to Eucken, the economic system is the characteristic feature of any economy by which the form and character of all economic activity at any period or place is determined, and without an understanding of which economic reality cannot be explained.[22] Eucken writes:

> [T]he task of the scientific economist is to get a knowledge of actual economic systems [...]. As the course of everyday economic life proceeds differently according to the form of the economic system, the knowledge of the different kinds of systems is the first step towards a knowledge of economic reality (Ibid, p. 90).

---

[22]The economic order or system is a central theme in all of Eucken's work. In his *Foundations*, he defines it as to "comprise the totality of forms through which the everyday economic process at any particular time or place, past or present, is actually controlled (Eucken 1950b, p. 227). He further remarks that only few economic systems have been intentionally designed on the basis of certain constitutional principles or a comprehensive plan, while most evolved in the course of history and were shaped, among others, by existing natural and technical conditions, the motivations and interests of economic actors, or the rules, conventions and institutions which emerged in the course of the everyday economic process. In contrast, constitutions or legal systems rarely determine the character of an economic system, but rather codify already existing elements of the economic system.

Yet, the differences between Eucken's approach and Spiethoff's concept of economic styles as regards the central position of the economic system in the research agenda of economists appear to be much smaller than conceived by Eucken. Elements of the economic system are actually captured in most parts of the scheme that Spiethoff devised as a framework for the identification and expression of specific economic patterns as an economic style.[23] For instance, the economic spirit and attitudes of economic actors, the constitution of society, or the forms of organisation and governance of economic activity are all elements that help the economist to get a grasp of the character of an economy's order or system. Eucken accuses the constructors of stages and styles of failing to start from the question about the structure of the economy (*Ordnungsgefüge*). But in applying Spiethoff's scheme, economists are actually bound to recognise and analyse elements and occurrences of the economic system by which economic relations in a specific time and context are governed. Economists thus have the economic system vividly in mind when applying a style-theoretical approach to the analysis of economic reality.

Apart from his criticism of the procedures by which economic stages and styles are constructed, Eucken was especially dismissive of all efforts to overcome the tension between history and theory by formulating theories that are limited in their application to a particular period or context – an aim that both stage theorists and style builders pursued, and which probably represents the closest commonality of Spiethoff's style-economic approach with earlier stage theories. Using the example of the style of the medieval "city" or "town" economy, Eucken asks:

> Is it possible to build a particular theory for it? The answer is "no", because the concept tells us nothing about the structure of the "city" economy. There can be no doubt that the everyday economic life of a city proceeds differently according to the economic system existing. Have all the guilds in the city a monopoly position, or are they altogether forbidden, or controlled by the town administration, or does the town administration intervene directly in supplying the inhabitants with goods, and if so, which goods? Without an answer to all these questions, it is impossible to attack the problem of how the economic process of a city fits together (Ibid, p. 100).

However, the scheme developed by Spiethoff (see Table 12.2) is actually by no means ignorant of these questions. It presents a framework that guides the researcher to identify the causal elements that determine the character of economic life in a particular context by asking, for instance, what the attitudes and motivations of economic agents are, what forms of organisation of economic activity have evolved from these, by what rules they are governed, or how the economic process is constrained by elements of the physical environment. Not all of the categories in Spiethoff's scheme will be relevant in all contexts, just as new ones may be added if considered essential for the understanding of the problem at hand. But in any case, the scheme can help the researcher to develop an idea about the governing principles that shape the economic system of a particular economy, and is thus instrumental in tackling the two central problems emphasised by Eucken: The question of "how everyday economic life hangs together", and "the problem of the

---

[23] See Table 12.2.

structure of the economic system under which everyday economic life proceeds" (Ibid, p. 102).

An important question that remains to be answered is how then to derive theoretical conclusions from knowledge about the style characteristics of a particular economy. Every theory contains propositions about significant relationships that are valid under certain sets of conditions. These conditions, which make up the assumptions of a theory, are embodied in the specific occurrences of attributes of economic life. For the theoretical analysis of their relationships, the economist has, in Spiethoff's view, to abstract all essential and uniform elements from a complex reality to obtain a "real type" model that expresses the characteristic elements of an economy's specific economic style. Eucken, by contrast, thought to have found in the study of economic history certain pure forms out of which all economic systems, past and present, are made up. He thus saw the task of the economist in working out a limited number of pure forms through historical research (which he referred to as a morphological study of the different prevailing economic systems), and to use these as a basis to theoretically explain the course of the economic process.[24] These forms do not purport to be pictures of actual reality. Instead, they are "ideal type" models, which each are obtained by the one-sided exaggeration[25] of a single aspect of economic reality.[26] Both approaches are not mutually exclusive, though. Spiethoff did see the explanatory value of analysing isolated relationships with the help of ideal type models, but proposed their use for heuristic purposes as means of the investigation, and not as their end.

The quest for identifying in the study of economic history certain pure forms of economic systems made Eucken dismissive towards the idea that markedly different forms of economic organisation and governance could represent distinct economic styles that warrant the development of time- and context-conditioned theories. However, his research interest was primarily in the economic development of Europe, and in particular that of Germany in the years before and after World War II. Although this was a time of rapid change, it still took place within the same cultural context. The observation of a certain constancy of form, which made Eucken confident in obtaining a precise understanding of the real world by studying ideal types of it, may not necessarily hold across different cultural contexts and for different stages of development. Pure forms of economic life will rather have to be identified for each context anew.

For all his discontent with earlier stage theories and, by inference, with the concept of economic styles, Eucken shared common ground especially with the "youngest"

---

[24]Moreover, he urged economists to approach the theoretical analysis of complex economic phenomena by breaking them down into their different components, namely into the subsystems which have evolved through time, and which only function as part of a particular economic order or system, and thus can only be understood in the context of the structure of this larger system.

[25]In German original, Eucken spoke of this method as *"pointierend hervorhebende Abstraktion"* (Eucken 1950a, p. 123).

[26]On a discussion of the methodological difference between real types and ideal types see footnote 5 and Sect. 12.2.1.

Historical School. On the methodological level, he was concerned not to lose contact with reality, and thus endorsed the historical-contextual nature of economic phenomena. And even though he wanted to advance from inductive research to theoretical analysis that arrives at "ideal types" by a method of one-sided exaggeration, he insisted that ideal, pure forms must be identified with reference to observable reality. In Eucken's view, this could be achieved by a morphological study of the actual forms and occurrences of economic systems that always has to precede the theoretical analysis. Furthermore, Eucken complemented Spiethoff's work in important respects. In particular, he reminded economists that the explorative and observational research of real facts can only be performed in a significant way if definite problems have first been formulated. In this regard, he cautions that the desire to "record reality in all its fullness and to observe and describe it simply by amassing material on climate, land, people, and the legal and economic systems" (Ibid, p. 61) leads to nowhere if it does not start from a problem, which, in Eucken's view, must be put in a general form and treated theoretically in order to discover the interrelationships in an economic system.

12.3.2 The Concept of Economic Styles in the Contemporary Literature

During and immediately after Spiethoff's own creative period, some German economists continued to use the concept of economic styles as a basis for their own research. Bechtel (1930), whose works had also had an influence on Spiethoff's own research, applied the concept broadly as a tool of economic history and with a view to understanding the connections between different aspects of life, like religion and arts, and their interrelations with economic forms of life. Weippert (1943) provided a careful reflection on the evolution and theoretical foundations of the concept of economic styles and developed it further. Müller-Armack (1941), finally, used the concept to elaborate on the economic and cultural characteristics of economic life in Europe from early civilisation until the eighteenth century. His main interest was in explaining how ideologies in each period shaped the development of its economic and political institutions. Müller-Armack chose a style-economic approach because he considered it as the most appropriate framework for expressing, in a genealogical manner, the influences from all political and social spheres of life. Later, Müller-Armack (1946) applied the concept of economic styles to distil, from a comparative analysis of the (liberal) market economy (*Marktwirtschaft*) and the planned economy (*Lenkungswirtschaft*), his concept of the social market economy (*Soziale Marktwirtschaft*), which he defined as an own economic style characterised by the combination of functions of a market-based economy with the pursuit of socio-economic policy objectives.

Beyond these early contributions by German authors, the concept of economic styles fell largely into oblivion in the second half of the twentieth century. The reasons for this were numerous: With the raise of neoclassical theory as the dominant

12.3 The Concept of Economic Styles in the Literature Since Spiethoff

paradigm in economics, the method and scope of economics narrowed significantly, leaving many fields that had previously been studied in the framework of historical economics to neighbouring disciplines such as economic history or economic sociology. Moreover, the neoclassical theory's claim for universal validity let recourses to time- and context-conditioned theories appear dispensable.[27] Apart from these reasons, the contributions on economic styles were closely tied to the German-language literature and hence remained hardly noticed in the Anglo-Saxon world.[28]

The transition process of former communist countries in the 1990s brought about a revival of interest in the style-economic approach as the importance of cultural, political and social factors for understanding processes of institutional change was gradually rediscovered. The use of the concept of economic styles re-emerged especially in comparative economic studies, a field that previously was concerned mainly with the comparison of socialist and capitalist economic systems, and now turned to the comparative analysis of different capitalist models and their distinct cultural origins. Backhaus (1997), for instance, applied the concept of economic styles, along with the concepts of economic governance and of the (political) entrepreneur, to explain the dynamic causes of structural change in former communist countries, and to predict the specific structures and economic forms that their transition to market-based economies could bring about. Klump (1996) edited a collection of contributions from various disciplines to research on economic culture, all of which use the concept of economic styles as a common framework for their analysis.

Schefold and Peukert (1992) took up the concept of economic styles in a far-reaching research project in which they investigated the economic systems in different cultural contexts and historical epochs. Moreover, Schefold (1994/1995) dedicated two volumes to a discussion of the origins and nature of the defining elements of economic styles, which he discovers already in ancient Greek philosophy. While his first volume features the particular property of style-theoretical research of making historical and cultural influences accessible for economic analysis, the second volume focuses on the applicability of the concept of economic styles to the analysis of technological, environmental and social concerns, and especially the responsiveness of an economic system to social and technological change. Likewise did Gioia (1997) reflect on methodological and epistemological contributions by Spiethoff and evaluated them with reference to his business cycle theory. The genesis of the style-economic approach is traced from the works of Weber and Sombart to that of Spiethoff in a contribution by Kaufhold (1996).

---

[27] The demise of the Historical School's contextual economics in favour of the isolated analysis of neoclassical economics also has its reason in the conservation of economic forms and systems on both sides of the Iron Curtain during the Cold War. This situation kept economic systems and their interrelations with other areas of societies relatively stable, and hence favoured the isolated analysis of economic phenomena without consideration of context-specific influences from political, social or cultural spheres on economic outcomes.

[28] The only texts by Spiethoff available in English are the translations by Fritz Redlich (see Spiethoff 1952, 1953; Redlich 1970).

Moreover, several authors have applied the concept of economic styles for specifying the characteristics of individual countries.[29] Among these, the attempt by Hermann-Pillath (2005) at defining a Chinese economic style comes closest to the idea of using the concept of economic styles as an analytical framework for research on the specific characteristics of developing countries. Notable in the same respect is also a study by Nienhaus (1999) in which he compares a style-based framework with other approaches for explaining the influence of cultural factors on the evolution of distinct economic systems in developing countries.

12.4 Parallel Contributions of the "Old" Institutional School of Economics

Intellectual support for a context-specific economic theory can also be borrowed from the "old" Institutional School of Economics, the American parallel to the German Historical School. While the interested reader may gain a wealth of additional insights from a more thorough study of American institutionalism, all that is feasible here is to point out its relevance and additional value for the study of institutional change and development in low-income countries on the basis of an introduction to the works of Thorstein Veblen (1857–1929).[30]

The son of farmers who had emigrated from Norway to the United States, Veblen grew up in a culture that differed widely from the culture of modern America. The experience of cultural differences certainly stimulated his choice of questions, and shaped his evolutionary approach to economics. Veblen defined culture as complexes of "prevalent habits of thought with respect to particular relations and particular functions of the individual and of the community" (Veblen [1912] 1899, p. 190). His main question was how these habits did develop into the forms that can be observed in a specific environment. Following Darwin's work in evolutionary biology, Veblen conceives the activities in which individual engage as the main formative force behind the evolution of their habits of thought. Since the engagement in economic activities in order to make a living occupies most of people's time, the structure of economic life must play a significant role in the evolution of people's habits, rules and cultural beliefs, and the institutions that govern their economic relations.

This evolutionary view on economics as a science of cultural change was, of course, very different from the classical economists' definition of their subject as a

---

[29] See, for instance, Ludwig (1988) on Spain; Ammon (1994) on France; Stemmermann (1996) on Italy; Ackermann (1996) on Japan; Nienhaus (1996) on Islamic countries; Rudner (1996) on Mexico; Hickmann (1996) on France, Germany and Russia; Müller-Pelzer (1997) on France; Hermann-Pillath (2005) on China; Rossi (2006) on France and Italy; and Wrobel (2007) on Europe, Russia and China.

[30] Additional reading on the works of Thorstein Veblen, John R. Commons, Wesley C. Mitchell, John M. Clark and other American Institutionalists can be found in Grunchy (1947). Hodgson (2004) offers a contemporary account of the rise, fall and potential rebirth of old institutional economics.

12.4 Parallel Contributions of the "Old" Institutional School of Economics

science dealing with production, exchange and the effect of prices on the distribution of income. In asking why economics was not an evolutionary science, Veblen (1898) criticises classical economics for its inability or refusal to incorporate insights from anthropology, ethnology and psychology into the explanation of economic realities, which prevented classical economics "to handle its subject matter in a way to entitle it to standing as a modern science" (Ibid, p. 373).[31] Related to this fundamental criticism of economic theory is Veblen's charge that classical and neoclassical economists have worked with a faulty conception of human nature, which he described in the following famous quote:

> In all the received formulations of economic theory, whether at the hands of English economists or those of the Continent, the human material with which the inquiry is concerned is conceived in hedonistic terms; that is to say, in terms of a passive and substantially inert and immutably given human nature. The psychological and anthropological preconceptions of the economists have been those which were accepted by the psychological and social sciences some generations ago. The hedonistic conception of man is that of a lightning calculator of pleasures and pains who oscillates like a homogeneous globule of desire of happiness under the impulse of stimuli that shift him about the area, but leave him intact. He has neither antecedent nor consequent. He is an isolated definitive human datum, in stable equilibrium except for the buffets of the impinging forces that displace him in one direction or another (Ibid, p. 389).

Veblen's notion of active man is closely associated with his definition of the subject of evolutionary economic analysis: Instead of studying satisfactions and sacrifices (i.e. pleasures and pains), and their supposed influence on economic behaviour, economists should study the process of human behaviour itself. This implies the need to understand how, in Veblen's terms, "usages, customs, conventions, preconceptions, [and] composite principles of conduct" evolve from human habits and routines, and how these habits are, in turn, determined by the "cumulative body of knowledge" that an individual acquires through tradition and education, and from the preconceptions and values that prevail in the cultural environment or community in which he grows up (Veblen 1914, p. 39). Economic change thus happens if people's methods of getting a living (i.e. the habits or routines involved in economic activity) change. And such change in economic behaviour, in turn, happens when individuals encounter new experiences and accumulate new knowledge. Therefore, institutions cannot be understood by only inquiring into how they work at a given point in time. What have also to be accounted for are the human habits and routines from which an institution evolved.

Veblen's evolutionary approach to the explanation of economic and cultural change exhibits clear parallels with the method and results of research by the

---

[31] In spite of the common ground that the German Historical and the American Institutional Schools of Economics share, Veblen also refused to consider the Historical School a modern, evolutionary science. That was, however, not because he did not recognise their understanding of the evolutionary nature of economic processes. Rather did Veblen consider their historical-empirical research as falling short of being science due to the lack of theoretical formulation of their results – a shortcoming that in particular Spiethoff and other members of the "youngest" Historical School saw and sought to overcome.

German Historical School.[32] Both schools defined economic behaviour as the main object of observation, and derived their behavioural assumptions from a model of active, creative man. They are also similar in the interdisciplinary scope of their research in that they considered a wide range of economic as well as psychological, cultural and historical factors in their explanation of economic processes.

Beyond these commonalities, the relevance of the "old" Institutional School of Veblen for a context-sensitive approach to development economics lies especially in its clear emphasis of the institutional dynamics involved in economic change: the idea that institutions are the product of daily routines, and that they evolve and change in response to the needs of the agents whose economic activities they support. "Old" American institutionalists thus remind modern development economists that appropriate institutions cannot be build independent of the economic structure into which they are grafted, and thereby reinforce the importance of studying the relevant context in order to understand the specific need for an institution that precedes its creation.[33]

---

[32] See Sect. 13.1 for a discussion of the methodological contributions of the Historical School of Economics.

[33] This conclusion draws on a comment by Erik Reinert to an earlier version of this book, and I am very grateful to him for pointing out to me the additional support for a context-sensitive economic theory that the old American Institutional School of Economics can provide.

Chapter 13
The Relevance of the Historical School for the Study of Low-Income Countries

Development economics seems to stand at a crossroads. On the one hand, development economists have hitherto been heavily dependent on the neoclassical framework of rational choice with all its auxiliary assumptions about actors' utilities, expectations and preferences. Even the contributions from institutional theory and early studies in behavioural economics that allow accounting for the consequences of imperfect information, positive transaction costs or limited information processing capabilities remain within the framework of rational choice theory. And with this framework, also its methodological foundations have been maintained, above all the deductive method of research and the precept of methodological individualism.

On the other hand, the growing evidence in support of the conjecture that economic behaviour and outcomes in low-income countries are to a large extent influenced by noneconomic factors, and vary significantly with different contexts, confronts development economists with new challenges. Advances in behavioural economics and intriguing results from experimental research are bringing into question the empirical validity of the basic axioms of conventional economic theory. Moreover, the failure of simple and universal policy prescriptions highlights the importance of finding context-specific solutions, which can only originate from a qualitative understanding of a country's historical and cultural characteristics, that is, of factors that lie outside the confines of the standard neoclassical framework, and can hardly be captured by a process of deductive reasoning alone.

The challenge that development economists are confronted with is to decide whether they believe in the flexibility of the neoclassical approach and continue testing to the limits its fundamental assumptions and axioms. Or if they are willing to make cultural, psychological or historical factors a living part of their analysis. The first option entails the risk that attempts at extending the scope and applicability of the rational choice framework to the study of low-income countries make model structures inconsistent in their assumptions and thus yields ambiguous conclusions. By contrast, the risk of venturing into new directions, and thus leaving the familiar ground of neoclassical analysis, is that development economics may diffuse into a multitude of separate disciplines without knowing if and how their findings can be integrated into a coherent analytical framework. Banerjee (2005, p. 4343) recently assessed with a view to the puzzling results from experimental and behavioural development economics that "[the problem] is not just that we do not have a theory within which these results can be interpreted – it is not even clear how we would begin to build that theory".

For a new generation of development economists, learning from the Historical School may provide relevant inspiration for going further from this point. At the methodological level, the historical-inductive method represents a full-fledged alternative to the deductive method of conventional economics, while at the theoretical level, its contextual approach can help to improve the explanatory power and policy relevance of research findings. Specifically, the contextual economics of the Historical School provides modern development economists with an analytical framework for capturing the interdependencies between the economic system and the social, political and cultural spheres of life. It emanates from the persuasion that to explain the driving forces of economic growth and development, economists have to gain a qualitative understanding of the dynamic interrelations of economic, political, social and cultural change. On the contrary, an isolating economics, which takes the relations between the economic system and society as given, will not advance to the deep determinants that are essential to understand differences in the performance of societies.[1]

A particularly useful device for applying the Historical School's contextual economics to the study of economic realties in low-income countries is the concept of economic styles. An economic style synthesises common features of economic, political, social and cultural systems during a particular period of time and in a specific context, and allows distinguishing between different paths of economic development that result from differences in the economic, social, cultural and political style characteristics of economies. It offers a framework that differs from neoclassical and hybrid models in respect to both the nature of the conclusions it yields, and the process by which it reaches at these conclusions. As such, the concept of economic styles allows development economists not only to gain a qualitative understanding of how living in poverty and without functioning markets and state institutions influences economic behaviour by affecting the constraints that people face in making economic choices. The concept also illuminates how economic behaviour itself is determined by the institutional environment and cultural underpinnings of different countries or societies.

As it is hoped to show in this chapter, the concept of economic styles embraces in a single theoretical concept the demands on a new framework for the study of

---

[1] It is a matter of an open debate whether the contemporary relevance of the methods and concepts of the Historical School holds beyond their application for the study of developing countries. The view that the contributions by the "older" and "younger" Historical Schools indeed qualify as a full-fledged alternative to the neoclassical framework in general is taken by "The Other Canon" project initiated by Erik Reinert. It aspires for "the study of the economy as a real object, not defined in terms of the adoption of core assumptions and techniques. A production-based economic theory where economic development is an intrinsically uneven process" (www.othercanon.org, accessed on 15 July 2008).

low-income countries, and accommodates in surprising correspondence many of the emerging new directions in modern development economics that have been discussed in Chap. 10. As such, it offers the prospect of integrating the various contemporary contributions from institutional and behavioural economics and neighbouring social sciences to the study of development into a coherent framework.

13.1 Methodological Contributions

A central conclusion from the retrospective review of development theories and policies in Part II was that a new generation of development economists will have to focus more than previous ones on questions of *how* to do development research and policy advice, rather than on *what* to research and advise on. Finding out what works in assisting the development of low-income countries cannot be confined to debating the relative importance for economic growth of, say, capital accumulation, education, institutions or geographical factors alone. The success of growth-igniting strategies is above all decided at the level of the methods of empirical and theoretical research that development economists apply for identifying, within the context of a given country, what factors actually determine the organisation and governance of economic activity, and which of these factors constitute binding constraints for private economic activity to prosper in a particular country context.

The prevailing method of contemporary empirical research in development economics has aptly been described by Mookherjee (2005, p. 4329) as the habit "to explicitly specify the hypothesis to be tested, derive their observable implications, use these in inference and test as far as possible assumptions required for the validity of the inference". As discussed in Chap. 9, this research agenda misses a crucial step, with important implications for the policy-relevance and context-sensitivity of research results. This step is about placing any attempt at theory formulation on sound empirical foundations from the onset. It describes a pre-theory stage of careful observation and explorative empirical analysis of the phenomenon of interest and of the specific context within which it emerges. Theoretical propositions and hypotheses can then be formulated on the basis of the empirical regularities identified in the first stage. These can finally be evaluated or tested by any method of empirical research depending on the structure of the problem of interest and the availability of statistical data.

The purpose of this section is to demonstrate that in designing and applying such a research methodology, development economists can learn from the scientific method of the Historical School. What follows is a tentative compilation of relevant insights from the inquiry into the contributions of the Historical School and suggestions for their application in modern development economics.

13.1.1 Inductive and Deductive Reasoning

Members of the Historical School have followed an unashamedly inductive approach. Most of their writings can be assigned to the pre-theory stage of research that is concerned with observing and describing empirical facts and identifying regularities in the behaviour of a phenomenon. But this approach is not hostile to theoretical deduction. It rather encourages recognising that any attempt at deductive reasoning requires considerable pre-existing knowledge about the phenomenon of interest. Members of the Historical School, in fact, considered deductive reasoning the more appropriate a method of research, the more advanced a science is and the more is hence known about the economic phenomena in question. Adopting a deductive approach to economic problems on which very little prior knowledge exists – as is the case with many economic phenomena in a context of low-income countries – can instead lead economists to being overly confident of the relevance and explanatory power of their general models. It is against this background that recent confessions of humility and modesty in development research, that have been discussed in Sect. 10.1, are to be understood.

The inductive method differs from deductive reasoning not only in the process by which it reaches at theoretical conclusions but also in the nature of the conclusions it yields. The focus of theoretical deduction is on verifying the validity of a predetermined result concerning the problem in question. By contrast, the outcome of inductive research is open and solely influenced by what the observation of reality reveals. Deductive logic may result in the definition of an economic system in terms of a single criterion like "subsistence" vs. "exchange", "formal" vs. "informal", or "traditional" vs. "modern", whereas a likely conclusion from applying inductive reasoning could be to characterise an economic system by a blend of institutional forms and modes of economic interaction.[2] The concept of economic styles clearly exemplifies an outcome of this open-ended approach. As will further be shown in Sect. 13.2, it is therefore particularly relevant to uncover significant but sometimes hidden structures that govern economic activity in low-income countries.

13.1.2 Positive and Normative Research

The objectivity and openness to results of the inductive, empirical-historical method makes it an instrument of economics as a descriptive or positive science.

---

[2] A related reason for such differences in the nature of research findings stems from the often conjoint use of the deductive method with partial analytic research in which an understanding of the whole economic system is sought by breaking it down in to pieces and studying each individual element and its behaviour individually while holding all other influences constant. This contrasts with the conception in contextual economics of the economy as a dynamic and open system that evolves in interrelation with the social, cultural and political spheres of societal life.

Schmoller, for instance, emphasised that the process of observation must be free from any subjective influence or personal opinion. Correct scientific observation of economic phenomena thus means that repeated observations by the same or different observers lead to similar results. At the same time, research by members of the Historical School was always motivated by a concrete problem of their time, and was meant to contribute in some way to the welfare of society. The motivation of drawing relevant policy conclusions from an theoretical understanding of real phenomena gives economic research a prescriptive role in which value judgement are inevitable. But they are permissible if grounded in a descriptive analysis of the relevant context, rather than in an abstract view of the world as the researcher sees it. Modern development economists can learn from earlier applications of the empirical–historical method that for ensuring the policy-relevance of their findings, normative statements cannot be independent of positive research. Normative proposals of growth-igniting strategies for low-income countries will therefore have to rest upon propositions about a respective country's individual binding constraints, which can only be identified by observation of its specific conditions and structures. It applies especially in the field of development economics that one has to understand what is, in order to conceive of what ought to be.

13.1.3 Nature and Scope of Research

Like no other school in economics, German Historism provides an example for the logical connectivity of inductive reasoning, sensitivity to context and interdisciplinary research. An important step in its research programme had been to analyse any observed phenomena in the context of the larger system of related phenomena, and to compare it with theses in order to identify similarities and difference, in order to finally arrive at insights about causal relations among the observed phenomena. Beyond this approach, which is increasingly approximated by exponents of an emerging fourth generation of development economists today, a precise understanding had developed within the Historical School of what exactly constitutes the context of a phenomenon. For Schmoller, economic phenomena are twofold conditioned: First, by material (i.e. physical, technical, natural or geographic) factors, and second, by mental (i.e. psychological, moral, cultural or ethical) influences. By stressing the pivotal influence of psychological factors such as values, attitudes and mental models on economic outcomes, Schmoller makes the link between context-specific analysis and the need for interdisciplinary research explicit. The review of past development theories has shown how the lost unity of the social sciences in the heyday of neoclassical economics has led development economists and policymakers astray. Research in development economics gradually returns to a more interdisciplinary approach today. The broadening of its scope began with the application of North's New Institutional Economics to development research with its explicit emphasis on the role of informal constraints that originate from people's attitudes, mental models and ideologies, and find expression in the norms, values and conventions that govern their economic interactions.[3] It continued with the good governance agenda that fosters interdisciplinary exchange with legal, political and historical sciences (see Sect. 8.4), and is finally reinforced by the increasing emphasis on the "deep determinants" of growth and development such as a country's social and political institutions, as well as its geography, history and culture.

13.1.4 Models of Man and Behavioural Assumptions

It follows from the German Historical School's interdisciplinary scope of research that its proponents repudiated economics as a science of quantities that is devoid of any qualitative meaning. Their objects of economic inquiry were not the quantifiable results of economic actions and behaviour (like prices or quantities of products produced and exchanged), but economic behaviour itself. This focus on human behaviour with all its methodological implications originates from the German economists' distinctive model of man, the philosophical foundations of which Reinert (2005, p. 52) aptly describes as follows:

> At its most fundamental level, the contrast between English and German economics lies in the view of the human mind: To John Locke, Man's mind is a blank slate – a *tabula rasa* – with which we are born, and which passively receives impressions throughout life. To Leibniz, we have an active mind that constantly compares experiences with established schemata, a mind both noble and creative.[4]

This view of human agency not only led members of the Historical School to consider a wide range of both economic and noneconomic (or, in Schmoller's words, material and mental) influences on economic behaviour. It also clearly highlights the evolutionary nature of their approach to economic development and institutional change.[5]

These tenets of German economics make its approach particularly relevant for modern development research. In that it defines the actions and behaviour of individuals and groups as its main object of analysis, and thereby also considers noneconomic influences on economic behaviour, the Historical School comes very

---

[3] See Denzau and North (1994), North (2005) and Sect. 8.2.
[4] The rationalist philosophy of Gottfried Wilhelm Leibniz (1646–1716), as that of his disciple Christian Wolff (1679–1754), had much influence on the German Historical School. This relates, in particular, to the legal tradition of Natural Law (*Naturrecht*), on which German economics was based in the eighteenth century. It maintains that Man has moral obligations, the origins of which are to be found in nature. While representing the law regardless of creed, the Natural Law tradition recognises every human being as the creation of God, and derives from this that every human being himself has the pleasurable duty to be creative and to invent (Reinert 2005).
[5] Note that the German Historical School's evolutionary notion of development is quite akin to Schumpeter's emphasis on the correspondence of economic and socio-cultural evolution. See, for instance, Ebner (2000) for an attempt to prove the consistency of Schumpeterian economics with the Schmollerian approach.

13.1 Methodological Contributions

close to modern notions of behavioural economics. Its dynamic model of man offers an approach for dealing with the challenge that intriguing results from recent behavioural and experimental research pose. As discussed in Sect. 10.3, this challenge arises from the sentiment that newer experimental evidence about economic behaviour in low-income countries cannot anymore fully be understood in the framework of rational choice based theories.

From the evolutionary perspective of a dynamic model of man, rationality and self-interested behaviour are not seen as inherent traits of human behaviour, but have rather to be understood as the result of a process of learning from the feedback that people receive when making choices in the institutional framework that governs their economic interactions. The market is certainly the most effective mechanism for feedback triggering rational behaviour.[6] The rationality assumption, although simplifying, may thus deliver a good approximation of individual behaviour in the presence of (nearly) perfect competition and efficient markets. Such conditions can indeed be assumed to hold for several markets in advanced economies, but they are rarely to be found in low-income countries. In a developing markets context, the use of the rationality assumption therefore often incorrectly specifies actual circumstances. As has been shown in the descriptive analysis of Part I, economic interactions in low-income countries are more likely to be based on personal trust, reputation and norms of morality. These forms of relation-based contracting can result in the development of behavioural traits that deviate from the precepts of rational choice theory, even though they may prove to be rational in the sense that they are effective in supporting economic activity in the context of the economic realities in low-income countries. Following this line of reasoning, evidence of apparently irrational behaviour looms less as a puzzle if one reckons that for the rationality postulate to hold, a number of concomitant assumptions have to apply about the existence of appropriate information- and feedback-processing institutions that make learning of rational, utility-maximising behaviour possible in the first place. To understand the results from recent research in behavioural economics, development economists might thus have to consider more closely the formative effects of institutions on behaviour beyond their role in minimising transaction costs of economic exchange and production relations.[7]

---

[6] The role of the market (and of the price mechanism) in inducing rational behaviour is an old theme in economics. Hayek (1945) was strongly convinced about the indispensability of the price system for any rational calculation, which he justified by "the unavoidable imperfection of man's knowledge and the consequent need for a process by which knowledge is constantly communicated and acquired" (Ibid, p. 530).

[7] The importance of learning for the formation of economic behaviour may further be elucidated by understanding that choices are the observable manifestation of individual preferences. Preferences can be understood as social constructs that result from a learning process. For instance, the relationship between the attributes of a good and one's preference for it are established in transactions that involve that good. It can generally be said that the more experience a consumer has with a certain type of good, the more accurately defined will his preferences concerning that good be, and the more rational can his choice behaviour be expected to be. For a discussion of the theoretical implications of the assumption of endogenous preferences, see, for instance, Bowles (1998).

The formation of economic behaviour through learning from repeated interactions within a given institutional context has been a vital part in the research programme of the Historical School. By also accounting for the noneconomic, and in particular cultural influences on economic behaviour, their programme moreover offers a framework that accommodates the factors that influence learning, the evolution of preferences and hence economic choices in contexts in which theories that are based on the standard axioms of rational choice tend to yield inaccurate predictions. The findings from this contextual approach have been reinforced, for instance, by the sociology of knowledge, which conceptualises learning as the intergenerational transfer of knowledge, mental model, cultural values and norms that people internalise in the course of their socialisation and through the experiences they make in their local environment. Accordingly, different cultural influences can result in separate institutionalised wisdom, each with its own inbuilt "rationality".[8]

In this context, the criticism by Karl Polanyi of the universal model of man as a rational economic actor, who tries to achieve the highest possible individual gain with the least possible effort, deserves mention here.[9] In *The Great Transformation* ([1944] 2001), he set out to show that in all previous human history, individual gain had never been the dominant incentive for engaging in economic activity, and explained that actors in the modern market economy have been conditioned to respond to economic motives of individual gain, which are in no way inherent in human nature. Polanyi thus argued that the economic principle is a far too narrow concept to understand how people became economically active in different historical circumstances. He classified economic systems according to three dominant patterns of integration of economic activity, namely reciprocity, redistribution and exchange. Each of these forms is conditional on the existence of specific social institutions into which economic life is embedded. Polanyi believed that every form of integration therefore has its own "rationalities", and that it makes little sense to define the behaviour of economic agents in a redistributively integrated economy, or an economy based on reciprocity, in terms of the rationality of market actors.

The recognition that cultural influences play a central role in the formation of economic behaviour introduces a new dimension into the economic analysis of behaviour that further challenges the applicability of conventional rational choice-based models of man. These models may be flexible enough to accommodate the effects of external constraints in the structures of low-income countries on economic behaviour. But they fail to elucidate how economic structures and institutional

---

[8] For a treatise in the sociology of knowledge, see Berger and Luckmann (1966). Of relevance here is also the sociological concept of "system rationality", which maintains that economic rationality is not universal, but determined by the specific values and mental models of a given cultural system (Luhmann 1968). More recently, the question of how mental models and cultural beliefs evolve and how they shape economic behaviour and choices has also been restated in the New Institutional Economics literature (see, for instance, Denzau and North 1994; North 2005), even though they had also already clearly been formulated in the evolutionary economics of the "old" Institutional School (see Sect. 12.4).

[9] See also Sect. 13.2.1 for a further discussion of Polanyi's work.

patterns within a given context affect the process of learning and decision-making itself. A new theoretical framework for the analysis of economic behaviour in low-income countries thus has to go beyond the present state of development economics, the guiding model of man of which is the *homo economicus*, even if he is assumed to live in a world with imperfect information, positive transaction costs and limited cognitive capacities.

Among the contributions of the Historical School, the concept of economic styles stands out in that it takes the culture and history of societies as a criterion to distinguish and explain different patterns of economic behaviour. Contrary to recent attempts at modifying and extending the assumptions of the rational choice model, the concept of economic styles thus seeks explanations for differences in economic behaviour not just in the external structural environment, or in the influence of different material circumstances and constraints people's choices. It rather offers a framework for the identification and methodologically sound consideration of cultural influences on the forms and processes of economic decision-making itself. As the next section shows, theoretical predictions about causes and implications of economic behaviour in low-income countries are possible without universal acceptance of the rationality assumption if only observed behaviour is reasonably consistent in its adaptations to institutional change, and reveals that people responds to incentives.

13.2 The Style-Based Approach to the Understanding of Economic Activity in Low-Income Countries

The concept of economic styles provides a useful framework for the reconstruction of a contextual economics that can be applied to the study of qualitative differences in contemporary economic life across different cultural and historical contexts. This concept, as well as the larger methodological contributions on which it is founded, accommodates many of the demands on a new economics of development that have been formulated in Chap. 9 in terms of lessons and conclusions from previous paradigms in development economics. Its relevance as a framework for the analysis of economic realities in low-income countries stems especially from the following properties of the style-economic approach.

The concept of the economic style epitomises the characteristic elements by which the order, structure and ultimately the performance of an economy are determined. These elements comprise the institutions, technologies and endowments of an economy, but also the "spirit" by which economic behaviour and institutions are shaped, and which finds expression in such culturally induced elements as the norms, values, motivations and attitudes of economic actors. By taking the idea of the style as an "unity of expression and attitude" from the cultural sciences, the concept is instrumental in showing how prevailing mental models, forms of organisation and governance of economic activity, the methods of production, and the constitutions of social and cultural life fit together and interact in a given place or time. Invoking a style-theoretical approach in development economics is not, in the first place, done for purposes of classifying the diversity of economic life throughout the world into different economic styles, or to describe the course of history as a succession of individual style periods. Instead, applying a style-economic approach to the analysis of any given research question can do two main things: First, it can help to clarify and delimit the sphere of influence of the factors that are significant and essential for understanding economic phenomena and outcomes in a given place and time. The approach thus helps the economist to arrive at a definite subject for his research, as well as a clear idea about the scope of applicability of his theoretical findings. Second, the concept of economic styles applied to the study of a particular country or region elucidates how economic outcomes are determined in a process of interactions between the economic system and the social, political and cultural systems that govern societal life in a given context.

It is important to note that not primarily an economic outcome has to satisfy a particular style, but rather the process by which it has been reached at.[10] Thinking in terms of economic styles provides the researcher with a framework for understanding the process and context-specific forces that have brought an economic phenomenon into being, and thus enables him to go beyond the explanation of static economic outcomes through investigating correlations between sets of aggregate data. Style models reflect the specificity of economic life as a causal complex – a system held together by the interaction of its elements. Aggregate statistical data can neither convey the original facts of economic life, nor the causes from which they originate in the specific contexts of individual countries. While cross-national accounts are useful for the investigation of general relationships especially at the macroeconomic level, a style-based approach can help to arrive at a qualitative understanding of why and how a particular relationship came about and how it is determined by both economic and noneconomic influences on individual behaviour.

The aim of applying a style-theoretical approach in development economics is to obtain an analytical framework for studying the specificity of forms and patterns of economic life in low-income countries by systematically taking account of the interdependencies between elements of the economic, as well as of the social, political and cultural systems of society. This framework can also help to structure and integrate the growing number of recent interdisciplinary attempts at broadening explanatory approaches in development economics beyond purely economic accounts. Most importantly, however, the concept of economic styles provides development economists with an analytical device for introducing cultural influences on economic behaviour and outcomes into economic analysis, and to think systematically about the role of culture in the process of institutional change and development.

---

[10] Spiethoff originally used the notion of the economic style in two different ways, namely, for a system of elements and institutional patterns held together by interaction, and for the conceptual models that are designed to analyse this institutional set-up.

13.2.1 Culture and Style in Economic Analysis

By examining the economic characteristics of low-income countries in Part I of this study, it has been shown that private economic activity emerges in a multitude of forms that function despite the lack of formal market-supporting institutions. By discussing this observation, the importance of cultural aspects of economic life became evident. In particular, cultural factors entered the analysis by way of recognising that the exercise of cultural norms through trust, reciprocity or moral obligations towards the community, can enable private economic activity in spite of conditions of weak formal governance of economic relations by markets and the state that can be found in many low-income countries (see Sect. 4.1). Moreover, development economists in the new institutionalist tradition are coming to understand that it is primarily the cultural underpinnings of a country's institutions that shape the form that these institutions take, and that the proper functioning of formal institutions is a function of how well they are embedded in a society's informal social and cultural structures (see Sect. 8.2.2). Finally, the importance of cultural influences on economic behaviour is increasingly conjectured on the basis of results from recent research in behavioural development economics and evidence from experimental studies (see Sect. 10.3). This makes evident the need in development economics for an analytical framework that accounts for the cultural foundations of institutional and economic change, and thus allows for a richer understanding of the forms and outcomes of economic activity in low-income countries.

The conjecture that culture matters has given rise to a growing number of attempts at introducing cultural explanations into the analysis of economic development.[11] However, many of these studies have been carried out within the methodological framework of conventional neoclassical economics. By broadly generalising cultural effects, they risk arriving at stereotypical assertions about the influence of culture on economic behaviour. While acknowledging that culture matters, these contributions fail to recognise that cultural phenomena influence economic structures in many different ways, and can issue into a large variety of forms of economic activity across different contexts. Therefore, an important implication of integrating cultural factors into the analysis of economic processes is that the scope of analysis, and hence the validity of results, inevitably narrows to the specific context to which a particular cultural effect applies. The context-specificity that comes along with culturally determined phenomena thus limits the scope for broad generalisations that provide for first-best models of the economy and recourse to universal economic principles.

The revival of culture-based explanations in economics has especially been spurred by the more recent New Institutional Economics literature.[12] It recognises cultural influences on economic outcomes by emphasising the interdependencies of

---

[11] See, for instance, Harrison and Huntington (2000); Rao and Walton (2004); Knack and Keefer (1997b); or Licht et al. (2007).

[12] See, for instance, North (2005) and Leipold (2006), as well as Sect. 8.2.2.

informal institutions like people's mental models, value orientations, attitudes, customs and traditions, with formal institutions in the process of economic change. However, these informal institutions are mostly seen as exogenous, thus making processes of institutional change culturally path-dependent in the sense that the pace and direction of institutional change is determined by the cultural legacy of a society. Applied to the analysis of development problems in low-income countries, this literature shows a tendency to blame the predicament of the poor on the deficient and persistent nature of their own regressive cultures. As Zweynert (2006) notes, such cultural fatalism could be warranted if regions or countries developed in complete isolation. However, a significant characteristic of today's low-income countries is that they are facing various pressures for change, for instance, as a result of interrelations with the world economy (e.g. through trade, foreign investment, migration or remittance flows), because they are under direct pressure to reform from foreign donors and international development institutions, or as a consequence of internal or external shocks. Similarly, informal institutions are incrementally changing as a result of human learning, either through adjustments in people's expectations and preferences in response to past experiences, or through the influence of education on people's cultural habits and traditions, as well as the impact of political groups or the media on people's ideologies and beliefs.

If development economists are to take advantage of the potential of cultural analysis, they will not only have to recognise the significance and variety of noneconomic influences on the evolution of institutions and modes of economic activity but also have to understand that a cultural perspective on development can only be of explanatory value if it carefully defines the concepts of culture it uses in relation to a given phenomenon's specific context. The problem is thus as much one of taxonomy, namely to define what exactly is meant by cultural influences on development, as it is one of the methodology in the sense that consideration for noneconomic factors requires clarifying the scope and context to which assumptions and theoretical conclusions about specific cultural influences apply.

With the concept of economic styles, development economists are provided with an analytical device that satisfies demands for both methodological and taxonomical clarity. Thinking in terms of economic styles enables economists to distil from a complex reality those patterns that are typical characteristics of economic life, while at the same time preventing them from generalising these patterns beyond the sphere of the economic style in which they have a significant and clearly specified effect on economic behaviour and outcomes. The contextual research approach, on which the concept of economic styles is based, thus ensures the methodologically sound consideration of cultural factors in economic analysis. Moreover, with the application of a style-based approach, ideas such as "economic spirit" and other foundations of a society's culture are given a concrete meaning. Cultural influences enter the analysis explicitly through consideration of the effects of people's moral motivations, attitudes and mental models on economic outcomes. The concept of culture adopted is thus a cognitive one, which is less broad than the normative understanding of culture as the entirety of a way of life, but more comprehensive than the functional view that restricts culture to the study and practice of acts and spiritual life. This cognitive understanding has not only already influenced Max Weber's notion of culture; it is also the basis of most research in the younger literature in economic sociology.[13] At the same time, culture is conceptualised as a criterion to distinguish between different institutional forms and governance structures of economic activity, which in turn are expressions of different economic styles.

Empirical evidence of how different cultural beliefs can lead to diverse trajectories of societal organisation is, for instance, provided by Greif (1994) in a historical study of collectivist and individualist societies.[14] His results can be explained within the framework of a style-economic approach in that individualist and collectivist forms of societal organisation can be understood as different occurrences of cultural attributes that describe different constitutions of society, which in turn represent elements of different economic styles. Greif (1994) suggests that collectivist cultural beliefs dominate in most developing countries, whereas social and economic relations in advanced Western economies are rather founded on individualistic cultural beliefs. He goes on to note that in collectivist societies, social and economic structures tend to be segregated in the sense that interactions are guided by cultural values and norms that are shared within specific groups. These shared cultural beliefs capture people's expectations with respect to others. They are relatively stable in intra-group relations, but at the same time limit the scope for cooperation with members of other groups. The institutional functions that support economic activity are mainly achieved through informal, self-enforcing institutional forms. On the contrary, social and economic structures in individualist societies tend to be integrated in the sense that interactions are governed by specialised formal institutions and take place irrespective of the exchange partners' cultural identity. Using the example of different forms of contract enforcement institutions, Greif concludes that collective enforcement systems are more effective than individualistic ones if the division of labour and trade opportunities are relatively limited, whereas individualist cultural beliefs are more conductive to the emergence of integrated systems of economic activity in which contract enforcement is delegated to a formal third party. These results support two main propositions that follow from the application of a style-economic approach: They show how distinct cultural characteristics of societies influence the form that institutions take; and they demonstrate that different sets of institutions may be optimal under different economic conditions.

Of clear relevance in the context of this discussion is also the work of Karl Polanyi.[15] He used economic anthropology and early economic history to dismantle

---

[13] For the recent literature in economic sociology that adopts a cognitive approach to culture, see, for instance, DiMaggio (1997) or Hofstede (1991). For a detailed definition of the cognitive and alternative views on culture, see Leipold (2006, Chap. 2).

[14] The study compares institutional forms that have emerged to support economic activity in two pre-modern societies, the Maghribi traders, which were part of the Muslim world in the eleventh century, and the Genoese traders, which were part of the Latin world in the twelfth century. For further discussion of this and related studies, see Sect. 4.2.3.

[15] I am grateful to Erik Reinert for bringing the conceptual kinship of Karl Polanyi's work to the style-theoretic approach to my attention. Of particular relevance in this context are Polanyi ([1944] 2001), Polanyi et al. (1957) and Dalton (1968).

the presumption from classical economics that the self-regulating market is a ubiquitous and invariable form of economic organisation, as well as the related perception of the economic system as the main determinative influence on a society's social organisation and culture. To Polanyi, these were wrong generalisations from the special case of laissez-faire capitalism, which had to be dropped if economists are to understand the organisation of economic activity outside the context of the Western liberal market economy. From extensive research into non-market exchange in pre-modern societies he found that it is kinship, tribal affiliation, political rule and religious obligation that govern economic activity in non-capitalist contexts. Furthermore, he showed that throughout human history, economic activity was a "by-product" of social life, controlled by rules of reciprocity, redistribution and mutual obligation rather than by anonymous market exchange and economic motives of individual gain. It was only when technological progress and new modes of industrial production led to the commodification of land, labour and money that the place of the economy in society changed radically. One of Polanyi's main theses is that this great transformation brought about the subordination of society to the requirements of the market economy, and with it the danger of an erosion of the web of social relationships that held human society together.[16]

A main objective of Polanyi was to develop a theory for explaining the organisation of economic activity in a society that provided an alternative to the market-centred models of classical liberalism. In *The Great Transformation*, Polanyi ([1944] 2001, chapter 4) identified reciprocity (e.g. gift-giving between kin and friends), redistribution (e.g. obligatory payments to a political or religious authority for its own maintenance) and exchange (on markets) as three main organising principles by which different patterns of integration of the economy in society can be distinguished. These forms of integration are likely to coexist in all systems of economic organisation. But economic systems may still be classified according to which of these patterns represents the dominant form of integration. For instance, markets exist in all societies, but their role in society can differ markedly depending on whether exchange is motivated by norms of reciprocity or the pursuit of material self-gain. Furthermore, a capitalist system, in which market-based exchange dominates, can only be sustainable if market exchanges are embedded in social and political institutions that regulate, stabilise and legitimate market outcomes.[17]

Polanyi's description of the transformation from pre-modern societal life to the dominance of market-based relations in the wake of the industrial revolution in Europe can downright be read as an account of the transition from a pre-modern to a capitalist economic style. Even though Polanyi never invoked the concept of

---

[16]This warning has never been more topical than in the context of contemporary globalisation, as well as in the present global financial crisis, and makes Polanyi required reading far beyond studies in economic sociology and anthropology.

[17]It is important to note that nothing in Polanyi's theory implies that the three forms or integration replace or follow each other in the course of history. Polanyi–Levitt (2005, p. 165) later emphasised that "Polanyi's approach was comparative. There was, in his work, no suggestion of progress or any implication that modern societies are more advanced or more developed than those of the past".

economic styles in his work, the key elements by which the economic style of any given society can be defined, like the ethical motivations that guide people's actions, the constitution of society or the forms of organisation and governance of economic activity, all feature prominently in his work. Moreover, modern economists are vigorously reminded by the work of Polanyi not to forget the interdependencies between the economic system on the one hand, and the social, political and cultural institutions of a society on the other – a concern that is central in recent attempts at reconstructing a contextual approach to development economics.

Profound insights into the cultural characteristics of non-Western societies, and the implications of their cultural beliefs and worldviews for the evolution of their own economic styles, are provided by Büscher (1988) at the example of contemporary African societies.[18] In a study in which he combines findings from own field research in South-Eastern Africa with a review of the relevant, mostly African literature, he describes the following culturally determined patterns of thought, and resulting structures, that are characteristic for many (traditional) African societies:

(i) *Concepts of time:* In the context of most African cultures, time has a meaning only in relation to the experience of concrete events. Unlike the Western concept of time as a linear, structured and predictable process that can be planned in a forward-looking manner, African cultures experience time predominantly in relation to past events. The future is unpredictable and hence irrelevant. Life is not focussed at realising a desirable state in the future; rather do people find orientation for their lives in the history of their traditions. This focus implies that time is not considered a constraint that determines and structures the course of life, but an abundant resource that can be created and used by man as he sees fit.[19]

(ii) *Religion:* The African concept of time is integral part of the religious ontology of African societies. Religion is omnipresent in African traditions, but in such a natural way that differentiations into secular and sacral spheres of life are virtually impossible. According to their spiritual worldview, God is creator and upholder of man and all life, the spirits, both supernatural beings and the spirit of ancestors, determine human destiny and function as mediators between God and men. Man stands at the centre, surrounded by nature and all material things. Beyond these categories, a central element of African ontology is the "vital force", an energy that upholds all life and with which all people are freely

---

[18] Equally interesting insight can also be gained from ontological studies of other cultural areas. For instance, the Islamic culture features many discrete institutional forms and structures that could allow for the identification of an Islamic economic style. For a comprehensive study of the interacting economic and cultural characteristics of Islamic countries, see Leipold (2001).

[19] The fact that Africans are often flatly denounce as "tardy", or as to "idly wasting their time" is an unintended consequence of the ignorance for the concept of time that people in a traditional African context have internalised and which is hence part of their normal course of life.

endowed owing to a generous universe. For Africans, a rich and happy life means to obtain as much of this vital force as possible.

(iii) *Cultural motivations for economic activity*: The generation of vital force is also a main purpose of acquiring material goods, and of the performance of productive labour. In the context of an African subsistence economy, production and consumption is directed towards safeguarding the material basis for recreating and sustaining the vital force of all members of the community. Economic activity is thus embedded in a spiritual context, in which the self-interested, profit-maximising pursuit of economic activity would have to be considered a deviation from shared norms and beliefs. This does not imply that principles of reciprocity or effort and reward are unknown in African cultures. They do exist, for instance, with regard to collectively performed work, in gift exchanges, in the form of mutual support, or in the bride price paid by the groom or his family to the parents of a woman in exchange for the bride's family's "loss" of her labour and fertility within her kin group.

(iv) *African communalism*: At the centre of the African spiritual worldview stands man in his community. The individual defines himself in the first place as part of his extended family or community. These bonds are not only based on kinship and shared values and norms, but also on economic ties. It is characteristic for the practice of reciprocity in African communities that give-and-take relationships do not lead to an instant and exact compensation. Instead, a certain imbalance is consciously kept up to maintain the relationship in that a remaining liability obliges the exchange partner, or his family, to provide a future service in return when the other partner comes in need of it. Here, the economic symmetry between effort and reward, or service and service in return, that characterises Western economic rationality is modified to fulfil a social integration function of economic exchange relations, the rationality of which can only be understood against the background of the values and norms that govern African communal life. Another economic implication of African communalism is the priority that is given to the needs of the community over the satisfaction of individual wants. While this does not necessarily preclude possibilities for specialisation, it inhibits incentives for the individual accumulation of capital as returns are predominantly claimed by the extended family or community.[20]

(v) *The emergence of dualist structures*: The juxtaposition of traditional African structures and formal institutions adopted on Western models has led to the emergence of parallel systems of governance in many parts of Africa.

---

[20]Limited possibilities for capital accumulation and long-term investments are also often claimed as reasons for the widespread practice of subsistence production in many parts of Africa. Beyond this explanation, an analysis of the cultural determinants of the subsistence economy can furthermore reveal the deep causes for the persistence of this type of production. Accordingly, subsistence farming has primarily to be seen as a consequence of the cultural belief that man is entitled to take from nature what is necessary to satisfy his wants, while these wants are in the first place those of the community. Moreover, as land is, on the same cultural grounds, considered as communal property, it cannot by used by the individual farmer as collateral for a loan from a formal bank.

The countries of Sub-Saharan Africa have inherited from their colonial powers a nation state with a central government the political leaders of which were supposed to serve the society as a whole. But the traditional political core in an African society has always been the tribe, whereas the organisation of the state with a central government and public administration has no structural roots in African history and culture. Consequently, the state has often only limited power in governing economic and social relations, while informal institutions rule at the community level. Unlike imported formal institutions, these informal arrangements are rooted in shared cultural norms and traditions, which render them actual legitimacy and internal stability. Where these opposed cultural levels converge, dependence and loyalty relationships often intermingle and create a basis for what Western observers usually identify as corruption, favouritism or cronyism. A related consequence is that the ruling of the African state is often dominated by rival networks of political groups that are more committed to their own reference group than to the well-being of the nation as a whole. Political power is thus used to benefit the particular interest of the members of their kin or community, while discriminating against members of rival groups.

These attempts at analytically approaching the essence of African culture and traditions are certainly incomplete and need empirical validation through further observational and explorative research of each concrete case. But even the basic characteristics conveyed in the above findings can give an idea of what cultural factors are all about, and how culture matters in the evolution of an economic style. The findings also show that cultural characteristics, as expressed in different worldviews and hence attitudes, behaviour and motivations, are no abstract, isolated and quantifiable variables, but elements of an actually experienced reality. They cannot adequately be captured by conventional modelling approaches. If expressed as elements of a particular economic style, however, their consideration as endogenous factors in the economic analysis of different institutional forms and paths of development becomes a real possibility.

The failure to understand how cultural variations account for context-specific differences in social and economic structures has also had important ramifications for the practice of international development cooperation. Without knowledge of people's cultural beliefs, motivations, attitudes and, by implication, their preferences and constraints, it is hardly possible to predict how local target groups will respond to the incentives that emanate from a development measure, and thus to accommodate the compatibility of incentives in the programme design. Moreover, effective development assistance requires a common understanding by donors and beneficiaries of the notions and concepts that are implied in the objectives of a development measure. For instance, the demand for sustainability that is a guiding principle of all international development assistance actually reflects Western concepts of time and future, the validity of which cannot be taken for granted in the context of low-income countries (Offe 2007). Sustainability implies to forego current gains in favour of expected benefits to future generations. The concept is based on the belief that the actions of the present generation have some influence on the welfare of future generations. But, as for instance in African cultures, the future is seen as destiny, implying a much higher time preference for present gains than demanded by the concept of sustainability. Similar consequences of different concepts of time and attitudes towards the future also apply with regard to peoples' saving and investment decisions. As discussed above, the liner, mathematical division of time in amortisation periods, repayment plans etc. must appear foreign to Africans, whose concept of time is oriented at the actual experience of present and past events. This applies especially to the poorest parts of society, and the mainly rural population that is rooted in traditional communal life. Moreover, the time preference of individuals in these parts African societies has important implications for the choice of an appropriate discount rate for evaluating public investments and development programs. If differences in cultural beliefs concerning concepts of time and future are indeed substantial, then discounting practices currently used in development planning and project appraisal are probably poor representations of actual intertemporal preferences of people in low-income countries.[21]

13.2.2 *Economic Style and Institutional Diversity*

Besides providing a framework for the identification and distinction of varied occurrences of cultural elements in economic life in different contexts, the concept of economic styles helps to gain a qualitative understanding of how the cultural, social and political institutions of a society interrelate with the economic system. This is particularly valuable for the study of low-income countries where cultural, political and economic spheres of life are much more intertwined than in advanced liberal market economies. The purpose of this section is to show that a framework for analysing the interdependencies between the economic system and the cultural and political areas of societal life is a prerequisite for also understanding the dynamic interplay between informal and formal institutions in the process of economic change and development. Understanding the process of economic change is, in turn, a necessary condition for the success of all attempts at deliberately improving the economic performance of low-income countries.

The application of a style-based framework can help development economists to anticipate and counteract many of the problems that inhere in attempts at transplanting formal institutions or governance systems from the confines of one economic style into another. Development policies that aim at assisting low-income

---

[21] For evidence on the actual time preferences in low-income countries, see Poulos and Whittington (1999). On the time discounting methods used in the development project appraisals, see Sect. 7.3.3. On the implications of different culture-specific concepts and perceptions of time for development cooperation, see GTZ et al. (2005). Implications of similar significance also arise from the multitude of concepts of progress that prevail across different cultures (see GTZ et al. 2004 Donner, 2004).

countries in implementing elements of the formal institutional structures of economically more advanced countries exhibit large variations in their effectiveness and sustainability. Externally assisted institutional reform programmes often tend to remain ineffective even if efforts are made to adapt the imported formal institutions to the conditions of the local economic environment. What is, in fact, often missing is a strategy to ensure the compatibility of formal institutional patterns with prevailing informal values and norms that convey the influence of people's mental models and cultural beliefs on economic outcomes. But since these cultural orientations are relatively stable, change of informal institutions is slow and often impossible to achieve from the outside. It often takes local actors – politicians, religious leaders or traditional authorities – who are able to "sell" an institutional reform project to their communities, and thereby harness the prevailing informal institutions as legitimising and stabilising forces in the process of formal institutional change.[22] Without such cultural compatibility between a formal institutional design and people's entrenched beliefs, traditions and customs, the formal institution may be rejected even if it has proven to be effective in other cultural contexts.

If the evolution or deliberate building of formal institutions depends on a society's cultural orientations that underpin its informal institutions, then this fact also explains why institutions that perform similar functions can emerge in widely varying forms in different cultural contexts. Development economics has reached a stage at which the role of institutions in economic development is widely accepted. But institutions are still operationalised through variables that can be used to measure their impact by means of quantitative cross-country regressions. There is only little understanding of the analytical and practical consequences of institutional diversity. Here, again, the concept of economic styles can help to increase the explanatory power and policy relevance of development research. Within a style-based framework, institutional diversity can be dealt with by perceiving specific institutional forms as expressions of a given economic style. This means that, albeit these institutions can be functional equivalents, their particular forms represent characteristic occurrences of attributes of a distinct economic style, and can thus only be analysed and understood in a meaningful way in the context of that particular style.

The contextual development economics that an application of the style-theoretic framework provides for goes beyond contemporary mainstream analysis in

---

[22] Culturally sensitive approaches that emphasise the role of local actors in "pulling in" a reform are encouraged by the German Development Cooperation since the 1990s (GTZ 1990). Principles for working with, and from within, communities and faith-based organisations in areas such as human rights, reproductive health, women's empowerment, adolescents and youth, humanitarian assistance and HIV/AIDS have since recently also been explored by the United Nations Population Fund (UNFPA 2004,2008). However, these attempts mostly aim at fostering sensitivity towards local cultures and habits in the course of international development cooperation, rather than being derived from a qualitative understanding of the interdependencies between cultural and economic elements of societal life in a given context, and their influence on economic change.

economics in that it allows for gaining a qualitative understanding of the context-specific factors by which the emergence of diverse institutional forms and trajectories of societal organisation can be explained. Thereby, the contextual approach to development economics does not, however, deny the existence of universal economic principles that have to be honoured in any context if broad-based economic growth is to be promoted. These include, in the first place, the general functions that institutions perform to enable and support private economic activity, albeit in a diversity of different, context-specific forms. These functions are, among others, the creation of trust, the provision of incentives for compliance in contractual relations, the provision of incentives for engaging in socially beneficial private economic activities, the legitimisation and regulation of economic outcomes and the maintenance of social cohesion within a society. These functions relate to further economic principles, the implementation of which is commonly attributed more to the formal institutions of the state, like an undistorted supply of physical capital, labour and land, the effective provision of education, health and infrastructure services, secure property rights and the rule of law, as well as sound macroeconomic management.

It is generally recognised that any economic order, irrespective of its form, should accommodate these economic principles, and the historical evidence shows that most successful countries have indeed adhered to them. But, as has been tried to show in this study, the challenge that development economists have to accept is that the diversity of context-specific institutional forms and modes of economic organisation in low-income countries defies the possibility for inferring universal policy solutions from these general principles. The development of sustainable market economies is an incremental process in which informal institutional change legitimises and stabilises formal institution building. Unlike in technology development, there are hardly any possibilities for societies to "leapfrog" from a traditional straight into a modern market-based economic system. The promotion of free trade has indeed long, but erroneously, been assumed to represent such a leapfrog strategy for poor countries to prosperity. But to benefit from free trade, low-income countries have to go through a transitional phase in which different kinds of strategies have to be adopted that are more commensurate with initial conditions of low-income countries. How could such transitional policies look like? Erik Reinert (2005) found that rich countries from Renaissance Italy to the modern Far East have been successful in transforming from low-income economies into high-income countries through a combination of government intervention, protectionism and strategic investment in increasing returns industries that enabled them to diversify their domestic industries beyond the sole dependence on exporting raw materials or cash crops.[23] He considers these mercantilist policies as a "mandatory passage point" that all hitherto poor countries have passed in their transitions out of poverty. These policies are context-specific in the sense that they are appropriate only at a particular stage in a country's development. Once they have been effective in

---

[23] See also Reinert and Reinert (2005).

helping to transform a country into a diversified industrialised economy, the promotion of free trade can follow as a more appropriate policy option in this new context. However, as the sobering experience with import-substitution policies in Latin America in the 1970s has shown, the success of such transitional policies is not universally guaranteed. Throughout history, mercantilist policies have been adopted in a variety of forms. It is here where the method and approach of contextual development economics can guide policymakers and development institutions in identifying fitting policy designs and implementation strategies that work for a given context.

13.2.3 Some Applications and Fields for Further Research

The operationalisation of culturally derived factors in economic analysis as criterion to distinguish between different institutional forms and governance structures of economic activity opens up important fields of applications for a style-theoretical approach in development research. The following examples describe some unrecognised or unresolved concerns, which can be elucidated within this framework:

- Determination of the goodness of fit between formal and informal institutions: The deliberate building of formal institutions through government intervention is, besides technological progress, an important source of exogenous structural change. The formal institutions of today's low-income countries have indeed rarely evolved endogenously. Instead, they have largely been transplanted from more advanced countries during the colonial area or in the course of international development cooperation. But unlike local institutions that have evolved endogenously from existing practices and conventions, the successful intersociety adoption of institutions requires a strategy for ensuring the coalescence of the imported rules and structures with existing norms and traditions into a coherent whole. Therefore, an essential part of development policy has to be concerned with the determination of the goodness of fit between formal and informal institutions within a given context. This requires an understanding of both, the cultural underpinnings of a society's informal institutional structure, and the interplay between this structure and a given formal institutional innovation. The concept of economic styles provides an appropriate framework for gaining such an understanding.[24]
- Restoration of social cohesion in the course of institutional reform: A related area of application concerns the search for ways to restore social cohesion in the course of institutional change where traditional ties begin to loosen while new relations are not yet internalised in actors' preferences, motivations and beliefs. Within a style-economic framework, social cohesion is addressed as an attribute

---

[24]See Goldschmidt and Zweynert (2006) for an analysis of the process of institutional transplantation in the course of Central and Eastern Europe's economic and political transition.

of the constitution of society, and recognised as a product of the dynamic interdependencies between societal and economic life.
- Addressing the implications of weak economic governance by the state: Main characteristics of low-income countries stem from the weak governance that formal state institutions exert on economic activity, as well the private governance mechanisms that have evolved as functional equivalents instead. As a result, enforcement power, and hence markets, tend to be fragmented while the perceived legitimacy of the centrally enforced system of formal legal rules is limited. Privately governed, relation-based exchanges rely heavily on culturally derived norms, values and motivations that are shared by all parties to an exchange. It has often been argued that these cultural orientations make institutional change path-dependent and therefore inhibit the transition to a modern system of formal rules that supports anonymous exchange across diverse ethical groups. In effect, development economists have for long perceived informal arrangements and formal legal systems as two conflicting modes of governance, or even associated informality with outright chaos and disorder. While a formal legal system with the state as a central third-party enforcement power has undoubtedly a comparative advantage in supporting the expansion of trade and investment to their efficient levels, one needs to consider the interdependencies between economic and cultural life to understand that a strong functional complementarily is actually implied between informal norms and formal rules in promoting economic activity and development. The evidence discussed in Sect. 4.4.3 suggests that even in advanced market economies, trust and reputation-based modes of governance are important complements to the functions that a formal legal system performs. There are actually many different ways in which formal rules can evolve from informal arrangements, and many channels through which informal and formal rules reinforce each other. These different ways correspond with different economic styles. Attempts at predicting the individual paths of institutional change described by the transition from private modes of governance to more formalised and general governance regimes are therefore most likely to succeed in an analytical framework that accounts for the interacting economic, cultural and political elements of any given economic style. This approach can finally also help to disprove the conception of informal arrangements as a threat to order and stability, which has often resulted in the proposal of policies that actually discriminate against the economic activities of the poor.
- Harnessing alternative modes of economic governance for private sector development: The style-economic approach allows identifying and analysing private forms of governance as functional equivalents to the economic governance functions of the state if the latter is absent or ineffective. Thereby, it provides a framework for designing innovative modes of private sector development that start from the problem of needed economic governance rather from the presumption that the performance of state institution will first have to be improved before private sector activity can thrive. A direct way of reducing uncertainty in contractual relations is to acquire economic governance from

outside jurisdictions. This can be done, for instance, through the integration of firms from low-income countries into the global value chains of multinational corporations that operate on the basis of international standards and the legal framework of an advanced country. Global value chains link production, processing, wholesale and retailing firms into a network of privately governed relations.[25] This private governance structure makes trade and exchange possible even in a context of limited external governance of economic transactions through domestic legal and state institutions. Global value chains thus have the potential to enhance domestic growth and employment in spite of difficult framework conditions in low-income countries. Additionally, they support the linkage of local firms with foreign markets, thus providing the prospect of sharing the benefits of globalisation with the world's poorest people.

---

[25]Whether these ties are exploitative or mutually beneficial depends on the design of their underlyingforms of long-term contracting. In this respect, an issue of particular importance is the application of global norms and standards as basis of these privately governed relationships.

Chapter 14
Conclusions

The application of a style-based framework has been suggested in the preceding analysis as a way to make development economics a more realistic, context-minded science again. Behind this approach lies the idea to conceptualise discrete sets of interdependent economic, cultural and political factors as elements of a particular economic style, and to define the context to which the elements of that style apply as the domain within which generalisations about the behaviour of economic phenomena are possible. While this approach challenges the usefulness of a universal model of behaviour, the possibility of a common framework for explaining economic behaviour in different cultural contexts is retained.

The style-based approach lays out such a framework. Theoretical research within this framework does not presuppose the validity of universal laws and axioms. Instead, it distils context-specific conclusions from empirically identified regularities in economic behaviour and processes with the objective to guide development economists to more relevant and appropriate theories especially in contexts to which conventional economic assumptions hardly apply. The development theories that emanate from the style–economic framework can be said to belong, from the perspective of standard economic theory, to the domain of the economics of the second-best.[1] They are typically concerned with "sub-optimal" or "inefficient" situations, but yet acknowledge that in the contexts of low-income countries, these arrangements are indeed often the most efficient available options for economic activity to take place. While style-based theories may not compare in their elegance to general equilibrium theory, they raise the prospect of significant advances in the understanding of economic processes in low-income countries, and in turn for more relevant, context-specific policy solutions.

---

[1] The theory of the second-best was first laid out by Lipsey and Lancaster (1956) who showed that the absence of any of the jointly necessary theoretical conditions for an optimal allocation of resources does not imply that the next-best allocation is secured by the presence of all the other optimality conditions. Rather, the second-best scenario may require changing other variables away from the ones that were originally assumed to be optimal. This implies that the second-best interactions may significantly differ from those predicted by the first-best model. Unlike in theoretical models, economists may not know, in practical situations, the necessary and sufficient conditions for achieving an economy-wide, first-best allocation of resources.

For all the differences between this approach and conventional methods of reasoning, economic styles are not meant to be regarded as counter concept to the general models of neoclassical theory. Rather, the two approaches represent different ways of understanding and explaining economic reality that each has its use depending on the problem under investigation, and the context to which it relates. It is a matter of sound economic research to always verify if the assumptions of a theory bear significant relation to the realities that they are supposed to explain. If they do not, theoretical conclusions and policy recommendations of better accuracy may be achieved from an alternative theory. It has been a main purpose of this book to demonstrate that the economic characteristics of low-income countries, and their context-specific determinants, warrant an alternative, contextual approach to development economics. The style–economic framework has been developed as an approach to the formulation of contextual development theories appropriate to meet the demands that economic realities in low-income countries make. The essential distinctions between this approach and mainstream thinking in development economics are indicated in Table 14.1. Albeit greatly simplified, it is intended to summarise the main results from the theoretical and methodological analysis from Part III of the book.

The purpose of applying the concept of economic styles to the analysis of economic realities in low-income countries is actually not already served by constructing economic style models of particular low-income countries. The style–economic approach is instead most useful if a definite problem or a concrete question has first been formulated, which can then be dealt within a style–theoretical framework. Several such problems, which arise against the backdrop of the specificity of economic realities in low-income countries, have been identified throughout this book, and some concrete fields of application have been proposed. They are by no means exhaustive, but are rather intended to exemplify areas where new insights can be expected from applying a style–economic framework. Further research is needed to uncover the "hidden rationalities" of economic behaviour in low-income countries, to gain from these a better understanding of how institutional forms and economic systems evolve, to establish causal relationships between them and other phenomena that influence economic activity, and finally to derive from this analysis policy-relevant conclusions that translate into more effective assistance towards igniting and sustaining processes of broad-based growth in today's poorest countries.

Beyond the application of the style–economic framework for finding context-specific solutions to concrete development problems, thinking in terms of economic styles could also provide a new perspective on the great conundrums that the persistence of poverty and the limited effectiveness of development assistance still pose. Especially with regard to Africa south of the Sahara, this situation can be interpreted from a style–economic perspective as the consequence of tensions that arise from the collusion of the Western economic style with the specific styles of organising economic and societal life in African economies. The entire development assistance exercise has been based on the implicit assumption that convergence in living standards between rich and poor countries presupposes convergence of poor countries' economic and societal systems with those that have led Western economies

14 Conclusions

Table 14.1 Methodological differences between mainstream and contextual approaches to development economics

	Mainstream development economics	Contextual development economics
Economic discipline	Neoclassical economics and extensions thereof ("hybrid" models)	Institutionalism; behavioural economics; economic sociology
Concept of economics	Akin to physical / mathematical science	A cultural / behavioural approach
Type of economics	Isolating economics	Contextual economics
Scope of research	Narrowly economic	Interdisciplinary across social sciences
Scope of theories	General theories	Time- and context-conditioned theories
Degree of abstraction	High level of abstraction	Level of abstraction chosen according to problem under investigation
Scientific method	Deductive	Inductive
Standard of excellence	Formal elegance and precision	Theoretical accuracy and policy-relevance
Empirical techniques	Cross-country regressions	Analytic narratives, participatory observation, explorative research
Empirical data	Mostly quantitative	Mostly qualitative
Mode of understanding	Mechanistic	Qualitative, irreducible only to numbers
Object of observation	Commodities and (relative) prices	Economic behaviour and interactions
Unit of analysis	Individual (Methodological Individualism)	Transaction / interaction between two or more economic agents
Model of man	Rational man, bound by external constraints	Creative man, whose rationality evolves through learning and in response to incentives of the institutional environment
Motives of economic agents	Self-interest	Self in relation to others
Motivation for economic activity	Profit maximisation	Satisfaction of wants; pursuit of varied motives conditioned by context
Role of society	Economy largely independent of society	Economy firmly rooted in society
Approach to culture	Exogenous	Endogenous; acceptance of values ideologies, mental models and beliefs
Sources of economic governance	The market and market-supporting institutions	The economic system (or order); individuals' shared norms and values
Analysis of change	Comparative static	Dynamic, evolutionary
Postulated outcome of economic process	Equilibrium	Multiple equilibria; disequilibrium
Targeted policy option	First best	Second best
Approach to policymaking	"Best-practice" approaches, universal recipes	Context-specific solutions

Source: Own research; format based on Reinert (2007, pp. 305ff)

to prosperity. As almost all outside development efforts, from colonial times to the era of development cooperation, were guided by this view, the room for manoeuvre of African leaders to embark on development paths in line with their distinct economic styles was restricted from the onset. Instead, the intermingling of Western systems and structures with African traditions and worldviews has led to the emergence of dual structures including multiple levels of loyalty, dysfunctional formal institutions, corruption, nepotism, rising inequality and civil conflict. Ultimately, the collusion of elements from these markedly different economic styles not only forestalled the possibility for African economies to develop along their own indigenous trajectories of societal organisation, but also impeded the successful adaptation and internalisation of Western institutions and modes of governing and organising economic activity within the framework of international development cooperation.

These are unconventional hypotheses that still require further research and empirical verification. But they do give a sense of how thinking about economic realities in low-income countries from a style–economic perspective could help development economists to move beyond the status quo of viewing the local institutions, traditional practices and indigenous knowledge of low-income countries as either irrelevant or hostile to their development. But the novel and unconventional nature of the style–economic approach also makes it vulnerable to misinterpretations. One problem arises in connection with confusing description and advocacy (or, for that matter, positive and normative statements). By their very nature, economic styles are descriptive models that capture regular and essential patterns of economic and societal life in a specific time and place. As such, they are part of economics as a positive science. But once the elements of specific economic styles have been identified and exhibited, the question inevitably arises as to whether these characteristics can be advocated. Is the kin system a promising social practice in spite of its seemingly negative impact on people's impetus for personal achievement? Should African communalism be accepted even if it is typically associated with fragmented markets and limited competition? Can informality be considered an efficient form of organising economic activity under conditions of weak formal governance even if it erodes the tax base of the government? Questions like these abound in academic and policy debates. Actually, however, they reflect a habit prevalent among outside observers, namely that of making tacit value judgements about observed regularities in low-income countries by unwittingly contrasting them with experiences and outcomes of Western-style economies. But these questions misconceive the rationale behind the style–economic approach. The main purpose of this approach is to rigorously identify and describe the realities of low-income countries and to assume regular and essential characteristics that describe the elements of a particular economic style as empirical facts. The purpose of normative research is then to conceive, based on these facts, the possible development paths that could lead to improvements in economic outcomes with the specific conditions of a given economic style.

A related danger is that the framing of realities in low-income countries as expression of specific economic styles may be seen as an apology of their existing order (or disorder). However, economic styles are not static models of economic life, but are rather able to capture the dynamic interdependencies between cultural, social and economic change. The possibility of cultural adaptations and hence development along style-specific paths is thus recognised. The traditional and culturally determined elements of African economic styles mentioned in Sect. 13.2.1 earlier have been undergoing changes throughout history, resulting from people's cumulative efforts to deal with uncertainty and solve the problems they face, or through adjustments in their preferences and expectations in response to changes in their external institutional environment. It would therefore be wrong to conclude from their specific cultural characteristics that African economic styles are static and therefore *per se* incompatible with the Western or any other style of organising and governing economic activity. But it would be equally mistaken to deem the adoption of a Western economic style as the only possible way of achieving convergence of African living standards with those in advanced economies. It has to be emphasised again that any economic style is primarily constituted by the ways and modes in which certain outcomes are achieved, rather than by the outcomes themselves. African economies may well evolve into modern market economies, but they are likely to do so along different development paths, involving different processes of cultural and institutional change, than those followed by Western economies. International development assistance still has an important role to play in helping low-income countries on their paths of building market economies. But it has to be recognised that cultural and hence economic change is an endogenous process in which outside assistance can be effective only if it bears on an understanding of prevailing structures, traditions and beliefs.

The knowledge about the discovery of realities in low-income countries as distinct economic styles may appear disturbing. But, to argue with Hirschman (1984b), if these findings are disturbing, there is at least some chance that they constitute new knowledge. If development economists are able to use this knowledge, it may help them to better understand what exists and works in low-income countries, and hence to make their policy proposals and assistance programmes more compatible and responsive to the innate knowledge and local institutional forms that result from poor people's own creative efforts at improving their lives.

Bibliography

Acemoglu, Daron, Simon Johnson and James A. Robinson (2001a): The Colonial Origins of Comparative Development: An Empirical Investigation. *American Economic Review*, Vol. 91(5), pp. 1369–1401.
Acemoglu, Daron, Simon Johnson and James A. Robinson (2001b): Reversal of Fortune: Geography and Institutions in the Making of the Modern World Income Distribution. NBER Working Paper 8460. Cambridge: National Bureau of Economic Research.
Ackermann, Peter (1996): Japanische Kultur und japanischer Wirtschaftsstil. In: Rainer Klump (ed.), *Wirtschaftskultur, Wirtschaftsstil und Wirtschaftsordnung: Methoden und Ergebnisse der Wirtschaftskulturforschung*. Marburg: Metropolis-Verlag, pp. 141–160.
Altmann, Matthias (1999): *The Social Cost of Pollution: Theory and Measurement of Negative Externalities: The Case of Past Corporate Environmental Liabilities in Eastern Europe*. Final Thesis in International Economic Studies, Maastricht University, Mimeo.
Ammon, Günther (1994): *Der französische Wirtschaftsstil*, second edition. München: Eberhard.
Anderson, Kym (2009): *Distortions to Agricultural Incentives in Africa*. Washington: World Bank.
Andersson, Svea (2004): *Überleben am Manila Express. 360° – Die GEO Reportage, broadcasted on 04.09.2004 at Arte TV*. Berlin: FFP MedienKontor GmbH.
Appleton, Simon and Lina Song (1999): *Income and Human Development at the Household Level: Evidence from Six Countries*. Background paper for the *World Development Report 2000/2001*. Washington: World Bank.
Arrow, Kenneth J. (1969): The Organization of Economic Activity. Issues Pertinent to the Choice of Market versus Non-Market Allocation. In: *The Analysis and Evaluation of Public Expenditures: The PPB System*, Joint Economic Committee Compendium, 91st Congress, 1st Session, pp. 47–64.
Ascher, William (1983): New Development Approaches and the Adaptability of International Agencies: The Case of the World Bank. *International Organization*, Vol. 37(3), pp. 415–439.
Ayyagari, Meghana, Thorsten Beck and Asli Demirgüç-Kunt (2003): *Small and Medium Enterprises Across the Globe: A New Database*. World Bank Policy Research Working Paper 3127 (revised version). Washington: World Bank.
Backhaus, Jürgen G., ed. (1980): Homogenous Social Groups. *Rivista Internazionale di Scienze Economiche e Commerciali*, Vol. XXVII(1), pp. 21–28.
Backhaus, Jürgen G., ed. (1989): Schmollers Grundriss – ein Aktueller Klassiker. In: *Vademecum zu einem Klassiker der Historischen Methode in der Ökonomischen Wissenschaft. Gustav von Schmollers Lebenswerk: Eine Kritische Analyse aus Moderner Sicht*. Düsseldorf: Verlag Wirtschaft und Finanzen.
Backhaus, Jürgen G., ed. (1997): Wirtschaften im Umbruch: Ordnung, Unternehmer und Stil. In: Sylke Behrends (ed.), *Ordnungskonforme Wirtschaftspolitik in der Marktwirtschaft, Festschrift für Prof. Dr. H-R. Peters*. Berlin: Duncker & Humblot, pp. 311–374.

Backhaus, Jürgen G., ed. (2000): Constitutional Causes for Technological Leadership: Why Europe? In: P. Fishback, et al. (eds.), *Public Choice Essays in Honor of a Maverick Scholar: Gordon Tullock*. Boston: Kluwer Academic Publishers, pp. 53–69.

Backhaus, Jürgen G., ed. (2005): *Historische Schulen*. Wirtschaft Forschung und Wissenschaft, Vol. 11. Münster: Lit.

Bandura, Romina (2008): A Survey of Composite Indices Measuring Country Performance: 2008 Update. UNDP/ODS Working Paper. New York: United Nations Development Programme.

Banerjee, Abhijit V. (2005): New Development Economics' and the Challenge to Theory. In: Ravi Kanbur (ed.), New Directions in Development Economics: Theory or Empirics? A Symposium. *Economic and Political Weekly*, Vol. 40(40), pp. 4340–4344.

Banerjee, Abhijit and Esther Duflo (2008): *The Experimental Approach to Development Economics*. NBER Working Paper No. 14467. Cambridge: National Bureau of Economic Research.

Banerjee, Abhijit, Angus Deaton, Nora Lustig and Ken Rogoff (2006): *An Evaluation of World Bank Research, 1998–2005*. Washington: World Bank.

Bardhan, Pranab (2005): Theory or Empirics in Development Economics. In: Ravi Kanbur (ed.), New Directions in Development Economics: Theory or Empirics? A Symposium. *Economic and Political Weekly*, Vol. 40(40), pp. 4333–4335.

Barro, Robert J. (2002): Quantity and Quality of Economic Growth. Central Bank of Chile Working Papers 168.

Barro, Robert J. and Xavier Sala-i-Martin (1992): Convergence. *Journal of Political Economy*, Vol. 100(2), pp. 223–251.

Barzel, Yoram (2000): The State and the Diversity of Third-Party Enforcers. In: Claude Ménard (ed.), *Institutions, Contracts and Organisations: Perspectives from the New Institutional Economics*. Cheltenham: Edward Elgar, pp. 211–233.

Basu, Kaushik (2005): The New Empirical Development Economics: Remarks on Its Philosophical Foundations. In: Ravi Kanbur (ed.), New Directions in Development Economics: Theory or Empirics? A Symposium. *Economic and Political Weekly*, Vol. 40(40), pp. 4336–4339.

Bates, Robert H., Avner Greif, Margaret Levi, Jean-Laurent Rosenthal and Barry R. Weingast (1998): *Analytic Narratives*. Princeton: Princeton University Press.

Bates, Robert H., Avner Greif, Margaret Levi, Jean-Laurent Rosenthal and Barry R. Weingast (2000): Analytic Narratives Revisited. *Social Science History*, Vol. 24(4), pp. 685–696.

Batra, Geeta, Daniel Kaufmann and Andrew H. W. Stone (2003): *Investment Climate Around the World: Voices of the Firms from the World Business Environment Survey*. Washington: World Bank.

Bauer, Peter T. (1965): The Vicious Circle of Poverty. *Weltwirtschaftliches Archiv*, Vol. 95(1), pp. 4–20.

Bauer, Peter T. (1991): *The Development Frontier: Essays in Applied Economics*. Cambridge: Harvard University Press.

Bauer, Peter T. (2000): From Subsistence to Exchange. In: Peter Bauer (ed.), *From Subsistence to Exchange and Other Essays*. Princeton: Princeton University Press, pp. 3–14.

Bauer, Peter T. and Basil S. Yamey (1957): *The Economics of Under-Developed Countries*. London and Cambridge: James Nisbet & Co and Cambridge University Press.

Bechtel, Heinrich (1930): *Wirtschaftsstil des deutschen Spätmittelalters. Der Ausdruck der Lebensform in Wirtschaft, Gesellschaftsaufbau und Kunst von 1350 bis um 1500*. München: Duncker & Humblot

Becker, Gary S. (1976): *The Economic Approach to Human Behavior*. Chicago and London: The University of Chicago Press.

Becker, Gary S. (1981): *A Treatise of the Family*. Cambridge: Harvard University Press.

Beckert, Jens (2005): The Moral Embeddedness of Markets. MPIfG Discussion Paper 05/6. Cologne: Max Planck Institute for the Study of Societies.

Berger, Peter L. and Thomas Luckmann (1966): *The Social Construction of Reality: A Treatise in the Sociology of Knowledge*. Garden City: Anchor Books.

Besley, Timothy (1995): Nonmarket Institutions for Credit and Risk Sharing in Low-Income Countries. *Journal of Economic Perspectives*, Vol. 9(3), pp. 115–127.

Beynon, Jonathan (1999): 'Assessing Aid' and the Collier/Dollar Poverty Efficient Aid Allocations. DFID Economist Group Discussion Paper. London: Department for International Development.
Beynon, Jonathan (2003): Poverty-Efficient Aid Allocations – Collier/Dollar Revisited. ESAU Working Paper 2, London: Overseas Development Institute.
Bigsten, Arne, Paul Collier, Stefan Dercon, Marcel Fafchamps, Bernard Gauthier, Jan Willem Gunning, Abena Oduro, Remco Oostendorp, Cathy Patillo, Mans Soderbom, Francis Teal and Albert Zeufack (2000): Contract Flexibility and Dispute Resolution in African Manufacturing. *Journal of Development Studies*, Vol. 36(4), pp. 1–17.
Birchall, Johnston (2003): *Rediscovering the Cooperative Advantage: Poverty Reduction through Self-Help*. Geneva: International Labour Organisation.
BMZ (1999): Charakterisierung des informellen Sektors. Stellungnahme des Wissenschaftlichen Beirats, *BMZ Spezial* 101. Bonn: Bundesministerium für wirtschaftliche Zusammenarbeit und Entwicklung.
Borner, Silvio (1998): The Washington Consensus and Economic Institutions: The Neglected Dimension. In: Gudrun Kochendörfer-Lucius and Boris Pleskovic (eds.), *Development Issues in the 21th Century*. Villa Borsig Workshop Series. Berlin: Deutsche Stiftung für Entwicklung (DSE).
Boserup, Ester (1981): *Population and Technology*. Oxford: Basil Blackwell.
Bowles, Samuel (1998): Endogenous Preferences: The Cultural Consequences of Markets and Other Economic Institutions. *Journal of Economic Literature*, Vol. 36(1), pp. 75–111.
Bromley, Daniel W. (2003): Institutional Economics Revisited: Discussion. *American Journal for Agricultural Economics*, Vol. 75(3), pp. 837–839.
Buchanan, James (1975): The Samaritan's Dilemma. In: E. Phelps (ed.), *Altruism, Morality and Economic Theory*. New York: Russell Sage Foundation, pp. 57–62.
Bücher, Karl (1893): *Die Entstehung der Volkswirtschaft*, first edition. Tübingen: Verlag der Laupp'schen Buchhandlung.
Burki, Javed and Guillermo E. Perry (1998): *Beyond the Washington Consensus: Institutions Matter*. Washington: World Bank.
Burnside, Craig and David Dollar (2000): Aid, Policies and Growth. *American Economic Review*, Vol. 90(4), pp. 847–868.
Büscher, Martin E. H. (1988): Afrikanische Weltanschauung und Tiefenstrukturen der Probleme wirtschaftlicher Entwicklung. Zu Inhalt und Bedeutung kultureller Faktoren in der Entwicklungspolitik. Working Paper No. 22, Institute for Business Ethics, University of St. Gallen.
Calderisi, Robert (2006): *The Trouble with Africa: Why Foreign Aid Isn't Working*. New York: Palgrave Macmillan.
Cardenas, Juan Camilo and Jeffrey Carpenter (2008): Behavioural Development Economics: Lessons From Field Labs in the Developing World. *Journal of Development Studies*, Vol. 44(3), pp. 311–338.
Carr, Marilyn and Martha A. Chen (2002): Globalization and the Informal Economy: How Global Trade and Investment Impact on the Working Poor. Working Paper on the Informal Economy, Employment Sector. Geneva: International Labour Office.
Charmes, Jacques (2000): Informal Sector, Poverty and Gender. A Review of Empirical Evidence. Background paper for the World Development Report 2001. University of Versailles-St Quentin en Yvelines, Centre of Economics and Ethics for Environment and Development (C3ED).
Chen, Martha Alter, Renana Jhabvala and Reema Nanavaty (2004): "The Investment Climate for Female Informal Businesses: A Case Study from Urban and Rural India." Background paper for the World Development Report 2005.
Chen, Shaohua and Martin Ravallion (2008): The Developing World is Poorer than We Thought, But No Less Successful in the Fight Against Poverty. World Bank Policy Working Paper No. 4703. Washington: World Bank.
Chen, Shaohua, Martin Ravallion and Prem Sangruala (2008): Dollar a Day Revisited. World Bank Policy Working Paper No. 4620. Washington: World Bank.

Clark, Colin (1957): *Conditions of Economic Progress*. Third, largely rewritten edition. London: Macmillan.
Clark, Colin and Margaret R. Haswell: *The Economics of Subsistence Agriculture*. London: Macmillan.
Clay, Karen (1997): Trade without Law: Private Order Institutions in Mexican California. *Journal of Law, Economics, and Organization*, Vol. 13(1), pp. 202–231.
Coase, Ronald H. (1937): The Nature of the Firm. *Economica*, Vol. 4(November), pp. 386–405.
Coleman, James Samuel (1990): *Foundations of Social Theory*. Cambridge: Harvard University Press.
Collier, Paul (2002): *Making Aid Smart: Institutional Incentives Facing Donor Organizations and their Implications for Aid Effectiveness*. Forum Series on the Role of Institutions in Promoting Growth. Washington: Center for Institutional Reform and the Informal Sector (IRIS) and US Agency for International Development (USAID).
Collier, Paul and David Dollar (2004): Development Effectiveness: What Have We Learnt? *Economic Journal*, Vol. 114(496), pp. F244–F271.
Commission on Growth and Development (2008): *The Growth Report. Strategies for Sustained Growth and Inclusive Development*. Washington: World Bank on behalf of the Commission on Growth and Development.
Cooter, Robert D. (1994): Structural Adjudication and the New Law Merchant. A Model of Decentralized Law. *International Review of Law and Economics*, Vol. 14(2), pp. 215–231.
Cord, Louise, J. Humberto Lopez and John Page: *When I Use A Word... Pro-Poor Growth and Poverty Reduction*. Washington: World Bank.
Cross, John C. (1998): *Informal Politics: Street Vendors and the State in Mexico City*. Stanford: Stanford University Press.
Cullis, John and Philip Jones (1994): *Public Finance, Public Choice: Analytical Perspectives*. London: McGraw Hill.
Dalton, George, ed. (1968): *Primitive, Archaic and Modern Economics. Essays of Karl Polyani*. New York: Anchor Books.
Daspypta, Partha, Stephen Marglin and Amartya Sen (1972): *Guidelines for Project Evaluation*. New York: United Nations Industrial Development Organization.
De Alessi, Louis (1983): Property Rights, Transaction Costs and X-Efficiency: An Essay in Economic Theory. *American Economic Review*, Vol. 73(1), pp. 64–81.
Deaton, Angus (2004): Measuring Poverty in a Growing World (or measuring Growth in a Poor World). Review of Economics and Statistics Lecture, presented at Harvard University, 15 April 2003. Revised version February 2004. Research Program in Development Studies, Woodrow Wilson School, Princeton University.
Deininger, Klaus (2003): *Land Policies for Growth and Poverty Reduction*. World Bank Policy Research Report 2003. New York, Washington: Oxford University Press and the World Bank.
Deininger, Klaus and Lyn Squire (1996): A New Data Set Measuring Income Inequality. *The World Bank Economic Review*, Vol. 10(3), 565–591.
Demsetz, Harold (1968): The Cost of Transacting. *Quarterly Journal of Economics*, Vol. 82(1), pp. 33–53.
Denzau, Arthur and Douglass C. North (1994): Shared Mental Models: Ideologies and Institutions. *Kyklos*, Vol. 47(1), pp. 3–31.
De Soto, Hernando (2000): *The Mystery of Capital. Why Capitalism Triumphs in the West and Fails Everywhere Else*. New York: Basic Books.
DFID (2006): *Eliminating World Poverty. Making Governance Work for the Poor. A White Paper on International Development*. London and Glasgow: UK Department for International Development.
Dilthey, Wilhelm (1883): *Einleitung in die Geisteswissenschaften: Versuch einer Grundlegung für das Studium der Gesellschaft und der Geschichte*. Vol. 1. Leipzig: Duncker & Humblot.
DiMaggio, Paul (1997): Culture and Cognition. *Annual Review of Sociology*, Vol. 23(1), pp. 263–287.

Dixit, Avinash K. (2004): *Lawlessness and Economics: Alternative Modes of Governance.* Princeton: Princeton University Press.
Dixon, Huw (1999): Controversy: On the Use of the 'Hidden Economy' Estimates. *Economic Journal*, Vol. 109(456), pp. F335–F337.
Dollar, David and Aart Kraay (2002): Growth is Good for the Poor. *Journal of Economic Growth*, Vol. 7(3), pp. 195–225.
Dollar, David and Aart Kraay (2004): Trade, Growth and Poverty. *Economic Journal*, Vol. 114(493), pp. F22–F49.
Dollar, David and Lant Pritchett (1998): *Aid Effectiveness: What Works? What Doesn't? Why?* World Bank Policy Research Report. New York: Oxford University Press for the World Bank.
Dollinger, Philippe (1998): *Die Hanse*, fifth edition. Stuttgart: Alfred Kröner Verlag.
Donner, Franziska (2004): Was ist 'Fortschritt'? Ein interkultureller Näherungsversuch. *Internationale Politik*, Vol. 11/12, pp. 40–47.
Drechsler, Wolfgang (2007): Towards a Law & Economics of Development: Ragnar Nurkse (1907–1959). Paper presented at the 20th Workshop in Law and Economics, April 5, 2007, University of Erfurt.
Duflo, Esther (2006): Poor but Rational? In: Abhijit Vinayak Banerjee, Roland Bénabou and Dilip (eds.), *Understanding Poverty*. Oxford: Oxford University Press, pp. 367–378.
Duflo, Ester and Michael Kremer (2005): Use of Randomization in the Evaluation of Development Effectiveness. In: George Keith Pitman, Osvaldo N. Feinstein and Gregory K. Ingram (eds.), *Evaluating Development Effectiveness*. Vol. 7 of World Bank Series on Evaluation and Development. New Brunswick: Transaction Publishers, pp. 205–231.
Duflo, Esther, Michael Kremer and Jonathan Robinson (2007): Why Don't Farmers Use Fertilizer? Experimental Evidence from Kenya. Working paper, MIT and Harvard.
Duflo, Esther, Michael Kremer and Jonathan Robinson (2008): How High are Rates of Return to Fertilizer? Evidence from Field Experiments in Kenya. *American Economic Review*, Vol. 98(2), pp. 482–488.
Easterly, William (2001): *The Elusive Quest for Growth: Economists' Adventures and Misadventures in the Tropics*. Cambridge: MIT Press.
Easterly, William (2005): National Economic Policies and Economic Growth: A Reappraisal. In: Philippe Aghion and Steven Durlauf (eds.), *Handbook of Economic Growth*, Vol. 1. North-Holland: Elsevier, Chapter 15.
Easterly, William (2006): *The White Man's Burden: Why the West's Efforts to Aid the Rest Have Done So Much Ill and So Little Good*. New York: Penguin Press.
Easterly, William and Ross Levine (2003): Tropics, Germs and Crops: How Endowments Influence Economic Development. *Journal of Monetary Economics*, Vol. 50(1), pp. 3–39.
Easterly, William, Ross Levine and David Roodman (2003): *New Data, New Doubts: A Comment on Burnside and Dollar's 'Aids, Policies and Growth (2000)*.' Mimeo. Department of Economics, New York University.
Ebner, Alexander (2000): Schumpeter and the 'Schmollerprogramm': Integrating Theory and History in the Analysis of Economic Development. *Journal of Evolutionary Economics*, Vol. 10(3), pp. 355–72.
Eucken, Walter (1938): Die Überwindung des Historismus. *Schmollers Jahrbuch für Gesetzgebung, Verwaltung und Volkswirtschaft im Deutschen Reiche*, Vol. 62(2), pp. 63–86.
Eucken, Walter (1940): Wissenschaft im Stile Schmollers. *Weltwirtschaftliches Archiv – Zeitschrift des Instituts für Weltwirtschaft an der Universität Kiel*, Vol. 52, pp. 469–506.
Eucken, Walter (1950a): *Die Grundlagen der Nationalökonomie*, sixth edition. Berlin: Springer-Verlag.
Eucken, Walter (1950b): *The Foundations of Economics. History and Theory in the Analysis of Economic Reality*. Translation by T.W. Hutchison based on the sixth edition of Die Grundlagen der Nationalökonomie (1950). London: William Hodge and Company Ltd.
European Commission (2003): *Governance and Development. Communication from the Commission to the Council, the European Parliament and Social Committee.* COM(2003). Brussels: European Commission.

Fafchamps, Marcel (2003): Ethnicity and Networks in African Trade. *Contributions to Economic Analysis and Policy*, Vol. 2(1), pp. 1–51.

Fafchamps, Marcel (2004): *Market Institutions in Sub-Saharan Africa: Theory and Evidence*. Cambridge: MIT Press.

Fafchamps, Marcel and Bart Minten (2001): Property Rights in a Flea Market Economy. *Economic Development and Cultural Change*, Vol. 49(2), pp. 229–268.

Fehr, Ernst and Bettina Rockenbach (2003): Detrimental Effects of Sanctions on Human Altruism. *Nature*, Vol. 422(March), pp. 137–140.

Fehr, Ernst and Klaus Schmidt (2000): Fairness, Incentives and Contractual Choices. *European Economic Review*, Vol. 44(4–6), pp. 1057–1068.

Freedom House (2009): *Freedom in the World 2009: Zimbabwe*. Accessed August 3rd, 2009 on www.freedomhouse.org/template.cfm?page=22&year=2009&country=7737. Washington: Freedom House.

Friedman, Eric, Simon Johnson, Daniel Kaufman and Pablo Zoido-Lobatón (2000): Dodging the Grabbing Hand: Determinants of Unofficial Activity in 69 Countries. *Journal of Public Economics*, Vol. 76(3), pp. 459–493.

Friedman, Milton (1953): The Methodology of Positive Economics. In: Friedman, Milton (ed.), *Essays in Positive Economics*. Chicago: University of Chicago Press, pp. 1–43.

Fukuyama, Francis (2002): Social Capital and Development: The Coming Agenda. *SAIS Review*, Vol. 22(1), pp. 23–37.

Fukuyama, Francis (1995): *Trust. The Social Virtues and the Creation of Prosperity*. New York: The Free Press.

Furubotn, Eirik (2001): The New Institutional Economics and the Theory of the Firm. *Journal of Economic Behavior & Organization*, Vol. 5(2), pp. 133–153.

Furubotn, Eirik and Rudolf Richter (1997): *Institutions and Economic Theory*. Ann Arbor: University of Michigan Press.

Galal, Ahmed (2005): The Economics of Formalization: Potential Winners and Losers from Formalization in Egypt. In: Gudrun Kochendörfer-Lucius and Boris Pleskovic (eds.), *Investment Climate, Growth and Poverty*, Berlin Workshop Series. Berlin and Washington: Capacity Building International (InWEnt) and World Bank, pp. 39–52.

Gallup, John L., Jeffrey Sachs and Andrew Mellinger (1999): Geography and Economic Development. In: Boris Pleskovic and Joseph E. Stiglitz (eds.), *Proceedings of the Annual Bank Conference on Development Economics 1998*. Washington: World Bank, pp. 127–178.

Gambretta, Diego (1993): *The Sicilian Mafia: The Business of Protection*. Cambridge: Harvard University Press.

Gerschenkron, Alexander (1962): *Economic Backwardness in Historical Perspective. A Book of Essays*. Cambridge: Harvard University Press.

Gioia, Vitantonio (1997): Historical Changes and Economics in Arthur Spiethoff's Theory of Wirschaftsstil. In: Peter Koslowski (ed.), *Methodology of the Social Sciences, Ethics and Economics in the Newer Historical School*. Berlin: Springer, pp. 168–190.

Glaeser, Edward L., Rafael La Porta, Florencio Lopez de Silanes and Andrei Shleifer (2004): Do Institutions Cause Growth? NBER Working Paper No. 10568. Cambridge: National Bureau of Economic Research.

Goldin, Ian, Halsey Rogers and Nicholas Stern (2002): *The Role and Effectiveness of Development Assistance. Lessons from World Bank Experience*. Washington: World Bank.

Goldschmidt, Niels and Joachim Zweynert (2006): The Two Transitions in Central and Eastern Europe as Processes of Institutional Transplantation. *Journal of Economic Issues*, Vol. XL(4), pp. 895–916.

Greif, Avner (1993): Contract Enforceability and Economic Institutions in Early Trade: The Maghribi Traders' Coalition. *American Economic Review*, Vol. 83(3), pp. 525–548.

Greif, Avner (1994): Cultural Beliefs and the Organization of Society: A Historical and Theoretical Reflection on Collectivist and Individualistic Societies. *Journal of Political Economy*, Vol. 102(5), pp. 912–950.

Greif, Avner (1997): *Self-enforcing Political Systems and Economic Growth: Late Medieval*: Genoa: Stanford University, Department of Economics Working paper 97-037.

Greif, Avner, Paul Milgrom and Barry Weingast (1994): Coordination, Commitment and Enforcement: The Case of the Merchant Guild. *The Journal of Political Economy*, Vol. 102(4), pp. 745–776.

Griffin, Ronald (1991): The Welfare Analysis of Transaction Costs, Externalities and Institutional Choice. *American Journal of Agricultural Economics*, Vol. 73(3), pp. 601–614.

Gruchy, Allan G. (1947): *Modern Economic Thought: The American Contribution*. New York: Prentice-Hall.

Grün, Carola and Stephan Klasen (2003): Growth, Inequality and Well-Being: Comparisons across Space and Time. Discussion Paper, Ibero-Amerika Institut für Wirtschaftsforschung, Universität Göttingen.

GTZ (1990): *Die Sozio-Kulturelle Dimension in der Entwicklungsarbeit. Eine Lesemappe für GTZ Mitarbeiter*. Eschborn: Deutsche Gesellschaft für Technische Zusammenarbeit.

GTZ, Die ZEIT, Misereor (2005): Time-Zones. Development and the Factor Time. Conference held on 22 February 2005 in Berlin. Available at www.time-and-development.net/en/results.

GTZ, Goethe Insititut (2004): The Concept of Progress in Different Cultures. Series of regional conferences concluded by an international conference from 28 until 30 November 2004 in Berlin. Available at www.fortschritt-weltweit.de.

Hancock, Graham (1998): *Lords of Poverty. The Power, Prestige and Corruption of the International Aid Business*. New York: The Atlantic Monthly Press.

Harberger, Arnold C. (1978). On the Use of Distributional Weights in Social Cost-Benefit Analysis. *The Journal of Political Economy*, Vol. 86(2) Part 2: Research in Taxation, pp. S87–S120.

Harrison, Lawrence E. and Samuel P. Huntington, eds. (2000): *Culture Matters: How Values Shape Human Progress*. New York: Basic Books.

Hart, Stuart L. (2007): *Capitalism at the Crossroads: Aligning Business, Earth, and Humanity*, second edition. Upper Saddle River: Wharton School Publishing.

Hausmann, Ricardo (2008): Final Recommendations of the International Panel on Growth. The National Treasury, Republic of South Africa. Retrieved July 2008 from the World Wide Web: http://www.treasury.gov.za/publications/other/growth/default.aspx.

Hausmann, Ricardo and Dani Rodrik (2005): Self-Discovery in a Development Strategy for El Salvador. *Economía – Journal of the Latin American and Caribbean Economic Association*, Vol. 6(1), pp. 43–101.

Hausmann, Ricardo, Dani Rodrik and Andrés Velasco (2006): Getting the Diagnosis Right. *Finance & Development*, Vol. 43(1). Washington: International Monetary Fund, pp. 12–15.

Hausmann, Ricardo, Dani Rodrik and Andrés Velasco (2008): Growth Diagnostics. In: Narcis Serra and Joseph Stiglitz (eds.), *The Washington Consensus Reconsidered: Towards a New Global Governance*. Oxford: Oxford University Press, Chapter 15.

Hayek, Friedrich A. von (1937): Economics and Knowledge. *Economica*, Vol. 4(February), pp. 33–54.

Hayek, Friedrich A. von (1945): The Use of Knowledge in Society. *American Economic Review*, Vol. 35(4), pp. 519–530.

Heilmann, Sebastian (2008): Policy Experimentation in China's Economic Rise. *Studies in Comparative International Development*, Vol. 43(1), pp. 1–26.

Henderson, J. Vernon, Zmarak Shalizi and Anthony J. Venables (2000): *Geography and Development*. World Bank Policy Research Working Paper 2456. Washington: World Bank.

Henn, Volker (1999): Was war die Hanse? In: Jörgen Bracker (ed.), *Die Hanse. Lebenswirklichkeit und Mythos*. Lübeck: Verlag Schmidt Romhild, pp. 14–23.

Hennis, Wilhelm (1987): *Max Webers Fragestellung. Studien zur Biographie des Werks*. Tübingen: Mohr.

Herrmann-Pillath, Carsten (2005): Culture, Economic Style and the Nature of the Chinese Economic System. *China aktuell – Journal of Current Chinese Affairs*, Vol. 34(2), pp. 32–52.

Hickmann, Thorsten (1996): *Einheit oder Vielfalt in Europa: die Wirtschaftsstile Frankreichs, Deutschlands und Russlands in ihrer Binnen-und Außenwirkung*. Wiesbaden: Deutscher Universitäts-Verlag.
Hildebrand, Bruno (1848): *Die Nationalökonomie der Gegenwart und Zukunft*. Frankfurt am Main: Literarische Anstalt.
Hirschman, Albert O. (1958): *The Strategy of Economic Development*. New Haven: Yale University Press.
Hirschman, Albert O. (1961): Ideologies of Economic Development in Latin America. In: Albert O. Hirschman (eds.), *Latin American Issues. Essays and Comments*. New York: Twentieth Century Fund.
Hirschman, Albert O. (1981a): The Rise and Decline of Development Economics. In: Albert O. Hirschman (ed.), *Essays in Trespassing: Economics to Politics and Beyond*. Cambridge: Cambridge University Press, pp. 1–24.
Hirschman, Albert O. (1981b): *Essays in Trespassing. Economics to Politics and Beyond*. Cambridge: Cambridge University Press.
Hirschman, Albert O. (1984a): *Getting Ahead Collectively. Grassroots Experiences from Latin America*. New York: Pergamon Press.
Hirschman, Albert O. (1984b): A Dissenter's Confession: 'The Strategy of Economic Development' Revisited. In: G. F. Meier and D. Seers (eds.), *Pioneers in Development*. New York: Oxford University Press for the World Bank.
Hodgson, Geoffrey M. (2004): *The Evolution of Institutional Economics: Agency, Structure, and Darwinism in American Institutionalism*. London: Routledge.
Hoff, Karla and Arijit Sen (2006): The Kin System as a Poverty Trap? In: Samuel Bowles, Steven Durlauf and Karla Hoff (eds.), *Poverty Traps*. Princeton: Princeton University Press, pp. 95–115.
Hofstede, Geert (1991): *Cultures and Organizations: Software of the Mind*. London: McGraw-Hill.
Hussmanns, Ralf (2004): *Statistical Definition of Informal Employment: Guidelines Endorsed by the Seventeenth International Conference of Labour Statisticians 2003*. Geneva: Bureau of Statistics, International Labour Office.
ICA (2009): Statement on the Co-operative Identity. Accessed online on August 2nd, 2009 at www.ica.coop/coop/principles.html. Geneva: International Co-operative Alliance.
ILO Bureau of Statistics (2002): *ILO Compendium of Official Statistics on Employment in the Informal Sector*. STAT Working Paper No. 1-2002. Geneva: International Labour Organization.
ILO Bureau of Statistics (2003): *Key Indicators of the Labour Market*, third edition. Geneva: International Labour Organization.
IMF (2003): *World Economic Outlook 2003: Growth and Institutions*. Washington: International Monetary Fund.
International Labour Office (1991): "The Dilemma of the Informal Sector." Report of the Director-General, International Labour Conference, 78th Session. Geneva: International Labour Organization.
International Labour Office (2002a): *Decent Work and the Informal Economy*. Report VI, International Labour Conference, 90th Session. Geneva: International Labour Organization.
International Labour Office (2002b): *Women and Men in the Informal Economy: A Statistical Picture*. Geneva: International Labour Organization.
Jepma, Catrinus J. (1991): *The Tying of Aid*. Paris: OECD Development Centre.
Johnson, Simon, Daniel Kaufmann and Pablo Zoido-Lobatón (1998): *Corruption, Public Finances and the Unofficial Economy*. World Bank Discussion Paper 2169. Washington: World Bank.
Johnson, Simon, John McMillan and Christopher Woodruff (2002): Courts and Relational Contracts. *Journal of Law, Economics and Organization*, Vol. 18(1), pp. 221–277.
Johnson, Simon, Daniel Kaufmann, John McMillan and Christopher Woodruff (2000): Why Do Firms Hide? Bribes and Unofficial Activity after Communism. *Journal of Public Economics*, Vol. 76(3), pp. 495–520.

Jul-Larsen, Eyolf (1993): The Micro 'State' of the Popo in Pointe Noire. An Analysis of Local Governance, State Society Relations and Access to Resources. Centre for Development Studies, University of Bergen, Norway (mimeo).

Kahneman, Daniel and Amos Tvesky (1979): Prospect Theory: An Analysis of Decision Under Risk. *Econometrica*, Vol. 47(1–3), pp. 263–291.

Kanbur, Ravi, ed. (2002): Conceptual Challenges in Poverty and Inequality: One Development Economist's Perspective. Working Paper No 7242. Cornell University, Department of Applied Economics and Management.

Kanbur, Ravi, ed. (2003): Behavioural Development Economics. Notes at the conference on Economics for An Imperfect World in honour of Joseph Stiglitz, Columbia University, October 24–25, 2003.

Kanbur, Ravi, ed. (2005): New Directions in Development Economics: Theory or Empirics? A Symposium. *Economic and Political Weekly*, Vol. 40(40), pp. 4328–4346.

Kanbur, Ravi and Lyn Squire (2001): The Evolution of Thinking about Poverty: Exploring the Interactions. In: G. M. Meier and J. E. Stiglitz (eds.), *Frontiers of Development Economics: The Future in Perspective*. New York: Oxford University Press, pp. 183–226.

Kattel, Rainer, Jan A. Kregel and Erik S. Reinert, eds. (2009): *Ragnar Nurkse (1907–2007): Classical Development Economics and its Relevance for Today*. The Anthem Other Canon Series, London: Anthem.

Kaufhold, Karl Heinrich (1996): Zur Entwicklung des Wirtschaftsstildenkens in Deutschland. In: Rainer Klump (ed.), *Wirtschaftskultur, Wirtschaftsstil und Wirtschaftsordnung: Methoden und Ergebnisse der Wirtschaftskulturforschung*. Marburg: Metropolis-Verlag, pp. 21–37.

Kaufmann, Daniel, Aart Kraay and Massimo Mastruzzi (2007): Governance Matters VI: Governance Indicators for 1996–2006. World Bank Policy Research Working Paper No. 4280. Washington: World Bank.

Kaul, Inge and Pedro Conceição (2006): Why Revisit Public Finance Today? In: Inge Kaul and Pedro Conceição (eds.), *The New Public Finance; Responding to Global Challenges*. New York: Oxford University Press for the United Nations Development Programme, pp. 28–70.

Keynes, John Maynard (1939): Professor Tinbergen's Method. *Economic Journal*, Vol. 49(195), pp. 558–577.

Klitgaard, Robert (1988): *Controlling Corruption*. Berkeley: University of California Press.

Klump, Rainer, ed. (1996): *Wirtschaftskultur, Wirtschaftsstil und Wirtschaftsordnung: Methoden und Ergebnisse der Wirtschaftskulturforschung*. Marburg: Metropolis Verlag.

Knack, Stephen and Philip Keefer (1995): Institutions and Economic Performance: Cross-country Test Using Alternative Institutional Measures. *Economics and Politics*, Vol. 7(3), pp. 207–227.

Knack, Stephen and Philip Keefer (1997a): Why Don't Poor Countries Catch Up? A Cross-National Test of an Institutional Explanation. *Economic Enquiry*, Vol. 35(3), pp. 590–602.

Knack, Stephen and Philip Keefer (1997b): Does Social Capital Have an Economic Payoff? A Cross-Country Investigation. *Quarterly Journal of Economics*, Vol. 112(4), pp. 1251–1288.

Kraay, Aart (2006): When Is Growth Pro-Poor? Evidence from a Panel of Countries. *Journal of Development Economics*, Vol. 80(1), pp. 198–227.

Kremer, Michael (2002): *Incentives, Institutions and Development Assistance. Forum Series on the Role of Institutions in Promoting Growth. Forum 1: The Institutional Approach to Donor-Facilitated Economic Development. Session on New Institutional Economics Applications*. Washington: IRIS Center.

Kremer, Michael (2003): Randomized Evaluations of Educational Programs in Developing Countries: Some Lessons. *American Economic Review Papers and Proceedings*, Vol. 93(2), pp. 102–106.

Krugman, Paul (1994): The Fall and Rise of Development Economics. In: Lloyd Rodwin and Donald Schön (eds.), *Rethinking the Development Experience: Essays Provoked by the Work of Albert Hirschman*. Washington: Brookings Institution, pp. 39–58.

Kumi, Sylvanus Nana (2007): Africans Lack Confidence. *Ghana Daily Guide*, November 5, 2007, accessed online on November 11, 2007 at www.dailyguideghana.com.

Kuznets, Simon (1966): Economic Growth and Income Inequality. *The American Economic Review*, Vol. 45(1), pp. 1–28.
Laderchi, Caterina, Ruhi Saith Ruggeri and Stewart Frances (2003): Does it Matter that we Don't Agree on the Definition of Poverty? A Comparison of Four Approaches. Queen Elizabeth House Working Paper 107. Oxford: Oxford University.
Lane, Frederic C. and Jelle C. Riemersma (1953): Introduction to Arthur Spiethoff. In: Frederic C. Lane and Jelle C. Riemersma (eds.), *Enterprise and Secular Change*. Homeland, IL: Richard D. Irwin, pp. 431–443.
Leipold, Helmut (2001): *Islam, Institutioneller Wandel und wirtschaftliche Entwicklung*. Stuttgart: Lucius & Lucius.
Leipold, Helmut (2006): *Kulturvergleichende Institutionenökonomik. Studien zur kulturellen, institutionellen und wirtschaftlichen Entwicklung*. Stuttgart: Lucius & Lucius.
Levi, Margaret (2004): An Analytic Narrative Approach to Puzzles and Problems. In: Ian Shapiro, Rogers Smith and Tarek Masoud (eds.), *Problems and Methods in the Study of Politics*. New York: Cambridge University Press, pp. 201–226.
Lewis, Arthur (1954): Economic Development with Unlimited Supplies of Labour. *The Manchester School*, Vol. 22, pp. 139–192.
Li, Shuhe (2003): Relation-Based vs. Rule-Based Governance: An Explanation of the East Asian Miracle and Asian Crisis. *Review of International Economics*, Vol. 11(4), pp. 651–673.
Libecap, Gary D. (1994): *Contracting for Property Rights*. Cambridge: Cambridge University Press.
Licht, Amir N., Chanan Goldschmidt and Shalom H. Schwartz (2007): Culture Rules: The Foundations of the Rule of Law and Other Norms of Governance. *Journal of Comparative Economics*, Vol. 35(4), pp. 659–688.
Lipsey, Richard G. and Kelvin Lancaster (1956): The General Theory of the Second Best. *Review of Economic Studies*, Vol. 24(1), pp. 11–32.
List, Friedrich (1959): *Das Nationale System der Politischen Ökonomie*. Basel, Tübingen: Kyklos-Verlag Mohr (Siebeck).
Little, Ian M. D. (1957): *A Critique of Welfare Economics*, second edition. London: Oxford University Press.
Little, Ian M. D. and James A. Mirrlees (1969): *Manual of Industrial Project Analysis in Developing Countries*. Paris: Organisation for Economic Cooperation and Development.
Lomborg, Bjørn (ed.): *How to Spend $50 Billion to Make the World a Better Place*. Cambridge: Cambridge University Press.
Lopez, J. Humberto (2005a): *Pro-poor Growth: A Review of What We Know (and of What We Don't)*. Washington: World Bank.
Lopez, Ricardo A. (2005b): Trade and Growth: Reconciling the Macroeconomic and Microeconomic Evidence. *Journal of Economic Surveys*, Vol. 19(4), pp. 623–648.
Lucas, Robert E. Jr. (1988): On the Mechanics of Economic Development. *Journal of Monetary Economics*, Vol. 22(11), pp. 3–42.
Ludwig, Alexander (1988): *Der spanische Wirtschaftsstil: Genealogie und Relevanz im Hinblick auf den EG-Beitritt Spaniens*. Frankfurt am Main: Lang.
Luhmann, Niklas (1968): *Zweckbegriff und Systemrationalität. Über die Funktion von Zwecken in sozialen Systemen*. Tübingen: Mohr.
Lutz, Friedrich A. (1950): Introduction. In: Walter Eucken (ed.), *The Foundations of Economics. History and Theory in the Analysis of Economic Reality*. Translation by T. W. Hutchison. London: William Hodge and Company Ltd.
Macaulay, Steward (1992): Non-Contractual Relations in Business: A Preliminary Study. *American Sociology Review*, Vol. 28(1), pp. 55–67. Reprinted 1992 in R. Swedberg and M. Granovetter (eds.), *The Sociology of Economic Life*. Boulder, Colorado: Westview Press, pp. 265–284.
Mahoney, James (1999): Nominal, Ordinal and Narrative Appraisal in Macrocausal Analysis. *The American Journal of Sociology*, Vol. 104(4), pp. 1154–1196.
Mankiw, Gregoy N., David Romer and David N. Weil (1992): A Contribution to the Empirics of Economic Growth. *Quarterly Journal of Economics*, Vol. 107(2), pp. 407–437.

Marcouiller, Douglas and Leslie Young (1995): The Black Hole of Graft: The Predatory State and the Informal Economy. *American Economic Review*, Vol. 85(3), pp. 630–646.
Marshall, Alfred (1925): The Present Position of Economics. Reprinted in A. C. Pigou (ed.), *Memorials of Alfred Marshall*. London: Macmillan.
Meier, Gerald M. (2005): *Biography of a Subject: An Evolution of Development Economics*. Oxford: Oxford University Press.
Meier, Gerald M. and Dudley Seers (1984): *Pioneers in Development*. New York: Oxford University Press for the World Bank.
Menard, Claude and Mary M. Shirley, eds. (2008): *Handbook of New Institutional Economics*. Berlin: Springer.
Miguel, Edward and Michael Kremer (2003): Worms: Identifying Impacts on Education and Health in the Presence of Externalities. *Econometrica*, Vol. 72(1), pp. 159–217.
Milgrom, Paul, Douglass C. North and Barry Weingast (1990): The Role of Institutions in the Revival of Trade: The Medieval Law Merchant, Private Judges, and the Champagne Fairs. *Economics and Politics*, Vol. 2(1), pp. 1–23.
Mishan, Edward J. (1976). *Cost-Benefit Analysis. New and Expanded Edition*. New York: Praeger Publishers.
Mitullah, Winnie (2004): Street Vending in African Cities: A Synthesis of Empirical Findings From Kenya, Cote D'Ivoire, Ghana, Zimbabwe, Uganda and South Africa. Background paper for the WDR 2005.
Mookherjee, Dilip (2005): Is There Too Little Theory in Development Economics? In: Ravi Kanbur (ed.), *New Directions in Development Economics: Theory or Empirics? A Symposium*. *Economic and Political Weekly*, Vol. 40(40), pp. 4328–4333.
Moyo, Dambisa (2009): *Dead Aid: Why Aid Is Not Working and How There Is Another Way for Africa*. New York: Farrar, Straus and Giroux.
Mullainathan, Sendhil (2007). Psychology and Development Economics. In: Peter Diamon and Hannu Vartianen (eds.), *Behavioral Economics and its Applications*. [Based on the Yrjö Jahnsson Foundation 50th Anniversary Conference held on June 22–23, 2004, in Espoo, Finland]. Princeton: Princeton University Press, pp. 85–114.
Müller-Armack, Alfred (1941): *Genealogie der Wirtschaftsstile: die geistesgeschichtlichen Ursprünge der Staats-und Wirtschaftsformen bis zum Ausgang des 18. Jahrhunderts*. Stuttgart: Kohlhammer.
Müller-Armack, Alfred (1946): *Wirtschaftslenkung und Marktwirtschaft*. Hamburg: Verlag für Wirtschaft und Sozialpolitik.
Müller-Pelzer, Werner (1997): Der französische Wirtschaftsstil. In: Uschi Gröner, Henk Maarten de Jongste and Ulrich Kracke (eds.), *Wirtschaftswissenschaft: Anwendungsorientierte Forschung an der Schwelle des 21. Jahrhunderts*. Heidelberg: Decker, pp. 281–290.
Murphy, Kevin M., Andrei Shleifer and Robert W. Vishny (1990): The Allocation of Talent: Implications for Growth. NBER Working Paper w3530. Cambridge: National Bureau of Economic Research.
Musgrave, Richard A. (1969). Cost-Benefit Analysis and the Theory of Public Finance. *Journal of Economic Literature*, Vol. 7(3), pp. 797–806.
Myrdal, K. Gunnar (1957): *Economic Theory and Under-Developed Regions*. London: Duckworth.
Narayan, Deepa (1999): Bonds and Bridges: Social Capital and Poverty. Policy Research Working Paper 2167. Washington: World Bank.
Nenova, Tatiana and Tim Harford (2004): *Anarchy and Invention. How Does Somalia's Private Sector Cope Without Government? Public Policy for the Private Sector*, Vol. 280. Washington: World Bank Group Private Sector Development Vice Presidency.
Nienhaus, Volker (1996): Islamische Weltanschauung und Wirtschaftsstil. In: Rainer Klump (ed.), *Wirtschaftskultur, Wirtschaftsstil und Wirtschaftsordnung: Methoden und Ergebnisse der Wirtschaftskulturforschung*. Marburg: Metropolis-Verlag, pp. 191–207.
Nienhaus, Volker (1999): Kultur und Wirtschaftsstil – Erklärungsansätze für die Systemdynamik und Systemeffizienz in Entwicklungsländern? In: Thomas Apolte and Dieter Cassel (eds.), *Perspektiven der Systemforschung*. Berlin: Duncker & Humblot, pp. 89–113.

North, Douglass C. (1984): Transaction Costs, Institutions and Economic History. *Journal of Institutional and Theoretical Economics/Zeitschrift für die gesamte Staatswissenschaft*, Vol. 140(March), pp. 7–17.

North, Douglass C. (1986): The New Institutional Economics. *Journal of Institutional and Theoretical Economics/Zeitschrift für die gesamte Staatswissenschaft*, Vol. 142, pp. 230–237.

North, Douglass C. (1992): Institutions and Economic Theory. *American Economist*, Vol. 36(1), pp. 3–6.

North, Douglass C. (1995a): The New Institutional Economics and Third World Development. In: John C. Harriss, Janet Hunter and Colin M. Lewis (eds.), *The New Institutional Economics and Third World Development*. London: Routledge.

North, Douglass C. (1995b): Five Propositions About Institutional Change. In: Jack Knight and Itai Sened (eds.), *Explaining Social Institutions*. Ann Arbor: University of Michigan Press, pp. 15–26.

North, Douglass C. (1997): Transaction Costs Through Time. In: Ménard, Claude (ed.), *Transaction Cost Economics: Recent Developments*. Cheltenham: Edward Elgar, pp. 149–160.

North, Douglass C. (2005): *Understanding the Process of Economic Change*. Princeton: Princeton University Press.

North, Douglass C. and John J. Wallis (1994): Integrating Institutional Change and Technical Change in Economic History: A Transaction Cost Approach. *Journal of Institutional and Theoretical Economics/Zeitschrift für die gesamte Staatswissenschaft*, Vol. 150(4), pp. 609–624.

Nurkse, Ragnar (1935): *Internationale Kapitalbewegungen*. Beiträge zur Konjunkturforschung Nr. 8. Wien: Julius Springer.

Nurkse, Ragnar (1952): Growth in Underdeveloped Countries. Some International Aspects of the Problem of Economic Development. *American Economic Review*, Vol. 62(May), pp. 571–583.

Nurkse, Ragnar (1953): *Problems of Capital Formation in Underdeveloped Countries*, first edition, seventh impression 1960. Oxford: Basil Blackwell.

Nurkse, Ragnar (1957): Balanced and Unbalanced Growth. Reprinted in Ragnar Nurkse, Gottfried Haberler and Robert M. Stern, eds. (1961), *Equilibrium and Growth in the World Economy: Economic Essays*. Cambridge: Harvard University Press, pp. 241ff.

OECD DAC (2008): *Development Cooperation Report (Summary)*. Paris: OECD Development Assistance Committee.

Offe, Johanna (2007): *Kulturelle Konzepte von Zukunft und der Begriff der 'Nachhaltigkeit.' Zusammenfassung des Fachgesprächs am 05.12.2007*. Berlin: Deutsche Gesellschaft für Technische Zusammenarbeit.

Olson, Mancur (1993): Dictatorship, Democracy, and Development. *American Political Science Review*, 87(3), pp. 567–576.

Ostrom, Elinor (1990): *Governing the Commons. The Evolution of Institutions for Collective Action*. Cambridge: Cambridge University Press.

Ostrom, Elinor (1997): Investing in Capital, Institutions and Incentives. In: C. Clague (ed.), *Institutions and Economic Development: Growth and Governance in Less-Developed and Post-Socialist Countries*. Baltimore and London: The Johns Hopkins University Press, pp. 153–181.

Ostrom, Elinor, Joanna Burger, Christopher B. Field, Richard B. Norgaard and David Policansky (1999): Revisiting the Commons. Local Lessons, Global Challenges. *Science*, Vol. 284(5412), pp. 278–283.

Ostrom, Elinor, Clark Gibson, Sujai Shivakumar and Krister Andersson (2002): *Aid, Incentives and Sustainability. An Institutional Analysis of Development Cooperation*. Main report. Sida Studies in Evaluation Nr. 02/01. Stockholm: Swedish International Development Cooperation Agency (SIDA).

Pedersen, Karl Rolf (2001): The Samaritan's Dilemma and the Effectiveness of Development Aid. *International Tax and Public Finance*, Vol. 8(5–6), pp. 693–703.

Peirce, William Spangar (1981): *Bureaucratic Failure and Public Expenditure*. New York: Academic Press.
Perlman, Janice E. (2005): *The Myth of Marginality Revisited: The Case of Favelas in Rio de Janeiro, 1969–2003*. Washington: World Bank.
Platteau, Jean-Philippe (2000): *Institutions, Social Norms and Economic Development*. London: Routledge.
Pogge, Thomas and Sanjay G. Reddy (2005). "How not to count the poor." Available at SSRN:http://ssrn.com/abstract=893159.
Polanyi, Karl (2001): *The Great Transformation: The Political and Economic Origins of Our Time*, second edition. Boston: Beacon Press.
Polanyi, Karl, Conrad M. Arensberg and Harry W. Pearson (1957): *Trade and Market in the Early Empires. Economies in History and Theory*. Glencoe: Free Press.
Polanyi Levitt, Kari (2005): Karl Polanyi as a Development Economist. In: Kwame S. Jomo (ed.), *Pioneers of Development Economics. Great Economists on Development*. London and New York: Zed Books, pp. 165–180.
Poulos, Christine and Dale Whittington (1999): Individuals' Rates of Time Preference for Life-Saving Programs in Developing Countries: Results from a Multi-Country Study. Paper prepared for the Economy and Environment Program for South East Asia (EEPSEA).
Prahalad, Coimbatore K. (2010): *The Fortune at the Bottom of the Pyramid: Eradicating Poverty Through Profits*. Revised and updated 5th Anniversary edition. Upper Saddle River: Wharton School Publishing.
Prebisch, Raúl (1950): *The Economic Development of Latin America and Its Principal Problems*. New York and Santiago: United Nations Economic Commission for Latin America.
Prebisch, Raúl (1984): Five Stages in My Thinking on Development. In: G. M. Meier and D. Seers (eds.), *Pioneers in Development*. New York: Oxford University Press for the World Bank, pp. 175–191.
Putnam, Robert D., Robert Leonardi and Raffaella Y. Nanetti (1993): *Making Democracy Work: Civic Traditions in Modern Italy*. Princeton: Princeton University Press.
Qian, Yingyi (2003): How Reform Worked in China. In: Dani Rodrik (ed.), *In Search of Prosperity: Analytic Narratives on Economic Growth*. Princeton: Princeton University Press, pp. 297–333.
Rao, Vijayendra and Michael Walton, eds. (2004): *Culture and Public Action: A Cross-Disciplinary Dialogue on Development Policy*. Stanford: Stanford University Press.
Ratha, Dilip, Sanket Mohapatra and Ani Silwal (2009): *Outlook for Remittance Flows 2009–2011. Migration and Development Brief*, Vol. 10. Washington: World Bank.
Ravallion, Martin (2004a): Pessimistic on Poverty? Economic Focus, by Invitation. *The Economist*, Vol. 371(8370), p. 70.
Ravallion, Martin (2004b): *Pro-Poor Growth: A primer*. Policy Research Working Paper Series 3242. Washington: World Bank.
Ray, Anandarup (1984). *Cost-Benefit Analysis: Issues and Methodologies*. Baltimore and London: John Hopkins University Press for the World Bank.
Redlich, Fritz (1970): Arthur Spiethoff on Economic Styles. Translator's Introduction. *Journal of Economic History*, Vol. 30(3), pp. 640–652.
Reinert, Erik S. (1996): Diminishing Returns and Economic Sustainability: The Dilemma of Resource-Based Economies Under a Free Trade Regime. In: Stein Hansen, Jan Hesselberg and Helge Hveem (eds.), *International Trade Regulation, National Development Strategies and the Environment: Towards Sustainable Development?* Oslo: Centre for Development and the Environment, University of Oslo.
Reinert, Erik S. (2005): German Economics as Development Economics: From the Thirty Years' War to World War II. In: Kwame S. Jomo and Erik S. Reinert (eds.), *The Origins of Development Economics: How Schools of Economic Thought Have Addressed Development*. London: Zed Books, pp. 48–68.
Reinert, Erik S. (2007): *How Rich Countries Got Rich and Why Poor Countries Stay Poor*. London: Constable & Robinson.

Reinert, Erik S. and Sophus A. Reinert (2005): Mercantilism and Economic Development. Schumpeterian Dynamics, Institution-building and International Benchmarking. In: Kwame S. Jomo and Erik S. Reinert (eds.), T*he Origins of Development Economics: How Schools of Economic Thought Have Addressed Development Economics.* London: Zed Books, pp. 1–23.
Reuters (2006): World Bank Head for Africa Resigns Amid Shake-Up. Reuters, November 17, 2006. Retrieved June 2008 from the World Wide Web: http://africa.reuters.com/.
Rice, Susan E. and Stewart Patrick (2008): *Index of State Weakness in the Developing World.* Washington: Brookings Institution.
Ritzen, Jo, William Easterly and Michael Woolcock (2000): On 'Good' Politicians and 'Bad' Policies: Social Cohesion, Institutions and Growth. Policy Research Working Paper 2448. Washington: World Bank.
Rodríguez, Francisco (2007): *Policymakers Beware: The Use and Misuse of Regressions in Explaining Economic Growth.* Policy Research Brief No. 5. New York: United Nations Development Programme – International Poverty Centre.
Rodrik, Dani, ed. (2003): *In Search of Prosperity: Analytic Narratives on Economic Growth.* Princeton: Princeton University Press.
Rodrik, Dani (2005): Why We Learn Nothing from Regressing Economic Growth on Policies. Mimeo, Harvard University.
Rodrik, Dani (2006): Goodbye Washington Consensus, Hello Washington Confusion? A Review of the World Bank's 'Economic Growth in the 1990s: Learning from a Decade of Reform.' *Journal of Economic Literature*, Vol. 44(4), pp. 973–987.
Rodrik, Dani (2007): *One Economics, Many Recipes: Globalization, Institutions, and Economic Growth.* Princeton: Princeton University Press.
Rodrik, Dani (2008): The New Development Economics: We Shall Experiment, But How Shall We Learn? Paper Prepared for the Brookings Development Conference, May 29–30, 2008, Harvard University.
Rodrik, Dani, Arvind Subramanian and Francesco Trebbi (2002): Institutions Rule: The Primacy of Institutions over Integration and Geography in Economic Development. NBER Working Paper 9305. Cambridge: National Bureau of Economic Research.
Romer, Paul M. (1986): Increasing Returns and Long-Run Growth. *Journal of Political Economy*, Vol. 94(5), pp. 1002–1037.
Ros, Jaime (2005): The Pioneers of Development Economics and Modern Growth Theory. In: Kwame S. Jomo and Erik S. Reinert (eds.), *The Origins of Development Economics: How Schools of Economic Thought Have Addressed Development Economics.* London: Zed Books, pp. 81–98.
Roscher, Wilhelm G. F. (1878): *Principles of Political Economy.* Translation from the thirteenth (1877) German edition. New York: Henry Holt & Co.
Rosenstein-Rodan, Paul N. (1943): Problems of Industrialisation of Eastern and South-Eastern Europe. *Economic Journal*, Vol. LIII(June–September), pp. 202–211.
Rossi, Sandra (2006): *Wirtschaftsstil und Wirtschaftskultur: Italien und Frankreich im Vergleich.* Saarbrücken: VDM Müller.
Rostow, Walt Whitman (1952): *The Process of Economic Growth.* New York: W. W. Norton and Company.
Rostow, Walt Whitman (1960): *The Stages of Economic Growth. A Non-Communist Manifesto.* Cambridge: Cambridge University Press.
Rostow, Walt Whitman (1984): Development: The Political Economy of the Marshallian Long Period. In: G. M. Meier and D. Seers (eds.), *Pioneers in Development.* New York: Oxford University Press for the World Bank, pp. 229–267.
Rudner, Nicole (1996): *Der mexikanische Wirtschaftsstil. Schriften zu Lateinamerika 7.* München: Eberhard.
Sachs, Jeffrey D. (2003): Institutions Matter, But Not for Everything. The Role of Geography and Resource Endowments in Development Shouldn't Be Underestimated. *Finance and Development*, Vol. 40(2), pp. 38–41.

Sachs, Jeffrey D. (2005): *The End of Poverty: Economic Possibilities for Our Time*. New York: Penguin Press.
Sachs, Jeffrey D., John W. McArthur, Guido Schmidt-Traub, Margaret Kruk, Chandrika Bahadur, Michael Faye and Gordon McCord (2004): Ending Africa's Poverty Trap, *Brookings Papers on Economic Activity*, Issue 1. Washington: Brookings Institution Press.
Salin, Edgar (1927): Hochkapitalismus. *Weltwirtschaftliches Archiv*, Vol. 25, pp. 314–344.
Schefold, Bertram (1989): Schmoller als Theoretiker. In: *Vademecum zu einem Klassiker der Historischen Methode in der Ökonomischen Wissenschaft. Gustav von Schmollers Lebenswerk: Eine Kritische Analyse aus Moderner Sicht*. Düsseldorf: Verlag Wirtschaft und Finanzen.
Schefold, Bertram (1994/1995): *Wirtschaftsstile*, 2 Volumes (Volume 1: *Studien zum Verhältnis von Ökonomie und Kultur*; Volume 2: *Studien zur ökonomischen Theorie und zur Zukunft der Technik*). Frankfurt am Main: Fischer Taschenbuch Verlag.
Schefold, Bertram (2002): Reflections on the Past and Current State of the History of Economic Thought in Germany. *History of Political Economy*, Vol. 34(5), pp. 125–136.
Schefold, Bertram and Helge Peukert (1992): Wirtschaftssysteme im historischen Vergleich: ein Projekt. *Jahrbuch für Wirtschaftsgeschichte*, Vol. 1, pp. 243–254.
Schmoller, Gustav von (1884): Das Merkantilsystem in seiner Historischen Bedeutung: Städtische, Territoriale und Staatliche Wirtschaftspolitik. *Schmollers Jahrbuch für Gesetzgebung, Verwaltung und Volkswirtschaft im Deutschen Reiche*, Vol. VIII, pp. 15–61.
Schmoller, Gustav von (1923a): *Grundriß der Allgemeinen Volkswirtschaftslehre*, Vol. 1, second edition. München: Duncker & Humblot.
Schmoller, Gustav von (1923b): *Grundriß der Allgemeinen Volkswirtschaftslehre*, Vol. 2, second edition. München: Duncker & Humblot.
Schneider, Friedrich (2002): Size and Measurement of the Informal Economy in 110 Countries around the World. World Bank Research Working Paper. Washington: World Bank.
Schneider, Friedrich (2007): The Size of the Shadow Economies of 145 Countries all Over the World: First Results Over the Period 1999 to 2003. *Journal of Population Economics*, Vol. 20(3), pp. 495–526.
Schneider, Friedrich and Dominik H. Enste (2000): Shadow Economies: Size, Causes, and Consequences. *Journal of Economic Literature*, Vol. 38(1), pp. 77–114.
Schönberg, Gustav von (1869): Die Volkswirtschaft der Gegenwart. In: *Handbuch der Politischen Ökonomie*, Vol. 1.1.1, fourth edition. Tübingen: Verlag der Laupp'schen Buchhandlung.
Schultz, Henry (1938): *The Theory and Measurement of Demand*. Chicago, IL: University of Chicago Press.
Schumpeter, Joseph A. (1926): Gustav v. Schmoller und die Probleme von Heute. *Schmollers Jahrbuch für Gesetzgebung, Verwaltung und Volkswirtschaft im Deutschen Reich*, Vol. 50, pp. 337–388.
Schumpeter, Joseph A. (1954): *History of Economic Analysis*. London: George Allen & Unwin.
Schwettmann, Jürgen (1997): Cooperatives and Employment in Africa. Occasional Discussion Paper 97-1. Geneva: International Labour Organization.
Scott, Maurice (1990): Social Cost-Benefit Analysis. In: M. Scott and D. Lal (eds.), *Public Policy and Economic Development. Essays in Honour of Ian Little*. Oxford: Clarendon Press, pp. 310–335.
Seers, Dudley (1963): The Limitations of the Special Case. *Bulletin of the Oxford Institute of Economics and Statistics*, Vol. 25(2), pp. 77–98.
Selten, Reinhard (1988): *Models of Strategic Rationality*. Dordrecht: Kluwer Academic Publishers.
Sen, Amartya (1979): Interpersonal Comparisons of Welfare. In: Michael J. Boskin (ed.), *Economics and Human Welfare. Essays in Honor of Tibor Scitovsky*. New York: Academic Press, pp. 183–202.
Sen, Amartya (1999): *Development as Freedom*. New York: Anchor Books.
Sen, Amartya (2000): Introduction. In: Peter T. Bauer (ed.), *From Subsistence to Exchange and Other Essays*. Princeton: Princeton University Press, pp. ix–xi.

Shionoya, Yuichi, ed. (1989): Schmollers Forschungsprogramm: Eine Methodologische Würdigung. In: *Vademecum zu einem Klassiker der Historischen Methode in der Ökonomischen Wissenschaft. Gustav von Schmollers Lebenswerk: Eine Kritische Analyse aus Moderner Sicht*. Düsseldorf: Verlag Wirtschaft und Finanzen.
Shionoya, Yuichi, ed. (2001): *The German Historical School: The Historical and Ethical Approach to Economics*. London: Routledge.
Shleifer, Andrei and Robert W. Vishny (1998): *The Grabbing Hand: Government Pathologies and Their Cures*. Cambridge: Harvard University Press.
Shleifer, Andrei and Robert W. Vishny (2003): Corruption. *Quarterly Journal of Economics*, Vol. 108(3), pp. 599–618.
Simon, Herbert A. (1947): *Administrative Behavior*, second edition. New York: The Free Press.
Simon, Herbert A. (1987): Behavioral Economics. In: John Eatwell, Murray Milgate and Peter Newman (eds.), *The New Palgrave: A Dictionary of Economics*. London and Basingstoke: Macmillan.
Singer, Hans (1950): The Distribution of Gains between Investing and Borrowing Countries. *American Economic Review*, Vol. 40(2), pp. 473–485.
Singer, Hans (1971): The Distribution of Gains Revisited. Paper presented to a Conference at the Institute of Development Studies (IDS) in Sussex, May 1971. Reprinted in A. Cairncross and M. Puri, eds. (1975), *The Strategy of International Development*. London: Macmillan.
Singh, Anoop, Agnès Belaisch, Charles Collyns, Paula De Masi, Reva Krieger, Guy Meredith and Robert Rennhack (2005): Stabilization and Reform in Latin America: A Macroeconomic Perspective on the Experience Since the Early 1990s. IMF Occasional Paper. Washington: International Monetary Fund.
Smith, Vernon L. (1962): An Experimental Study of Competitive Market Behavior. *Journal of Political Economy*, Vol. 70(April), pp. 111–137.
Sombart, Werner (1916): *Der moderne Kapitalismus: Historisch-systematische Darstellung des gesamteuropäischen Wirtschaftslebens von seinen Anfängen bis zur Gegenwart, Vol. 1: Die vorkapitalistische Wirtschaft*. München and Leipzig: Duncker & Humblot.
Sombart, Werner (1925): *Die Ordnung des Wirtschaftslebens*. Enzyklopädie der Rechts-und Staatswissenschaft, Vol. XXXV. Berlin: Julius Springer.
Sombart, Werner (1929): Economic Theory and Economic History. *Economic History Review*, Vol. 2(1), pp. 1–19.
Spiethoff, Arthur (1925): Krisen. In: *Handwörterbuch der Sozialwissenschaften*, Vol. 6, fourth edition. Stuttgart and Tübingen: Gustav Fischer and J.C.B Mohr, pp. 8–91.
Spiethoff, Arthur (1932): Die allgemeine Volkswirtschaftslehre als geschichtliche Theorie. Die Wirtschaftsstile. *Schmollers Jahrbuch für Gesetzgebung, Verwaltung und Volkswirtschaft im Deutschen Reiche*, Vol. 56(2), pp. 891–924.
Spiethoff, Arthur (1938): Gustav von Schmoller und die anschauliche Theorie der Volkswirtschaft. *Schmollers Jahrbuch für Gesetzgebung, Verwaltung und Volkswirtschaft im Deutschen Reiche*, Vol. 62(II), pp. 16–35.
Spiethoff, Arthur (1948): Anschauliche und Reine Volkswirtschaftliche Theorie und ihr Verhältnis Zueinander. In: Edgar Salin (ed.), *Synopsis. Festgabe für Alfred Weber (in Honour)*. Heidelberg: Schneider, pp. 567–664.
Spiethoff, Arthur (1952): The 'Historical' Character of Economic Theories. Translation by Fritz Redlich of a formerly unpublished essay. *Journal of Economic History*, Vol. 12(2), pp. 131–139.
Spiethoff, Arthur (1953): Pure Theory and Economic Gestalt Theory; Ideal Types and Real Types. In: Frederic C. Lane and Jelle C. Riemersma (eds.), *Enterprise and Secular Change*. Homeland: Richard D. Irwin, pp. 444–463.
Srinivasan, John T. N. (2000): The Washington Consensus a Decade Later: Ideology and the Art and Science of Policy Advice. *The World Bank Research Observer*, Vol. 15(2), pp. 265–270.
Stemmermann, Klaus (1996): Gibt es einen italienischen Wirtschaftsstil? In: Rainer Klump (ed.), *Wirtschaftskultur, Wirtschaftsstil und Wirtschaftsordnung: Methoden und Ergebnisse der Wirtschaftskulturforschung*. Marburg: Metropolis-Verlag, pp. 93–123.

Stigler, George J. (1961): The Economics of Information. *Journal of Political Economy*, Vol. 69(3), pp. 213–225.
Stiglitz, Joseph E. (1985): Information and Economic Analysis: A Perspective. *Economic Journal*, Vol. 95(Supplement), pp. 21–41.
Stiglitz, Joseph E. (1986): The New Development Economics. *World Development*, Vol. 14(2), pp. 257–265.
Stiglitz, Joseph E. (1990): Peer Monitoring and Credit Markets. *World Bank Economic Review*, Vol. 4(3), pp. 351–366.
Stiglitz, Joseph E. (2002): Information and the Change in the Paradigm in Economics. *American Economic Review*, Vol. 92(3), pp. 460–501.
Tanzi, Vito (1999): Uses and Abuses of Estimates of the Underground Economy. *Economic Journal*, 109(456), pp. F338–F347.
Tarp, Finn ed. (2000): *Foreign Aid and Development: Lessons Learnt and Directions for the Future*. London: Routledge.
Temple, Jonathan (1999): The New Growth Evidence. *Journal of Economic Literature*, Vol. 37(1), pp. 112–156.
Tévoédjrè, Albert (1978): *La Pauvreeté, Richess des Peuples*. Paris: Éditions Économie et Humanisme, les Éditions Ouvrières.
The Economist (1999): Deep Discount. Economic Focus. *The Economist*, Vol. 351(26), p. 90.
The Economist (2005): Inside the Slums. *The Economist*, Vol. 374(8407), p. 43.
The Economist (2006): A Giant Leap Forward. *The Economist*, Vol. 378(8459), p. 39.
The Economist (2007a): Africa Calling. Face Value. *The Economist*, Vol. 383(8529), p. 74.
The Economist (2007b): The Strange Allure of the Slums. *The Economist, Special Report: Cities*, Vol. 383(8527), p. 5.
The Economist (2007c): What the World Bank Knows …And What it Only Thinks it Knows. Economic Focus. *The Economist*, Vol. 382, p. 67.
The Gringo Times (2009): Building Walls Around Favelas. The Gringo Times online edition, April 7th, 2009. Accessed at http://thegringotimes.com.
Tinbergen, Jan (1939): *Statistical Testing of Business-Cycle Theories*. Geneva: League of Nations Economic Intelligence Service.
Tinbergen, Jan (1967): *Development Planning*. London: World University Library.
Trueman, Chris (2008): Population and the Thirty Years' War. Retrieved July 2008 from the World Wide Web: www.historylearningsite.co.uk.
UN Millennium Project (2005): *Investing in Development: A Practical Plan to Achieve the Millennium Development Goals*. New York and London: United Nations Development Programme and Earthscan.
UNCTAD (2004): *The Least Developed Countries Report 2004*. New York and Geneva: United Nations.
UNCTAD (2008): *The Least Developed Countries Report 2008. Growth, Poverty and the Terms of Development Partnership*. Geneva: United Nations Conference on Trade and Development.
UNDP (2007): *Human Development Report 2007/2008: Fighting Climate Change: Human Solidarity in a Divided World*. New York: Palgrave Macmillan.
UNFPA (2004): *Working from Within: Culturally Sensitive Approaches in UNFPA Programming*. New York: United Nations Population Fund.
UNFPA (2008): *Culture Matters. Lessons from a Legacy of Engaging Faith-based Organizations*. New York: United Nations Population Fund.
United Nations General Assembly (2000): *United Nations Millennium Declaration 55/2*. Resolution adopted by the General Assembly, 18 September 2000. New York: United Nations.
Uphoff, Norman and Jerry Combs (2001): Some Things Can't Be True But Are: Rice, Rickets and What Else? 'Unlearning' Conventional Wisdoms To Remove Paradigm Blockages. Ithaca, New York: Cornell International Institute for Food, Agriculture and Development, Cornell University.

Veblen, Thorstein (1898): Why is Economics Not an Evolutionary Science? *Quarterly Journal of Economics*, Vol. 12, pp. 373–397.
Veblen, Thorstein (1899): *The Theory of the Leisure Class*. New York: The Macmillan Company.
Veblen, Thorstein (1914): *The Instinct of Workmanship and the State of Industrial Arts*. New York: The Macmillan Company.
Wade, Robert (1982): The System of Administrative and Political Corruption: Canal Irrigation in South India. *Journal of Development Studies*, Vol. 18(3), pp. 287–328.
Wallis, John J. and Douglass C. North (1986): Measuring the Transaction Sector in the American Economy 1870–1970. In: Stanley L. Engerman and Robert E. Gallman (eds.), *Long-Term Factors in American Economic Growth*, pp. 95–161.
Weber, Max (1904): Die 'Objektivität' sozialwissenschaftlicher und sozialpolitischer Erkenntnis. *Archiv für Sozialwissenschaft und Sozialpolitik*, Vol. XIX(1), pp. 22–87.
Weippert, Georg (1943): Zum Begriff des Wirtschaftsstils. *Schmollers Jahrbuch für Gesetzgebung, Verwaltung und Volkswirtschaft im Deutschen Reiche*, Vol. 67(1), pp. 417–478.
Werner, Heinecke (2003): *The Development Business D+C Magazine for Development and Cooperation, 4/2003*. Bonn: Internationale Weiterbildung und Entwicklung, pp. 161–163.
Williamson, John (1990): What Washington Means by Policy Reform. In: John Williamson (ed.), *Latin American Adjustment: How Much Has Happened?* Washington: Institute for International Economics.
Williamson, Oliver E. (1975): *Markets and Hierarchies: Analysis and Antitrust Implications*. New York: Free Press.
Williamson, Oliver E. (1979): Transaction Cost Economics: The Governance of Contractual Relations. *Journal of Law and Economics*, Vol. 22(October), pp. 233–261.
Williamson, Oliver E. (1990): A Comparison of Alternative Approaches to Economic Organization. *Journal of Institutional and Theoretical Economics/Zeitschrift für die gesamte Staatswissenschaft*, Vol. 146(1), pp. 61–71.
Williamson, Oliver E. (1996): *The Mechanisms of Governance*. New York: Oxford University Press.
World Bank (1997): *World Development Report 1997: The State in a Changing World*. Washington: World Bank.
World Bank (1998): *Assessing Aid: What Works, What Doesn't and Why*. New York: Oxford University Press for the World Bank.
World Bank (2000): *The Quality of Growth*. Report Carried out by Vinod Thomas, Mansoor Dailami, Ashok Dhareshwar, Daniel Kaufmann, Nalin Kishor and Ramón López Yan Wang. New York: Oxford University Press for the World Bank.
World Bank (2001a): *World Development Report 2000/2001: Attacking Poverty*. New York: Oxford University Press for the World Bank.
World Bank (2001b): *World Development Report 2002: Building Institutions for Markets*. New York: Oxford University Press.
World Bank (2002): *Poverty Reduction and the World Bank. Progress in Operationalizing the WDR 2000/2001*. Washington: World Bank.
World Bank (2004): *World Development Report 2005: A Better Investment Climate for Everyone*. New York: Oxford University Press for the World Bank.
World Bank (2005): *Economic Growth in the 1990s. Learning from a Decade of Reform*. Report prepared by a team led by Roberto Zagha. Washington: World Bank.
World Bank (2007): *Strengthening Bank Group Engagement on Governance and Anticorruption*. Washington: World Bank.
World Bank (2008): *African Development Indicators 2007*. Washington: World Bank.
World Bank (2009): *2008 World Development Indicators Database*, Online query at http://devdata.worldbank.org/data-query. Accessed on 09.03.2009.
World Bank and IFC (2004): *Doing Business in 2004: Understanding Regulation*. Washington: World Bank, International Finance Corporation, and Oxford University Press.

World Bank and IFC (2008): *Doing Business in 2009: Creating Jobs*. Washington: World Bank, International Finance Corporation, and Palgrave Macmillan.

Wrobel, Ralph M. (2007): Culture and Economic Transformation: 'Economic Style' in Europe, Russia and China. In: Mica Jovanovic (ed.), *System Transformation in Comparative Perspective*. Münster: LIT, pp. 163–185.

Yanikkaya, Halit (2003): Trade Openness and Economic Growth: A Cross-Country Empirical Investigation. *Journal of Development Economics*, Vol. 72 (1), pp. 57–89.

Yunus, Muhammad and Alan Jolis (1999): *Banker to the Poor. The Story of the Grameen Bank*. London: Aurum Press.

Zattler, Jürgen (2004): Post-Washington-Consensus – Einige Überlegungen. BMZ-Diskurs. Discussion Paper. Bonn: Bundesministerium für wirtschaftliche Zusammenarbeit und Entwicklung.

Zweynert, Joachim (2006): Wirtschaftskultur und Transformation. *Wirtschaftsdienst*, Vol. 86(12), pp. 801–808.

Author Index

A
Acemoglu, Daron, 144, 145
Ackermann, Peter, 222
Altmann, Matthias, 202
Ammon, Günther, 222
Anderson, Kym, 189
Andersson, Svea, 55
Appleton, Simon, 24
Arrow, Kenneth J., 34
Ascher, William, 167
Ayyagari, Meghana, 90

B
Backhaus, Jürgen G., 40, 52, 69, 196–198, 209, 221
Bandura, Romina, 148
Banerjee, Abhijit V., 156, 193, 225
Basu, Kaushik, 146
Bates, Robert H., 188, 189
Batra, Geeta, 33
Bauer, Peter T., 16–18, 105, 114–116
Bechtel, Heinrich, 220
Becker, Gary S., 151, 185
Beckert, Jens, 47, 48
Berger, Peter L., 162, 232
Besley, Timothy, 57, 163
Beynon, Jonathan, 156
Bigsten, Arne, 55, 56
Birchall, Johnston, 84
Borner, Silvio, 143
Boserup, Ester, 39
Bowles, Samuel, 231
Bromley, Daniel W., 138
Buchanan, James, 151, 169, 200
Bücher, Karl, 204, 205

Burki, Javed, 143, 171
Burnside, Craig, 149, 155, 156, 164
Büscher, Martin E. H., 239
Bush, George W., 156

C
Calderisi, Robert, 182
Campos, J. Edgardo, 178
Cardenas, Juan Camilo, 186
Carpenter, Jeffrey, 186
Carr, Marilyn, 77, 86
Charmes, Jacques, 83
Chen, Martha A., 14, 77, 86
Chen, Shaohua, 1, 14, 15
Clark, Colin, 100–101, 105, 222
Clay, Karen, 61
Coase, Ronald H., 30, 151
Coleman, James S., 22
Collier, Paul, 133, 156, 164, 167
Combs, Jerry, 167
Conceição, Pedro, 6
Cooter, Robert D., 69, 70, 89
Cord, Louise, 155
Cross, John C., 75
Cullis, John, 132

D
Dalton, George, 237
Daspypta, Partha, 125
De Alessi, Louis, 185
De Soto, Hernando, 62, 75, 76, 90
Deaton, Angus, 24, 156
Deininger, Klaus, 25, 63
Demsetz, Harold, 34
Denzau, Arthur, 140, 230, 232

Dilthey, Wilhelm, 215
DiMaggio, Paul, 237
Dixit, Avinash K., 43, 45, 65, 67
Dixon, Huw, 83
Dollar, David, 149, 155, 156, 164
Dollinger, Philippe, 59
Domar, Evsey, 119
Donner, Franziska, 242
Drechsler, Wolfgang, 99
Duflo, Esther, 186, 187, 192, 193

E

Easterly, William, 145, 156, 164, 165, 168, 180–182, 184
Ebner, Alexander, 230
Enste, Dominik H., 78, 87
Eucken, Walter, 216–220

F

Fafchamps, Marcel, 49, 55, 163
Fehr, Ernst, 185, 187
Friedman, Eric, 88
Friedman, Milton, 122, 123
Furubotn, Eirik, 185, 186

G

Galal, Ahmed, 89
Gallup, John L., 145
Gambretta, Diego, 65
Gerschenkron, Alexander, 100–101, 163
Gioia, Vitantonio, 221
Glaeser, Edward L., 145, 156
Goldin, Ian, 164
Goldschmidt, Niels, 245
Greif, Avner, 59–61, 237
Griffin, Ronald, 64
Grün, Carola, 25
Grunchy, Allan G., 222

H

Hamilton, Alexander, 111
Hancock, Graham, 170, 182
Haq, Mahbub ul, 27
Harberger, Arnold C., 125, 129
Harford, Tim, 45
Harrison, Lawrence E., 178, 235
Harrod, Roy, 119

Hart, Stuart L., 19
Haswell, Margaret R., 100
Hausmann, Ricardo, 180, 190, 191
Hayek, Friedrich A. von, 151, 200, 201, 231
Heilmann, Sebastian, 194
Henderson, J. Vernon, 145
Henn, Volker, 59
Hennis, Wilhelm, 200
Hermann-Pillath, Carsten, 222
Heston, Alan, 25, 118
Hickmann, Thorsten, 222
Hildebrand, Bruno, 196, 203
Hirschman, Albert O., 93, 94, 102–105, 153, 157, 158, 160, 163, 253
Hodgson, Geoffrey M., 222
Hoff, Karla, 68
Hofstede, Geert, 237
Huntington, Samuel P., 235
Hussmanns, Ralf, 78

J

Jepma, Catrinus J., 165
Jevons, William Stanley, 200
Johnson, Simon, 68, 88, 170
Jolis, Alan, 57, 182
Jones, Philip, 132
Jul-Larsen, Eyolf, 61

K

Kahneman, Daniel, 185
Kanbur, Ravi, 21, 27, 137, 138, 186
Kattel, Rainer, 99
Kaufhold, Karl Heinrich, 221
Kaufmann, Daniel, 147
Kaul, Inge, 6
Keefer, Philip, 144, 178, 235
Kessides, Ioannis, 178
Keynes, John Maynard, 105, 154
Klasen, Stephan, 25
Klitgaard, Robert, 170
Klump, Rainer, 221
Knack, Stephen, 144, 235
Knies, Karl, 196
Kraay, Aart, 155
Kravis, Irving, 25, 118
Kremer, Michael, 168, 192, 193
Krugman, Paul, 118

Kumi, Sylvanus Nana, 160
Kuznets, Simon, 100–101, 151

L
Laderchi, Caterina, 15
Lancaster, Kelvin, 249
Lane, Frederic C., 196, 205, 206
Lateef, Sarwar, 178
Leibniz, Wilhelm, 230
Leipold, Helmut, 235, 237, 239
Levi, Margaret, 189, 190
Levine, Ross, 145
Lewis, Arthur, 94, 96–97, 105, 120, 151
Li, Shuhe, 66, 67
Libecap, Gary D., 63
Licht, Amir N., 235
Lipsey, Richard G., 249
List, Friedrich, 111–114, 203
Locke, John, 230
Lucas, Robert E. Jr., 120, 121
Luckmann, Thomas, 162, 232
Ludwig, Alexander, 200, 201, 222
Luhmann, Niklas, 232
Lutz, Friedrich A., 216

M
Macaulay, Steward, 70
Mahoney, James, 189
Mankiw, Gregory N., 121, 144
Marcouiller, Douglas, 88
Marglin, Stephen, 125
Marshall, Alfred, 122
Marx, Karl, 141, 206
McNamara, Robert, 13
Meier, Gerald M., 105, 118
Menard, Claude, 140
Menger, Carl, 198, 200, 216
Miguel, Edward, 193
Milgrom, Paul, 50, 51, 59–61, 69
Mill, John Stuart, 115
Minten, Bart, 49
Mishan, Edward J., 125, 129, 132
Mitullah, Winnie, 75, 84
Möller, Hero, 210
Montiel, Peter, 178
Mookherjee, Dilip, 161, 188, 227
Moyo, Dambisa, 182
Mullainathan, Sendhil, 186, 193
Müller-Armack, Alfred, 220

Müller-Pelzer, Werner, 222
Murphy, Kevin M., 20
Musgrave, Richard A., 129
Myrdal, K. Gunnar, 102, 104–105, 124, 151, 157, 163

N
Nankani, Gobind, 178, 179
Narayan, Deepa, 22
Nenova, Tatiana, 45
Nienhaus, Volker, 222
North, Douglass C., 33, 34, 38, 50, 51, 61, 69, 89, 135, 138–143, 151, 230, 232, 235
Nurkse, Ragnar, 97–99, 103, 104, 157, 158

O
Offe, Johanna, 241
Olson, Mancur, 64, 143
Osei Tutu II, Otumfuo, 160
Ostrom, Elinor, 22, 63, 168–170

P
Patrick, Stewart, 46
Pedersen, Karl Rolf, 169
Peirce, William Spangar, 164, 166
Perlman, Janice E., 76
Perry, Guillermo E., 143, 171
Peukert, Helge, 221
Platteau, Jean-Philippe, 39, 47, 48, 51, 61
Pogge, Thomas W., 14
Polanyi Levitt, Kari, 238
Polanyi, Karl, 39, 232, 237–239
Poulos, Christine, 242
Prahalad, Coimbatore K., 19
Prebisch, Raúl, 102, 103, 105, 107–112
Pritchett, Lant, 155, 178
Putnam, Robert D., 22, 53, 54

R
Ramachandran, S., 178
Rao, Vijayendra, 235
Ratha, Dilip, 85
Ravallion, Martin, 1, 14, 15, 24, 150
Ray, Anandarup, 129
Reddy, Sanjay G., 14
Redlich, Fritz, 205, 210, 212, 221
Reinert, Erik S., 111, 115, 195, 196, 215, 224, 226, 230, 237, 244, 251

Reinert, Sophus A., 244
Ricardo, David, 124, 190, 196, 200
Rice, Susan E., 46
Richter, Rudolf, 185
Riemersma, Jelle C., 196,
    205, 206
Ritzen, Jo, 22
Robert Mugabe, 68, 88
Rockenbach, Bettina, 187
Rodríguez, Francisco, 156
Rodrik, Dani, 43, 44, 132, 145, 146, 152,
    153, 156, 167, 178–181, 183, 184,
    189–191, 194
Romer, Paul M., 120, 121
Ros, Jaime, 121
Roscher, Wilhelm G. F., 196
Rosenstein-Rodan, Paul N., 95–97,
    99, 105
Rossi, Sandra, 222
Rostow, Walt Whitman, 100–101,
    105, 163
Rudner, Nicole, 222

S
Sachs, Jeffrey D., 145, 165, 183, 184
Salin, Edgar, 210
Schefold, Bertram, 204, 215, 221
Schmidt, Klaus, 185
Schmoller, Gustav von, 196–200, 204, 206,
    207, 210, 229, 230
Schneider, Friedrich, 78, 80, 82, 83, 87
Schönberg, Gustav von, 204
Schultz, Henry, 154
Schumpeter, Joseph A., 105, 123, 124, 162,
    198–200, 230
Schwettmann, Jürgen, 84, 85
Scott, Maurice, 125, 126
Seers, Dudley, 94, 105
Selten, Reinhard, 185
Sen, Amartya, 22, 25, 114, 125, 128,
    147, 151
Sen, Arijit, 68
Serra, Antonio, 115
Serven, Luis, 178
Shionoya, Yuichi, 196, 199
Shirley, Mary M., 140
Shleifer, Andrei, 64, 170
Shvets, Oleksiy, 178
Simon, Herbert A., 151, 166, 185
Singer, Hans, 107–109, 112, 210
Singh, Anoop, 178
Smith, Adam, 112, 200

Smith, Vernon L., 185
Solow, Robert, 119–121, 151
Sombart, Werner, 203, 205–207, 210, 213,
    215, 221
Song, Lina, 24
Spence, Michael, 179
Spiethoff, Arthur, 105, 203,
    205–223, 234
Squire, Lyn, 21, 25
Srinivasan, John T. N., 161
Stemmermann, Klaus, 222
Stigler, George J., 151, 185
Stiglitz, Joseph E., 57, 136, 137,
    151, 163, 185
Summer, Robert, 25, 118

T
Tang, Helena, 178, 181
Tanzi, Vito, 83
Tarp, Finn, 164
Temple, Jonathan, 156
Tévoédjrè, Albert, 14, 163
Tinbergen, Jan, 105, 125,
    151, 154
Trueman, Chris, 195
Tvesky, Amos, 185

U
Uphoff, Norman, 167

V
Veblen, Thorstein, 139, 222–224
Velasco, Andrés, 180, 190
Vishny, Robert W., 64, 170

W
Wade, Robert, 170
Wallis, John J., 33, 34, 38
Walras, Léon, 200
Walton, Michael, 235
Weber, Max, 123, 200, 205, 213,
    215, 221, 237
Weingast, Barry, 50, 51,
    59–61, 69
Weippert, Georg, 220
Werner, Heinecke, 162
Williamson, John, 132
Williamson, Oliver E., 30, 31, 43, 132,
    139, 185

Author Index

Wolfensohn, James, 13
Wolff, Christian, 230
Wolfowitz, Paul, 179
Wrobel, Ralph M., 222

Y
Yamey, Basil S., 114
Yanikkaya, Halit, 155

Young, Leslie, 88
Yunus, Muhammad, 57, 182

Z
Zagha, Roberto, 178
Zattler, Jürgen, 143
Zweynert, Joachim, 236, 245

Subject Index

A

Adverse selection, 49, 57, 137. *See also* Information
Afghanistan, 46
African Development Bank (AFDB), 102
Africa south of the Sahara, 1, 15, 17, 20, 54, 56, 75, 83, 150, 172, 183, 241, 250
Agriculture, 17, 26, 39, 55, 57, 68, 75, 77, 78, 80, 83, 85, 100, 109–112, 154, 163, 203
Algeria, 2
Altruism, 47, 48, 185
American Institutional School, 222–224
Andean Community of Nations, 110
Angola, 73, 150
Anthropology, 223, 237, 238
Asia, 1, 15, 19, 55, 68, 76, 77, 83, 106, 111, 132, 133, 149
Asset specificity, 227
Austrian School of Economics, 198, 200, 201

B

Backwardness model (Alexander Gerschenkron), 101
Bangladesh, 19, 38, 57, 58, 167, 182
Base of the Pyramid (BoP), 19, 20
Behavioural economics, 184–187, 225, 227, 231, 235
Belarus, 38
Belgium, 113
Benin, 14, 61, 73
Bertelsmann, 148
Big Push industrialisation, 95, 96, 103, 183
Botswana, 20, 179, 189
Brazil, 63, 76, 109, 132, 179, 189
Brookings Institution, 46
Bureaucratic failure, 151, 163–171, 173

Burundi, 45, 55
Business cycle theory, 210, 221

C

Cambodia, 147
Cameralism, 40, 41, 196
Capability approach, 27
Capital, 5, 16, 18 20, 22, 23, 33, 36, 39, 53, 54, 64, 74, 75, 85, 90, 93, 95–100, 106, 110, 113, 115, 117, 119–121, 124, 127, 129, 132, 135, 139, 144, 152, 153, 155, 157, 178, 183, 191, 204, 217, 221, 227, 238, 240, 246. *See also* Investment
Capitalism, 5, 96, 97, 206, 217, 221, 238
Caribbean, the, 113
Causation, 104–105, 118, 145, 155, 184. *See also* Reverse causality
  circular, 104–105, 118, 184
Celtel, 17
Central African Republic, 45–46
Central American Common Market, 110
Central American Common Market (CACM), 110
Ceteris paribus, 124
Chad, 150
Chile, 4, 109
China, 4, 5, 15, 38, 54, 55, 76, 111, 147, 179, 189, 194, 222
Classical Economics, 29, 105, 112, 124, 196, 222, 223, 238
Climate change, 128
Cognitive science, 140, 185, 233, 236, 237
Colonialism, 39, 41, 55, 68, 94, 113, 114, 241, 245, 252
Columbia, 109, 110

Commission on Growth
  and Development, 179
Common pool resources, 63
Comparative advantage, 62, 77, 246
Congo, Democratic Republic, 39, 45,
  61, 150
Congo, Republic, 61
Constitution, 30, 31, 34–36, 39, 44, 51,
  55–59, 63, 69, 70, 151, 152, 209,
  218, 239, 244, 246
Contract
  first-party enforcement of, 58
  formal enforcement of, 36, 47, 50–53, 56
  relation-based, 23, 31, 46, 66–70, 170,
    231, 246
  second-party enforcement of, 58, 59
  third-party enforcement of, 49, 58, 67,
    69, 246
Cooperatives, 57, 84–86
Copenhagen Consensus, 127, 128
Corruption, 2, 37, 38, 45, 64, 74, 88,
  143, 144, 147, 148, 156, 170, 182,
  241, 252
Costa Rica, 81
Côte d'Ivoire, 55
Culture, 5, 17, 80, 112, 142, 159, 160, 162,
  163, 170, 178, 197, 203, 204, 221, 222,
  235–243
  cultural beliefs, 40, 46, 47, 49, 50,
    52, 89, 142, 170, 222, 232, 237,
    239, 241–243

D
Deduction, 3, 4, 159–161, 195, 196, 198, 199,
  210, 212, 215, 225, 226, 228
Dependency theory, 108. *See also*
  Structuralists
Deutsche Bank, 148
Development assistance, 1, 4, 13, 18, 99, 149,
  156, 157, 163–171, 173, 180, 182,
  241–243, 245, 250, 253. *See also*
  Foreign aid
Development Economics, 1–5, 7, 8, 13, 17, 61,
  93–173, 177–201, 224–227, 229, 231,
  233–235, 239, 243, 245, 249–251
  contextual, 2–5, 8, 226, 232, 239,
    243–245, 250
  neoclassical, 117–121, 167
Development policy, 101, 121, 150–152,
  157, 158, 160, 163, 171, 172, 177,
  179, 183, 245
Discriminating alignment hypothesis
  (Oliver Williamson), 30

Dispute settlement, 3, 35, 56
Djibouti, 73
Dominican Republic, 81
Dual sector model (Arthur Lewis), 94,
  96–97, 120
Dubai, 76

E
Eastern Europe, 95, 132, 136, 209, 245
Econometrics, 79, 143–145, 154, 155, 161,
  164, 173, 188, 189
  cross-country regressions, 36, 90, 100,
    118, 120, 144, 145, 154–156, 190,
    193, 243
  endogeneity of explanatory
    variables, 144, 156 (*see also*
    Reverse causality)
  instrumental variable, 144, 145, 188
  proxy variable, 79
Economic methodology, 5, 15, 24, 25,
  121, 124, 151, 158, 194, 198, 210,
  212, 214, 220, 225, 226, 235
  of development research, 121, 151,
    158, 227
  of the Historical School, 196, 216,
    227–229
Economic spirit, 113, 117, 179, 206, 212, 214,
  218, 233, 236, 239
Economic style, 4, 5, 8, 175–253
Economies of scale, 62, 69, 74, 85, 95, 96,
  109, 119, 121
Ecuador, 110
Education, 16, 20–21, 25, 27, 33, 48, 75, 105,
  132, 146, 150, 153, 158, 193, 223, 227,
  236, 244
  adult literacy, 27
  school enrolment, 27
Efficiency, 40, 61, 66, 68, 103, 116,
  117, 119, 125, 129, 136, 140, 159,
  178, 186, 188
  adaptive, 140
  allocative, 117, 129, 140, 186
  distributive, 129
  Pareto, 136
Egypt, 60
Electricity, 20, 38, 76, 79, 80, 126
El Salvador, 191
Equatorial Guinea, 150
Equilibrium analysis, 123. *See also*
  Neoclassical economics
Ethiopia, 84
Ethnology, 223
European Commission, 147

Subject Index

Evolutionary Economics, 232
Exchange economy, 17, 29, 115
Experimental economics, 185, 186

F
Failed states, 45, 46
Family, 14, 21, 23, 24, 53, 54, 68,
    73, 123, 162, 185, 204, 237,
    238, 240
Favelas (Brazil), 76
Foreign aid, 4, 6, 93, 95, 99, 115, 116, 142,
    145, 149, 155, 156, 163–166, 168, 169,
    171, 180, 182, 183. *See also*
    Development assistance
  conditionality of, 133
  effectiveness of, 6, 99, 155, 156, 164
  fungibility of, 169
  tying of, 165
France, 54, 222
Fraser Institute, 148
Freedom, 6, 13, 16, 22, 88, 148, 162, 182
Freedom House, 88
Functional equivalent, 2, 3, 54, 58, 148,
    243, 246

G
Gambia, The, 114
Game theory, 67, 122, 185
Genoese traders, 61, 237
Georgia, 38
German Development Cooperation (GTZ),
    242, 243
German Federal Ministry for Economic
    Cooperation and Development
    (BMZ), 88
Germany, 54, 59, 111, 113, 195, 196,
    219, 222
Gestalt theory, 210–214
Ghana, 14, 63, 75, 114, 160
Globalisation, 77, 204, 238, 247
Governance
  formal, 45, 52, 68, 71, 235, 246, 252
  good, 33, 99, 146–148
  indicators, 147, 148
  informal, 66, 68, 70, 73, 86
  private, 2, 3, 6, 31, 43–71, 73, 84,
    86, 246, 247
Government failure, 117, 147, 163
Grameen Bank, 19, 57, 58, 85, 182
Great Antinomy (Walter Eucken),
    216, 217
Great Britain, 111–114

Growth, 1, 20, 21, 24, 54, 88, 95, 100, 101,
    118–120, 132, 135, 142, 144, 145, 147,
    150, 151, 155, 156, 158, 163, 165, 178,
    179, 204, 226, 227, 244
  balanced, 97–99, 102–104, 115
  pro-poor, 21, 150
  unbalanced, 102–104
Growth diagnostics, 178, 180,
    190–192, 194
Growth theory, 119–121, 144
  endogenous, 14, 18, 20, 47, 121,
    140, 141, 146, 150, 181, 188, 231,
    241, 245, 253
  Keynesian, 93, 94, 100, 119
  neoclassical, 120, 144
Guatemala, 64
Guinea, 150

H
Hanseatic League *(Hanse)*, 59
Harrod-Domar model, 119. *See also*
    Growth theory
Health, 16, 19–21, 25, 27, 70, 86, 105, 132,
    142, 188, 192, 243, 244
  life expectancy, 16, 27
  malnutrition, 20, 128, 193
Heritage Foundation, 148
Hicks-Kaldor welfare criterion,
    130, 131
Historical School of Economics, 4, 7, 112,
    163, 195–201, 204, 205, 211, 215,
    216, 221–247
HIV/AIDS, 20, 21, 128, 243
Holland, 113
Homo economicus, 138, 213, 233
Honduras, 81
Hong Kong, 76, 179
Human Development Index (HDI), 27

I
Ideal type, 205, 213–214, 219, 220
Import-substituting industrialisation, 108–111,
    117, 245
Income distribution, 18, 19, 24, 25, 35,
    38, 57, 68, 77, 100, 105–108,
    128–132, 137, 184, 223,
    232, 238
India, 4, 15, 38, 55, 76, 85, 86, 168,
    179, 189
  Mumbai, 55, 76
Indonesia, 55, 63, 179
Induction, 173, 212

Informal sector, 20, 38, 46, 70, 73, 74, 78–80, 83–90, 111, 142. *See also* Informal; Institutions
  definition of, 74, 78
Information, 49, 57, 61, 136–138, 140, 167, 185, 186, 225, 233
  asymmetric, 49, 60, 118, 169, 170
  cost of, 35, 37, 136, 137
  imperfect, 49, 57, 136–138, 185, 225, 236
  pooling of, 51
  sharing of, 50, 51
Infrastructure, 21, 33, 35, 38, 39, 45, 74, 86, 88, 90, 95, 105, 132, 153, 157, 158, 191, 244
Insecurity, 2, 14, 16, 20, 22–23, 27
Institute for Liberty and Democracy (ILD), 62
Institutional change, 32, 33, 40, 71, 89, 139–144, 151, 171, 221, 222, 233, 234, 236, 244–246, 253
Institutional diversity, 3, 7, 172, 242–245
Institutional reform Institutions, 88, 89, 141, 178, 179, 243, 245
Institutions
  and economic growth, 143–147, 155
  formal, 3, 6, 21, 22, 39–41, 43, 46, 66, 69, 71, 73, 74, 83, 88, 89, 137, 139–142, 146, 153, 163, 169, 235, 241–245, 252
  informal institutions, 21, 22, 32, 66, 74, 89, 139–142, 153, 236, 241, 243, 245
  legal, 44–46, 52, 56, 62, 66, 88
  market-creating, 43, 182
  market-supporting, 159, 182, 235
  political institutions, 115, 204, 220, 230, 238, 242
Inter-American Development Bank (IDB), 76
Interdisciplinary research, 147, 167, 224, 229, 230, 234
International Comparison Program (ICP), 25, 118
International Co-operative Alliance, 84
International demonstration effects, 98
International Development Association (IDA), 102, 148. *See also* World Bank
International Finance Corporation (IFC), 36–38, 71. *See also* World Bank
International Labour Organization (ILO), 44, 48, 74, 76, 78, 80, 81, 83, 88, 184, 193, 215, 230
  ILO Bureau of Statistics, 83
  International Labour Office, 88
International Monetary Fund (IMF), 95, 102, 132, 143, 145, 178

Investment, 64, 125, 127, 191.
  See also Capital
  foreign, 33, 36, 99, 106, 107, 132, 236
  planned by state, 93, 95, 99, 104, 115, 127, 183, 242
Investment climate, 33, 38, 39, 64, 136, 142
Iraq, 46
Islam, 5, 47, 55, 60, 61, 222, 237, 239
Italy, 54, 196, 222, 244

J
Japan, 54, 179, 222

K
Kenya, 55, 64, 75, 186, 193
  Kibera (Nairobi), 87
Keynesian Economics, 93, 94
Keynes–Tinbergen debate, 154
Korea, Republic of, 54, 85, 111, 179
Kuznets curve, 100

L
Labour productivity, 20, 96–98, 158
Land reform, 56, 68
Latin America, 18, 76, 77, 83, 102, 106, 108–111, 132, 157, 178, 179, 245
Latvia, 38
Law Merchant, 61, 69
Least Developed Countries (LDCs), 102
Legal reform, 70, 89, 90, 141
Lesotho, 20
Liberia, 46
Linkages concept (Albert O. Hirschman), 103, 158
Little welfare criterion, 131
Logical Framework, 157

M
Macroeconomic policy, 22, 93, 114, 119, 132, 133, 153, 183, 189, 192, 194, 234, 244
Madagascar, 14, 84, 167
Maghribi traders, 60, 61, 237
Malaria, 20, 128, 184
Malawi, 6, 16–18
Malawi Agricultural Commodity Exchange (MACE), 17
Malaysia, 55, 114, 179

Mandatory passage point (Erik Reinert), 111, 244
Manufacturing, 2, 55, 75, 77, 85, 96, 101, 106, 107, 109–113, 115
Marginal utility theory, 23, 129, 200
Market economy, 4, 43, 49, 54, 163, 220, 221, 232, 238, 244
Mauritania, 189
Mercantilism, 41, 204, 244, 245
Methodenstreit, 198 200, 211, 216
Methodological individualism, 123, 138, 186, 225
Mexico, 109, 110, 132, 189, 222
  Mexico City, 75, 110
Micro-finance, 19, 85, 182
  group lending, 57, 58, 85, 182
Middle Ages, 44, 59, 61, 69, 196, 204, 205, 217, 218
Millennium Challenge Corporation (MCC), 148, 156
Millennium Development Goals (MDGs), 13, 25, 26, 183
Model of man, 213, 230–233
Modernisation theory, 94, 97, 99–102, 183
Moldova, 38
Monopoly, 20, 60, 62, 108, 126, 218
Monopsony, 18
Monterrey Consensus, 156
Moral hazard, 49, 57, 137, 169. *See also* Information
Morality, 14, 47–49, 52, 57, 58, 65, 67, 69, 80, 137, 141, 169, 185, 197, 209, 229–231, 235, 236
Morocco, 81
Mozambique, 84
Multinational corporations, 247

N
Namibia, 55
Natural Law, 230
Neoclassical Economics, 4, 7, 93, 104, 116–119, 121–124, 136–140, 143, 160, 167, 185, 200, 212, 216, 220, 221, 225, 226, 229, 235, 251
New Institutional Economics, 29, 136–143, 232, 235
Nicaragua, 63
Nigeria, 16, 64, 73, 114, 150
Normative theory, 196, 228–229, 236, 252
Norway, 222

O
Opportunism, 43, 49, 51, 53, 55, 56, 58–60
Organisation for Economic Co-operation and Development (OECD), 36, 37, 79, 125, 165

P
Palestine, 60
Pareto welfare criterion, 129–131, 136
Path dependency, 89, 141, 142, 236, 246
Peru, 110
Philippines, the, 55, 63
Physiocrats, 112
Policy reform, 3, 32, 36, 132, 133, 135, 141–143, 145, 149, 152, 153, 167, 171, 173, 179, 180, 189
Population density, 39
Positive theory, 196, 228–229, 252
Post-Washington Consensus, 135, 136
Poverty, 1, 2, 4–6, 13–27, 68, 73, 88, 98, 104–106, 111, 115, 137, 143, 149–151, 154, 155, 158, 164, 165, 172, 178, 181–183, 193, 226, 244, 250
  absolute, 14, 24
  measurement of, 14, 15, 23–27
  vicious circle of, 98, 104, 115
Poverty alleviation, 1, 2, 5, 6, 13, 14, 20, 25, 88, 143, 150, 155, 158, 164, 178
Poverty line, 14, 24, 25
Poverty penalty, 20
Poverty trap, 68, 137, 183
Prebisch–Singer thesis, 108, 109
PriceWaterhouseCoopers, 148
Principal–agent problem, 169, 170
Privatisation, 132, 133, 135
Property rights, 21
Protectionism, 64, 109, 110, 112, 113, 117, 244
Psychology, 186, 198, 203
Public Choice, 29
Purchasing Power Parity (PPP), 1, 14, 24, 25, 27, 118
Pure theory, 210–216

R
Rationality, 35, 69, 102, 138, 153, 159, 185, 187, 231–233, 240
  bounded, 35, 69, 138, 185
  hidden, 102, 103, 153, 250
  instrumental, 138
  system, 232

Real type, 205, 211, 213–214, 219
Reciprocity, 48, 49, 65, 185, 232, 235, 238, 240
Remittances, 85, 236
Rent-seeking, 20, 170
Reputation, 3, 47, 50–52, 59–61, 66, 68–71, 170, 185, 231, 246
   bilateral reputation mechanism, 50, 59, 66
   multilateral reputation mechanism, 51, 60
Reuters, 179
Reverse causality, 20, 90, 131, 144, 146, 155, 156, 158, 160, 188, 189
Ricardian Vice, 124, 199
Rostowian take-off model, 100
Rule of law, 22, 50, 97, 144, 146, 147, 153, 244
Russia, 5, 38, 112, 132, 147, 222

S

Samaritan's dilemma, 164
Savings, 33, 85, 96, 98, 99, 119, 154, 155, 159, 169, 186, 187, 242
Scitovsky welfare criterion, 131
Second best, 139, 140, 148, 153, 172, 249
Senegal, 73, 85
Shadow prices, 126, 127
Sharecropping, 57, 136, 137
Sierra Leone, 14, 55, 114
Singapore, 55, 111, 179
Small and medium-sized enterprise (SME), 90
Social cost-benefit analysis, 129
Social exclusion, 16, 21–22, 27, 51
Social norms, 3, 47, 50, 52, 58, 67, 71, 182
Social structure, 53, 54, 60
Sociology, 22, 162, 200, 210, 232, 237, 238
   economic, 200, 237, 238
   of knowledge, 162, 232
Solow model, 120. *See also* Growth theory
Somalia, 45
South Africa, 1, 17, 20, 55, 75, 76, 86, 172, 191, 250
Spain, 60, 222
Special United Nations Fund for Economic Development (SUNFED), 102
Squatter settlements, 55, 76, 103

Stage theory, 100, 101, 112, 121, 203–224, 227, 228
Street vendors, 75, 84–86
Structuralists, 94, 101–116, 119, 158
Subsistence economy, 2, 16–18, 24, 73–75, 96, 97, 115, 120, 123, 150, 182, 204, 206, 228, 240
Sudan, 46, 55, 84, 150
Sustainability, 60, 166, 168, 170, 173, 241–243
Swedish International Development Cooperation Agency (SIDA), 168
Syria, 55

T

Taiwan, 85, 111, 179
Tanzania, 84
Telecommunication, mobile, 17, 19
Thailand, 63, 179
Theoretical abstraction, 69, 121, 159, 194, 199, 210, 212–215
Theoretical generalisation, 4, 114, 140, 159, 172, 173, 193, 194, 199, 205, 212, 214, 235, 238, 249
Thirty Years' War, 40
Trade
   fair, 18
   foreign, 106, 133, 236
   informal, 17, 76
   internal, 17, 18, 20, 41, 115
   liberalisation of, 39, 77, 128, 132, 135, 140, 155
   terms of, 103, 106–109, 158
Transaction costs, 29–41, 138, 139, 141, 142
Transparency International, 148
Treaties of Westphalia, 40
Trickle down effect, 129
Trust, 3, 21, 31, 43, 45, 47, 49–50, 52–54, 67–69, 71, 83, 170, 231, 235, 244, 246
Tunisia, 60
Turkey, 132

U

Uganda, 14, 75, 85
UK Department for International Development (DFID), 147
United Nations Conference on Trade and Development (UNCTAD), 102
United Nations Department of Economic and Social Affairs (UN DESA), 102

Subject Index

United Nations Development Programme (UNDP), 26, 27, 102, 164, 183
United Nations Economic Commission for Africa (UN ECA), 148
United Nations Economic Commission for Europe (UNECE), 102
United Nations Economic Commission for Latin America (UN ECLA), 102, 108
United Nations General Assembly, 165
United Nations Industrial Development Organization (UNIDO), 125
United Nations International Children's Emergency Fund (UNICEF), 102
United Nations Population Fund (UNFPA), 243
United Nations World Food Programme (WFP), 102
United States, 14, 34, 54, 70, 77, 94, 112, 120, 164, 222
UN Millennium Project, 183, 184
Uruguay, 109

V
Value chain, global, 75, 77, 247
Venezuela, 109, 110, 189
Vietnam, 4, 147

W
Washington Consensus, 132–133, 135, 136, 143, 145, 161, 167, 178–180, 190, 191
Welfare Economics, 125–132
World Bank, 13–15, 20, 21, 23, 25, 27, 33, 36–38, 40, 63, 64, 73, 85, 90, 95, 102, 118, 132, 143, 147–150, 155, 156, 164, 167, 178, 179, 182
World Development Report, 118, 143, 147

Z
Zain Group, 17
Zambia, 14, 55, 64, 84, 182
Zimbabwe, 20, 46, 55, 56, 68, 75
Zollverein (Germany), 111–114

Lightning Source UK Ltd.
Milton Keynes UK
29 November 2010

163631UK00006B/11/P